Bc

The Soviet-American
Competition in
the Middle East

The Soviet-American Competition in the Middle East

Edited by

Steven L. Spiegel
University of California, Los Angeles

Mark A. Heller
Tel Aviv University

Jacob Goldberg
Tel Aviv University

Institute on Global Conflict and Cooperation
University of California
Jaffee Center for Strategic Studies
Tel Aviv University
**Moshe Dayan Center for Middle Eastern
& African Studies**
Tel Aviv University
Center for International and Strategic Affairs
University of California, Los Angeles
Lexington Books
D.C. Heath and Company/Lexington, Massachusetts/Toronto

Library of Congress Cataloging-in-Publication Data

The Soviet-American competition in the Middle East.

  Includes index.
  1. Middle East—Relations—United States. 2. United
States—Relations—Middle East. 3. Middle East—
Relations—Soviet Union. 4. Soviet Union—Relations—
United States. 5. United States—Foreign relations—
Soviet Union. 6. Soviet Union—Foreign relations—
United States. 7. United States—Foreign relations—
1981- . I. Spiegel, Steven L. II. Heller, Mark.
III. Goldberg, Jacob.
DS63.3.U5S6 1988   956'.05   86-46313
ISBN 0-669-15357-5 (alk. paper)
ISBN 0-669-16891-2 (pbk. : alk. paper)

Published simultaneously in Canada
Printed in the United States of America
Casebound International Standard Book Number: 0-669-15357-5
Paperbound International Standard Book Number: 0-669-16891-2
Library of Congress Catalog Card Number 86-46313

The paper used in this publication meets the minimum requirements of American National
Standard for Information Sciences—Permanence of Paper for Printed Library Materials, ANSI
Z39.48-1984. ∞™

88 89 90 91 92 8 7 6 5 4 3 2 1

Contents

Preface and Acknowledgments

This project was initiated by the Institute on Global Conflict and Cooperation (IGCC) of the University of California. The institute, founded in 1983 and based at the university's San Diego campus, is a unique program that combines the resources of all nine campuses of the University of California in an effort to pursue research on means of controlling international hostilities and promoting cross-country collaboration.

As part of its efforts to pursue innovative approaches to existing security problems, the institute has embarked on specific programs in which American scholars work with their counterparts in another counterparts in another country to analyze a particular issue. In this program, Professor Steven Spiegel of the UCLA political science department was asked to chair the effort vis-à-vis Israel. He gained the collaboration of the two institutes at Tel Aviv University: the Moshe Dayan Center for Middle Eastern and African Studies and the Jaffee Center for Strategic Studies. This volume is the outcome of the research collaboration that resulted. The papers published were delivered at conferences held at Tel Aviv University in July and at UCLA in September 1986, where the conferees were hosted by the Center for International and Strategic Affairs.

In an international effort of this magnitude, many individuals contributed their time and talents. Herbert York, head of the IGCC, conceived of the enterprise and gave his full support. Itamar Rabinovich, head of the Dayan Center, and Aharon Yariv, head of the Jaffee Center, participated personally in the practical and conceptual planning of the project. Mark Heller assumed responsibility for the Jaffee Center's contribution, while Jacob Goldberg became Dayan's chairman for the project. Sanford Lakoff, chairman of the IGCC publications committee, was instrumental in initial plans and became the central figure in arrangements for publication with Lexington Books.

With respect to the initial conference in Israel, Amira Margalith of the Dayan Center performed her usual miracles in facilitating the smooth functioning of the program. We wish to thank Joshua Teitelbaum of the Dayan Center for his devotion and assistance in editing a number of the articles in the volume. We also thank the Senator E. Leon Kolber Fund at the Dayan Center for its assistance.

The director of UCLA's Center for International and Strategic Affairs, Professor Michael Intriligator, also contributed his personal interest to the project. Thanks to this concern, his administrative assistant, Gerri Harrington, took charge of the conference at UCLA and the prodigious task of collecting papers from authors dispersed across three continents. Because of her remarkable efforts, the manuscript was actually submitted early. Richard Bitzinger of the UCLA Center exercised his impressive talents in personally editing the entire manuscript. We are grateful for the contributions of all these individuals, as well as the coordination of Dr. Helen Hawkins at IGCC and Jamie Welch-Donahue at Lexington Books. Without the extraordinarily effective cooperation of the staffs of four institutes, this volume would not have been possible. We also wish to thank the authors themselves for their prompt and effective participation in this volume. Their willingness to make revisions and meet deadlines in a convivial spirit of collaboration repeatedly eased our task. All of us only hope that this project will contribute in some small way to the amelioration of conflict in the most strife-torn region of the world, the Middle East.

Introduction

This book has been designed to provide perspective on the nature of the Soviet-American competition in the Middle East and the possible means of controlling it. Although we present a multiauthored volume, the consequence of two conferences, all contributors have employed a common framework. A system of mutual critiques was used to encourage commonality in the focus of individual chapters.

Chapter 1, by Steven L. Spiegel, provides a short history of the Soviet-American competition in the Middle East and should serve as background to the more detailed articles that follow. The text has been organized according to the primary instruments of superpower policy: military, economic, and political-diplomatic.

We begin with three chapters on arms transfers to the area. Robert Harkavy and Stephanie Neuman present an analysis of the superpower arms race and focus on the quantitative record of U.S. shipments, the reasons for Washington's policies, and the changes that have occurred over time. Abraham Becker provides a research note on Soviet transfers and attempts to evaluate the benefits to Moscow of its large arms transfer program. Alan Platt deals with the impact that growing nonsuperpower arms shipments have had on the Soviet-American competition. Harkavy and Neuman as well as Platt also address the possibilities of controlling arms transfers to the area.

Part III is directed at the technological dimension of the Soviet-American interaction with the area. Gerald Steinberg describes the increasingly advanced military technologies provided by the superpowers and analyzes the military, political, and economic effects on the nations of the region and their relations with each other. Shai Feldman focuses on one critical aspect of the technological impact, the possibility of nuclear proliferation in the Middle East, and also assesses U.S. and Soviet policy on nonproliferation.

Another factor in the superpower competition is the place of the Middle East in superpower strategic doctrines. In Part IV Dore Gold traces the evolution of U.S. power projection policies vis-à-vis the Middle East from the aftermath of World War II to the late 1970s, culminating in the Carter Doctrine. Sanford A. Lakoff concentrates on the policies of the Reagan administration and demonstrates the centrality of the Reagan Doctrine to an understanding of U.S. Middle East policy.

Efraim Karsh and Francis Fukuyama discuss Soviet military policies. Karsh begins with a historical review of Soviet approaches to peacetime presence and wartime engagement. His exploration of Soviet doctrines and actions leads him to conclude that even though military engagement in Middle Eastern wars has intensified since the late 1960s, the Soviets have actually been reactive, defensive, cautious, and incremental. Against this background, Fukuyama focuses explicitly on the evolution of the Soviet power projection mission, arguing that despite retrenchment, Moscow remains anxious to protect its relationships with established clients.

This part concludes with a discussion of one special area of superpower involvement in the region: terrorism. Brian Jenkins examines U.S. counterterrorism efforts, with special reference to the April 1986 attack on Libya as a test of the relative effectiveness of U.S. policy. U.S. and Soviet methods concerning terrorism differ more sharply than those concerning any other issue studied in this book. This contrast clearly emerges in Ariel Merari's analysis of the pragmatic and selective Soviet support for Middle Eastern terrorism, as reflected in Soviet policy vis-à-vis South Yemen, the Palestine Liberation Organization (PLO), Libya, and Syria.

Part V concentrates on the economic dimension of the Soviet-American competition. Eliyahu Kanovsky reviews the impact of the oil crisis of the 1970s and early 1980s on U.S. problems in the area and then examines the impact of the decline in oil prices in the 1980s on Egypt, Syria, Jordan, and Israel. Kanovsky reaches some intriguing conclusions concerning the effect of the oil crash on Soviet-American competition.

Gur Ofer and Joseph Pelzman follow with a cost-benefit analysis of Soviet strategic interests in the region and argue that the Soviets initially scored significant gains in the region. Later, however, the level of net Soviet economic activity declined, and the geographical focus of Soviet economic activity shifted. Like Kanovsky, Ofer and Pelzman also attempt to estimate the impact of declining oil revenues.

Part VI deals with the political-diplomatic context of the superpower competition. Barry Rubin's review of the Soviet-American record during Arab-Israeli wars analyzes the dynamics of relations between each superpower and its clients as well as the dangers of direct confrontation between Moscow and Washington. Rubin focuses on the 1967, 1973, and 1982 wars in the area.

Ambassador Samuel W. Lewis looks at the other side of the competition. Soviet and American attitudes toward the Arab-Israeli peace process. Lewis describes the superpowers' contrasting interests, the internal contradictions each attempts to overcome, and the resulting contrasts in their approaches toward peacemaking, and he applies these differences to a discussion of peacekeeping efforts after 1967. Lewis argues that the overall balance of strengths and weaknesses tends to favor the United States, and he considers the possible impact of a Soviet-Israeli rapprochement on this balance.

While both Rubin and Lewis refer to ambiguities and contradictions in the superpower approach toward the Middle East, Mark A. Heller must deal with a minefield of internal tensions: Soviet and American attitudes toward the Iran-Iraq war. Heller points out the dangers to vital superpower interests of an ongoing war in the Persian Gulf and analyzes why neither superpower has succeeded in bringing the war to an end, despite the fact that both advocate a negotiated settlement.

The failure of Soviet and U.S. war termination efforts reflects the limits of superpower influence in the area.

The next three Chapters address the regional problems raised by the global competition between Moscow and Washington. Jacob Goldberg concentrates on the impact of superpower rivalries on local conflicts and argues that the effect of the Soviet-American competition has been both to ameliorate and to escalate local tensions. Goldberg deals with the consequences of superpower competition for the Arab-Israeli conflict, inter-Arab relations, the Iran-Iraq war, and the Lebanese crisis.

Two case studies illustrate the processes discussed by Goldberg. Itamar Rabinovich and Asher Susser deal with patterns of mutual encroachment and describe how the United States attempts to make inroads in Syria (a state closely aligned with the Soviet Union), while the Soviets try to whittle away at one of the United States' most consistent Arab supporters, Jordan. Both the fluidity and consistency of superpower involvement in the Middle East are amply documented in this analysis.

Bruce Jentleson then examines the Soviet-American competition with respect to a specific crisis—the Lebanon war. Jentleson explains why U.S. intervention in Lebanon was unsuccessful and why the Soviets were able to take only limited advantage of this failure. His study returns to a persistent theme of this book: the limits on superpower influence.

One often neglected aspect of the Soviet-American competition is the effect of regional conflicts on bilateral relations between the two countries. Abraham Ben-Zvi examines the problems of Soviet and U.S. policymakers in managing their own competition. Ben-Zvi explores how they reconcile the fundamental discrepancy between their roles as partners and superpowers, their coercive and accommodative tactics, the ad hoc ground rules they have developed for involvement in the area, and the lessons for future conflict management and conflict resolution that may be learned from past experience.

The book concludes with a comprehensive overview by Aharon Yariv of the patterns and lessons that emerge from the collective analysis of the Soviet-American competition in the Middle East undertaken here. Yariv places the military, economic and political instruments in perspective and integrates the analyses of the complex patterns of interaction examined by individual authors. In so doing, he underscores the basic objectives of this book: to analyze the impact of the United States and the Soviet Union on the Middle East, but also to contribute to a reconsideration of superpower efforts in conflict management and limitation.

Part I
Background

1

Soviet-American Competition in the Middle East: A Profile

Steven L. Spiegel

The Middle East is one of the world's truly unique regions: A host to ancient cultures and peoples, it is a cauldron of creativity and conflict, deep beliefs and terrible hatreds. It is also located at a critical juncture of three continents and occupies the world's richest oil fields. Religious, ideological, and political movements sweep the area, and charismatic leaders emerge to espouse them—confusing past alliances and upsetting previous balances of power.

Not surprisingly, since World War II this region has been the source of continuing competition and frequent frustration for the two superpowers. The bitter local conflicts and deep hostilities between and within countries, movements, and peoples have made it difficult to achieve lasting success or develop reliable clients. Instead, tactical adjustments and even new strategies have necessitated by the winds of change that seem to blow regularly across the area. Neither the United States nor the Soviet Union has been able to establish a clear sphere of influence in the region, and it is a Mideast axiom that even an apparent victory can be overturned. Nonetheless, neither Moscow nor Washington has been prepared to relinquish unchallenged the fruits of involvement to its adversary. The importance of oil supplies and the routes through which they are shipped have been too critical, the region's location too inviting as a basis for broader influence, the objective of gaining support in the United Nations and other international councils from a majority of states in the area too appealing. Most important, each superpower has hoped that it could contain the gains that its adversary might achieve. Both, however, have consistently stopped short of engaging in a direct confrontation that might escalate beyond their control, accompanied by the danger of nuclear war.

The Politics of the Competition

As the politics of the superpower competition in the area have evolved, it has often been said that the states of the region cannot make war without the Soviet Union or make peace without the United States. This aphorism summarizes the strengths and weaknesses of both countries in the region. The Soviet Union is geographically adjacent, and, as the challenger, it has been more prepared to pursue danger-ous policies that might escalate conflict in the region. Yet its policies have lacked vision and imagination, hobbled by ideological blinders and the limited economic means at its disposal. In contrast, the United States has been more internally di-vided and less consistent, but after 40 years it has also been more successful, as judged by the criterion of maintaining close relations with the largest possible number of states in the region.

The reasons for the contrasting styles and achievements can be seen in the nature of the two societies and their political systems. Moscow has seen the area largely in instrumental terms, as a vehicle for gaining the warm water ports and control in the area that the Russian people have pursued for centuries, accom-panied by the newer objective of gaining greater control over oil supplies. This latter goal has political, military, and, especially, economic benefits. The Kremlin also has sought to exclude—or at least weaken—the United States (and earlier, Great Britain) in a region that the Western powers could use for political or mili-tary advances at the Soviet Union's expense.

In pursuit of a larger role in the region, the Soviets have abandoned any pre-tense of concern for the future of international communism. With the partial ex-ception of Israel, they have been prepared to align with any state in the area ready to cooperate. They have consistently ignored the suppression of local communist parties as long as the government in power was perceived to be serving their ends. Even then, they have often supported other opposition groups deemed to be more likely to come to power.

U.S. leaders also have been concerned about containing their superpower ad-versary and ensuring their own access to oil supplies. Yet unlike the Soviet Union, the U.S. approach to the area has been fundamentally ideological. Both Jews and Christians have shared a religious concern for the fate of the Holy Land, however much the intensity and attraction has differed among groups. Many involved Americans have been genuinely intrigued by the Arab and Persian worlds as the repositories of distant but exotic cultures. Many more have felt a deep sense of moral commitment to Israel. The belief that the United States has a fundamental obligation to support democracies also has created a continuing attraction to Israel.

These romantic fascinations have not prevented serious tensions between the United States and many states in the region and the development of fundamentalist and terrorist movements committed to the United States' departure and the defeat of its clients. Yet the United States still enjoys genuine popularity throughout the area. Unlike the Soviets, Americans have retained their mythical quality as a model and source of inspiration.

Like most bureaucracies around the world, the Soviet system continues to weigh influence by concrete measures (such as demographics, geography, and re-sources). As Premier Alexei Kosygin asked President Lyndon Johnson at their Glassboro Summit in June 1967, how could the United States continue to support 3 million Israelis when there were more than 100 million Arabs? In the Soviet

Union, this attitude is not tempered by domestic lobbies or ideological sensitivities; indeed, deep-rooted antisemitism reinforces it.

By contrast, in the United States pro-Israeli nongovernmental groups, ideological roots, and the preferences of individual leaders have blocked the pro-Arab policies favored by national security bureaucrats. The United States has, therefore, been forced to curry favor with both Arabs and Jews, with the result that it has discovered an intriguing reality of Mideast politics. A close relationship with Israel does not prevent improved relations with many Arab states, and, indeed, it might become an impetus to closer ties. Thus, the U.S. political system, so long seen as an impediment to a successful policy in the Middle East, has actually given the United States an advantage in its competition with the Soviet Union.

A History of Competition

The Soviet-American competition began gradually in the Middle East, but there were early indications that the nineteenth-century confrontation between the British and Russians might be re-created. Thus, it was the United States, not Britain, that blocked Moscow in Northern Iran in 1946 and prevented Soviet efforts to gain control over the Dardanelles. With the Truman Doctrine of 1947, the United States in effect declared that it would now play the role of guardian of the Soviet Union's southern gates. On the other hand, with their political and material support of Palestine's Jews in 1948, the Soviets demonstrated that they would use any available means to weaken the West in the region. Nevertheless, in 1950 the United States reached an agreement with the British and French in the Tripartite Declaration to limit arms transfers to the region and to assume that the policy would work without the participation of Moscow.

The Soviet-American competition as we know it today evolved in the mid–1950s as a consequence of new policies pursued by President Dwight Eisenhower and Soviet Premier Nikita Khrushchev. Until this period, U.S. engagement in the region had largely been economic—the product of American companies seeking expanded involvement, often at the expense of European competitors. This policy was epitomized when, in 1953, the Eisenhower administration sponsored a coup in Iran that ousted the Mossadegh government. The real losers were British companies, not Soviet influence, but the immediate objective was the containment of the Soviet Union. Moreover, as the Truman Doctrine and Truman's earlier, abortive attempt to create a Middle East defense organization suggested, the United States was beginning to expand its horizons. As suggested by the brief dalliance between the CIA and Egyptian President Gamal Abdel Nasser, covert means would not be excluded.

Eisenhower and Secretary of State John Foster Dulles believed that there was a fundamental threat from expanded Soviet involvement and influence in the region. To stop this, they devised a multifaceted strategy: (1) the British could no

longer be trusted to protect U.S. interests in the area, so the United States would
have to assume direct responsibility for the Middle East; (2) the United States
would encourage a group of states in the area to organize a "mini-NATO" (later
known as the Baghdad Pact); (3) arms sales to the Arabs (especially Iraq and hopefully Egypt) would be stepped up; (4) the United States would keep its distance
from Israel and try to settle the Arab-Israeli dispute. As it began to implement this
strategy, the United States expanded its instruments of involvement to include
both diplomatic and military policy, although the military implements largely consisted of arms transfers and the use of intelligence operations.

Eisenhower and Dulles had correctly identified the threat of Soviet involvement, and they had developed a sophisticated strategy. Unfortunately, it did not
work. Khrushchev, anxious to develop a strategy for challenging the West in the
Third World, simply "jumped over" the Maginot Line that Eisenhower and Dulles had created in the form of the Baghdad Pact when he began selling arms to
Egypt and Syria in 1955. During the Suez crisis the following year, the Soviet
leader was able to pose as the protector of the Arabs while threatening to punish
the British, French, and Israelis. The United States pressured all three to cease
their activities and eventually to withdraw; the Soviets got the credit. By tying his
fate to the nationalist Arab movement led by Nasser, Khrushchev had catapulted
the Soviet Union into a central role in the area. When a radical coup overthrew
the pro-Western government in Iraq in July 1958, the Soviet role appeared to
constitute an even wider menace. In response, Eisenhower intervened in Lebanon.

The vicissitudes of internal Arab rivalry (especially between Iraq and Egypt)
had blocked Eisenhower's designs for organizing the area against the Soviet Union.
Now Khrushchev too suffered from conflicts between these two key Arab states.
The new government of Iraq, although radical and prepared to buy Soviet arms,
was not ready to align with Cairo. In addition, Nasser and Khrushchev were dis-
covering that their new relationship was not devoid of tensions. Nevertheless, by
the end of the 1950s, the Soviets were pursuing large programs of arms transfers
to Egypt, Iraq, and Syria; they were engaged in demonstrative aid projects such
as the Aswan Dam; and larger numbers of Arab students were traveling to Moscow. The United States, although heavily involved in the region, had no effective
means of countering Soviet inroads and was attempting to bolster regimes still
ready to align with the West.

In the 1960s, the Kennedy administration attempted to build new bridges
back to Nasser but was thwarted by the Yemen war, which held the prospect of
Soviet influence and Egyptian troops at the border of oil-rich Saudi Arabia. In
response, the Johnson administration began to expand arms sales to several conservative Arab states and to Israel. During this period, the Soviets had gradually
increased their involvement in the region, especially through continuing military
aid, yet they too were hindered by quarreling Arab clients. Particularly after 1966,
a new radical Syrian government began calling for a national liberation campaign

against Israel and complained that Nasser's involvement in this struggle was marginal. To resolve these divisions, the Soviets began warning Nasser of imminent Israeli plans to attack Syria. This action was consistent with the Soviet pattern of stirring up local conflicts for their own political gains. All parties knew this accusation was false, and Nasser at first ignored it. By May 1967, however, with his army bogged down in Yemen and his economy deteriorating, Nasser flirted with the tides of history by ordering a partial withdrawal of the United Nations Emergency Force, which had been stationed in the Sinai since 1957, thus setting in motion the events that led to the Six Day War three weeks later.

From Moscow's perspective, the consequences of the war were horrifying, and it has never fully recovered its former position in the region. The two Arab states most closely associated with the Soviet Union, Egypt and Syria, were soundly defeated. Both lost significant pieces of territory; their armies were decimated. As these horrors occurred, the Soviets could do little but lobby in support of their Arab clients at the United Nations and increase their presence in the Mediterranean. Even their confrontation with the United States in protecting Syria during the last hours of the war appeared to be little more than posturing.

Yet in the immediate aftermath of the war, the balance did not appear totally negative from the Kremlin's perspective. Although the Israelis won their victory largely with French rather than U.S. weapons, the Untied States was blamed. As a consequence, several Arab states broke off diplomatic relations with Washington, and French President Charles de Gaulle's abrupt snubbing of Israel forced the United States for the first time into the position of protector of Jerusalem. Moscow's enormous resupply of weaponry to the Arabs partially compensated for the dismal showing of the Soviet Union and its arms during the war. It forced the United States to step up its arms transfers to Israel in order to maintain the regional balance of power. By 1969, when Nasser started his War of Attrition along the Suez Canal, the Soviets could justifiably argue that the return of Arab power had begun under their sponsorship. They were also heavily engaged in training and support for the Palestine Liberation Organization (PLO), which intensified its terrorist attacks against Israel after 1967.

The Six Day War certainly increased the immediate dependence of key Arab states on Moscow and of Israel on the United States. In more subtle terms, however, the nature of the Soviet-American competition was altered. For the first time, the means of Soviet involvement in the region had contracted and U.S. options had expanded. In frustration at the successful Israeli attack and its inability to reverse the outcome of the war, Moscow broke diplomatic relations with Israel. It was to prove a terrible blunder. Henceforth, the United States was the only superpower in close touch with both sides. Since the results of the war necessitated diplomatic discussions on conditions under which Israel might return the occupied Arab territories, a negotiating process of some kind was inevitable. The Soviets, however, always fearful of losing their Arab support purchased largely arms transfers, continued to maintain a posture equivalent to the lowest common denominator radical Arab position, thereby proving themselves irrelevant in serious negotiations.

The changed atmosphere could be seen immediately after the war. It was the United States that took the lead in trying to reach some kind of modus vivendi, a process that led to U.N. Security Council Resolution 242, in which an agenda for discussions was set. In 1969 it was the United States that promulgated the first major post–1967 peace plan for the area, the Rogers Plan, and it was the United States that arranged the cease-fire that ended the War of Attrition in August 1970. When Syrian tanks invaded Jordan the following month, the United States and Israel demonstrably maneuvered to strengthen Jordan's King Hussein, and the Syrians and their Palestinian allies were defeated. By 1972 Nasser's successor, Anwar Sadat, with the overwhelming support of his countrymen, expelled the large contingent of Soviet advisors who had entered Egypt during the War of Attrition.

During 1973 the Soviets attempted to recoup their weakened position to Cairo by shipping additional sophisticated weapons to Egypt. They risked a break in the new détente with Washington by not properly warning the Nixon administration that an Arab attack on Israel was imminent. When the war began, Soviet arms in the employ of Syria and Egypt initially defeated U.S. arms used by Israel. The Soviets cheered their Arab clients on, initiated an airlift, encouraged an oil embargo, and saved the Egyptian army by working with U.S. Secretary of State Henry A. Kissinger when defeat finally seemed certain. They even risked confrontation with the United States in order to save the Egyptian Third Army trapped in the Sinai.

In response, Sadat turned to Kissinger, whose own manipulation of a stalemate had outmaneuvered Moscow and created the basis for a strengthened U.S. role in the area. Over the next several months, Sadat switched superpower alliances and concluded a disengagement accord with Israel; the Geneva Conference format in which the Soviets participated was bypassed; and even the Syrians were forced to deal through Kissinger to gain the withdrawal of Israeli troops from territory captured in 1973. Kissinger's strategy had worked: Key Arab states were forced to recognize that only the United States held the answer to a possible settlement. For all their accomplishments, the Soviets were only spoilers. They could sell arms or train terrorists in the Middle East; they had become a superpower for troublemakers.

In the light of the energy crisis and the superpower confrontation that ended the October 1973 war, however, the new Carter administration's perception of the Soviet role was very different. The new team hoped to achieve a comprehensive settlement of the Arab-Israeli dispute to avert a worsening of the energy crisis. It also hoped to defuse the global competition with the Soviet Union by engaging Moscow in a variety of cooperative endeavors, including the Middle East peace process. Finally, the new administration proposed to recognize the Soviets' role in the area by inviting them to cochair a Geneva conference under whose rubric a settlement could be achieved. However, when the administration reached agreement with Moscow on October 1, 1977, on a set of principles for reconvening the conference, the strategy unraveled.

The idea of legitimizing the Soviet role in the region in order to persuade them to encourage their clients, especially Syria and possibly the PLO, to come to the peace table was novel. Yet there was no evidence they would or could deliver these reluctant clients. In any case, we will never know what might have happened if the strategy had been tried. The domestic protest in response to the communiqué was vociferous, particularly in Congress. After Kissinger's successful crippling of the Soviet Mideast position, Americans were not prepared to acquiesce in inviting them back in. Even worse for the Carter administration's plans, the new Begin government in Israel was so vehemently opposed to the joint superpower communiqué that there appeared to be a genuine danger that it would refuse to attend the conference. Therefore, within days Carter was forced to reach an agreement with Israeli Foreign Minister Moshe Dayan on a working paper for a conference that was unacceptable to the Arab parties, especially Syria, that his administration had been trying to attract.

Not only Israel rejected a Soviet role; Anwar Sadat ended any possibility of a near-term Soviet involvement in the peace process by traveling to Jerusalem in November 1977. Thus, ironically, even when the U.S. government was prepared to involve the Kremlin as cochairman of the Geneva conference, domestic and external constraints mitigated against it. Most important, the two parties ready to enter into direct peace talks, Egypt and Israel, would not accept Soviet participation. The events leading to Camp David, the Egyptian-Israeli peace treaty, and the autonomy talks left the Soviets as outsiders once again. When, in 1981, they petulantly refused to endorse a U.N. peacekeeping force for the Sinai (called for in the Egyptian-Israeli peace treaty), Secretary of State Alexander Haig negotiated a multinational force that was outside the U.N.'s auspices and therefore did not require Moscow's approval.

By then any hint of possible Soviet-American cooperation in the peace process had long been history. The fall of the Shah of Iran, the hostage crisis, the Iran-Iraq war, and the increased threat of Islamic fundamentalism had all combined to complicate enormously the Soviet-American competition in the area. Events in Iran represented a major defeat for the United States—in and of itself a victory for the Soviets—but the Kremlin was unable to turn either this or the Iran-Iraq war into an asset because of the Khomeini regime's inherent distrust of Soviet communism. The possibility that the fundamentalist contagion might also spread to Islamic areas of the Soviet Union was itself a deficit to Soviet interests and a potential source of domestic tension.

Islamic fundamentalism also represented a challenge to U.S. interests. If the Shah could be overthrown, which U.S. clients might be next? The temporary occupation of the Great Mosque in Mecca, the assassination of Anwar Sadat in

October 1981, and the general nervousness in the area were exemplary signs that the traditionally strong U.S. position in the region could be undermined. The second oil crisis in 1979—caused by panic buying after the fall of the Shah—seemed to indicate that the U.S. position in the area was deteriorating.

These events all represented a weakening of the United States, but it was unclear how the Soviets might benefit as a consequence. The Soviet invasion of Afghanistan altered this calculation. Whatever the reason for the invasion, it was interpreted by many Americans as a bid to take advantage of the West's travails and possibly even to capture the major Persian Gulf oil fields. The United States now seemed to face a twin threat to the Gulf states from both Teheran and Moscow. The Carter administration's response was to identify an "arc of crisis," stretching from Ethiopia (which had recently fallen to a pro-Soviet regime) to Pakistan (now threatened as a refuge for Afghans fleeing from Soviet troops). The declaration of the Carter Doctrine expanded the U.S. security umbrella to the Persian Gulf, and the United States set about trying to create a nexus of facilities in countries such as Oman, Kenya, Somalia, and Egypt to serve as possible staging points for a Rapid Deployment Force that could move to the area in an emergency.

The implication of these developments was that the Soviet-American competition had expanded to the Persian gulf and might require the use of U.S. troops. These issues extended far beyond the Palestinian question per se, although some analysts persisted in arguing that its resolution would solve the bulk of U.S. problems in the area. Yet this prescription progressively seemed impossible to achieve. With the Soviets establishing new strong points in Ethiopia, South Yemen, and Afghanistan, in addition to their influence with the PLO, Syria, and Libya, by 1981 their challenge to U.S. interests appeared to be more serious than ever. These developments in the region served to shatter the detente of the 1970s and create a sharper and more tense Soviet-American relationship.

The new Reagan administration came to office determined to address these perceived challenges. It hoped to create a "strategic consensus" between both the Arabs and Israelis and to convince them to set aside—at least temporarily—the sharp edge of their dispute in favor of parallel actions against the common Soviet foe. The critical medium for this new policy was military. The Rapid Deployment Force would be reinforced both with increased U.S. military expenditures and with bases in the area, hopefully including Saudi Arabia. Arms sales to the Arab states would be increased, especially the sale of sophisticated AWACS to Riyadh. A strategic cooperation agreement would be reached with Israel.

The policy did not work. The Arabs, especially the Saudis, were not prepared to play an activist role with the United States in its confrontation with the Soviet Union. The Israelis were alarmed by the administration's intention to strengthen the Arabs and progressively set out on their own. Their relations with Washington were strained by their independent actions in Lebanon, their destruction of the

Iraqi nuclear plant, the application of Israeli law to the Golan Heights, their invasion of Lebanon, and, finally, the Sabra and Shatila massacres of September 1982.

In response to its initial failures, the administration took two key initiatives in the summer of 1982 designed to salvage its strategy of confronting both the Soviet and fundamentalist threats. Both backfired. To secure a Lebanese cease-fire, it moved to insert U.S. troops into the thick of the Arab-Israeli conflict by volunteering their service in a multinational force in Lebanon. The U.S. presence in Beirut created a direct challenge to both Syria and the Kremlin, to which Moscow responded by dramatically rearming Syrian forces defeated in the 1982 war—which by 1986 created the potential for a new Syrian-Israeli war. The Syrians responded by initiating a proxy terrorist war, which enabled them to reject the May 1983 Lebanese-Israeli accord brokered by the United States and to force the Americans from Lebanon.

The administration's experiment with the notion that U.S. problems could be overcome through resolving the Palestinian question fared no better. The Reagan plan for a settlement based on a Palestinian entity on the West Bank and the Gaza Strip in political association with Jordan was stillborn. Negotiations could not be arranged. Jordan's King Hussein would not act alone, and he could not come to an agreement with PLO leader Yasser Arafat on a joint negotiating posture, despite repeated attempts between 1982 and 1986.

It is testimony to the increased complexities of the Soviet-American competition in the Middle East that Moscow could not take advantage of Washington's travails. First, Afghanistan proved to be a political-military disaster, with the Soviet Army bogged down through the 1980s in fighting Islamic fundamentalist rebels. Second, the Israelis succeeded in destroying the PLO infrastructure in Lebanon, and the war was followed by increasing splits within the Palestinian camp. The Soviets were confronted by a continuing conflict between two of their chief clients—Syria's Assad and Arafat—which they were helpless to control. Third, events continued to prove their irrelevance for the Arab-Israeli peace process. They could only encourage spoilers who would create roadblocks, but even this strategy failed to produce an enhanced Soviet position. Even when Jordan and Israel both agreed in theory to attend an international conference in October 1985, the conditions were discussed solely with the United States. Jordan insisted on greater Arab backing; Israel demanded renewed diplomatic relations with Moscow and emigration of Soviet Jews in large numbers.

Finally, the growing evidence of international terrorism also proved to be an embarrassment to the Soviet Union. Its clients, Libya and Syria, and the potpourri of radical Palestinians, were the prime sponsors. The attacks on civilian facilities, especially in Europe, meant that any connection with Moscow would prove detrimental to improved relations with the West. When the Reagan administration challenged Libya in the Gulf of Sidra and in bombing attacks against suspected terrorist facilities in early 1986, however, Moscow merely protested. The Soviets thereby proved to be as much a paper tiger in their passive policy toward Libya as the Americans had been in their activist approach to Lebanon.

Perspective on the Competition

By the mid–1980s, the Middle East had become too crucial to avoid and too dangerous for both superpowers to pursue consistently and effectively. Therefore, both the United States and the Soviet Union were engaged in phantom policies, carefully testing where they might make advances without undue commitments. For example, by the spring of 1987, a combination of factors combined to provide the Soviets under Mikhail Gorbachev with new opportunities. Encouraged by King Hussein and Israel's Shimon Peres, there was increasing talk of an international conference as an umbrella for peace negotiations. Moscow had worked to encourage renewed PLO unity and to improve its relations with several Persian Gulf states. The Reagan administration was mired in controversies over the Iran arms scandal and efforts to protect Kuwaiti ships in the Gulf. Soviet advances, however, remained in a stage of cautious incipiency.

The United States still maintained its stronger position in the competition. It had lost Iran, its Egyptian client remained fragile, and the credibility of its commitments were jeopardized by its erratic behavior in Lebanon and its secret arms deal with Iran. The Reagan administration also had introduced a new instrument, a willingness to use military force, which had at best been employed with mixed results. Yet in terms of the other instruments of involvement, diplomatic and economic, the United States was clearly the premier superpower. After 30 years of Soviet-American competition, the states of the area knew that only the United States could seriously assist with the peace process or with economic advancement. On both the diplomatic and economic levels of involvement, the United States was more creative and more flexible. Only in the area of arms sales did the Soviets have greater maneuverability, and here the Europeans—not the Kremlin—were increasingly replacing the United States when it failed to offer weapons.

Not surprisingly, the Soviets were left with a motley collection of unreliable or unstable clients: Iraq, obviously beleaguered and anxious to move back toward the Western camp; Syria, whose Assad could never be totally trusted by any patron; the PLO, in disarray; and South Yemen, where even Moscow's supposed control could not prevent a civil war in early 1986. Yet the energy glut, which had dramatically increased Western flexibility in the area, was also creating the economic disruption that could lead to renewed Soviet strength. The inherent instability and fragility of politics in the area mean that neither superpower can be sure of any of its positions, with the exception of the U.S. connection to Israel. Thus, in increasing fashion both superpowers are losers in the Middle East; both suffer problems even maintaining their positions; and reversals of fortune as a consequence of events both between and within states are ever possible.

It remains to be seen how both superpowers will react to the increasing complexity of a region in which the effect of political, military, and economic instruments of policy are progressively uncertain and frustrating. This complexity creates the incentive for at least tacit means of limiting the competition. The area's instability, and its accompanying unpredictability, however, mean that the danger of reversals and hope for gains are a constant incentive for vigilance and involvement. In the future Washington and Moscow are likely to be employed in dealing with problems among their clients and in adjusting to regional developments. Their policies are likely to be aimed at damage limitation rather than at major breakthroughs. The uncertainties over the Iran-Iraq war and the consternation that the upheavals in Iran have caused the Carter and Reagan administrations epitomize the vicissitudes of the new era. With the exception of the possibility of a major crisis (most likely between Syria and Israel), the growing confusion in the area is likely to diffuse the competition even while the region continues to attract the superpowers' attention and engagement.

Part II
Arms Transfers:
Quantitative Factors

2

U.S. Arms Transfer
and Arms Control Policies:
The Middle East

Robert E. Harkavy
Stephanie G. Neuman

The recent imbroglios over arms sales to Saudi Arabia and Jordan, U.S. financing of the Israeli fighter aircraft project, and the covert transfers of arms to Iran are but the latest episodes in what has long been a complex core issue in U.S. foreign policy—that of military sales and aid to the Middle East. That issue has been at the very vortex of the more general dilemmas of U.S. Middle Eastern policy, which include balancing the competing requirements of Israeli security and survival; maintaining access to Persian Gulf oil and related trade and monetary considerations, particularly with regard to Saudi Arabia; and blocking Soviet penetration into the Middle East and the adjoining regions of South Asia and East Africa.

In pursuit of these policy goals, the United States, in recent years, has depended increasingly on military assistance as a policy instrument. Between 1973 and 1982, at the peak of U.S. arms transfer activity in the Middle East, the United States delivered more than $65 billion worth of military equipment and related services to the area. As of this writing, depressed oil revenues and unstable economic conditions in non-oil-producing Middle Eastern countries, combined with the efforts of the Reagan administration to cut expenditures, augur a decline in the absolute value of U.S. sales to the region. But if recent trends are any indication, the proportion of U.S. military transfers to the Middle East relative to other regions of the world will remain high.

What factors have brought the United States to its current position of dominance as a supplier to the region? How can its increased military assistance activities be explained? This chapter will first examine U.S. military transfers in relation to those of other suppliers to the Middle East and then describe trends in the U.S.

military assistance program, as well as the specific events and policy rationales that have prompted the changes and continuities in it.

A Word about the Data

The tables in this chapter are intended to provide an overview of arms transfer patterns and trends for the Middle East by pointing out the comparative roles of major suppliers, the distribution of U.S. transfers to various Middle Eastern recipients, and the share of global transfers accounted for by the Middle East. To draw a complete picture, no single table will suffice. What is provided here are several diverse, complementary angles on the Middle East arms market, based on information derived from several sources.

The dollar values for U.S. transfers presented here are drawn from the Defense Security Assistance Agency (DSAA) Fiscal Year Series, which includes all U.S. transfers: commercial, Military Assistance Program (MAP, grant aid), and Foreign Military Sales (FMS).[1] We have also tried, wherever possible, to present the dollar values of deliveries—that is, what the countries actually received as opposed to what was ordered. Because states, for a variety of reasons, often change their minds, deliveries provide a more accurate picture of who actually got what from whom when. Unfortunately, information on deliveries is not always available, so in tables 2–8 and 2–10–2–11 orders have been used instead. For comparative purposes an attempt has been made to control for inflation by providing constant dollar figures whenever possible.

The dollar values for other suppliers and all estimates of military expenditures are drawn from U.S. Arms Control and Disarmament Agency (ACDA's) *World Military Expenditures and Arms Transfers*.[2] These, too, have been converted into constant dollars. Some of the import figures, because they were not available elsewhere, were drawn from a non-U.S. source—the Stockholm International Peace Research Institute's (SIPRI) arms transfer registers.[3]

We have attempted to present the data in as comparable a form as possible. Nevertheless, because some data were derived from different sources, they are subject to question with regard to relative accuracy, comparisons of current dollar versus constant dollar, deliveries versus orders, and so on. While these methodological problems are not insignificant and may loom large for some scholarly disputations, they are of marginal importance here. The interest here is in the elucidation of very broad trends and comparisons, and for these purposes the data presented, although not perfect, are adequate.

The term *Middle East* also has been subject to a variety of disputations. It has been used as a generic concept to designate a region that, depending on the analyst, has included a shifting number and variety of countries. By and large, we have adopted the ACDA definition of the region, with two exceptions: Libya has been added, and Cyprus is not included. For the purposes of this analysis, then, the Middle East is composed of a core of sixteen countries: Bahrain, Egypt, Iran, Iraq, Israel, Jordan, Kuwait, Lebanon, Libya, Oman, Qatar, Saudi Arabia, Syria, United Arab Emirates, Yemen (Aden), and Yemen (Sanaa).

Overview: Trends in Arms Transfers to the Middle East

The first and most obvious trend is the enormous continual increase, as measured in constant dollars, in the volume of arms coming into the Middle East from all sources since 1966 (see table 2–1). This correlates, of course, with the large rise in military expenditures for the region, itself a reflection of the fact that the Middle East has become the most volatile, conflict-prone area of the world (see table 2–2).

In the Middle East, military expenditures (MILEX) have risen some 1,600 percent since 1963. From a total of $4 billion in 1963 (constant 1985 dollars), military expenditures escalated to around $68 billion in 1983. Between 1973 and 1983 alone, the rate of increase (7.6 percent) was double that of NATO. And although declining oil revenues have cut the previous rate of growth, military expenditures are still rising at an annual rate of 3.7 percent. By 1983 the Middle East accounted for about 8 percent of the world's military expenditures, up from around 1 percent in 1963 and 4.2 percent in 1973 (see table 2–2).

The volume of arms delivered to the Middle East has likewise escalated. Even when the dollar values are controlled for inflation by using constant dollars, it is clear that the quantity of arms coming into the Middle East has grown steadily and incrementally. Thus, the dollar value of imports for the late 1960s dwarf those for the 1950s, and those for the 1970s and 1980s dwarf those of previous decades. During the period 1973 to 1983, for example, the Middle Eastern share of world arms imports increased from 27 percent in 1973 to around 43 percent in 1983. Overall, since the mid-1960s there has been about a 400 percent increase in Middle Eastern military imports (see table 2–1).

A look at the numbers and quality of discrete major weapons systems pouring into the region (see various published registers of U.S. transfers to the Middle East not included here for reasons of space)[4] reveals a similar picture. The increasing unit cost of individual systems (well beyond the rate of inflation), a trend now 50 or more years in evidence, has resulted in increased costs for virtually all nations in the procurement of smaller numbers of ships, aircraft, tanks, and so on, which are more modern and have much more capability.[5]

Looked at from another angle (see table 2–1), it is apparent that not only have transfers into the region vastly increased in absolute terms, but they also have greatly increased relative to other Third World regions. In 1966 the region's arms

Table 2-1
Values of Imports of Major Weapons by the Third World
(by region, 1966–1985[a])

Region[b]		1966	1967	1968	1969	1970	1971	1972	1973
Middle East	A	440	1063	1258	1212	1462	1758	1076	2211
	B	718	883	1087	1351	1353	1544	1869	2282
South Asia	A	391	271	297	312	300	499	409	289
	B	250	297	314	336	363	362	374	349
North Africa	A	122	135	83	87	121	123	167	145
	B	92	102	110	110	116	129	157	285
South America	A	138	128	208	158	148	222	310	352
	B	127	148	156	173	209	238	296	392
Far East (excl. Vietnam)[c]	A	497	199	266	586	271	419	162	302
	B	339	378	364	348	341	348	281	354
Sub-Saharan Africa (excl. S. Africa)	A	93	81	55	71	121	134	89	152
	B	78	79	84	92	94	113	176	199
Central America	A	21	16	8	10	6	47	35	56
	B	19	15	12	17	21	31	46	72
South Africa	A	92	78	45	46	77	69	25	37
	B	90	89	68	63	52	51	96	117
Oceania	A	—	—	—	—	—	—	—	—
	B	—	—	—	—	—	—	—	—
Total (excl. Vietnam)[d]	A	1794	1971	2220	2482	2506	3272	2273	3545
	B	1715	1990	2195	2490	2551	2816	3295	4050
Vietnam	A	237	494	473	298	433	435	1200	82
	B	274	315	387	427	568	490	467	384
Total[d]	A	2031	2465	2693	2780	2939	3707	3473	3627
	B	1989	2305	2582	2917	3118	3305	3762	4435

Source: Stockholm International Peace Research Institute, *World Armaments and Disarmament, SIPRI Yearbook 1986* (Oxford: Oxford University Press), pp. 354–355.

Note: Figures are SIPRI trend indicator values, as expressed in millions of U.S. dollars, at constant 1975 prices. Five-year moving averages are calculated from the year arms imports began, as a more stable measure of the trend in arms imports than the often erratic year-to-year figures.

[a]The values include licensed production of major weapons in Third World countries. For the values for the period 1950–1956, see *SIPRI Yearbook 1976*, pp. 250–251; and 1957–1965, *SIPRI Yearbook 1978*, pp. 254–255.

imports were smaller than those to the Far East (even excluding Vietnam), only slightly greater than those to South Asia, and only about three times more than the combined figures for South and Central America. By the end of the 1970s the picture had changed dramatically. Between 1974 and 1978, the Middle East absorbed 56 percent of world deliveries (see table 2-3). By the early 1980s (1979–1983), arms transfers to the Middle East had dropped somewhat but still amounted to 49 percent of world deliveries (see table 2-4) and were larger than those imports

1974	1975	1976	1977	1978	1979	1980	1981	1982	1983	1984	1985
2836	3527	3613	5190	4018	3512	4859	3480	4332	4446	5165	3928
2653	3475	3837	3972	4238	4212	4040	4126	4456	4270	NA	NA
373	177	414	663	1077	541	765	938	971	749	780	1006
332	383	541	574	692	792	858	793	841	889	NA	NA
228	761	929	948	1337	2281	1524	1164	1357	690	579	391
444	602	841	1251	1404	1451	1533	1403	1063	836	NA	NA
446	630	710	826	713	798	649	816	769	1006	993	476
490	593	665	735	739	760	749	808	847	812	NA	NA
249	640	1035	653	2367	1964	1180	876	659	872	748	810
478	579	989	1332	1440	1408	1409	1110	867	793	NA	NA
386	232	432	1148	1269	299	788	709	603	459	774	414
258	470	693	676	787	843	734	572	667	592	NA	NA
87	137	58	60	110	80	605	453	470	252	159	105
75	80	90	89	183	262	344	372	388	288	NA	NA
274	179	118	211	253	120	80	10	11	73	2	2
127	164	207	176	156	135	95	59	35	20	NA	NA
—	—	3	—	3	3	1	2	4	9	2	2
—	—	—	2	2	2	3	4	4	4	NA	NA
4878	6284	7312	9699	11147	9598	10451	8448	9176	8558	9202	7134
4858	6344	7864	8807	9641	9869	9764	9246	9167	8503	NA	NA
185	20										
—											
5064	6304	7312	9699	11147	9598	10451	8448	9176	8558	9202	7134
5156	6401	7905	8810	9641	9869	9764	9246	9167	8503	NA	NA

bThe regions are listed in rank order according to their five-year average values in the column for 1983.

cVietnam is included in the figures for the Far East after 1975, the year the Vietnam War ended.

dItems may not add up to totals due to rounding.

— = nil.

NA = Not applicable.

into other Third World regions: more than eight times those to South Asia, six times those to Latin America, and four times those to East Asia. The proportion of imports rose to about one-half of the Third World total during 1979–1983.[6]

Viewed from still another perspective, from 1973 to 1983, the seven largest arms importers among Third World countries were *all* from the Middle East: Iraq, Libya, Iran, Syria, Saudi Arabia, Israel, and Egypt. Using a broader definition of that region, one finds that Morocco, Algeria, and Afghanistan are also among the

Table 2–2
Military Expenditures of the Middle East as a Proportion of World Military Expenditures, 1963–1983
(1985 constant dollars, in billions)

Years	World MILEX	Middle East MILEX	Percent
1963–1967	2398.6	25.27	1.2
1968–1972	2815.8	54.18	1.9
1973–1977	3414.67	237.72	7.0
1978–1982	3928.71	324.25	8.2
1983	870.03	72.52	8.3

Source: U.S. Arms Control and Disarmament Agency (ACDA), *World Military Expenditures and Arms Transfers, 1985* (Washington: ACDA Publication 123, August 1985).

top 20 (see table 2–5). In short, not only have military expenditures and imports risen, but the region has come to dominate global arms transfers to an astonishing degree.

Patterns of U.S. Military Assistance to the Middle East

Turning now to a discussion of U.S. military assistance to the Middle East, at the risk of some simplification, one perceives several discrete phases in U.S. arms transfer policy in this region. These phases can be related to changes in overall U.S. global arms transfer policies since the end of World War II, as well as to specific regional developments. Of the latter, wars have had a particularly significant impact on U.S. aid to the area.

The earliest phase corresponds more or less to the first 10 years of the postwar period, in which U.S. arms sales to the region were quite modest.[7] That was in part a function of continued British influence in the region and U.S. concern with the rebuilding of Europe as a bulwark versus the Soviet Union. But it also was a function of the relatively low level of demand from regional states whose financial wherewithal was nowhere near what it would later become. From 1953 to 1957, for example, the proportion of U.S. military transfers to the Middle East was only 1.2 percent of its worldwide deliveries (see table 2–6).

In the second phase, from the late 1950s to the 1967 war—a period that saw strong Soviet penetration of arms markets, first in Egypt and Syria and then in Iraq—U.S. arms sales were concentrated in those "forward" nations—in and near the core Middle Eastern region—Iran, Turkey, and Pakistan—that had become alliance partners in the rimland geopolitical defense against the Soviet Union. Even then, U.S. military assistance to the Middle East averaged only about 4

Table 2-3
Military Assistance Deliveries to the Middle East by Supplier, 1974–1978
(1985 constant dollars, in millions)

Recipient	Total	Supplier										
		Soviet	U.S.	France	U.K.	FRG	Italy	Czech.	China	Rumania	Poland	Others
Bahrain	11.		2.	9.								
Egypt	2031.	750.	113.	453.	192.	297.	17.	52.		70.		87.
Iran	18461.	541.	14902.	349.	733.	820.	610.					506.
Iraq	9244.	6279.	0.*	750.	35.	262.	122.	157.		17.		1570.
Israel	9251.		9050.	35.	105.		52.					9.
Jordan	1259.		1040.	9.	52.	9.						149.
Kuwait	1364.	87.	632.	262.	331.	35.						17.
Lebanon	105.		36.	17.	17.	9.		9.				17.
Libya	8571.	5930.	7.	471.	35.	244.	576.	314.			384.	610.
Oman	655.		10.		576.		9.					70.
Qatar	71.		2.		17.						52.	
S. Arabia	12673.		10065.	52.	1265.		157.					663.
Syria	5757.	4709.	2.	488.	52.	35.		366.				
UAE	642.		15.	262.	209.	157.	35.					209.
S. Yemen	662.	645.						0.				17.
N. Yemen	377.	87.	151.	87.								52.
Mideast	71135.	19028.	36027.*	3601.	3619.	1868.	1578.	898.	87.	**	436.	3993.
Percent		26.7	50.6	5.1	5.1	2.6	2.2	1.2	—	—	—	5.6

World Total 127,249

Mideast percent 55.9

Source: For non-U.S. deliveries: U.S. Arms Control and Disarmament Agency, (ACDA) *World Military Expenditures and Arms Transfers, 1985*, table II (Washington: ACDA Publication 123, August 1985); for U.S. deliveries: Department of Defense Security Assistance Agency (DSAA), *Fiscal Year Series, as of September 30, 1985* (Washington: Data Management Division, Controller, DSAA).

Note: Conversion factor used to convert ACDA current dollars into 1985 constant = 1.7442.

*Deliveries of less than $1 million.

**Rumania is included in "Others."

Table 2–4
Military Assistance Deliveries to the Middle East by Supplier, 1979–1983
(1985 constant dollars, in millions)

Recipient	Total	Supplier										
		Soviet	U.S.	France	U.K.	FRG	Italy	Czech.	China	Rumania	Poland	Others
Bahrain	144.		12.	48.		48.	12.					24.
Egypt	7077.	48.	3163.	1448.	694.	253.	386.		362.		60.	663.
Iran	8251.	1176.	3228.	24.	169.	6.	181.	48.	227.	6.	48.	3136.
Iraq	21255.	8685.	0.*	4584.	338.	169.	495.		1809.	483.	1025.	3619.
Israel	6193.		6187.									6.
Jordan	4307.	277.	1346.	1206.	1327.	6.	133.		12.			133.
Kuwait	797.	36.	472.		60.	84.	12.					12.
Lebanon	474.		299.	109.	12.							36.
Libya	12095.	5800.	0.	850.	40.	380.	700.	575.	310.	310.	230.	2900.
Oman	684.		99.	24.	519.		12.		6.			24.
Qatar	923.		12.	531.	374.							6.
S. Arabia	30073.		21599.	3016.	2292.	633.	241.					2292.
Syria	12702.	11098.	0.*	241.	217.	48.		567.	109.	24.	36.	362.
UAE	752.		28.	422.	109.	133.	36.	0				24.
S. Yemen	1821.	1809.	0.*									12.
N. Yemen	2826.	1448.	226.	36.		12.	6.			302.	12.	784.
Mideast	110374	30377.	36671.	12539.	6151.	1772.	2214.	1190.	2885.	1125	1417.	14033.
Percent	100	27.5	33.2	11.4	5.6	1.6	2.0	1.1	2.6	1.0	1.3	12.7

World Total 223,987
Mideast percent 49.3

Source: For non-U.S. deliveries: U.S. Arms Control and Disarmament Agency, (ACDA) *World Military Expenditures and Arms Transfers, 1985*, table II (Washington: ACDA Publication 123, August 1985); for U.S. deliveries: Department of Defense Security Assistance Agency (DSAA), *Fiscal Year Series*, as of September 30, 1985 (Washington: Data Management Division, Controller, DSAA).

Note: Conversion factor used to convert ACDA current dollars into 1985 constant = 1.2063.

*Deliveries of less than $1 million.

Table 2–5
Major Third World Arms Importers, 1973–1983

Rank Country	Value 1982 (millions of dollars)	Percent Developing Country	Cumulative
1 Iraq	27,713	10.4	10.4
2 Libya	21,065	7.9	13.3
3 Iran	20,446	7.7	26.0
4 Syria	19,416	7.3	33.3
5 Saudi Arabia	17,925	6.7	40.0
6 Israel	11,930	4.5	44.5
7 Egypt	9,587	3.6	48.1
8 India	8,188	3.1	51.2
9 Vietnam	7,186	2.7	53.9
10 Algeria	6,362	2.4	56.3
11 South Korea	4,947	1.9	58.2
12 Cuba	4,557	1.7	59.9
13 Jordan	4,507	1.7	61.6
14 Taiwan	4,338	1.6	63.2
15 Morocco	3,483	1.3	64.5
16 Pakistan	3,462	1.3	65.8
17 Peru	3,241	1.2	67.0
18 Ethiopia	3,044	1.1	68.1
19 Yemen (Sanaa)	2,849	1.1	69.2
20 Afghanistan	2,679	1.0	70.2
Total Third World	266,509		

Source: For non–U.S. deliveries: U.S. Arms Control and Disarmament Agency, (ACDA) *World Military Expenditures and Arms Transfers, 1985,* table II (Washington: ACDA Publication 123, August 1985); for U.S. deliveries: Department of Defense Security Assistance Agency (DSAA), *Fiscal Year Series, as of September 30, 1985* (Washington: Data Management Division, Controller, DSAA).

percent of its worldwide deliveries—again a reflection of the limited pre-OPEC buying power of the region (see table 2–6).

In the aftermath of the 1967 war—a third phase—a constellation of forces propelled the United States into the role of primary supplier to Israel. The French wartime embargo on arms sales to Israel became fixed and permanent around 1968–1969, and the *de facto* British embargo was continued into the postwar period. Filling the vacuum, the United States began it supply relationship with Israel, which gradually expanded until Israel became a major recipient of U.S. military aid. Whereas Israel consumed 10 percent of total U.S. military aid to the region between 1963 and 1967, during the next five years its share rose to 34 percent. Iran remained a major U.S. client, consuming another one-third of U.S. exports to the region between 1968 and 1972 (see table 2–7).

During the fourth phase, after the 1973 war, the distribution of military transfers to U.S. clients changed again, along with the method of payment. U.S. arms delivered to Iran increased, and more significant sales to Saudi Arabia were initiated. Iran's share of U.S. transfers rose to 42 percent between 1973 and 1977, and

Table 2-6
U.S. Military Assistance Deliveries to the Middle East, 1953–1985
(1985 constant dollars, in millions)

Years	U.S. Mideast	U.S. World	Percent of World Total
1953–1957	989.5	79245.3	1.2
1958–1962	2054.0	49489.7	4.1
1963–1967	2035.2	46224.4	4.4
1968–1972	6640.0	62332.7	10.6
1973–1977	27709.232	70801.8	39.1
1978–1982	36979.2	70244.2	52.6
1983–1985	19387.3	44781.5	43.3
1984			39.3
1985			39.3

Source: Derived from Table 2–7.

the Saudis' increased from 16 percent in 1963–1973 to 24 percent in 1973–1977. In addition, in response to the vast accumulations of petrodollars by OPEC, sales, not grants (MAP), of equipment and services became the major form of U.S. military assistance. Since the early 1960s a desire to reduce its foreign aid burden prompted the United States to reassess its military assistance program with a view toward decreasing the grant-aid component.[8] Prior to OPEC, however, the Middle East lacked sufficient resources, and many countries' programs continued to be subsidized. The changing fortunes of its clients in 1973 made it possible for the United States to implement its preferred policy. By 1974 MAP deliveries to Iran had virtually stopped, and even the U.S. grant-aid training program for Saudi Arabia was terminated. In terms of the focus of U.S. arms transfer policy, this shift was significant. Until 1964 Europe, Japan, Canada, and Australia accounted for 80 percent of U.S. FMS sales each year. By 1974 only 14 percent of total U.S. arms sales went to these countries, and Iran had become the largest recipient of FMS, purchasing 45 percent of the arms sold by the United States.[9]

During this period, the United States also increased its military transfers to Israel and began a patron-client relationship with Egypt after President Sadat's expulsion of the Soviets. As trade with the regional oil-rich nation grew, however, Israel's proportionate share of U.S. exports dropped, and even with the huge U.S. resupply effort after the 1973 war, its share fell from 34 percent in the previous five-year period to 29 percent between 1973 and 1977.

In the fifth phase, beginning in the late 1970s, the dollar value of U.S. exports to the region remained high but began to level off, reflecting the end of the U.S.-Iranian supply relationship, the United States' low profile as a supplier during the Iran-Iraq war, and the increasing economic difficulties of traditional U.S. clients in the region. As a result, this period witnessed major fluctuations, with some countries expanding their military imports while others reduced them. The staggering sales to Saudi Arabia are a case in point, averaging around $3 to $4 billion annually for the period 1978 to 1982 and amounting to 51 percent of total U.S. regional deliveries. Egypt's U.S. deliveries also increased from virtually nothing, when its major supplier was the Soviet Union, to 5.4 percent of U.S. Middle Eastern exports and by 1983–1985, it had actually exceeded Israel's share. During that three-year period, Israel's share dropped to 10.2 percent while Egypt's grew to 12.1 percent.

Unlike Saudi Arabia and Egypt, the ratio of Israeli and Iranian military imports relative to their region as a whole declined. Israel's share slipped to 19.2 percent between 1978 and 1982, and Iran's fell to 17.5 percent (with U.S. deliveries to the latter ending in 1981.) Jordanian deliveries also dropped during this period. Although never a major recipient compared to Iran, Saudi Arabia, and Israel, Jordan's share of total U.S. exports to the region was not insignificant in the mid-1960s and early 1970s, and between 1963 and 1972 it received approximately 9 percent of total U.S. Middle East deliveries. By the 1970s and 1980s, however, Jordan's share had fallen to approximately 3 percent. Since 1984, the absolute value of Jordan's U.S. arms imports also has declined—no doubt reflecting both Jordan's economic difficulties and congressionally mandated controls that have prompted Jordan to diversify suppliers. During the period 1979 to 1983, its acquisitions from France and the United Kingdom were almost equal to the U.S. figures (see table 2–4) a striking contrast to the 1974–1978 period (see table 2–3).

In general, diversification of supply became a more common pattern of procurement during this period. As U.S. deliveries began to decline, those from other suppliers increased. Whereas the United States dominated the Mideast market between 1973 and 1978, with 51 percent of all arms imports, by 1979 to 1983, although still the largest single supplier, it only provided about one-third of the Mideast's military deliveries (see tables 2–3 and 2–4). Soviet and British shares remained flat, but the absolute value of their deliveries almost doubled, and the proportion of French transfers rose in relative as well as in absolute dollar value— the latter more than tripling between the two periods.[10] Whereas combined European aid to the Middle East amounted to less than one-third the dollar value of U.S. aid (30 percent) between 1974 and 1978, it had increased to almost two-thirds (62 percent) of the U.S. Middle East total by the period 1979 to 1983.

If the U.S. data are disaggregated by type of program (that is, MAP, FMS, FMS construction, and commercial exports), significant differences among the recipients' procurement patterns emerge[11] (see tables 2–8 through 2–11). Jordan, for example, between 1950 and 1975 obtained about 44 percent of its military equipment through the MAP program and accounted for more than 76 percent of total U.S. grant aid to the region. Since then, Jordan has continued to receive what little MAP aid the United States gives to the Middle East, although as in other Middle Eastern states, since the mid-1970s FMS has been the major vehicle for

Table 2-7
U.S. Military Assistance Deliveries to the Middle East, 1953–1985
(1985 constant dollars, in millions)

Year	Bahrain	Egypt	Iran	Iraq	Israel	Jordan	Kuwait	Lebanon	Libya
1953	.000	.000	142.106	.000	.000	.000	.000	.000	.000
1954	.000	0.569	201.704	0.000	1.232	0.000	0.000	0.000	0.000
1955	.000	0.093	108.209	27.944	0.493	0.000	0.000	0.000	0.000
1956	.000	0.127	114.135	29.770	0.191	0.000	0.000	0.000	0.000
1957	.000	0.057	198.889	67.772	0.029	0.000	0.000	11.071	0.000
Subtotal	.000	0.846	765.043	125.486	1.945	0.000	0.000	11.071	0.000
%M.E. total	0.00	0.09	77.3	12.7	0.2	0.00	0.00	1.1	0.00
1958	.000	0.036	321.093	101.406	0.113	40.457	0.00	5.906	5.662
1959	.000	0.040	422.744	2.560	2.312	9.338	0.00	16.774	1.275
1960	.000	0.030	395.359	0.030	3.605	12.590	0.00	0.723	4.371
1961	.000	0.376	221.144	0.047	3.194	8.585	0.00	4.015	1.317
1962	.000	0.059	122.037	0.076	1.409	11.226	0.00	0.074	5.159
Subtotal	.000	0.541	1,482.377	104.119	10.633	82.196	0.000	27.492	17.784
%M.E. total	0.00	0.03	72.2	5.1	0.52	4.0	0.00	1.3	0.87
1963	.000	0.083	302.621	1.751	1.522	12.118	0.00*	0.590	3.519
1964	.000	0.098	129.284	5.477	4.570	39.203	.00*	0.383	7.486
1965	.000	0.047	249.544	4.332	67.939	45.716	0.00*	0.553	10.382
1966	.000	0.011	271.783	16.080	72.649	99.795	0.00*	0.655	8.105
1967	.000	0.051	275.746	19.715	58.500	93.027	0.00*	.250	10.492
Subtotal	0.000	0.290	1228.978	47.355	205.180	289.859	0.00	2.431	39.984
%M.E. total	0.00	0.014	60.4	2.3	10.1	14.2	0.00	0.1	2.0
1968	.000	0.000	324.260	.683	95.346	48.164	0.00*	2.054	25.902
1969	.000	0.000	456.329	.092	230.433	82.814	0.00*	3.368	38.050
1970	.000	0.000	428.079	.000	640.684	163.466	0.00*	3.348	18.773
1971	.060	0.002	316.248	.710	948.101	85.701	0.005	4.959	4.061
1972	.007	0.00*	679.732	.000	714.878	89.914	0.00*	1.086	80.944
Subtotal	0.067	0.002	2204.648	1.485	2629.442	470.059	0.005	14.815	167.730
%M.E. total	0.001	0.00	33.2	0.02	33.9	7.1	0.00	0.2	2.5
1973	.006	0.00	32.087	0	518.805	118.140	.014	21.273	2.220
1974	.127	0.001	1491.207	0.00	2250.839	126.978	.325	3.940	2.874
1975	.100	0.063	2054.147	0.00	1548.153	173.707	15.511	3.592	2.614
1976	.701	1.269	3717.873	.054	1866.384	259.260	41.711	10.234	.498
1977	1.182	20.206	4399.723	.108	1878.331	193.901	270.765	.714	.342
Subtotal	2.116	21.539	11.695.037	.162	8062.512	871.986	328.326	39.753	8.548
%M.E. total	0.0	0.08	42.2	0.0	29.1	3.1	1.2	0.1	0.03
1978	0.336	91.764	3239.609	.221	1506.640	286.564	304.061	17.919	.483
1979	1.054	283.913	3216.353	.014	753.769	181.125	109.243	17.417	0.000
1980	0.285	276.250	9.245	.001	1103.433	360.843	101.562	22.513	.291
1981	2.406	243.360	0.00	0.000	2607.288	258.924	78.719	16.667	0
1982	3.324	1093.594	0	0	1120.143	212.078	100.295	42.601	0
Subtotal	7.405	1988.881	6465.207	.236	7091.273	1299.534	693.880	117.117	.774
%M.E. total	0.02	5.4	17.5	0.0	19.2	3.5	1.9	0.3	0.0
1983	3.278	1265.513	0	0	601.938	332.989	81.973	199.458	0
1984	4.319	406.683	.055	.013	661.168	106.947	114.808	226.466	0
1985	13.021	671.108	2.102	.001	717.385	153.252	48.658	54.124	0
Subtotal	20.618	2343.304	2.157	.014	1980.491	593.188	245.43 9	480.048	0.00
%M.E. total	0.1	12.1	0.01	0.00	10.2	3.1	1.3	2.5	0.00
Total	30.206	4,355.403	23,843.447	278.875	19,981.476	3,606.822	1267.650	692.727	234.820
Percent	0.03	4.5	24.9	0.29	20.86	3.77	1.32	0.72	0.25

Source: Department of Defense Security Assistance Agency (DSAA), *Fiscal Year Series, as of September 30, 1985* (Washington: Data Management Division, Controller, DSAA).
*Less than $500.

Oman	Qatar	Saudi Arabia	Syria	UAE	Yemen (Aden)	Yemen (Sanaa)	Total M.E.	U.S. Total Worldwide	% Mideast of U.S. World
.000	.00	5.348	.00	.00	.00	.00	147.454	20095.093	0.7
0.000	0.00	4.771	.00	.00	.00	.00	208.276	18115.385	1.1
0.000	0.00	12.985	.00	.00	.00	.00	149.724	12675.422	1.2
0.000	0.00	55.161	.00	.00	.00	.00	199.384	15186.878	1.3
0.000	0.00	6.878	.00	.00	.00	.00	284.696	13172.564	2.2
0.00	0.000	85.143	0.000	0.000	.000	0.000	989.534	79245.342	1.2
0.00	0.00	8.6	0.00	0.00	0.00	0.00	100.0		
0.00	0.00	243.455	0.00	0.00	0.00	0.00	718.128	12639.201	5.7
0.00	0.00	18.919	0.00	0.00	0.00	0.00	473.962	10754.036	4.4
0.00	0.00	13.539	0.00	0.00	0.00	0.00	430.247	9758.919	4.4
0.00	0.00	31.911	0.00	0.00	0.00	0.00	270.589	7563.985	3.6
0.00	0.00	20.989	0.00	0.00	0.00	0.00	161.029	8773.590	1.8
0.000	0.000	328.813	0.000	0.000	0.000	0.000	2,053.955	49,489.731	4.1
0.00	0.00	16.0	0.00	0.00	0.00	0.00	100.0		
.00	0.00	24.033	.00	0.00	0.00	0.00	346.237	10916.477	3.2
.00	0.00	23.582	.059	.00	0.0	0.00	210.142	7595.909	2.8
.00	.00	26.034	0.72	.00	0	0.00	404.619	8970.833	4.5
.00	.00	48.242	.065	.00	0	0.00	517.385	9009.495	5.7
.00	.00	99.050	.016	.00	0	0.00	556.847	9731.706	5.7
0.00	0.00	220.941	.212	0.00	0.00	0.00	2035.230	46224.420	4.4
0.00	0.00	10.9	0.01	0.00	0.00	0.00	100		
0.000	0.000	125.394	.002	0.000	0	0.00	621.805	10909.588	5.7
0.000	0.000	103.704	.000	0.000	0	0.00	914.790	11570.150	7.9
0.000	0.000	96.245	.000	0.000	0	0.00	1350.595	11521.795	11.7
0.037	0.003	380.729	.035	0.016	0	0.00	1740.667	14103.360	12.3
0.448	0.00*	420.936	.000	1.162	0	0.00	1989.107	14227.769	14.0
0.485	0.003	1127.008	.037	1.178	0.00	0.00	6616.964	62332.662	10.6
0.01	0.00	17.0	0.00	0.02	0.00	0.00	100		
.154	.012	512.604	.058	.159	0.00	0.00	1205.532	16,825.437	7.2
.087	0.000	762.710	.234	.275	0.0	0.00	4639.597	12,800.940	36.2
4.235	0.42	696.721	.147	.512	0	3.603	4503.147	11,925.043	37.8
1.871	.062	1896.367	.195	4.793	0	1.031	7802.303	14,176.310	55.0
1.977	.995	2744.965	.068	1.571	0	43.805	9558.653	15,074.207	63.4
8.324	1.111	6613.367	.702	7.310	0.00	48.439	27709.232	70,801.937	39.1
0.03	0.0	23.9	0.0	0.03	0.0	0.2	100.0		
2.310	.461	3964.584	1.324	8.258	0.00	103.013	9527.547	15,118.387	63.0
0.946	4.785	3643.017	.278	2.712	0.00	91.233	8305.859	14,318.266	58.0
10.497	1.365	3431.014	.001	7.070	0	59.061	5383.431	12,706.083	42.4
20.570	1.283	3547.750	0	6.949	0	28.297	6812.213	13,899.714	49.0
36.188	2.515	4303.794	0	5.235	0	28.469	6948.236	14,201.728	48.9
70.511	10.409	18890.159	1.603	30.224	0.00	310.073	36977.286	70,244.159	52.6
0.2	0.02	51.1	0.0	0.08	0.0	0.8	100.0		
31.221	1.566	6673.146	.008	5.919	.016	18.799	9215.824	18,531.077	49.7
10.249	4.026	3916.473	.006	22.465	0	11.450	5485.308	14,315.489	38.3
4.226	1.856	2991.830	.132	16.323	0	12.078	4686.096	11,934.972	39.2
45.876	7.448	13581.449	.146	44.707	.016	42.327	19387.228	44,781.538	43.3
0.2	0.04	70.1	0.00	0.2	0.08	0.2			
125.196	18.971	40,846.880	2.700	83.419	0.16	400.839	95,769.429	423,119.808	22.6
0.13	0.19	42.65	0.002	0.09	0.00	0.42	100		

Table 2-8

U.S. Military Assistance Program, 1950–1985

(in millions of dollars)

Fiscal Year	Egypt	Jordan	Kuwait	Saudi Arabia	Other[a]	Total Arab	Israel
1950–1975		261		24	58	342	
1976		51				51	
1977		51				51	
1978		55				55	
1979		42				42	
1980		28				28	
1981		1				1	
1982							
1983							
1984							
1985							
Total		490		24	58	572	0

Source: Seth Carus.

[a]Other includes Iraq, Libya, and Syria.

its U.S. transfers. Israel, on the other hand, despite its large FMS procurements, has availed itself, out of all proportion to its neighbors, of U.S. commercial exports by buying directly from U.S. military industries (see table 2–9). In recent years only Saudi Arabia has begun to use commercial sales to a similar degree. Prior to 1976, FMS construction agreements made up the largest proportion of its military

Table 2-9

U.S. Commercial Military Exports, 1950–1985

(in millions of dollars)

Fiscal Year	Egypt	Jordan	Kuwait	Saudi Arabia	Other[a]	Total Arab	Israel
1950–1975				68	31	100	242
1976	1		6	93		100	190
1977	1	4		44		50	222
1978	7	9	2	166	1	186	123
1979	1	4	3	44		53	174
1980	7	54		29		90	272
1981	4	42	1	72		119	267
1982	15	50	5	50		120	150
1983	103	28	4	252		387	300
1984	69	17	61	360		507	418
1985	50	7	1	186		244	186
Total	257	215	84	1,364	33	1,953	2,542

Source: Seth Carus.

[a]Other includes Iraq, Libya, and Syria.

Table 2-10
U.S. Foreign Military Sales Agreements, 1950–1985
(in millions of dollars)

Fiscal Year	Egypt	Jordan	Kuwait	Saudi Arabia	Other[a]	Total Arab	Israel
1950–1975		332	383	3,683	41	4,439	4,664
1976	76	344	187	1,827		2,434	954
1977	1	94	16	1,123		1,234	464
1978	160	64	65	1,312		1,601	1,347
1979	404	72	11	5,450		5,936	760
1980	2,055	292	121	2,954		5,422	517
1981	308	320	44	1,043		1,714	130
1982	1,860	116	114	5,347		7,438	598
1983	691	49	147	891		1,778	2,313
1984	917	26	155	2,840		3,939	118
1985	455	120	94	2,791		3,460	95
Total	6,927	1,830	1,334	29,261	41	39,395	11,960

Source: Seth Carus.
[a]Other includes Iraq, Libya, Syria.

purchases. Comprising about 40 percent of the Saudis' U.S. military transfers since 1950, these sales reflect both their decision to build a military-related infrastructure first (roads, harbors, and so on) and their inability to absorb large amounts of military equipment because of Saudi Arabia's relatively small trained manpower base.

Table 2-11
U.S. Foreign Military Sales Construction Agreements, 1950–1985
(in millions of dollars)

Fiscal Year	Egypt	Jordan	Kuwait	Saudi Arabia	Other[a]	Total Arab	Israel
1950–1975				6,902	1	6,903	
1976			1	5,451		5,452	
1977				590		590	
1978				647		647	
1979				1,021		1,021	3
1980				1,591		1,591	
1981			1	877		878	
1982	20			1,888		1,908	
1983				716		716	
1984	30			263		293	
1985	28			743		771	
Total	78	1	1	20,690	1	20,771	3

Source: Seth Carus.
[a]Other includes Iraq, Libya, and Syria.

A review of the arms trade registers (not included here) reveal other differences in the types of military assistance received by U.S. Middle Eastern customers. For example, from 1950 to 1985 weapons and ammunition amounted to about 60 percent of all Israeli and Egyptian military aid from the United States (65 percent and 59 percent, respectively). On the other hand, only about 14 percent of Saudi Arabia's procurement has been for weapons and ammunition. (Seventy-two percent has been for support services, including construction, 7 percent for support equipment, and 7 percent for spare parts and modifications.)

Qualitatively, however, U.S. customers in the Middle East today receive more sophisticated hardware relative to their own early history and compared to U.S. customers in other less-developed regions of the world. As a region, there are more similarities than differences in this regard. During the past decade or so, U.S. arms recipients in the Middle East have been acquiring very up-to-date systems, often simultaneous with the supply of regular U.S. forces in Western Europe and elsewhere. This has actually been part of a global trend, evidenced by the more modern transfers by other suppliers to the Middle East (note current Soviet transfers to Syria of T-72 tanks, MiG-29 aircraft, SA-5 and SS-21 missiles, and so on).[12] Clearly, the financial clout and associated political leverage of OPEC states and the U.S. policy of attempting to maintain a qualitative edge for Israel in the face of its huge quantitative disadvantage in forces and weapons have encouraged this development.

The registers also reveal that in the early postwar period, most U.S. transfers to the region consisted of World War II surplus or otherwise rather obsolete equipment. Israel's early aircraft purchases from the United States in 1950–1951 (when the United States was well into the era of jet fighters) consisted of propeller-driven T-6 Harvard and Boeing-Stearman trainers. Iran during the 1950s got Sherman and Chaffee tanks and M–8 armored cars dating back a decade or more.[13]

In recent years, however, Israel, Saudi Arabia, Egypt, and (earlier) Iran have received the most modern U.S. weapons platforms, albeit often minus their most sensitive components. Egypt and Israel have acquired F–16s; Israel and Saudi Arabia F-15s; Iran (during the Shah's regime) the U.S. Navy's F-14s. Saudi Arabia has acquired E-3A AWACS, and Egypt and Israel the less expensive E-2C battle management aircraft. Some of the most modern missiles in the U.S. arsenals in all categories—air-to-surface, air-to-air, antitank, ship-to-ship—have entered the region's inventories. Saudi Arabia has Stingers, Improved TOWs, Maverick AGMs, AIM 9-L&P, Harpoons, etc. Israel has all these plus Shrike antiradiation missiles, Walleyebombs, Lance surface-to-surface missiles, cluster bomb units, Cobra gunships, and so on. Iran received long-range Phoenix air-to-air missiles to go with its F-14s—the only country other than the United States to have them in inventory. The same trends have been evidenced across the board in all major classes of weaponry, which have not been matched in any other region of the world. Whether these trends will be maintained, if OPEC's wherewithal and clout decline in the future, remains to be seen.

The Basis for U.S. Arms Transfer Policies

Analysts have made numerous efforts to list, sort out, and weigh the various motivations or rationales for arms sales, beyond what is conveyed by so-called "declaratory policies." Those motivations are seen to vary somewhat between suppliers (or classes of suppliers) and differ according to time, circumstance, and the nature of the recipients. Most analysts, however, divide the arms transfer motives of suppliers into two broad categories, political and economic. Some concentrate on one or the other, while others incorporate both into an analytic model.

SIPRI, for instance, has espoused a division between *hegemonial* and *commercial* national arms sales policies.[14] The former applies to the superpowers, which are locked in a global competition for influence and access, and the latter to the more market-oriented, second tier suppliers, mostly in Western Europe. Leslie Gelb, however, concentrates on the political category, breaking it down into nine specific subcategories:

1. preventing nuclear proliferation
2. self-sufficiency (making a country strong enough to defend itself without direct U.S. intervention)
3. Internal security and human rights
4. alliance relationships with industrialized states
5. the strategic balance of power
6. regional balances of power
7. conflict resolution
8. base and transit rights
9. general political influence.[15]

Still others provide a breakdown of counterpart economic rationales, such as balance of payments, employment, access to raw materials, corporate profits, maintenance of a "warm base" for domestic arms production, and amortization of research and development costs.[16]

These political and economic rationales need not be mutually exclusive, as applied either to a major power's overall arms sales doctrine or to its policies for given regions or individual clients. In the effort to distinguish between supplier policies, one ought to remain aware that the differences may often be matters of emphasis and nuance, since in a general sense, all suppliers pursue some mix of political and economic goals.

Because of alterations in the global environment and in the political circumstances of individual suppliers, however, one can often discern some broad shifts in the rationales for arms supplies over a period of time. The Untied States, for instance, has been forced by the rise of OPEC and by trade rivals in Japan and in

Europe into a greater concern for the economics of arms sales. The following discussion, then, will utilize Gelb's categories as well as the economic rationales cited above to identify some of the changes and phases of U.S. arms transfer policy. The above caveat about relative differences, however, must be kept in mind.

The Cold War Period: A Geopolitical Emphasis

The early part of the Cold War period, up through the late 1950s, saw an obviously geopolitical emphasis in U.S. Middle Eastern arms sales policy, during a period in which the United States was energetically constructing a rimland alliance system around the Soviet Union (an alliance network the United States earlier hoped would include Egypt and Iraq). In this period, the United States gave extensive arms aid to clients, perhaps in part because its too-favorable balance of payments' situation dictated new, temporary measures to assist others in rectifying their payments imbalances.[17] The major emphasis, however, was geopolitical—arms aid to forward states, primarily Turkey, Iran, and Pakistan, but also to Jordan, Lebanon, and Iraq. The main rationales involved alliances, the strategic balance of power, and basing rights (Turkey and Iran were used for intelligence bases, the staging of U-2 flights, and so on). Even Saudi Arabia, which allowed the United States use of its air base at Dhahran, was given some outright aid as well as FMS financing during this period, well before the beginning of its OPEC cornucopia. Libya also received aid in the late 1950s and early 1960s, at a time when the United States made extensive use of Wheelus Air Force Base.[18]

Nonproliferation had not yet arrived as a major issue in connection with arms transfers. That would await the surfacing of the Israeli nuclear program in the early 1960s. Then, too, the United States attempted to remain somewhat aloof from maintaining a regional (Arab-Israeli) arms balance, preferring to leave that task in part to other suppliers and in part to the arms restraint effort embodied in the 1950 Tripartite Declaration involving the United States, France, and the United Kingdom. Economic rationales for arms sales to this region also remained relatively minor, as reflected in the ratio of aid to trade and in the modest proportions of U.S. global arms transfers to the Middle East. During the 1950s the United States was a net exporter of oil, which meant that although access to oil was a major consideration, it reflected a concern for the welfare of U.S. allies rather than U.S. national economic interests.

The Growing Importance of Economic Factors

The 1960s—especially during the latter part of that decade—and the early 1970s saw a gradual change in the rationale for U.S. arms sales. During this period industrial competition from Japan, Western Europe, and other rising economic powers in the Far East, the increasing imports of oil and other raw materials, and the negative U.S. trade balance in civilian goods (a condition that remained permanent through the late 1980s) all served to make arms sales a major policy instrument for helping to ameliorate these economic problems. As a result, the ratio of sales to aid shifted dramatically, beginning with the Kennedy administration and peaking in the 1970s, when arms sales to the Middle East—as reflected in the annual figures provided by *Directions of International Trade*, published by the World Bank and the International Monetary Fund (IMF)—helped maintain a fairly level U.S. trade balance with that region, even as oil imports soared.[19]

Of course, geopolitical reasons for arms sales remained important during this period as well. Although economic considerations grew in importance, they never dwarfed geopolitical rationales and were in fact seen as integral to those concerns, including the growing pressure on the United States to maintain the Arab-Israeli balance, nuclear proliferation considerations, and the Vietnam fiasco and its domestic political repercussions. In response to these issues, as well as to the economic ones cited above, various new policy initiatives were introduced, of which the Nixon Doctrine was one. It dictated the arming of friends (preferably those wealthy enough to pay for it themselves) who could then serve as guardians of U.S. regional security interests. With such a rationale in mind, Iran in the late 1960s and later Saudi Arabia (and to some extent the less-solvent Egypt) became heavy recipients of U.S. arms. The emphasis was on finding a regional policeman to protect Western oil interests at a time when direct U.S. military intervention there or anywhere else appeared increasingly unlikely.[20]

After the French embargo on Israel in the late 1960s, the United States took on the major responsibility of providing Israel with arms and, hence, of preserving a regional balance between Israel and its Arab foes. From that point on, sales to Jordan, Saudi Arabia, and (later) Egypt would be justified by successive administrations on those grounds. Indeed, this question of a balance became politicized because measuring that balance was (and remains) a highly uncertain, subjective issue. Generally, it involved matching Israel's qualitative edge (a matter transcending mere comparisons of the weapons' order of battle) with the quantitative edge held by the Arabs in manpower and major weapons systems.

The nuclear proliferation rationale, in the form of the so-called "doves' dilemma" (involving trade-offs between proliferation controls and arms transfers) became a factor at the beginning of the Kennedy administration, when the ultimate implications of the Dimona reactor became clear. The Kennedy administration was later to initiate Hawk SAM sales to Israel as a trade-off for Israel's allowing U.S. inspections of Dimona.[21] These inspections apparently petered out in later years. Later, around 1968, when the United States, with the initial transfer of F-4 fighters, assumed the role of primary arms supplier to Israel, it was reported that some officials within the U.S. administration had unsuccessfully advocated tying those sales to nuclear proliferation controls.[22] Although they did not prevail, from that point on U.S. arms sales policies to Israel have had to take this matter into account, it being tacitly understood by all parties that failure by the United States to help maintain a conventional balance on behalf of Israel would, in all likelihood, bring the latter's nuclear arsenal into play, at least forcing Israel to make it more overt so as to enhance the credibility of its threat.

In recent years, U.S. arms sales policies toward Pakistan also have had to take proliferation into account. Here the doves' dilemma has been dealt with in a relatively more overt fashion, but the results are as yet inconclusive, and those policies are now enmeshed in the U.S. effort to funnel arms to Afghan rebels via Pakistan.[23]

With the election of Jimmy Carter in 1976, U.S. Middle Eastern arms transfer policies shifted emphasis again. This period witnessed the only concerted effort by any post–World War II administration to downgrade geopolitical and economic considerations in favor of ideological factors. During the early phases of the Carter administration, there was the halting attempt at controls embodied in Presidential Directive 13, involving annual ceilings, leprosy clauses for corporate arms marketing, human rights considerations, and so on. However, that had little eventual impact on sales agreements—this was, after all, the high-water mark of OPEC, and the requirements of petrodollar recycling and the fact of a buyer's market simply overrode those of arms control, particularly after it became apparent that other suppliers would not contribute to a multilateral control effort.

The Dominance of Geopolitical Factors—Again

Toward the end of both the Carter administration and the 1970s, the twin shocks of Afghanistan and the Iranian hostage crisis stimulated a reemphasis of geopolitical concerns. This period produced the Carter Doctrine, which focused on the defense of the Persian Gulf area, which in turn required basing access for the newly conceived Rapid Deployment Force (RDF) which was charged with its defense. Access was successfully sought in Oman, Kenya, Somalia, Egypt, Morocco, and Turkey, but it was mostly denied in Saudi Arabia[24] (leaving open the question of what would occur in some contingencies or crises) and was considered but ultimately rejected by the United States (for political reasons) in the case of Israel. Utilizing a geographically broad construction of the Middle East, basing access became a major consideration for arms transfer policies. After the U.S. Central Command was established, the Pentagon also attempted to move toward a more centralized, coordinated control of Middle Eastern arms sales with a view toward encouraging a strategic consensus in the Middle East directed against the Soviet Union.

Utilizing Gelb's terminology, *conflict control* in the Persian Gulf as well as in the Arab-Israeli dispute also became a more important rationale during this period. Note that by the end of the Carter administration, massive military and economic aid for Egypt and Israel had come to constitute the bulk of overall U.S. foreign aid and was justified in terms of underwriting the Camp David process.

These policies were continued by the Reagan administration, although some subtle shifts in the motivation for regional arms transfers can be discerned. This is particularly true of the second Reagan administration. In general, this administration has tended to take a more overtly global, geopolitical perspective, downplaying some of the more idealistic and economic components previous administrations had emphasized. Although there were obvious continuities, even some of the geopolitical rationales shifted as the Reagan administration appeared to tilt in a more pro-Israel direction. These changes may have had less to do with ideological differences between administrations, however, than with the changing geopolitical environment. The decline of OPEC had lessened the economic imperatives associated with regional transfers, and a series of more or less accidental changes in high-level foreign policy positions from 1983 to 1986 may have been responsible for the administration's more pro-Israel policy direction.[25]

By 1986 the urgency earlier associated with the RDF and associated arms transfer policies appeared to decline. The Pentagon seemed less focused on protracted war/horizontal escalation scenarios emerging from a hypothetical crisis in the Persian Gulf, although these considerations were by no means absent and remained formally reflected in the Defense Department's various defense planning documents.[26] Congress had become more assertive, however, blocking new arms deals with Jordan, limiting those with Saudi Arabia, and imposing human rights restrictions on Iraq (related to terrorism), thus thwarting some elements in the administration who wished to sell arms to these countries in order to build a strategic consensus within a moderate (that is, Pro-Western) Arab coalition (to include Egypt, Jordan, Iraq, Saudi Arabia, and the other Gulf Arab states). In line with this strategy, the administration, at least on an overt level, blocked Israeli arms transfers to Iran in a weak effort at conflict resolution and in a stronger effort at alliance formation. (At the covert level, policy was more complex, clearly involving an effort to reestablish some links with the Iranian military with rather bizarre Saudi connivance).[27] The Reagan administration continued the older policy of evenhandedly arming Israel and Egypt, so as to maintain a balance and the peace in the Arab-Israeli dispute. In 1985–1986, the administration appeared more willing to assist Israel's indigenous arms development and production capabilities, in part so as to remove the contingent dilemma of U.S. resupply in case of war, which had been demonstrated in 1973.[28]

Economic motives were not absent from the Reagan administration's arms transfer policies, but Congress again interceded to prevent their implementation. By mid-1986, figures were emerging that showed the U.S. balance-of-trade deficit growing to ominous proportions—the worst in history, despite a 30 percent or so drop in the dollar in one year—and a falling oil import bill. Thus, in spite of the (visible) decline in the need for one-to-one balancing of oil imports with matching arms exports, the need for increased exports to balance industrial imports from the Far East and Europe had never been greater. However, Congress, then pushing for more combative import restrictions but more concerned with geopolitical factors, moved anyway to restrict arms transfers to Saudi Arabia, Jordan, and Iraq, causing each to seek and retain alternative suppliers. Perhaps more than anything else this appeared to demonstrate that U.S. Middle Eastern arms export policy—in clear distinction to the policies of European powers and perhaps even relative to the Soviet Union—retained a strong geopolitical flavor, with an emphasis on conflict control, maintaining regional balances, stanching nuclear proliferation, as well as a concern for moral issues, specifically terrorism.

Access to bases remained important despite the perceived reduction of urgency about the defense of the Persian Gulf. Some of the initial aspirations from the late 1970s were not realized, however. Egypt allowed joint exercises on its soil with U.S. forces and port visits but not the permanent facility earlier envisaged at Ras Banas[29]; Saudi Arabia also stonewalled, although it apparently shared the control and use of AWACS based on its territory. Still, continuing high levels of arms transfers to these countries could be viewed as an investment for contingencies or crises, without the need for a permanent U.S. presence.

In one sense at least, related to bases, arms transfers had been rendered less important by the onrush of technological developments. In the late 1970s the loss of Iranian facilities for monitoring Soviet missile test telemetry had seemed critical—they were one major rationale for U.S. arms sales there—and alternate facilities were sought in Turkey, China, and Pakistan. By 1986 new satellites, such as the Rhyolite series, with advanced Sigint capabilities had rendered this particular rationale less important.[30] Meanwhile, Israel, as part of its wished-for role as a strategic asset to the United States, now allowed not only port visits and perhaps the prepositioning of materiel but also a Voice of America transmitting unit, which, because of political sensitivities, might not easily find a home elsewhere in the Middle East.[31]

In sum, one can see nuanced emphasis on one or another of Gelb's categories of political rationales, supplemented at times by economic considerations. Policy toward Iran in the late 1960s and the 1970s was primarily dictated by the desire to find self-sufficient U.S. regional allies who could then act as local policemen. U.S. policy toward Israel has stressed regional balances, conflict resolution, nuclear proliferation, and general political influence. In the case of Saudi Arabia, economic rationales, along with that of internal security, have been dominant, as they have been in regard to other Gulf states, with the overall strategic balance and denial to the Soviet Union a key factor in that policy. Policy toward Egypt has been based on some of the same rationales, with a stress on political influence to the detriment of Soviet Union. The regional balance of power, conflict resolution, and human rights as reflected by the terrorism issue have been important motives in the recent cases of Iraq, Iran, and Lebanon.

Yet despite these differences in approach to arms transfers to individual countries at different periods of time, on a regional level the continuity of U.S. military assistance has been quite striking. Unlike other suppliers in the arms trade, since the end of World War II geopolitical factors have dominated the U.S. policymaking process. Even when economic motives are domestic political concerns have become more prominent, they have been quickly superseded by what has been perceived by U.S. decision makers as more pressing global and regional political-military considerations. It is this continuity that distinguishes U.S. arms transfer policy in the Middle East.

Arms Control Policies

A short history of U.S. arms control policies toward the Middle East would, in a truly comprehensive effort, have to be dealt with along several dimensions, involving basic divisions between multilateral and unilateral measures and between declaratory policies and tacit or implicit (that is, unannounced) policies. Historically, there have been various arms control initiatives representing the whole spectrum of these categories, even though, in retrospect, not much that has been accomplished has been durable.

In the mid-1930s, as a result of the Nye Committee hearings and some well-publicized, unsavory activities by private arms manufacturers in connection with the Chaco War between Paraguay and Bolivia, the U.S. Congress passed the Neutrality Acts, which, in effect, compelled the U.S. government to embargo or quarantine participants in wars, regardless of who was the aggressor. That legislation worked to the disadvantage of France and Britain at the outset of World War II. The acts were overturned by the Lend-Lease Agreement, which provided for arms aid to beleaguered Britain,[32] but the Neutrality Acts nevertheless established a mind-set in connection with U.S. arms transfers to conflict-ridden regions.

Although U.S. arms transfer policy after 1945 was less inhibited and much more purposeful on behalf of foreign policy aims, such as blocking the extension of Soviet power and influence, the echoes of the old Neutrality Acts could be heard in U.S. handling of arms transfers to the belligerents in Israel's War of Independence. The United States declared an evenhanded embargo on both sides, in actuality adhering to a U.N. embargo decreed by the Security Council, then dominated by the United States and the United Kingdom.

Most analyses of that period assert that the embargo effectively put Israel at a disadvantage because its Arab foes possessed quantities of surplus materiel left behind in the wake of the British departure. They further assert that the U.S. government was well aware of that but demurred to British pressure and to the internal pressures of Arabists in the State Department. As it turned out, Israel managed to acquire sufficient arms—from Czechoslovakia (with Soviet approval) and through a variety of clandestine, black market, and private sources, involving dummy airlines and masked ship charters—to ensure its victory and survival.[33] It also would appear that the U.S. government did not really exert itself in enforcing the embargo and may actually have winked at some known illegal arms transfers.

Multilateral Controls

In the aftermath of the War of Independence, the U.S. embargo, in coordination with the United Kingdom and France, was effectively extended in the form of the Tripartite Declaration of 1950. Thus, according to one congressional report:

> During the course of a Foreign Ministers' meeting in London in 1950, the three principal suppliers of arms for the Middle East—the United States, the United Kingdom, and France—formally restated the Middle East arms policy that they had announced in 1949. Recognizing the need of the Arab states and Israel to maintain a certain level of armed forces to protect their security, the three Western powers reaffirmed their opposition to an arms race between the two sides and declared that all applications for arms from these countries would be regarded in the light of defense needs of the area as a whole and the necessity for self-defense purposes. They pledged that they would take immediate action, "both within and outside the United Nations" to prevent the violation of frontiers or armistice lines by any of these states.[34]

Luttwak and Horowitz have summarized the impact of this declaration as follows:

> The Tripartite Declaration of 1950 amounted to a virtual embargo on arms supplies to the Middle East. Issued by Britain, France and the United States it opposed any forcible change in the 1949 armistice lines and called for limits on arms supplies to the Middle East. As long as the embargo applied to the Arabs as well, some sort of balance was maintained.[35]

As it happened, the Tripartite Declaration did not altogether stanch the flow of arms—not even major weapons systems—into the core Arab-Israeli arena. From 1950, prior to the 1955 Soviet arms deal with Egypt and Syria which formally signaled the end of the Tripartite arrangement, Israel received some 25 surplus Mustang fighters from Sweden, 20 Mosquitos and 25 Gloster Meteors from the United Kingdom, and 375 surplus tanks (Shermans, Cromwells, M-9s, and M-7s) from the three major western powers. During the same period, Jordan acquired about 100 tanks from the United Kingdom, while Egypt received from the British about 100 combat aircraft (Avro Ansons, Spitfires, Gloster Meteors, and DeHavilland Vampires) and more than 300 tanks (Charioteers, Centurions, Shermans, Valentines, and AMX-13s) from all three Western powers.[36] Then, in 1954, the United States agreed to grant military aid to Iraq in connection with the formation of the then-nascent Baghdad Pact. That was one factor impelling Egypt toward a client relationship with the Soviet Union after it learned it could not unconditionally receive arms from the United States, due to the Tripartite arrangement.

There have been other efforts at multilateral controls to which the United States has been a party. The United Nations adopted a U.S. cease fire resolution during the 1956 war that included an arms embargo. Still another embargo was announced at the outset of the 1967 war, embedded within the Johnson proposal, which called for registration and limitations of arms shipments into the area. In addition, between 1967 and 1972, the United States made several attempts, both through diplomatic channels and public appeals, to interest the Soviet Union in a joint undertaking to limit the flow of arms to the Middle East, all of which were to no avail, even when coupled with some (temporary) U.S. unilateral restraints on arms sales to Israel.[37]

More recently, in 1977–1978, the possibilities for supplier restraints on arms shipments to the Middle East were at least discussed in the U.S.-Soviet Conventional Arms Transfer Talks (CATT).[38] Nothing concrete emerged, however, as the Soviets were solely interested in capping U.S. shipments to Israel. Since then there has been little if any multilateral activity in this area.

Unilateral Controls

Much more deserving of serious attention have been the various U.S. unilateral control efforts, some of them informal, tacit, or ad hoc and not easily revealed to the reader of declaratory statements. Categorization of these efforts becomes even more complicated when one attempts to distinguish between those imposed by the executive branch and those imposed by Congress. With respect to Middle Eastern diplomacy in general but also to arms transfers in particular, Congress's tilt toward Israel has long acted as a counterweight to executive branch tendencies toward evenhandedness, underpinned by the traditional pro-Arab tilt within the State Department (consistently) and the Pentagon (more recently).[39]

The unilateral control efforts can be divided into several categories. Some, involving new, sensitive, or advanced weapons, are general policies applicable to all recipient nations or, in some cases, to those outside of NATO. Others are temporary restrictions—qualitative or quantitative—on sales, particularly to Israel in connection with political pressures intended to produce withdrawals, peace negotiations, and so on. These generally originate in the executive branch. Congress has, of course, also often placed roadblocks in the way of arms sales to Arab states, sometimes involving only components or accessories or strictures about the locations in which arms might be stationed. Other controls have been applied to technology transfer and third-party sales (in some cases where only U.S. components are involved), either to or from Middle Eastern states. There are so many examples in the above categories that we can do little more here than briefly note some salient cases of unilateral controls.

In July 1970, amid the tense Canal war with Egypt and during a period of rapidly escalating Soviet arms shipments to Egypt, the United States held up on Israeli requests for arms (most importantly, electronic countermeasures [ECM] to deal with Soviet air defenses) in order to nudge Israel toward acceptance of the Rogers Plan. Then, during the 1973 war, the United States delayed arms resupply for more than a week, hoping to achieve a cease fire in place, which might then lead to further negotiations (although when that policy failed, an all-out airlift was initiated).[40] Later in the war it was the U.S. threat to withhold further arms that forced Israel to abjure a more total victory—a march on Cairo or at least the destruction of the surrounded Egyptian Third Army in Sinai, which had, in turn, precipitated Soviet threats to intervene.[41] Later threats to withhold U.S. arms transfers were used to pressure Israel into phased withdrawal from the Sinai. Some arms sales also were delayed in response to the Israeli raid on the Iraqi nuclear reactor in Baghdad.

Other U.S. controls regarding Israel have involved sensitive technology that the Pentagon has not wished transferred to Israel. Sales of forward-looking infrared systems (FLIR) and some inertial navigation systems, for instance, were delayed in the 1970s. Some weapons systems, such as cluster bombs and rapid-firing miniguns for helicopters, have been denied on allegedly moral grounds as inhumane.[42] One also could point to the restrictions regarding nuclear use at least nominally in force in connection with the potentially dual-purpose (conventional and nuclear) Lance missiles.

There have also been some unilateral control measures applied to U.S. transfers to Arab nations, for the most part imposed by Congress in opposition to the desires of the executive branch. The blocking of sales of Stinger missiles to Saudi Arabia and the shelving of a large proposed arms deal with Jordan have been recent examples.[43] Earlier, one could point to the restrictions imposed on bomb racks and fuel tanks for the Saudi F-15s, limitations on the capabilities of AWACS going to Riyadh, and restrictions on the mobility of I-Hawks sold to Jordan. The United States also initially moved very slowly on arms sales to Egypt, even after the latter's severing of its client ties with the Soviet Union, and despite strong Egyptian pressures, there was an early emphasis on relatively benign transfers such as C-130 aircraft. Another recent example has been that of U.S. restrictions on sales of arms to Iraq for use against Iran. That too has clearly pitted pro-Israeli elements in Congress against the administration, with the former emphasizing Iraq's role as a supporter of terrorist groups.

The use of unilateral controls in connection with third-party transfers has been an interesting and sometimes contentious issue. This is, of course, a complex subject. Third-party transfers are often encouraged or winked at because a major supplier, such as the United States, wishes to lower its visibility and cushion the political fallout from certain transactions. Thus, in the early 1960s the United States encouraged German sales of U.S.-origin tanks to Israel in an effort to deflect an anti-U.S. reaction in the Arab world.[44] Generally, however, U.S. controls on such transfers to Arab countries, particularly where only U.S. components have been involved, have been rather lax. French and Italian arms going to U.S.-embargoed Libya, for example, are full of U.S. technology.[45]

The United States has collaborated with Israel in third-party transfers to Iran, notwithstanding U.S. declaratory policy, which forbids such transactions. On the other hand, the United States has restrained the development of Israel's indigenous arms industry by blocking Israeli arms exports, such as the sale of Kfir fighters to Ecuador or Taiwan. (There are indications that this was part of a broader strategy by the Carter administration to fray U.S.-Israeli ties.) Initial U.S. stalling on the transfer of the technology for composite materials needed for the Lavi fighter aircraft constitutes another example.[46]

Sometimes, of course, the relaxation of unilateral controls on arms transfers may be utilized for other arms control purposes. The United States initiated Hawk SAM sales to Israel during the Kennedy administration—really the first major U.S. arms deal with Israel—because it thought it could thereby stall Israel's nascent drive toward nuclear weapons.[47]

Recently, as oil prices have dropped and OPEC's purchasing power has declined, there has been renewed talk about multilateral controls on arms shipments to the region, whether formally negotiated or not. (This might be in Israel's and the Arab countries' interest, given their common budgetary problems.) Nothing yet has come of this idea, however. Practically speaking, the serious questions deal with whatever tacit arrangements exist between the Soviet Union and the United States involving high-performance, state-of-the-art technology. Recent Soviet transfers of more modern aircraft, tanks, SAMs, and Scud missile warheads configured for use with chemical weapons do not augur well for the future of such arrangements.[48]

Meaning for U.S.-Soviet Competition in the Middle East

As has been amply discussed elsewhere in this volume, the U.S.-Soviet competition in the Middle East can be perceived in a number of dimensions: general aspects of influence and leverage over various regional actors; differing interests and perspectives concerning regional stability, balance, peace, and so on; basing access and alliances, as contributors to the global strategic balance; and access to oil and export markets. Arms transfers are seen as the primary instrument for the achievement of these ends. In addition, the export earnings and other economic benefits from arms sales are themselves an end in the competition, given the Soviet need for Western currency and the U.S. requirement for petrodollar recycle.

It is important to note in this context that although arms transfers affect all areas of this competition, the two superpowers rarely compete head-to-head for influence in a particular country using this instrument. Clearly, most arms transfer patterns follow from a priori political relationships and are correlated with a variety of other measures of international cohesion, including U.N. votes, overall trade patterns, basing access, and formal alliances. When a nation's allegiance switches from one bloc to another following a coup or other political upheaval, arms transfers usually follow in its wake. Note, for example, the double *volte-face* by Somalia and Ethiopia at the time of their 1977–1978 war.

In numerous cases, past and present, certain regional clients in the Middle East have had sole or predominant supplier relationships with one of the superpowers, which have been predictable on the basis of broader political orientations. Syria and South Yemen have long been solid Soviet clients; so was Iraq up to 1973, although it has been increasingly less so since. Iran under the Shah received most of its weapons from the United States, as has Israel since 1968. Those patterns are consistently predictable in an era of comprehensive government controls over the destination of arms, a half century or more beyond the era when corporate arms producers and traders were able to operate on a free market basis outside the lines of political alignment and official government controls.

In the Middle East, however, these standard patterns have been somewhat complicated and muddied by specific circumstances, which in turn have influenced the nature of the superpower competition. First, there is the anomaly of Israel as a pariah state, dependent on external grant aid for financing its arms purchases. This raises the issue of reluctant suppliers—namely, those who are willing to be suppliers even if at a cost to interests elsewhere. Then, OPEC oil wealth, in conjunction with U.S. restrictions on sales to Israel's foes, provided leverage for some Arab states (and, earlier, Iran) to play off the superpowers, even where political/ideological alignments would appear to dictate a sole or predominant supplier/recipient relationship. Still other cross-pressures, such as hostilities between clients of one or the other superpower, have resulted in unpredictable patterns. Hence, the superpower competition has sometimes become complicated and the political lines blurred.

Jordan, chagrined at U.S. restrictions, has gone to the Soviet Union for air defense weapons (as well as to France and the United Kingdom, which has put pressure on the United States and Soviet influence. Iran under the Shah, although allied with the West, bought Soviet armored personnel carriers (APCs) and air defense weapons. Kuwait has done the same. On the flip side, Iraq, long a Soviet client, has bought arms from France, Italy, and Brazil and since the onset of the Iraq-Iran war, has sought U.S. arms as well. Syria, between the 1973 and 1982 wars, bought helicopters and missiles from France, thus distancing itself a bit from the Soviet Union and putting the latter under pressure to be more forthcoming, which it did.

Generally, the Soviet Union has been able to use the fact of U.S. support for Israel as a way of increasing its influence in some states willing to acquire Soviet arms. The United States (and the West in general), however, is able to dangle the benefits of Western-oriented trade, technology transfer, and economic assistance to shift political relationships and arms transfers; hence, the massive shift by Egypt and the halting moves by Iraq (and Algeria) toward a more pro-Western orientation.

On one point, of course, the U.S.-Soviet competition has heretofore seen a considerable divergence of perspectives and policies. The United States, painfully aware that the continued festering of the Arab-Israeli dispute works against its influence in the region, tries to use arms transfers as an instrument of balance and conflict control. It arms Israel so as to deter Arab attacks but holds a club over the former (relevant in preventive war or preemptive contingencies) in the form of resupply and continued transfers where Israel has no alternative suppliers. The Soviet Union, however, is normally thought to have a vested interest in continued high levels of conflict and tension (but not in war), which is all the better if the situation frustrates the Arabs and diminishes U.S. influence. Massive Soviet transfers before the 1956, 1967, and 1982 wars may be said to have been contributing factors to those wars, prompting Israel to initiate a preventive war in 1956 so as to forestall a shift in the military balance, and then to preempt in the 1967 crisis so as to take advantage of its more rapid mobilization capacity.

For the Soviets, these matters can be a double-edged sword. If their clients are defeated, resentment can result, perhaps in the form of denigration of Soviet arms and training. In part for such reasons, Egypt abandoned Soviet clientship after 1973,[49] while Israel's success in 1973 with U.S. arms technology served to lure Cairo into its *volte-face*. Granted, there were other reasons, such as economic reform, which required Western capital and a more Western orientation. Thus, as this chapter has demonstrated, arms transfer patterns are an outcome as well as an instrument of U.S.-Soviet competition in the Middle East.

Looking to the future, one hesitates to venture predictions that might involve significant change from present patterns or from their approximate extrapolations. One key, of course, is the future of OPEC and the oil markets, which, in turn, will largely dictate the volume of Middle Eastern arms transfers as well as the Arabs' (and the Israelis') leverage relationship with the United States. Another important unknown has to do with emerging conventional military technologies (such as stealth aircraft, battle-management aircraft, assault-breaker systems vis-a-vis armored formations, and electronic warfare gear) and, in turn, the question of whether the superpowers will be as willing as they have been in the past to transfer the most up-to-date systems. That too may ultimately hinge on the oil markets. In addition, the Vanunu affair (resulting in startling disclosures about Israel's nuclear capabilities) and recent rumors concerning Pakistan's nuclear program appear to presage a larger role for nuclear proliferation in arms transfer decisions.[50] One way or another, arms transfers promise to remain at the heart of the U.S.-Soviet competition in the Middle East.

Notes

1. For a review of problems associated with measurements, methodology, definitions, etc., in connection with arms transfers, see Richard Wilcox, "Twixt Cup and Lip: Some Problems in Applying Arms Controls," in S.G. Neuman and R.E. Harkavy, eds., *Arms Transfers in the Modern World* (New York: Praeger, 1979), chapter 2; and Edward Fei, "Understanding Arms Transfers and Military Expenditures: Data Problems, *ibid.,*

chapter 3. See also the U.S. Arms Control and Disarmament Agency's *World Military Expenditures and Arms Transfers* (Washington: GPO), published annually, utilizing both constant and current dollar values, with data time-lagged about 2 to 3 years back from date of publication.

2. Such registers are published annually in SIPRI's annual Yearbook, *World Armaments and Disarmament* (London: Taylor and Francis).

3. For registers spanning the period 1950 to 1973, see SIPRI, *Arms Trade Registers* (Cambridge, MA: The MIT Press, 1975).

4. In addition to the previously cited SIPRI registers, see also the International Institute for Strategic Studies' annual, *The Military Balance* (London), which also provides annual order-of-battle information for the world's nations. For this chapter, we were also availed of unpublished registers provided by Seth Carus of the America-Israel Public Affairs Committee (AIPAC), Washington, D.C.

5. This trend is noted and analyzed in R.E. Harkavy, *The Arms Trade and International Systems* (Lexington, MA: Ballinger, 1975), esp. pp. 21–22.

6. U.S. Arms Control and Disarmament Agency, *World Military Expenditures and Arms Transfers: 1985* (Washington: ACDA Publication 123, August 1985).

7. For relevant analyses of the early postwar period, see, among others, George Thayer, *The War Business* (New York: Simon and Schuster, 1969); and Lewis Frank, *The Arms Trade in International Relations* (New York: Praeger, 1969), esp. pp. 98–121.

8. See Thayer, chapter 4.

9. Paul Y. Hammond, David J. Jouscher, Michael D. Salamone, and Norman A. Graham, *The Reluctant Supplier* (Cambridge, MA: Oelgeschlager, Gunn, and Hain, 1983), pp. 59–60.

10. For a more focused analysis of France's role, see Edward Kolodziej, "French Arms Trade: Economic Determinants," in SIPRI, *World Armaments and Disarmament: SIPRI Yearbook 1983* (London: Taylor and Francis, 1983), pp. 371–390.

11. These data, as disaggregated into MAP, FMS, FMS construction, and commercial, were provided by Seth Carus. A similar breakdown on a more global basis for U.S. transfers is provided by Hammond et al., *The Reluctant Supplier,* esp. chapter 4.

12. This is discussed in "Syrians' Armed Forces: Playing Waiting Game?" *New York Times,* 7 January 1984, p. 4; and "Threat from the East," *Near East Report,* 31 12 January 1987), p. 7.

13. See SIPRI, *Arms Trade Registers,* under the relevant recipient listings.

14. See SIPRI, *The Arms Trade with the Third World* (New York: Humanities Press, 1971), chapter 3, under "Factors Influencing the Supply of Weapons."

15. Leslie Gelb, "Arms Sales," *Foreign Policy,* 25 (Winter 1976–77), pp. 3–23.

16. See, for instance, as earlier applied to the Middle East, Mary Kaldor, "Economic Aspects of Arms Supply Policies to the Middle East," in Milton Leitenberg and Gabriel Sheffer, eds., *Great Power Intervention in the Middle East* (New York: Pergamon, 1979), pp. 206–230. See also, for a more general analysis, John Stanley and Maurice Pearton, *The International Trade in Arms* (London: Chatto and Windus, 1972).

17. Robert Gilpin, *U.S. Power and the Multinational Corporation* (New York: Basic Books, 1975), esp. chapter 6; and Joan Spero, *The Politics of International Economic Relations,* 2d ed. (New York: St. Martin's, 1981), chapters 1, 3.

18. For an analysis of the arms transfer/basing nexus in the early postwar years, see R.E. Harkavy, *Great Power Competition for Overseas Bases* (New York: Pergamon, 1982), chapter 4.

19. *Direction of International Trade* (New York), annual, published jointly by the United Nations, International Monetary Fund, and the International Bank for Reconstruction and Development.

20. See, among others, Lewis Sorley, *Arms Transfers under Nixon* (Lexington, KY: The University Press of Kentucky, 1983), chapter 7, particularly with respect to Nixon and Iran.

21. This is noted in, among other sources on the Israeli nuclear program, Fuad Jabber, *Israel and Nuclear Weapons* (London: Chatto and Windus, 1971), pp. 36–39; and R.E. Harkavy, *Spectre of a Middle Eastern Holocaust* (Denver: University of Denver Press, 1977), Monograph Series in World Affairs, pp. 6–7.

22. See William Quandt, *Decade of Decisions: American Policy Toward the Arab-Israeli Conflict, 1967–1976* (Berkeley, CA: University of California Press, 1977), pp. 66–67.

23. See, among other sources, "Caravans on Moonless Nights: How the CIA Supports and Supplies the Anti-Soviet Guerrillas," *Time,* 11 June 1984, pp. 38–40. Also see "Needless Offense to India," *New York Times,* 25 November 1986, p. A27, which reports that the United States, for the first time since 1966, is monitoring Soviet missile tests with ground-based electronic intelligence facilities in Pakistan; and "The World is Watching Pakistan's Nuclear Program," *International Herald Tribune,* 29 July 1986, p. 4.

24. See "Saudis to Let U.S. Use Bases in Crisis," *New York Times,* 5 September 1985, p. A1, wherein: "Saudi Arabia has told the United States that it will allow American military forces to use its bases in case of Soviet aggression or if it is unable to handle a Persian Gulf crisis on its own."

25. Inside Washington scuttlebutt has it that the Reagan administration's somewhat pro-Arab tilt in 1981–1982 was due in great measure to the influence of William Clark, James Baker, and Michael Deaver, all of whom were removed from foreign-policy decision making during 1983–1986, as the influence of relatively more pro-Israel Robert McFarlane and John Poindexter rose. But the changes following the Iran/Contra imbroglio in 1986–1987 might foreshadow still another shift. For a general analysis, see "After Low Period, Israel Finds Its Influence at Apex," *International Herald Tribune,* 7 August 1986, p. 1. See also "U.S.-Israeli Military Pact to Start Soon," *New York Times,* 15 January 1984, p. A10, which discusses National Security Decision Directive 111, which provided for closer American military cooperation with Israel; and "Cheap Oil and Weaker OPEC Are Easing Israel's Burdens," *New York Times,* 24 March 1986, p. 1.

26. On an unclassified basis, this can be traced from year to year in the annual "posture statement" published for each fiscal year by the Organization of the Joint Chiefs of Staff.

27. For a discussion of the use of surrogates by the United States in the arms trade see: Stephanie G. Neuman, *Military Assistance in Recent Wars: The Dominance of the Superpowers* The Washington Papers, No. 122 (Washington, D.C.: Center for Strategic and International Studies, with Praeger Publishers, 1986), chapter 6; and "Arms and Superpower Influence: Lessons From Recent Wars," *Orbis* (Winter 1987) pp. 711–729.

28. The pros and cons of U.S. policy in this area are discussed in Robert E. Harkavy and Stephanie G. Neuman, "Israel," in James E. Katz, ed., *Arms Production in Developing Countries* (Lexington, MA: D.C. Heath, 1984), chapter 10. See also "Lavi Passes Test," *Near East Report,* 31 (12 January 1987), p. 7, wherein U.S. financial assistance to the Lavi project is discussed as well as the (new) possibility of Israel's coproduction of the F-16.

29. See "U.S.-Egyptian Base Scrapped," *Near East Report,* 29 (28 January 1985), p. 13.

30. See Jeffrey T. Richelson, *The U.S. Intelligence Community* (Cambridge, MA: Ballinger, 1985), esp. pp. 118–121.

31. See "Congress Expands U.S.-Israel Ties," *Near East Report*, 30 (27 October 1986), p. 171.

32. See Harkavy, *The Arms Trade and International Systems*, p. 225; and Elton Atwater, *American Regulation of Arms Exports* (New York: Carnegie Endowment, 1941), pp. 208–257.

33. Edward Luttwak and Dan Horowitz in *The Israeli Army* (New York: Harper and Row, 1975), p. 65, noted that "Czechoslovakia was the only legal government-to-government source of arms for the Israelis." See also Larry Collins and Dominique LaPierre, *O' Jerusalem* (New York: Simon and Schuster, 1972), pp. 476–477.

34. "The International Transfer of Conventional Arms," A Report to the Congress from the U.S. Arms Control and Disarmament Agency, 12 April 1974 (Washington: GPO, 1974), Annex C, p. 9.

35. Luttwak and Horowitz, *The Israeli Army*, p. 128.

36. SIPRI, *Arms Trade Registers*.

37. These, in addition to the Johnson proposal, are outlined in "The International Transfer of Conventional Arms," Annex C. pp. 6–8.

38. CATT is discussed in Hammond, et all., *The Reluctant Supplier*, chapter 6, under "The Carter Experiment in Control and the Reagan Response."

39. This is discussed in Wolf Blitzer, *Between Washington and Jerusalem: A Reporter's Notebook* (New York: Oxford University Press, 1985), chapters 1, 2.

40. See, among numerous sources, Matti Golan, *The Secret Conversations of Henry Kissinger* (New York: Quadrangle, 1976); and the Insight Team of the London Times, *The Yom Kippur War* (New York: Doubleday, 1974), part 30.

41. *Ibid.*, part 5.

42. See, for example, "Halting Weapons Spread," *New York Times*, 15 July 1986, p. A10, wherein it is stated, "Israel lost its access to American cluster weapons after it was accused of using them against populated areas or civilian targets (in Lebanon)." See also "U.S. Aides Say Policy Stands on Cluster Weapon Exports," *New York Times*, 10 July 1986, p. A18.

43. See "Big Missile sale to Saudi Arabia Opposed by Key Congress Panels," *New York Times*, 24 April 1986, p. A1.

44. See Thayer, *The War Business*, pp. 223–226.

45. Italy, for instance, has transferred Agusta Bell helicopters, which incorporate considerable U.S. technology. See *The Military Balance 1985-1986* (London: IISS), p. 81.

46. "The U.S. Nears Lavi Transfer Approval," *Aviation Week and Space Technology*, 10 January 1983, pp. 20–23; and "Israeli Request for Help in Building Lavi Plane gives Reagan Problems and Divides Contractors," *The Wall Street Journal*, 7 April 1983, p. 58.

47. See Shai Feldman, *Israeli Nuclear Deterrence* (New York: Columbia University Press, 1982), p. 211.

48. "Syrian Chemical Arms," *Near East Report* 30 (15 December 1986, p. 197.

49. Alvin Rubinstein, *Red Star on the Nile: The Soviet-Egyptian Influence Relationship since the June War* (Princeton, NJ: Princeton University Press, 1977), chapters 8, 9; and Robert O. Freedman, *Soviet Policy Toward the Middle East Since 1970*, 3d ed. (New York: Praeger, 1982).

50. See "Israel Holds Technician Who Sold Atom Secrets," *The New York Times*, 10 November 1986, p. A10.

3

A Note on
Soviet Arms Transfers
to the Middle East

Abraham S. Becker

Active Soviet involvement with the Third World after Stalin's demise was inaugurated with the Egyptian-Czech arms deal of 1955. Since that event Soviet arms transfers have grown rapidly and have continued to be the primary Soviet instrument of penetration into the noncommunist developing world. This much at least is evident and generally recognized by Western analysts. Proceeding beyond these generalizations, however, involves disagreement and controversy even on the basic data of size and distribution of Soviet transfers. It seems worthwhile, therefore, to attempt some clarification of the data foundations for any analysis of the Soviet arms transfer relationship.[1]

This chapter begins with an examination of the data on Soviet arms transfers to the Third World as a whole before proceeding to the Middle East component. It is a measure of both the paucity of data and the uncertainties in the data available that the discussion of transfers to the less-developed countries (LDCs) as a group takes more space than the consideration of transfers to the Middle East alone. A summary view of military personnel relations between the Soviet bloc and the Third World concludes the substantive discussion.

Soviet Arms to the Third World

At the outset, one should perhaps make the obvious explicit: The Soviets publish almost no information at all on their arms dealings with other countries. All the information we have is derived from the recipients or represents estimates by Western sources. Because the components of such estimates are difficult to obtain and often shrouded in secrecy, there is considerable room for dispute.[2] Estimates have been made by various government and private sources at different times, but this chapter focuses on the best known and the longest time series, those published by the U.S. government and by three independent research institutions—the Stockholm International Peace Research Institute (SIPRI), Wharton Econometric Forecasting Associates, and PlanEcon (the last two located in Washington, D.C.).

Table 3-1
Soviet Arms Transfers to LDCs, 1955–1985
(millions of dollars)

	CIA		SIPRI	Vanous	Efrat
	Total Transfers, Current Prices		Major Weapons, 1975 dollars	Total Transfers, Current Prices	Total Transfers, Current Prices
	Agreements	Deliveries	Deliveries	Deliveries	Deliveries
1955–1966	4,500	3,575	n.a.	n.a.	6,060–7,270
1967	525	500	1,545	n.a.	↑
1968	450	505	1,116	n.a.	│
1969	360	450	834	n.a.	│
1970	1,150	995	1,136	891	│
1971	1,590	865	1,515	780	│
1972	1,680	1,215	1,225	1,155	│
1973	2,890	3,135	1,537	2,331	│
1974	5,735	2,225	1,930	2,199	│
1975	3,185	2,035	2,160	2,227	│
1976	6,140	3,110	1,554	2,669	n.a.
1977	9,645	4,815	2,156	4,504	│
1978	2,700	6,075	3,526	5,364	│
1979	8,835	8,340	4,565	5,585	│
1980	14,860	8,125	5,265	5,570	│
1981	6,535	8,175	3,514	6,440	│
1982	10,960	8,660	2,986	8,100	│
1983	2,535	7,495	3,404	8,040	│
1984	9,155	7,205	1,863	7,330	│
1985	2,130	5,530	n.a.	5,520	↓
1967–1973	8,645	7,665	8,908	n.a.	15,212–18,255
1974–1982	68,595	51,560	27,656	42,658	75,579–90,690
1955–1982	81,740	62,800	n.a.[a]	n.a.	96,851–116,215
1967–1985	91,060	79,455	41,831[a]	n.a.	n.a.
1955–1985	95,560	83,030	n.a.	n.a.	n.a.

Sources: Columns 1 and 2: 1955–1966 and 1967—CIA, *Communist Aid to the Less Developed Countries of the Free World, 1976,* August 1977; 1968–1971—*Handbook of Economic Statistics 1978,* October 1978, p. 73; 1972–1973—Department of State, *Soviet and East European Aid to the Third World, 1981,* February 1983, p. 4 (the State Department series in other years essentially coincides with CIA estimates); 1974—CIA, *Handbook of Economic Statistics 1984,* September 1984, p. 109; 1975—CIA, *Handbook of Economic Statistics 1985,* September 1985, p. 109; 1976–1985—CIA, *Handbook of Economic Statistics 1986,* September 1986, p. 111.

Column 3: *World Armaments and Disarmament SIPRI Yearbook 1985,* (London and Philadelphia: Taylor and Francis, 1985), pp. 372–373.

Column 4: Estimates by Jan Vanous, under the auspices of Wharton Econometric Forecasting Associates (WEFA) and, later, PlanEcon Inc., both of Washington, DC: 1970–1977—Vanous, "Soviet and Eastern European Foreign Trade in the 1970's: A Quantitative Assessment," *East European Economic Assessment. Part 2—Regional Assessments,* U.S. Congress Joint Economic Committee, 1981, pp. 691–692; 1977–1979—WEFA estimates cited in Laure Despres, "Les Retombees des Ventes d'Armes Sovietiques et Est-Europeenes sur les Relations Economiques Est-Ouest," *Le Courier des Pays de l'Est,* no. 297, July–August 1985, p. 51; 1980–1981—"Developments in Soviet Arms Exports and Imports," WEFA, *Centrally Planned Economies Current Analysis,* (15 August 1984); 1982–85—"Soviet Foreign Trade Performance in 1985," *PlanEcon Report* 2 (7 April 1986).

Column 5: Moshe Efrat, "The Economics of Soviet Arms Transfers to the Third World," in Peter Wiles and Moshe Efrat, *The Economics of Soviet Arms* (London: Suntory-Toyota Centre for Economics and Related Disciplines, London School of Economics and Political Science, May 1985), p. 34a of part II.

[a] 1967–1984

n.a. = not available

Table 3–1 assembles estimates of total Soviet sales and deliveries of arms, under a variety of trade or aid arrangements, to the noncommunist Third World over the past three decades. The first two columns present CIA estimates, while SIPRI data on deliveries are shown in the third column. The SIPRI figures differ in at least four respects from the CIA numbers:

1. The latter are in current dollar prices, while the SIPRI figures are in constant 1975 dollars.

2. The SIPRI estimates cover deliveries of major weapons, whereas the CIA attempts total coverage, including supporting equipment, munitions, maintenance support, and associated services (training and technical assistance and military construction).[3]

3. SIPRI prices the Soviet export according to the Western weapon most closely matching the Soviet system,[4] whereas the CIA valuation goal is apparently actual contract prices.[5]

4. The SIPRI figures explicitly include transfers to Vietnam (and perhaps to Cuba, North Korea, and Mongolia as well), whereas the CIA coverage excludes communist developing states.[6]

Whether these methodological differences fully explain the divergences between the two series in the table is, however, somewhat doubtful. Consider the respective series in terms of subperiods as follows (in millions of dollars):

	CIA Deliveries	SIPRI Deliveries
1967–1970	$ 2,450	$ 4,631
1971–1975	9,475	8,367
1976–1980	30,465	17,066
1981–1984	31,535	11,767

One might expect values for the late 1960s in 1975 prices to exceed those in current prices, despite the difference in commodity coverage and valuation basis. Also, because of the almost continuous inflation in arms prices, a constant price series based on an earlier year should, all other things equal, diverge increasingly from a series in current prices. The SIPRI figures, however, are less than 60 percent of the CIA numbers in the last half of the 1970s and only 37 percent as high in the early 1980s. In neither case is it self-evident that price inflation, commodity coverage, and valuation standard are a plausible explanation.[7]

Two other U.S. government agencies publish data on Soviet arms transfers. The Defense Intelligence Agency (DIA) does so intermittently, the Arms Control and Disarmament Agency (ACDA) regularly. A recent DIA statement[8] may be compared with the CIA estimates as follows (in billions of dollars):

	1974–1979	1980–1985
DIA: Soviet military deliveries excluding those to six Warsaw Pact countries, Vietnam, and Cuba (sixty-seven countries)	$29.4	$49.4
CIA: Soviet military deliveries to noncommunist LDCs	26.6	45.2

The DIA figures are roughly 10 percent higher than those provided by the CIA. The probable inclusion by the DIA and exclusion by the CIA of deliveries to Laos, North Korea, and Mongolia accounts for some but far from all the difference between the two sets of numbers. The DIA numbers are not explained further.

ACDA publishes an annual report of arms transfers and military expenditures for all countries. Figures relating to the Soviet Union are said to be "estimates by U.S. government sources" and are qualified as "approximations based on limited information." The ACDA figures, however, differ considerably from the CIA numbers, if we consider only the two latest ACDA reports (in billions of dollars)[9]:

	Agreements		Deliveries	
	ACDA*	CIA*	ACDA*	CIA*
1973–1976	$20.7	$18.0	$13.2	$10.5
1977–1980	42.5	36.0	35.2	27.4
1981	8.3	6.5	10.0	8.2
1982	13.9	11.0	10.4	8.7
1983	4.8	2.5	8.9	7.5
1984	10.6	9.2	8.6	7.2
1985	9.5	2.1	7.6	5.5

*ACDA—transactions with all developing countries; CIA—transactions with noncommunist developing countries.

The ACDA figures are uniformly higher than those of the CIA and by varying margins, although the relative differences for deliveries seem somewhat more stable than those for agreements. In its regional breakdowns, ACDA does distinguish between communist and other developing states, but the aggregate totals shown above include transfers to Bulgaria, China, Cuba, Kampuchea (Cambodia), Laos, Mongolia, North Korea, Vietnam, Yugoslavia, and even Greece, all of which are included in the developing country category. Exclusion of transactions with these countries would result in ACDA numbers considerably closer to the CIA data. Unfortunately, ACDA publishes a country breakdown only for deliveries and only for varying subperiods—1981–85 in the most recent report (its Table III). For that interval the CIA and ACDA data are much closer (in billions of dollars):

	Deliveries 1981–1985
ACDA	$38.6
CIA	30.1

With the same country coverage the two aggregates are within 4 percent of each other. Note that if Afghanistan is excluded from the ACDA aggregate, on the hypothesis that the CIA estimates now also exclude that country, the CIA and ACDA figures would be identical.

Soviet official data on trade with the (nonsocialist) LDCs contain large unidentified residuals. Several Western scholars have hypothesized that the residuals conceal Soviet arms exports.[10] A time series estimated by Jan Vanous from these residuals and other data is shown in column 4 of table 3–1. The Vanous estimates are relatively close to the CIA figures on deliveries except in 1978–1981, where the latter are a third larger than the former. The reasons for the sharp divergence in these four years are not known.

Moshe Efrat is critical of the estimates of the U.S. government as considerably too low, which he infers to be the result of inadequate and inconsistent pricing methodologies. His own calculations (column 5 of table 3–1) are based on estimates of the unit values of Soviet arms, conceived as official export prices and derived from Arab sources. Since he can only estimate major weapons deliveries, he inflates them to total transfers by a coefficient developed from a variety of sources. It is not clear, however, how he obtained the quantities of major weapons deliveries. In any case, Efrat's estimates far exceed anyone else's.[11]

Because of the length and availability of the annual total series published by the CIA and the general closeness to calculations based on Soviet trade residuals, these data are preferred. The CIA estimates show a cumulative total for the entire period of $95.6 billion in extensions or agreements and $83.0 billion in deliveries, roughly $3 billion a year on the average. The initial levels were low, however, running $600 million (agreements) or $300 million (deliveries) annually in the interval 1955–1966, whereas in the late 1970s and first half of the 1980s arms deliveries were at the $5 to $9 billion level, and extensions in 1980 reached the unprecedented level of $15 billion. The annual average levels of deliveries in the early 1980s of about $7.5 billion were twenty-five times higher than those of the initial interval, 1955–1966.

Economic aid once figured as heavily as arms transfers in Soviet Third World activities. In the first half of this 30-year period, economic and military aid agreements came to almost $7 billion each, although deliveries on military account were considerably larger, about $6 billion, compared to $3.6 billion for economic aid.[12] Since 1970, however, arms transfers have far outpaced economic aid by ratios of more than 3 to 1 for agreements and 6 to 1 for deliveries.

The extraordinarily rapid growth of Soviet arms transfers is largely associated with the oil price revolution of the mid–1970s. The Middle East crisis of the Six Day War and its aftermath had brought a boom in Soviet deliveries, but the Soviets were often selling less-than-first-line equipment to governments with constrained budgets. The explosion in oil prices brought sudden wealth to states with growing appetites for arms or those that had an interest in financing the appetites of neighbors. Increasing competition from the West for petrodollars moved the Soviet Union to offer the developing countries more sophisticated military equipment, while at the same time exploiting the increased demand to raise supply prices. In addition, new opportunities for arms transfers and military involvement developed in sub-Saharan Africa (Angola, Ethiopia, and Mozambique).

Transfers to the Middle East

Unfortunately, the CIA has published no regional breakdown of arms transfers since 1980.[13] The DIA's (Defense Intelligence Agency) information releases on recipients of Soviet transfers are irregular and highly aggregated. Thus, a 1986 DIA contribution shows the destinations of total Soviet deliveries for 1974–1979 and 1980–1985 as six Warsaw Pact countries in aggregate, nine individual Third World countries, and a residual package of sixty others. SIPRI publishes no regional distribution either. The only regularly published regional breakdowns are those by the ACDA. Table 3–2 combines CIA and ACDA data for a view of changes in the gross regional distribution of Soviet military deliveries.[14]

Soviet arms transfer relations with the Third World began with the Czech-Egyptian arms deal in 1955, and the Middle East and North Africa have remained the chief recipients of Soviet military deliveries.[15] From this initial $250 million venture with Egypt, Soviet agreements rose to an average annual level in 1975–1979 of $4 billion (2.5 billion in the Middle East alone and perhaps as much as a billion dollars more in the area in 1979–1985). Deliveries to the Middle East and North Africa, which averaged about $500 million in 1956–1974, jumped to more than $3 billion in 1975–1979 ($2 billion for the Middle East) and $5–6 billion in 1979–1985 (around $4 billion for the Middle East). The 1970s thus brought a sharp transformation in the value size of Soviet arms deliveries to the Middle East. The value of contracts concluded in the last decade was triple or more that concluded in the first two, as a consequence of a steep increase in prices and stepped-up LDC demand.

The Middle East's share of Soviet arms transfers to the Third World was sharply reduced in 1975–1979, to the benefit of Africa, both North and sub-Saharan. These were the years of the huge deals with Libya and the Soviet involvement in Angola and Ethiopia. Also, with the Cairo-Moscow split in the early and mid-1970s, Egypt ceased to be a significant buyer of Soviet military equipment. Some rebound in the Middle East share took place in the early 1980s, primarily at the expense of North Africa and principally due to major arms agreements with

Table 3–2

Regional Distribution of Soviet Arms Transfers to the Third World, Varying Periods

	North Africa	Sub-Saharan Africa	Middle East	South Asia	Latin America	Total [a]
	Billions of Dollars					
Agreements						
1956–1974	2.805	0.715	11.980	2.330	0.205	18.035
1975–1979	8.155	3.920	12.465	3.080	0.765	28.385
1979–1981	< 14		> 10	5	1	30.23
1982–1985	5		12 1/2	8	1	24.78
Deliveries						
1956–1974	0.665	0.410	9.375	2.130	0.030	12.610
1975–1979	6.500	3.120	9.300	2.280	0.645	21.845
1979–1983	9.000	4.910	20.375	5.250	0.540	40.075
1981–1985	7.800	6.075	18.375	5.730	0.650	38.630
	Percent of Total					
Agreements						
1956–1974	16	4	66	13	1	
1975–1979	29	14	44	11	3	
1979–1981	> 50		39	> 6	< 6	
1982–1985	< 46		33 +	17	3	
Deliveries						
1956–1974	5	3	74	17	—	
1975–1979	30	14	43	10	3	
1979–1983	22	12	51	13	1	
1981–1985	20	16	48	15	2	

Sources: *Agreements:* 1956–1974 and 1975–1979—CIA, *Communist Aid Activities in Non-Communist Less Developed Countries, 1979 and 1954–79,* October 1980, p. 14; 1979–1981 and 1982–1985—CIA, *Handbook of Economic Statistics 1986,* September 1986, p. 15 (figures read from a chart). *Deliveries:* 1956–1974 and 1975–1979—same as for Agreements; 1979–1983—ACDA, *World Military Expenditures and Arms Transfers, 1985,* August 1985, table III; 1981–1985—ACDA, *World Military Expenditures and Arms Transfers, 1986,* April 1987, Table III.

[a] Excluding East Asia.

Iraq and Syria. Together, North Africa and the Middle East accounted for 68–73 percent of Soviet arms deliveries in both the late 1970s and the early 1980s, a little below their combined share in the roughly two decades of 1956–1974.

Three countries now completely dominate Soviet arms transactions with the Middle East and North Africa—Iraq, Libya, and Syria. These three hold the record for receipt of Soviet arms with values around $10 to $15 billion each.[16] Together they probably accounted for three-quarters or more of all Soviet arms transfers to the region in the past decade. Far behind these three in size of sales or delivery comes Algeria, and still farther back are Iran and North and South Yemen.

The rationale of this hierarchy and pattern of transfer seems reasonably straightforward. The Soviet Union appears ready to sell arms to almost anyone: witness its deals with Iran under both the Shah and the Ayatollah, with Kuwait (1976 and 1982), and with Jordan (1981). Its largest clients, however, share some combination of the following characteristics:

Involvement in a regional conflict with "anti-imperialist" overtones.

Subjection to internal dissidence, again with ties to "nonprogressive" forces.

Congruence of foreign policy interest with the Soviet Union, perhaps symbolized by conclusion of a treaty of friendship.

Capability of paying for Soviet arms in hard currency, goods (such as oil) or services (bases or basing rights).

One might guess that Libya's main attraction to the Soviet Union has been the last-named quality, although some of the mischief Muammar Qaddafi has perpetrated has suited Soviet purposes. Syria's development as a major client relates to the first and third elements. From the mid-1970s until recently, however, Moscow was exacting hard currency payment from Damascus too (the bill being footed by Saudi Arabia and the Gulf states), and Syrian ports have been used by Soviet naval forces. Iraq is another old client originally developed largely on political grounds but whose oil wealth made it a favored market. In the first year of the Iran-Iraq war, the Soviets cut off the arms flow to Baghdad out of concern for their position in Iran. But they have since resumed their supply relationship with Iraq's Saddam Hussein, after apparently becoming convinced that there was little chance of gaining or retaining a foothold in Teheran.

The entries in tables 3–1 and 3–2 are values in current dollars. Neither the CIA nor the DIA publishes time series of arms transfers in constant prices. In its 1986 submission to the Senate's Proxmire subcommittee, the DIA presented a truncated distribution of deliveries in both current and 1984 dollars.[17] These data indicate an estimate of about 70 percent price increase in deliveries to Iraq, Libya, and Syria between 1974–1979 and 1984 and somewhat less in deliveries to Algeria; a roughly 10 percent price increase is estimated to have taken place in the first half of the 1980s. This suggests that the real value of deliveries to North Africa probably did not change between 1975–1979 and 1979–1983, as contrasted with the indicated growth of 38 percent, and that real deliveries to the Middle East increased around 40 percent instead of the nominal 119 percent. By the same token, the growth in average annual delivery values between the period 1956–1974 and the past decade was considerably smaller than is implied in table 3–2.

The capability and general quality of the equipment involved rose substantially over these years. Shipments to Syria of the SA-5 surface-to-surface and SS-21 short-range surface-to-surface missile systems after the 1982 Lebanon war at the time represented the only appearance of such weaponry outside the Warsaw Pact area. Libya has since also received the SA-5 as well as MiG-25 fighters and MI-24 helicopters. Iraq was the first country in the Third World to receive the SU-25 ground attack aircraft, and Iraq and Syria are receiving, or are expected to receive shortly, MiG-29s.[18]

The DIA data remind us that Soviet asking prices climbed steeply in the 1970s, no doubt at least in part in recognition of the new petrodollar wealth of the Arab oil producers. The implication is that the Middle Eastern clients were getting more capable systems than in the past but that the quantities delivered were considerably smaller than the nominal dollar values suggest.

The Kremlin has definitely been more forthcoming in supplying sophisticated modern weaponry than it was in the 1950s and 1960s, but Moscow is still selective with respect to both client and type of hardware. Weapons sent to Syria are not available to the Yemens, or even to Libya; nuclear weapons are still rigidly withheld everywhere.

Eastern Europe is, of course, a much smaller player in the arms transfer game, but its role is not negligible. Eastern European arms transfers added another 15 percent to total Soviet arms sales or deliveries in all regions over the past three decades, and in the first half of the 1980s the ratio was closer to 20 percent. The same big three of Soviet transfers—Iraq, Libya, and Syria—also dominate Eastern European transactions with the Middle East. Despite reaching out into new regions of the globe, the Soviet bloc continues to concentrate on the arc of countries from North Africa to India, which are, to cite language made familiar in Soviet official justifications of involvement in the Middle East, close to the Soviet Union's southern frontiers.

Since the 1955 Soviet breakthrough into the Third World, increasing numbers of LDC military personnel have been sent to the Soviet Union and Eastern Europe for advanced training, while large numbers of Soviet bloc military technicians and advisors have been dispatched to the LDCs to upgrade the latter's forces. Over these three decades, more than eighty thousand Third World military personnel have been trained in Eastern Europe and the Soviet Union, 85 percent of them in the Soviet Union. About a third of this total came from the Middle East and another 15 percent from North Africa, together composing almost half of the aggregate total.[19] The Middle East/North African shares, individually and in aggregate, are lower for military trainees than for receipts of arms deliveries, however, indicating that these regions felt less need, relative to the size of their arms relationship with the Soviet bloc, than other Third World recipients to have their military trained by their benefactors in the Soviet Union or Eastern Europe.[20]

More than 18,000 military technicians from the Soviet Union and Eastern Europe spent at least one month in the Third World field in 1985; 34 percent (6,260) were assigned to the Middle East and another 21 percent (3,915) to North Africa.[21] Again, these proportions are smaller than the regional shares in Soviet arms transfers, owing to the large number of bloc technicians dispatched to Afghanistan, Angola, and Ethiopia (31 percent of the total). However, the 1985 regional distribution of Eastern bloc military technicians in the Third World shows slightly larger weights for the Middle East and North Africa than was the case in 1979.[22] In addition, the 1985 military technician contingent in the Middle East is considerably smaller than it was in 1984, owing to a sharp reduction in the number of Soviet bloc technicians in Syria (from 5,300 to 2,300).[23] This contingent had been abruptly enlarged in connection with the reequipment of the Syrian armed forces after the 1982 Lebanon conflict. Soviet troops were heavily involved in Syrian air defense, especially with the SA-5. It seems likely that increasing local mastery of the new equipment enabled Moscow to reduce both its troops and the advisory force serving in Syria.

Conclusion

Sometime in the remainder of this decade, most likely the Soviets will have delivered $100 billion worth of arms and military services to the Third World. It is difficult to believe that any informed observer, in viewing the breakthrough Czech-Egyptian agreement at the time, would have forecast such an extraordinary growth. This was due in large measure, however, to a possibly unique event, the oil price shock. In other respects, the patterns of change would probably not seem so surprising to the 1955 observer. The recipients of Soviet arms at one time or another are scattered around the globe, but the bulk (about three-quarters) of the more than $85 billion worth of arms and services already delivered has been concentrated in the largely Arab fringe of North Africa and the Middle East. Within that regional concentration, three countries have continued to receive the lion's share of the allocation. Egypt has vanished from the favored list, but Syria is a charter member, and Iraq joined not much later. Only Libya is a relative newcomer. Add India to the list, and it is clear that, however broad the geographical range of Soviet arms transfers, a handful of countries (with limited change in composition) has always accounted for its essential weight.

How much profit, military and otherwise, the Soviet Union obtained from this very sizable and concentrated investment has been much debated in the West, and perhaps in the Soviet Union as well. This is not the place to attempt an independent balance or even to survey the efforts of others. It seems a reasonable assumption, however, that our 1955 observer would have predicted far more extensive political-military gains from such a sum than have, by anyone's estimate, actually been achieved. Undoubtedly, the same could be said about counterpart Western arms transfers. Perhaps this is a tribute simultaneously to the stubborn persistence of regional conflicts and the balancing forces that have preserved the maneuvering space of the superpower clients. It also suggests that, barring radical change in the superpower correlation of forces, the future growth of Soviet arms transfers, while perhaps not nearly as stormy as in the 1970s, will show essential continuities with the record of the past three decades.

Notes

1. This chapter elaborates and updates one section of the author's "The Soviet Union and the Third World: The Economic Dimension," *Soviet Economy* 2 (1986), pp. 233–260, also published in Andrzej Korbonski and Francis Fukuyama, eds., *The Soviet Union and the Third World: The Last Three Decades,* (Ithaca, NY: Cornell University Press, 1987).

2. The editor of a symposium on the Soviet role in the Middle East found it necessary to remind readers, through a footnote intervention in an article by Alexander J. Bennett, "Arms Transfers As An Instrument of Soviet Policy in the Middle East," *The Middle East Journal,* 39 (Autumn 1985), p. 745: "We must all remember that even official U.S. government figures are only estimates. This is particularly true when they relate to the USSR."

3. CIA, *Arms Flows to LDCs: US-Soviet Comparisons, 1974–77,* November 1978.

4. *World Armaments and Disarmament SIPRI Yearbook 1983* (New York: Taylor and Francis, 1983), pp. 361–362.

5. See CIA, *Arms Flows to LDCs,* which contrasts two dollar pricing models—Soviet export prices and equivalent U.S. production costs. The values in subsequent CIA documents, which are reproduced in table 3–1, evidently refer to the export prices.

6. But not Afghanistan, whose essential difference from Cuba or Vietnam seems obscure to this writer. Nor is it clear why Ethiopia should be considered a noncommunist state.

7. DIA data imply a 50-odd percent rise in the price level of Soviet military deliveries to the Third World (U.S. Congress, Joint Economic Committee, *Allocation of Resources in the USSR and China—1985,* Washington, DC, 1986, pp. 19–20, 112–113). Inflated by that amount, the SIPRI estimate in 1981–1984 would still be less than 60 percent of the CIA figure.

For SIPRI's critique of U.S. government estimates, see *World Armaments and Disarmament SIPRI Yearbook 1984* (London and Philadelphia: Taylor and Francis, 1984), pp. 180–183.

8. *Allocation of Resources in the USSR and China—1985, pp. 19–20.*

9. ACDA, *World Military Expenditures and Arms Transfers 1985,* August 1985, tables A and B (1973–1976, 1977–1980, and 1981 agreements); *World Military Expenditures and Arms Transfers 1986,* April 1987, Table IV (1981 deliveries; deliveries and agreements 1982–1985).

10. See, for example, Gur Ofer, "Economic Aspects of Soviet Involvement in the Middle East," in Yaacov Ro'i, ed., *The Limits to Power: Soviet Policy in the Middle East* (London: Croom Helm, 1979), p. 73, who cites Barry Kostinsky, *Description and Analysis of Soviet Foreign Trade Statistics,* Foreign Economic Reports, No. 5, U.S. Department of Commerce, Foreign Demographic Analysis Division, Washington, D.C., 1974, pp. 66–69. For a recent statement of the thesis and supporting evidence, see Wharton Econometric

Forecasting Associates (WEFA), *Centrally Planned Economies Current Analysis,* 4 (15 August 1984).

11. Efrat doubts the thesis that Soviet arms exports are included in total in the LDC trade residuals in official Soviet statistics. His calculation of the value of the residual yields a set of numbers considerably smaller not only than his own estimates but also relative to the CIA figures. This, plus some information on the institutional division of weapons and nonweapons transfers, leads him to speculate that official data exclude weapons transfers and cover only nonweapons sales.

12. See the sources for the CIA time series in table 3–1.

13. CIA, *Communist Aid Activities in Non-Communist Less Developed Countries, 1979 and 1954–79,* October 1980.

14. Note that the data for the 1970s, particularly the earlier part, were probably subsequently revised, but the revisions have not been published.

15. In both CIA and ACDA distributions, Egypt is included with the Middle East rather than North Africa.

16. The U.S. Department of Defense's *Soviet Military Power,* 3d ed., Washington, DC, 1984, p. 119, credits Libya with $15 billion and Syria with $13.8 billion. The DIA figures in *Allocation of Resources in the USSR and China—1985,* p. 19, show $14.8 billion for Syria, $14.2 billion for Iraq, and $11.2 billion for Libya in the period since 1974 alone.

17. *Allocation of Resources in the USSR and China—1985,* pp. 19–20, 112–113.

18. *Soviet Military Power,* 3d ed., 1984, p. 119, and 5th ed., 1986, pp. 133–135.

19. CIA, *Handbook of Economic Statistics 1986,* p. 122.

20. While Eastern Europe hosted 14 percent of the trainees sent from the Middle East to the Soviet bloc, it trained a third of those coming from North Africa. This is because Libya has preferred to send 60 percent of its trainees to Eastern Europe.

21. Ibid., pp. 124–125. It is not clear whether "military technicians" covers all military specialists—including advisors and support personnel—or is restricted to technicians. The numbers seem large enough to fit the broader concept.

22. 1979 data from CIA, *Communist Aid Activities in Non-Communist Less Developed Countries, 1979 and 1954–79,* p. 15.

23. CIA, *Handbook of Economic Statistics 1985,* p. 123.

4

European
Arms Transfers
and Other Suppliers

Alan Platt

Since the end of World War II, the United States and the Soviet Union have
been the world's two largest arms exporters to the Middle East as well as
elsewhere in the Third World. In recent years, the quantity and quality of
these transfers to the Middle East—from the superpowers as well as from European and other suppliers—have jumped in an unprecedented manner, with roughly
three-quarters of the total dollar value of all international arms sales agreements
in 1985 being for weapons for the Middle East.[1]

During the past 30 years, each war in the Middle East has been followed by
a significant increase in the inflow of major weapons. In the early 1950s, the arms
inflow to the Middle East averaged roughly $40 million annually. Following the
Suez war in 1956, this inflow moved up to roughly $200 million a year. It then
significantly increased after the June war of 1967 to around $600 million a year.
Most importantly, since the 1973 war and the early 1970s oil embargo, arms inflow to the Middle East has jumped to an unparalleled level.[2] According to a
spring 1986 Library of Congress study, the 1985 arms inflow to the Middle East
exceeded $20 billion, despite an overall drop in the value of new arms purchases
by Third World countries from $32.3 billion in 1984 to $29.9 billion in 1985.[3]

Whereas in most earlier periods in the postwar era the United States and the
Soviet Union were the preeminent suppliers of conventional arms to the Middle
East, in 1985 that was no longer the case. To be sure, the two superpowers were
still highly important arms suppliers—in terms of both the quantity of arms transferred and the unparalleled sophistication of the weaponry sold—with the Soviet
Union being the primary supplier of Iraq, Libya, and Syria, and the United States
supplying Saudi Arabia, Egypt, and Israel, among others. Nevertheless, in 1985
the big four Western European arms suppliers—France, Britain, West Germany,
and Italy—collectively led both the superpowers in concluding new arms agreements with the nations of the Middle East. Whether this was a one-time phenomenon remains to be seen. There is no question, though, that the principal countries

The views expressed herein are those of the author and do not necessarily reflect the thinking of the
RAND Corporation or the U.S. government.

of Western Europe are now and are likely to continue to be major arms suppliers to the Middle East.

How did this happen? Why is it that Western European arms suppliers now play such an important role in transferring arms to the Middle East? A number of factors might be cited, but two seem most salient. First, there are the blatant inconsistencies in recent overall U.S. arms sales policies, leaving Western-oriented Middle East arms recipients uncertain about the United States' reliability in the arms transfer field. Following the 1973 Middle East war, U.S. arms sales to the region jumped significantly, particularly to Iran. During the mid-1970s, for example, Iranian arms orders averaged $3.2 billion per year (in current dollars), or about 28 percent of all U.S. arms sales globally. In part because of this perceived excessive arms salesmanship, there was a negative popular reaction in the United States to the government's arms sale policies. Reflecting this reaction and acting out of frustration with the Nixon administration's seeming unwillingness to impose self-restraints, Congress passed the Nelson amendment in 1974, which laid out procedures by which the U.S. legislative branch could block significant proposed arms sales. Then in 1976 Congress enacted the Arms Export Control Act, the most comprehensive legislation enacted in this policy area since the early 1950s. This legislation sought to shift through its detailed provisions the focus of U.S. arms sales policy from that of selling arms to controlling arms sales and exports. Behind the oversight procedures laid out in this act was the general sense in Congress and in the country that the United States' interests would best be served if annual aggregate arms sales did not exceed current levels.[4]

When the Carter administration began in 1977, U.S. sentiments toward arms transfer restraint reached new heights. In May 1977 Carter issued Presidential Directive 13, which contained guidelines to effect such constraint. Among other things, this directive provided that:

1. There would be a dollar ceiling on the volume of new U.S. commitments for foreign military sales and military assistance programs, with the total for fiscal year 1978 to be less than for the previous year.

2. The United States would not be the first supplier to introduce into a region newly developed advanced weapons systems that would create a new or significantly higher combat capability.

3. The United States would not sell or coproduce newly developed advance weapons systems until they were operationally deployed with U.S. forces.

4. The United States would not produce or significantly modify advanced systems solely for export.

5. The United States would not permit coproduction agreements with other countries for significant weapons, equipment, and major components.

6. The United States would not allow U.S. weapons or equipment to be transferred to third parties without U.S. government consent.[5]

At the same time the United States undertook a policy of national arms transfer restraint in the mid-1970s, it attempted to pursue multilateral restraint as well. Implicit in this effort was the understanding that if the United States exercised unilateral restraint and there were no constraints on the other major arms suppliers, U.S. restraint objectives would not be attained and American geopolitical and commercial interests would be undercut. With this in mind, in the spring of 1977, the United States first attempted to enlist the support of the major European arms suppliers in multilateral discussions on global arms transfer restraint. When the Europeans indicated that Soviet participation in such discussions was a precondition to their involvement, the United States approached the Soviet Union about such talks. In the course of the summer of 1977, these bilateral superpower discussions led to the initiation of American-Soviet conventional arms transfer (CAT) talks in December 1977, and in 1978 three additional superpower sessions were held on this subject. No concrete agreements were reached, however. While there was substantial agreement concerning general principles governing possible arms transfer restraint, the talks foundered in significant part over the issue of to which regions of the world such agreement might apply. The United States favored regional discussions about arms transfer restraint solely concerning Latin America and sub-Saharan Africa, while the Soviet Union favored talks to restrain the transfer of arms to the Middle East and eastern Asia. At no time during this period did the big four European suppliers join in these talks about possible restraint.

In the wake of aggressive Soviet activities in the late 1970s in the Middle East and Persian Gulf, the Carter administration formally gave up the notion that arms sales were to be an "exceptional" instrument of policy, and by 1980 the Carter administration had essentially abandoned its national and international efforts to restrain the transfer of conventional arms. This course was taken even further when in July 1981 the Reagan administration replaced the Carter administration's Presidential Directive 13 with a new presidential policy directive aimed at "giving the Reagan administration greater flexibility in using the transfer of weapons as a tool of foreign policy." Henceforth, arms sales were to be "an integral component of the U.S. global defense posture and a key instrument of foreign policy." In the Reagan directive, it was also noted that the Soviet Union and other suppliers had shown "little or no interest" in agreements or understandings to restrain arms transfers and that thereafter the United States would not "jeopardize its own security needs through a program of unilateral restraint."[6] Accordingly, in the past five years Reagan administration policy has focused on the positive role that arms transfers could play as a tool of U.S. foreign policy around the world. Nevertheless, despite the Reagan administration's emphasis on the use of arms sales as a positive instrument of U.S. foreign policy, a number of White House–favored arms sales to the Middle East and Persian Gulf have either been stopped within the executive branch or significantly modified, largely due to congressional efforts.

The wide oscillations and vacillation in recent U.S. arms sale policies might not have had a significant impact on the flow of arms from Europe to the Middle

East were it not for the second key factor affecting contemporary arms sales in the area—a heightened interest and effort on the part of the major European nations to market more and more sophisticated arms abroad. While there have been some differences within and between the various European arms suppliers in their respective approaches to arms sales in the Middle East and elsewhere, the bottom line is that in each of the big four European arms-supplying countries, there has been discernible movement in recent years toward a more aggressive marketing stance to take advantage of a continuing high demand for arms in the Middle East.

France

Before the 1973 war and the 1974 OPEC oil price rise, most of the arms that France exported were sold to other Western industrial democracies. In the period since 1974, however, the pattern of French arms transfers has shifted, with France playing an increasingly important role in supplying arms to the developing world, including the Middle East. Indeed, during most of this period, France has consistently been ranked third behind the superpowers in transferring arms to the Middle East.

In the course of this past decade, as French arms sales to the Middle East have mushroomed, the arms-producing sector of the French economy has grown dramatically. Not only has the volume of French arms deliveries to the Middle East and elsewhere in the Third World more than quadrupled in the past 10 years, but now more than 300,000 people work in the French arms industry. Of French arms exports, the Middle East typically accounts for more than half of the weapons sold abroad in any given year.

There is, of course, an important relationship between the dramatic growth in recent French arms sales to the Middle East and the pattern of France's oil imports. Roughly 80 percent of France's oil imports come from the Middle East, with the largest suppliers being Saudi Arabia and Iraq—countries with which France has concluded its largest arms sales in recent years. For example, in 1980 the French concluded its largest arms deal ever, a $3.5 billion multiyear package to modernize and equip the Saudi Navy. In addition, France has supplied the Saudis with three hundred AMX-30 tanks, numerous armored personnel carriers and artillery pieces, and a number of the key components for an air defense system. Furthermore, as Iraq has gravitated away from its heavy dependence on the Soviet Union, France, despite the Iran-Iraq war, has sent Mirage F-1s, antiaircraft missiles, and AMX-30 and AMX-13 tanks to Iraq, while Iran has received missile-armed fast attack boats, antitank missiles, and large amounts of 150mm ammunition. In recent years France also has sold Mirage aircraft to Libya and Jordan, and Milan and HOT antitank missiles to Syria. Overall, it is estimated that earnings from arms sold to countries in the Middle East have paid for approximately 20 percent of the cost of recent French oil imports on an annual basis.[7]

While important, economic considerations only partly explain France's motivation in aggressively marketing arms to Middle Eastern countries. Political considerations have played an important role as well. France has long valued its independence in foreign policy. To carry out such a policy, founded on nuclear deterrence and the maintenance of a national capacity for developing and producing weapons, France needs its own defense industry. Given the size of the country's domestic arms market, however, this has meant that Paris must export weapons abroad to justify its relatively small defense industrial base and also to keep the unit cost of weapons at an affordable level for its own armed forces. As Andrew Pierre has pointed out, "[For France] arms exports make economically possible a basic political necessity of the country."[8]

Finally, it has been long-standing French policy to sell arms to foreign governments that wish to lessen their dependence on the two superpowers and maintain their own national military capability. Such a policy is seen not only as being justified by the sovereign right of countries to defend themselves but also as a prime way for France to exercise and maintain its influence in the world. As Jean Klein, a widely known French defense analyst, has written in explaining and defending his country's highly permissive arms sales policies, "In devoting herself to arming countries that desire to escape the hold of a powerful neighbor and in seeing to it that each country is assured a minimum military capability, France is not pursuing a despicable objective and it's therefore improper to identify her as the 'beast of the apocalypse.'"[9]

Great Britain

In the last few years, British arms sales to the Middle East and elsewhere around the world have followed the same dramatic, upward direction as those of France, with Great Britain particularly benefiting as a result of the performance of battle-proven equipment during the Falklands conflict. While Great Britain has typically continued to trail France in the dollar value of arms delivered to the Middle East on an annual basis, there has not been so great a difference in their respective levels of arms sales and deliveries that their rankings should not be considered fixed.

Like the United States, the Soviet Union, and France, Great Britain has sold a relatively wide range of military hardware to a number of Middle Eastern countries. Of these, the British weapons systems most exported have been aircraft, tanks, and naval vessels, with some of these weapons (such as Chieftain tanks) being designed essentially for export, at times to the disadvantage of the British military.

As in France, British arms exports have come to play an important role in the national economy, with 25 to 35 percent of all arms produced being exported and the number of British jobs dependent on arms exports now at about 100,000 people. The conservative government of Prime Minister Margaret Thatcher has been particularly interested in the economic benefits to be derived from an effective arms sales program. This expedient interest was starkly summarized in a Thatcher speech to the 1980 Farnsborough Air Show:

> Overseas sales of British defense equipment will this year earn $1.2 billion pounds in foreign currency. That's a handy sum. That's quite a large sum. . . . But it is not enough. The procurement budget of government and the skills of our people, if used to the best advantage, could bring the country far greater sums, greater benefits to both our armed services and to our industries, and more jobs at the same time.[10]

Moreover, while Britain has acquired a large financial stake in having its own arms export industry and needs to export a certain level of armaments to support its own defense procurement needs, there are some differences between the British and French approaches to arms sales. The notion of having a large, autonomous, arms-manufacturing capability is not commonly given the same importance as in France. In addition, the export of arms is not seen in London as having the same importance in foreign policy terms as in Paris. Finally, there is periodic questioning in Britain of certain arms sales on moral/political grounds, with the French being commonly thought of as "ruthless and indiscriminate arms pushers compared to the British."[11] Moreover, such questioning would undoubtedly increase significantly should the Conservatives be replaced in office.

In the near future, the British are likely to continue to market arms aggressively in the Middle East. Since the outbreak of the Iran-Iraq war, Britain has worked to increase its military supply role with a number of Arab and Gulf states—most notably Jordan, Kuwait, Oman, and the United Arab Emirates—and to expand its Saudi Air Force supply contract. Most significantly, the largest British arms sale in history was begun with Saudi Arabia in September 1985, when Great Britain, as the lead member of the British–West German–Italian consortium that manufactures Tornado fighter jets, reached an agreement to transfer seventy two of these warplanes to Riyadh. Concluded after a Reagan proposal to sell an additional forty F-15 fighters ran into congressional opposition and a tough head-to-head competition with the French Mirage, the deal was ultimately finalized in the winter of 1986 by the British Defense Ministry's Arms Sales Division. Of the seventy two Tornados to be transferred largely in exchange for Saudi oil, forty-eight are to be strike models and twenty-four interceptors. The package also includes the transfer of thirty Hawks, an advanced jet trainer/light strike aircraft, and thirty Swiss-built PC-9 aircraft, which will be outfitted in Britain before being shipped to Saudi Arabia. It has been estimated that this deal alone is worth between $5 and $6 billion, although the total amount will be spread over several years as deliveries are made.[12]

Oman, which earlier had placed an order for eight Tornados, is the only other country to which this consortium has so far exported Tornado aircraft, but negotiations have been underway for some time between the British Defense Ministry and Jordan to sell forty Tornados. Valued at roughly $1 billion, this potential deal picked up some momentum in the months since Congress forced the Reagan administration to withdraw plans to sell F-16/F-20 aircraft to Amman. The Tornado deal now under discussion is said to focus on the so-called Air Defense Variant, which could be used for air-to-air combat and not for ground strikes.[13] Other British efforts to sell Chieftain tanks, Hawk aircraft, Rapier surface-to-air missiles, Scorpion armored cars, and Land Rovers to various countries in the Middle East continue as well.

Federal Republic of Germany

Unlike the superpowers, France, and Great Britain, the Federal Republic of Germany has consistently maintained a set of restrictions on its export of weapons in recent years. In the wake of World War II, the German arms industry was completely dismantled and all German military production prohibited. In 1955, however, as the Federal Republic gradually regained its position as a European power and joined the Western European Union and NATO, German military production was resumed. Initially, the emphasis was on rearming West Germany's own armed forces. In time this led the Federal Republic to resume overt and covert military assistance programs with a number of countries, primarily to gain political support for Bonn's claim as the only German state. One of the countries to which West Germany shipped arms on a clandestine basis was Israel, and when in the early 1960s, this became public in the Arab world, ten Arab states broke diplomatic relations with the Federal Republic.

In large part because of these developments in the Middle East, West Germany in 1966 formally adopted a policy that placed restrictions on all arms sales to "areas of tension," including the Middle East. In 1971, two years after the Social Democrats and the Free Democrats regained office, the West German government reviewed its arms sale policies and ultimately announced even tighter guidelines to restrict the sale of arms outside the NATO area. A key part of the revised policy was that arms sales to areas of tension, as defined by the Foreign Ministry, were specifically prohibited. In Bonn it was widely understood that henceforth West Germany would seriously limit weapons sales to countries in crisis areas such as the Middle East.[14] One category of non-NATO countries— those at peace or of critical importance to West Germany and the West—was eligible under the tightened guidelines to receive German arms if the German government determined that to do so would be in its national interest and would not be in conflict with the law.[15]

During the 15-year period since the promulgation of these guidelines in 1971, West Germany has had an evolving and paradoxical stance on arms sales. On the one hand, West Germany's regulations concerning arms exports have remained in effect and are generally considered to be the strictest in the noncommunist world. Each proposed sale must be approved on a case-by-case basis and is subject to lengthy bureaucratic review by several ministries. Further, German, as opposed to French or British, companies are limited in their international arms marketing efforts. Still, by 1984, the last year for which complete statistics are currently available, German arms exports to the Middle East and elsewhere had grown significantly, with overall German arms exports approaching $2 billion annually. Constituting roughly 6.4 percent of the world total, this level of arms exports made the Federal Republic the world's fifth largest arms trader.[16]

What has happened is that German arms export policy has been interpreted, for economic and industrial reasons, in an increasingly permissive manner over the past 15 years. In part due to West Germany's need to import large quantities of oil and in part to growing economic pressure from the business and labor communities in the Federal Republic, successive governments have seen fit to relax the arms sale guidelines, or at least to interpret them loosely. Through a variety of circuitous means—export of entire plants, supply of component parts for assembly abroad, and development of joint products with other countries—West Germany has developed arms relationships with some 85 countries.[17]

Concerning their multinational weapons projects, West Germany has become most actively involved with both France and Great Britain, two nations with patently less restrictive arms export policies. For example, in the case of the Tornado, (a plane for which 42.5 percent of the work will be done in the Federal Republic), during the 1970s and early 1980s the Bonn government had doubts as to the wisdom of selling such aircraft to Saudi Arabia. In significant part as a result of these German doubts, the sale initially did not go through, as the original memorandum of understanding establishing the Tornado consortium gave any of the three participating countries a veto over any export sale. After Chancellor Kohl took office in 1982 and serious negotiations regarding the Saudi sale were resumed, Britain proposed an amendment eliminating this veto power, which the Bonn government chose not to oppose. Similarly, French-German close-support Alpha Jet aircraft are available for sale throughout the Middle East through the French, while antitank missiles such as the HOT, Milan, and Roland are produced by a French-German industrial consortium and marketed through the French-led Euromissile corporation.[18]

While German involvement in multinational arms projects burgeoned in recent years to roughly 60 percent of the equipment procured by Germany's armed forces, there has continued to be strong sentiment in Bonn for some restraint on arms transfers. Defined as shipments leaving the Federal Republic per se, German arms transfers continue to be particularly controversial when considered for areas of high tension, such as the Middle East. Nowhere has this ambivalence about arms sales been more clearly demonstrated than in West Germany's dealings with

Saudi Arabia. On the other hand, there continues to be a major ongoing controversy over the possible sale of three hundred Leopard-2 tanks, one thousand armored personnel carriers, and self-propelled guns to Saudi Arabia. Reluctant to turn down a lucrative arms request from Saudi Arabia, German's largest non-Western trading partner and a country from which Germany imports roughly 25 percent of its oil, Bonn has agonized over this sale for more than 5 years, and it is unlikely that the Leopard-2 deal will be completed anytime soon. At the same time, the Federal Republic has opted to allow the Saudi Tornado sale to go forward and has recently permitted two German companies, Rheinmetall and Thyssen Rheinstahl Fabrik, to try to negotiate a multibillion-dollar agreement with Riyadh to build a factory to manufacture terminally guided artillery ammunition. Overall, there is no reason to assume that Bonn will formally abandon its announced policy of arms transfer restraint concerning areas of high tension, although bulges in this policy seem increasingly likely in coming years.[19]

Italy

Like France, Great Britain, and West Germany, Italy's arms export practices have been and remain closely related to Italian military procurement policies and national economic needs. Like the Federal Republic of Germany, Italy's military production capabilities were severely restricted after World War II. In 1949, however, Italy joined NATO, and by 1951 most of these restrictions were lifted. As Italy gradually got back on its economic feet and its defense industry grew, so too did Italy's arms export efforts, especially as U.S. military aid declined during the 1950s and 1960s. By the mid-1980s, Italy, spurred by commercial needs and interests, ranked behind the United States, the Soviet Union, France, and Great Britain as a leading arms supplier to the Middle East. In the period from 1982 to 1985, for example, it has been estimated that Italy exported on the average significantly more than $1 billion a year to the Middle East and Persian Gulf region.[20]

Of particular importance to the general growth of the Italian arms export industry has been the virtual absence of government oversight. In stark contrast to the welter of legal and political regulations affecting German arms sales, Italian arms export companies are relatively free to export whatever they wish to almost any country in the world. To the chagrin of other arms suppliers, this has at times meant that Italian companies were free to fill orders for commercial purposes that other companies could not bring to fruition due to political considerations.[21]

Given this lack of government oversight on arms transfers, it is not surprising that two of the largest recipients of Italian weapons in recent years have been Iraq and Libya, in addition to Saudi Arabia. In 1979, in a deal worth more than $1.5 billion, Italy agreed to supply Iraq with virtually a made-to-order fleet, including four Lupo frigates armed with Italian ship-to-ship and antiaircraft missiles, six fully armed corvettes, and a supply ship. In recent years Italy also has played an important role in helping Libya, a country from which it purchased 16 percent of its total oil imports in 1985, meet its land, air, and naval military needs.[22]

As Italian companies have expanded their international marketing efforts throughout the developing world, they have made a noticeable effort to team up with leading international partners to ensure greater capital and more sophisticated technologies. For example, Aeritalia, Italy's leading producer of military and civil fighter aircraft, has joined with British and West German companies to build the Tornado and the prospective new European Fighter Aircraft (EFA); Aeritalia also has teamed up with Embraer of Brazil to build a new subsonic jet fighter, while, Agusta has joined an international consortium to build and market a new antitank helicopter.[23]

Other Suppliers

At the same time as the big four European arms suppliers have substantially increased their arms exports to the Middle East in recent years, so too have a number of nonsuperpower, non-European suppliers. Most notable of these is Brazil. Until the mid-1970 arms production in Brazil was negligible. At that time the Brazilian government consciously set out to develop an arms industry not primarily for self-defense or as a by-product of a growing military establishment but rather for commercial and national prestige, and in the intervening years, this plan has succeeded splendidly. According to Stockholm International Peace Research Institute (SIPRI) statistics, in less than a decade Brazil leaped from zero arms exports to roughly $1.3 billion in 1984.[24]

Selling arms with no strings attached and when other arms suppliers are often reluctant (only South Africa and Cuba are currently blacklisted) Brazil now has arms ties with a number of countries around the world. Unlike the United States, Brazil does not typically require clients to sign end-user agreements, under which manufacturers can block the resale or retransfer of their military goods. Not surprisingly, this has helped Brazilian companies pick up clients unable, either directly or indirectly, to obtain Western-manufactured weapons. For example, in the Iran-Iraq war, both sides are currently using Brazilian-made armored cars, which are the equal of anything the major powers manufacture. These armored cars have been obtained both directly and indirectly by the combatants. In addition, the Iraqis have been sold the first ten Brazilian-made Astros II rockets, while in Saudi Arabia, Brazil's new 40-ton tracked vehicle, the Ozorio, has recently won a head-to-head competition with France's AMX-40 armored vehicles. The Ozorio deal, which was clinched this spring after 18 months of field testing and negotiations, will likely lessen prospective Saudi interest in the Leopard-2, which is equipped with comparable technology. Furthermore, the Brazilians hope that the Ozorio deal will lead to a multibillion-dollar deal to produce five hundred to a thousand

Ozorio tanks in Jeddah. Other near-term Brazilian sales are likely to be made directly to Saudi Arabia, Libya, Iraq, Jordan, Tunisia, and Morocco and may include a range of military and civilian aircraft, guided missiles, ships, tanks, artillery, and small arms.[25]

Of course, Brazil is not the only developing country to find a useful commercial and political niche in exporting arms to the Middle East. There are a number of other important arms suppliers to the region, and more than thirty developing nations have homegrown arms industries.[26] Currently, the People's Republic of China sells fighter planes and tanks to Iran, Iraq, and Egypt, while Egypt sells aircraft, tanks, and armored vehicles to Iraq, Oman, Somalia, Sudan, and North Yemen, among others. South Korea sells attack boats, tanks, and small arms to several different countries, while North Korea sells attack boats and artillery to Egypt and Iran. Singapore sells ships and small arms to Iran, Iraq, Oman, and Saudi Arabia. India sells aircraft and guided missiles to Iran and Libya, among others. In so doing, these developing country arms exporters have clearly made the nations of the Middle East less dependent on the superpowers for all but some of the top-of-the-line systems. The consequences of this development are manifold and likely to be unpredictable. It is clear, though, as one U.S. State Department official recently lamented, that "the days are long gone when we [the United States] could control the flow of weapons. . . . It's Saturday-night-special time worldwide."[27]

Conclusions

Arms deliveries to the Middle East have risen dramatically in recent years, and there is little reason to assume that this inflow will not continue. While the superpowers have continued to sell and deliver arms to the region at generally high levels, recent arms inflow has been notably spurred by the increasing aggressive international marketing efforts of Western European and other arms suppliers. Overall, Western European suppliers in 1985 collectively accounted for a greater share of new Third World arms sales than either the United States or the Soviet Union.

Given economic pressures, the growth of international arms black and gray markets, and the overall international political situation, what are the prospects for restraints on the inflow of arms to the Middle East in the near future? In a word, dismal. In the next few years it seems likely that there will be a continuing high demand for arms in the region, and both superpowers, the big four European suppliers, and other important arms suppliers such as Brazil, Czechoslovakia, and the People's Republic of China are all likely to continue to transfer arms to the Middle East at high levels.

At least three crosscurrents, however, suggest that in a longer-term perspective, some highly limited international agreement on arms transfers to the region may be possible. First, it should be explicitly noted that despite record-level arms transfers to the Middle East in recent years, the efforts of the major arms suppliers have not been completely open-ended. There has been some self-denial, some tacit form of restraint on arms transfers to the Middle East. For example, the United States has been reluctant to transfer large quantities of top-of-the-line aircraft, as well as Stinger antiaircraft weapons and long-range surface-to-surface missiles, to most of the countries in the Middle East. At the same time, the Soviet Union, seemingly wary of provoking a superpower confrontation in the Middle East, has imposed on itself certain restraints on highly advanced systems. The West Germans have not been willing to transfer Leopard-2 tanks to Saudi Arabia, while virtually all the members of the European Economic Community have recently demonstrated a willingness to restrain their arms sales to Syria. In addition, none of the major suppliers has been inclined to transfer to the Middle East certain ingredients for the production of chemical weapons or materials to aid the manufacture of nuclear weapons. In short, some restraint, albeit very selective and typically limited to high-technology items, has existed.

Second, it is increasingly obvious in 1986 that there are important limits on the ability of recipient countries in the Middle East to continue to finance the importation of increasingly expensive sophisticated arms. These financial limits, due to a decline in the world economy, a perceptible drop in the availability of large amounts of credit, and the selective saturation of the arms market, have already had a perceptible influence on the importation of arms to the region and likely will have an increasingly significant impact in the future, despite innovative efforts by supplier and recipient countries to finance the importation of high levels of arms.[28]

Third, there are important general limits on the inclination and ability of most major arms suppliers to continue to export their most sophisticated weapons. As to inclination, there is growing concern among a number of the world's major arms suppliers that as the number of developing country arms suppliers get larger, so too will the competition. The realization that today's customers may be tomorrow's competitors is already having an inhibiting effect on certain arms transfers. Further, for countries such as Brazil, in regard to manufacturing arms there is a qualitative threshold regarding technological sophistication. For Brazil to continue to be competitive in the arms export market, in the words of Peter Lock, it will need to "significantly increase its research and development expenditures or associate with products from the major producer countries in NATO."[29] As evidence of this, it has been noted that in 1977 the Brazilian government canceled its military cooperation agreements with the United States so as to allow it to export arms freely. In 1984, however, Brazil saw fit to sign a new memorandum of understanding with the United States concerning military cooperation, under which Brazil is to be restrained in its arms transfer sales to Libya and the Middle East.

In the American-Soviet conventional arms transfer negotiation in 1977–1978, important progress was made between the two superpowers in agreeing on a framework of general principles to govern possible future transfers to the Middle East and elsewhere in the Third World. In brief, both sides were able to agree on the need for a three-part arms transfer restraint framework: commonly agreed upon political and legal criteria to determine recipients' eligibility; commonly agreed upon military and technical criteria to govern types and quantities of arms permitted to be transferred; and the need for arrangements to implement these principles and guidelines in specific regional situations. Such a framework was seen as a necessary step toward establishing "a common set of criteria and a common approach to their implementation, which (could) serve as models for both suppliers and recipients in framing arms transfer policies and designing regional restraint agreements."[30]

In time the U.S.-Soviet efforts to establish such a concrete framework foundered, although not before a number of specific criteria developed to govern prospective arms transfers. Given the current international political climate, the renewal of talks on conventional arms transfer restraints is highly unlikely in the near future. Nevertheless, against the backdrop of the superpowers' limited earlier progress, the above-identified crosscurrents affecting present and future patterns of international arms trade, and the legacy of costly and bitter conflict in the Middle East, a few points about possible efforts at arms transfer restraints might be made for future reference.

First, to be successful, future international restraint efforts will have to be multilateral, not bilateral. Especially given the increasingly prominent role that the big four European suppliers have played and are likely to play in transferring arms to the region, restrain efforts would have to include the major European countries and other suppliers to have any chance of being meaningful.

Second, restraint efforts would stand the best chance for success if they were carried out, at least initially, at the technical rather than the political level. Such efforts would be doomed to failure if they were seen and used as a way of trying to solve larger political issues in the region.

Third, in the beginning these efforts might best be focused on those weapons that suppliers have thus far been generally reluctant to transfer to the region anyway (for example, long-range surface-to-surface missiles, sophisticated weapons to abet terrorists, and certain chemical weapons). The idea would be to codify restraints that thus far have been largely tacit and, in so doing, create momentum for increasingly broad restraints. For the types of selective restraints envisaged here, economic dislocations among the world's major arms suppliers would be minimal.

Fourth, efforts to restrain suppliers would have to be carried out in coordination with the arms recipients in the Middle East. Without at least the forbearance of the major prospective recipients, supplier restraints would likely be doomed to failure, given the growing proliferation of conventional arms suppliers and the widespread growth of phenomena such as subcontracting and coproduction.

While likely to be helpful in bringing about a lasting peace in the Middle

East, international arms transfer restraints in regard to the region are improbable in the future. To note this, however, is not to suggest that such arms control is impossible over time. Indeed, one should remember that the United States, France, and Great Britain, concerned about a possible arms race in the Middle East after the fighting of the late 1940s, signed the Tripartite Declaration in 1950, in which the three major arms suppliers to the region undertook jointly to regulate the inflow of arms. This agreement lasted until 1955, when the Soviet Union negotiated an arms deal between Czechoslovakia and Egypt. Focused on the Middle East, the Tripartite Declaration continues to stand out as the one major arms transfer restraint agreement among the world's leading arms suppliers in the postwar era.

Notes

1. Richard Grimmett, *Trends in Conventional Arms Transfers to the Third World by Major Suppliers, 1978-1985*, Congressional Research Service, 9 May 1986, pp. 1–2.

2. See *World Military Expenditures and Arms Transfers, 1973-1983* (U.S. Arms Control and Disarmament Agency, 1985), pp. 7–11.

3. Grimmett, *Trends in Conventional Arms Transfers*, p. 3; and Michael Klare, "The State of the (Arms) Trade," *Journal of International Affairs*, Summer 1986, p. 4.

4. For further discussion of this point, see Andrew Pierre, *The Global Politics of Arms Sales* (Princeton, NJ: Princeton University Press, 1982), pp. 50–52.

5. "Statement on Conventional Arms Transfer Policy," White House Press Release, 19 May 1977.

6. Charles Mohr, "U.S. Seeks Flexibility in Arms Sales," *The New York Times*, 10 July 1981, p. 3. Also see James Buckley, "Arms Transfers and the National Interest," an address before the Aerospace Industries Association, 21 May 1986.

7. Pierre, *The Global Politics of Arms Sales*, pp. 83–85. Also see Roger Labrie et al., *U.S. Arms Sales Policy* (Washington DC: American Enterprise Institute, 1982), pp. 20–22.

8. Pierre, *The Global Politics of Arms Sales*, p. 86. For further discussion of this point, see Edward Kolodziej, "Determinants of French Arms Sales: Security Implications," in Patrick McGowan and Charles Kegley, Jr., eds., *Threats, Weapons and Foreign Policy* (Beverly Hills: Sage, 1980), pp. 165–167.

9. Jean Klein, "France and the Arms Trade," in Cindy Cannizzo, ed., *The Gun Merchants: Politics and Policies of the Major Arms Suppliers* (New York: Pergamon Press, 1980), p. 129.

10. Quoted in Paul Hammond et al., *The Reluctant Supplier: U.S. Decisionmaking for Arms Sales* (Cambridge, MA: Oelgeschlager, Gunn and Hain, 1983), p. 243.

11. Andrew Pierre, "Multilateral Restraints on Arms Transfers," in Andrew Pierre, ed., *Arms Transfers and American Foreign Policy* (New York: New York University Press, 1979), pp. 300–302.

12. "Britain Expects 1986 Exports to Reach Record of $7 Billion," *Aviation Week and Space Technology*, 10 March 1986, p. 93.

13. Peter Gumbel, "Britain in Talks to sell Jordan 40 Fighter Jets," *The Wall Street Journal,* 10 June 1986, p. 25.

14. Pierre, *The Global Politics of Arms Sales,* pp. 109–111.

15. For more discussion of this point, see Frederic Pearson, "Of Leopards and Cheetahs: West Germany's Role as Mid-Sized Arms Supplier," *Orbis,* Spring 1985, p. 172; and Eberhard Wisdorff, "Move to Change Guidelines Covering Weapons Exports," *German Tribune,* 8 May 1983.

16. Paul Chadwell, "West German Arms Export Policies," *National Defense,* February 1986, p. 12.

17. For a discussion of the evolution of contemporary German arms transfer policy, see Ulrich Albrecht, "West Germany and Italy: New Strategies," *Journal of International Affairs,* Summer 1986, pp. 129–142.

18. Pierre, *The Global Politics of Arms Sales,* pp. 112–113.

19. Pearson, "Of Leopards and Cheetahs," pp. 176–180.

20. "Italians Look for Larger Share of World Market," *Aviation Week and Space Technology,* 3 June 1985, p. 22.

21. See Albrecht, "West Germany and Italy," pp. 129–134.

22. For a discussion of past and prospective Italian sales to Libya, see James Russell, "Libya's Arms Aren't All Soviet," *Defense Week,* 13 January 1986, p. 14. Also see Marcello Di Falco, "The Volume of Trade," *Defense Today,* February 1986, pp. 25–27.

23. See "Italians Look for Larger Share of World Market," *Aviation Week and Space Technology,* 8 June 1981, p. 119.

24. *SIPRI Yearbook 1985: World Armaments and Disarmament* (London: Taylor and Francis, 1985), p. 331.

25. For a more detailed discussion of Brazilian arms sales to the Middle East, see "Brazil and the Middle East," *The Middle East,* June 1986, pp. 34–39. Also see Peter Lock, "Brazil: Arms for Export," in Michael Brzoska and Thomas Ohlson, eds., *Arms Production in the Third World* (London: Taylor and Francis, 1986), pp. 89–100; Alan Riding, "Brazil's Burgeoning Arms Industry," *The New York Times,* 3 November 1985; Michael Klare, *American Arms Supermarket* (Austin, TX: University of Texas, 1984), pp. 174–178.

26. See James Katz, ed., *Arms Production in Developing Countries* Lexington, MA: Lexington Books 1984. Also see Michael Moodie, "Defense Industries in the Third World: Problems and Promises," in Stephanie Neuman and Robert Harkavy, *Arms Transfers in the Modern World* (New York: Praeger, 1979), pp. 294–321.

27. "New Sellers in Arms Bazaar," *U.S. News and World Report,* 3 February 1986, p. 39. Also see *World Military Expenditures and Arms Transfers, 1973–1983.*

28. See Walter Kitchenman, *Arms Transfers and the Indebtedness of Less Developed Countries,* The Rand Corporation, N-2020-FF, December 1983; Stephanie Neuman, "Co-production, Barter and Countertrade: Offsets in the International Arms Market," *Orbis,* September 1985, pp. 183–213.

29. Lock, "Brazil: Arms For Export," p. 99.

30. Barry Blechman, Janne Nolan, and Alan Platt, "Negotiated Limitations on Arms Transfers: First Steps toward Crisis Prevention?" in Alexander George, ed., *Managing U.S.-Soviet Rivalry* (Boulder, CO: Westview Press, 1983), p. 267.

Part III
The
Technological
Dimension

5

The Impact of New Technology on the Arab-Israel Military Balance

Gerald M. Steinberg

While it would be a mistake to ascribe primary importance to the development and transfer of various technologies in explaining the outbreak of war and the maintenance of peace, these factors should not be underestimated. The Arab-Israel conflict has many primary causes rooted in geography, history and politics, and religion. The conflict existed well before the deployment of new technology to the region, and the disappearance of such systems would not solve the underlying issues. Nevertheless, like a pungent spice, the availability of new weapons enhances and highlights the role of these other factors and can contribute in a significant manner to the outbreak of fighting or the development of stability.

In this sense, military technology has played an increasingly significant role in the Arab-Israeli conflict. Aided by their respect superpower patrons, Israel, Syria, Egypt, Saudi Arabia, and, to a lesser degree, Jordan have emphasized the rapid introduction of new weapons and new generations of technology. Advanced technology played a significant role in determining the outcome of battles between Israel and Syria in 1982. Since then, a number of new systems have been introduced, including surface-to-surface and air-to-air missiles, along with new high-performance aircraft, missiles, and AWACS.[1] While in the past there was a delay in the introduction of new technology into the region so that the newest state-of-the-art systems were not quickly deployed, this delay has essentially disappeared.

These changes are in part the result of the degree to which the U.S.-Soviet competition for influence in the region is characterized by a contest in supplying weapons to clients. Ever-higher levels of military technology are offered by the superpowers in an effort to ensure continued allegiance or to lure local states to change allegiance. For example, in cementing its new alliance with Egypt in the

Research for this study was supported by a grant from the Leonard Davis Institute for International Relations.

1970s, the United States agreed to provide a large number of new advanced weapons, including combat aircraft and missiles. In addition to their military significance, such weapons play a very important political and symbolic role. These factors have been cited repeatedly by recent U.S. administrations to justify sales of weapons such as AWACS, Stinger missiles, and F-15 aircraft to Saudi Arabia and similar systems to Jordan.

At the same time, the economic importance of the sale of sophisticated weapons, particularly to the Arab states, has become significant. Profits from such sales have spurred the United States, the Soviet Union, and, increasingly, Western Europe to make increasingly sophisticated weapons available in the region.

The increase in the rate of introduction of advanced weapons technology can have a number of major military effects. In general, new weapons, such as bombers and missiles, can increase the scope of the conflict and number of casualties. Conversely, defensive technologies, precision-guided munitions, and more accurate counterforce applications of offensive technologies can limit damage. Relative technological advantages can offset a quantitative imbalance or create qualitative superiority. New defensive technology might strengthen stability, while offensive developments can lead to instabilities, increasing the probability of war. Longer ranges for weapons can expand the number of participants in a conflict, while various command, control, and communications systems (C^3) systems are important factors in facilitating or obstructing the termination of hostilities.

Changing military technologies also have a variety of political and economic effects. Most states in the region find it difficult to cope with the increasing costs of military research and development (R&D) and procurement. The military sector also diverts scarce scientific and technological resources (although the acquisition of this new technology might have positive spin-offs in the civilian sector). In addition, to the degree that the sources of new technologies are external, the recipient states have become increasingly dependent on the supplier states.

This rapid rate of technological change is, if anything, increasing, due to the development of new systems for use in the European central front and in other areas of potential superpower confrontation. NATO's emphasis on Follow-On Forces Attack (FOFA) capabilities, emerging technologies (ET), antitactical ballistic missile (ATBM) systems, integrated air-land battle systems, stealth technologies, and similar systems will quickly find its way to the Middle East.[2] These systems will incorporate technologies such as very large scale integrated circuits (VLSI), directed energy systems, and rapid large-scale information and communications systems, among others.

As the major suppliers of these systems, the superpowers contribute to the technology-based determinants of stability and the balance of power in the region. Since violence in the Middle East often results in superpower confrontation and affects the economic and political interests of the rest of the world, the introduction of new weapons into this theater is of general importance to the United States and the Soviet Union as well as the relationship between them.

Evolution of Military Technology in the Arab-Israeli Theater

The level of technology employed in the early phases of the Arab-Israeli conflict was relatively low. In the 1947–1949 War of Independence, neither Israel nor the Arab forces fielded anything that could be considered state-of-the-art weaponry. The outcome of most battles was determined by the number, deployment, and capabilities of the infantry.[3] During the later phases of the war, Israel managed to field weapons obtained from Czechoslovakia and other sources, but these were largely obsolete.

Following the war, however, both the Arabs and the Israelis sought to increase the level and sophistication of their weapons. In 1955 Egypt received large shipments of tanks, armored troop carriers, self-propelled guns, artillery, MiG-15 fighters, destroyers, and even submarines from the Soviet Union. In response, Israel purchased Mystere and Vautourjet fighters, light tanks, and a variety of other relatively advanced weapons from France. As will be discussed later, these arms shipments contributed to the Israeli decision to participate in the 1956 Suez campaign, but while some of these new weapons were employed in the war, the level of available technology was still limited.

Between 1956 and 1967 the Israeli Defense Force (IDF) placed continued emphasis on technological modernization. The Science Corps, which was founded in 1948, was expanded and divided into two groups, the R&D department within the IDF and the National Weapons Development Authority (Rafael). The air force received particular emphasis and became the first in the world to deploy only jet fighters. Its Mirage IIIs were locally reconfigured for interdiction and ground support, improving the versatility of these weapons. Egypt also continued to modernize its air force with the addition of MiG-21 fighters and Tu-16 and Il-28 bombers. The 1967 Six Day War and, in particular, the Israeli Air Force's (IAF) destruction of the Arab air forces on the ground demonstrated that Israel had assimilated the new technology and had become a modern army.[4] In contrast, it became apparent that the Arab states had not taken this step.

Prior to 1967 the Soviet Union had become the major weapons supplier to the Arab states. While the United States had provided Hawk antiaircraft missiles in 1962 to counter Egypt's deployment of Il-28 bombers, this was a unique exception to standing U.S. policy of not supplying significant arms to countries in the region.[5] After 1967, however, when France ceased to supply Israel with weapons and the Soviets, to compensate for their failure to prevent an Israeli victory, provided massive amounts of sophisticated weapons to their Arab clients, this policy changed, and the United States reluctantly agreed to sell Israel-comparable weapons. Superpower competition based on their role as arms suppliers in the region began.

This process resulted in the introduction of a new generation of military technology into the Arab-Israeli conflict, including electronics, missiles, and high-performance combat aircraft. In October 1967 Egypt used Soviet Styx ship-to-ship missiles to sink an Israeli destroyer, the *Eilat*. This was the first combat use of such weapons. In the 1969–1970 War of Attrition, Israel began to employ U.S.-made F-4 fighters and A-4 Skyhawks. The increased range and payload of the F-4 enabled the IAF to carry out raids deep into Egypt, extending the combat radius far beyond the Sinai region. In addition, the IAF took maximum advantage of the F-4's advanced electronics and improved air-to-air combat capabilities. The Skyhawk greatly increased the IAF's payload capability, serving as flying artillery. At the same time, Egypt deployed MiG-21 aircraft and Soviet-made SAM-3 and 23mm ZSU air defense systems. To operate these, fifteen thousand Soviet troops were stationed in Egypt. Soviet pilots also were used to fly Egyptian warplanes, and, in a battle that marked the climax of air combat during the War of Attrition, the IAF shot down five Soviet pilots.[6]

By 1973 technology had become a central determinant of the balance of power. Egyptian air defenses now included large numbers of mobile, low-altitude SAM-6 missiles, and similar air defense systems were deployed in Syria. In addition, these systems were deployed in densely packed configurations (based on experience gained during the Vietnam war[7]). In response to Israeli electronic countermeasures (ECM), the SAM-6 missile systems were equipped with multiple-channel guidance systems. These air defenses, which included radar-guided antiaircraft guns and a combination of high- and low-altitude SAM systems, led to the loss of 102 Israeli aircraft, one-quarter of the total IAF.

Furthermore, the Egyptian attack across the Suez Canal was facilitated by specific technologies. For example, the Soviets provided advanced, high-speed, heavy assault bridging systems. Massive deployment of rocket-propelled grenades (RPGs) and Sagger antitank missiles with a range of 3,000 meters blunted Israeli counterattacks on the ground. The advanced T-62 tanks in the Egyptian armored columns were protected from air attacks by portable heat-seeking SAM-7s (similar to the U.S. Redeye). Syrian tanks were equipped with advanced infrared and Star Light Systems (SLS) technology to facilitate night fighting.[8] Syria also used helicopter-borne assaults to attack Israeli positions on Mount Hermon.

To deter the kind of deep penetration raids that occurred during the War of Attrition, Egypt deployed SCUD surface-to-surface ballistic missiles, which had a range of 300 kilometers, and Kelt air-to-surface standoff missiles.[9]

Advanced naval technology also played an important role in the 1973 war. Israeli Reshef missile boats used Gabriel missiles and other systems to destroy eight Syrian missile boats and a number of Egyptian craft. This gave Israel extensive command of coastal areas in the combat zone.[10]

The decade between the Yom Kippur War and the 1982 war in Lebanon witnessed the continued acceleration of the rate at which new military technology was introduced into the region. That technology was exhibited primarily in the clashes between Israel and Syria. In July 1982 Israel used a combination of highly sophisticated weapons to destroy the large air defense system that the Soviets had installed in Syria. The IAF also downed eighty-five Syrian MiG-21 and MiG-23 fighters without sustaining a single loss.[11]

This effort demonstrated the IAF's mastery of a wide range of advanced equipment. Electronic countermeasures were used to confuse the Syrians and succeeded in "destroying enemy situation awareness."[12] Israeli remotely piloted vehicles (RPVs) gave ground-based commanders real-time video images of Syrian air bases. Enemy aircraft were tracked by Israeli airborne radar and control systems, including E-2C flying command posts, Boeing-707 electronic intelligence platforms, and the radars carried on F-15s. Overflights of drones led the Syrians to waste many missiles on these decoys. Various other systems, including highly accurate surface-to-surface missiles, also were used. Thus, by 1982 the level of technology in the Arab-Israeli theater had reached the state of the art in the United States and the Soviet Union and played an important role in determining events in the region.

Technology, Deterrence, and Stability

In any situation of crisis and confrontation, the nature of the technology and the weapons available to opposing armies play an important role in determining whether and how war breaks out. In this context it is important to distinguish between deterrence and stability. While some technologies may generally enhance deterrence, they may also be destabilizing in crisis situations. In the U.S.-Soviet context, some analysts cite the advent of nuclear weapons, deterrence, and mutual assured destruction as the basic obstacle to war between the superpowers. Similarly, in the Middle East the balanced deployment of strategic weapons, such as surface-to-surface missiles, could lead to mutual deterrence. For example, Kenneth Hunt, former deputy director of the International Institute for Strategic Studies, has argued that Arab deployment of such missiles would lead to a situation in which both sides' cities would be held hostage to the other's weapons, thus leading to self-deterrence and actually limiting the scope of damage.[13]

At the same time, however, some systems and deployments may be destabilizing. The outbreak of World War I has often been attributed, at least in part, to the destablizing impact of technology.[14] Analysts of nuclear strategy frequently characterize some technologies as relatively destabilizing, such as MIRV, while others are seen as stabilizing, such as ballistic missile submarines and reconnaissance satellites.

In the Middle East, technology has clearly played a similar role, and new systems, particularly those provided by the superpowers, have frequently contributed to instability and the outbreak of war. In 1955 Czechoslovakia, acting on behalf of the Soviet Union transferred large numbers of relatively advanced weapons (at least compared to the weapons available previously) to Egypt. To Israel, and to Prime Minister David Ben-Gurion in particular, these weapons represented a major, if not long-term, threat to Israeli security. Israel's decision to join the 1956 campaign was at least partially spurred by the desire to destroy these weapons before they could be assimilated into the Egyptian military.[15]

During the crisis of May 1967 the military threat to Israel from Egypt and Syria was based largely on the volume of tanks, artillery, and bombers massed on its borders. At the same time, however, the capabilities of these forces added to Israeli fears and specifically led to the Israeli decision to preempt. Egypt recently had added MiG-21 jets and surface-to-surface missiles to its arsenals, while Jordan's air force had deployed F-104 fighter-bombers. The Israeli strike was aimed largely at neutralizing the air forces of Egypt, Syria, Jordan, and Iraq.

In general, it is not only the existence of new technology but the particular form it takes that affects stability. Analysts such as Clausewitz, Liddell Hart, Gilpin, and, more recently, Quester have suggested that the introduction of offensive technology can in particular contribute to crisis instability and increased conflict.[16] In the 1967 crisis the perception of the superiority of offensive over defensive technology may have contributed to the Israeli decision.[17]

The introduction of advanced, effective, and clearly offensive weapons, such as surface-to-surface missiles, is seen by some as particularly destabilizing. In the first place, according to a variety of historical analyses, offensive superiority leads to increased aggression. Quincy Wright, for example, concludes that offensive superiority increases the probability of war.[18] As noted, offensive superiority or the deployment of significant new strategic systems also can increase the incentive to preeempt precisely to prevent employment of these systems. The recent deployment of SS-21 missiles in Syria, which have a range of 120 kilometers and are accurate to 250 meters, represents a threat to stability. This offensive system can target Israeli staging areas as well as population centers and thus, in a crisis situation, could lead to an Israeli preemptive attack on those missile sites. Conversely, just as the forward-based tactical nuclear weapons in Europe are subject to preemptive attack and are thus likely to be used early in a conflict, if Syria is faced with the possibility of an Israeli preemptive attack, there is a strong incentive to use those missiles before they are overrun or destroyed.

Tactically, the distinction between offensive and defensive weapons is also ambiguous. Ostensibly, defensive technologies can be used offensively, and their deployment can likewise be destabilizing and encourage preemption. In 1973 Egypt used large-scale advanced air defense systems to protect its offensive forces and to hold territory seized by its ground forces. The technologically advanced Syrian air defense system poses a similar threat. Since 1982 the Soviets have introduced long-range SAM-5s into Syria, marking the first time these missiles have been deployed outside the Soviet Union. With a slant range of 300 kilometers, this missile is capable of downing Israeli aircraft well inside Israeli territory, thus threatening the E-2C and B-707 platforms. According to Lambeth, this system will "require preemptive destruction by the IDF."[19]

If the Saudis are involved in any conflict, or rather if the IDF fears or perceives that the Saudi military or its newly acquired technology is likely to be used against Israel, this new technology may also be a likely target for a first strike. In addition to Saudi Arabia's formidable arsenal of F-15 aircraft and a variety of missiles, the use of its AWACS system against Israel would serve as a major threat, and these systems would be subject to preemptive Israeli attack.

New Technology and the Balance of Power

Just as the United States relies on technology and qualitative superiority to overcome Soviet quantitative advantages, so Israel seeks to use technology to offset the inherent demographic advantage of the combined Arab states. Indeed, since 1969 the Israeli technological lead has been largely a result of its U.S. weaponry. Recently, however, the U.S. technological edge has diminished, influencing both the U.S.-Soviet balance of power and the balance in the Arab-Israeli theater.[20] Until the past decade, the Arabs' Soviet-supplied technology lagged behind that of the United States. Electrical systems generally contained vacuum tubes instead of solid-state components, and early Soviet antitank weapons, such as the Snapper, were almost "no threat on the battlefield."[21] In addition, the Soviet Union was reluctant to give or sell its most advanced systems to Egypt and Syria. Indeed, Egypt's Anwar Sadat often complained about this policy and publicly cited refusal to provide advanced equipment as the basis for the expulsion of the Soviets in 1972. Today, however, not only has the Soviet Union narrowed the gap with the United States, but Syria, its major client in the region, receives the most advanced technology before most Soviet allies in the Warsaw Pact.[22] At the same time, the United States has sold increasingly advanced weapons to Saudi Arabia and Egypt, in some cases breaking an understanding that these states would not receive weapons more advanced than those available to Israel.[23]

To reach its stated goal of strategic parity with Israel, Syria has placed heavy emphasis on advanced technology. Its Soviet-made equipment, such as the SS-21 ballistic missile, has become increasingly sophisticated. In addition, Soviet replacements after Syria's heavy losses in 1982 gave Damascus a much more modern air force than it possessed before the war. While Syria lost several MiG-21s, the replacement MiG-23s have improved interception capabilities, long-range radar, and improved antiaircraft missiles. According to a book titled *The Middle East Military Balance: 1984,* the Syrian Air Force also has absorbed elecronic warfare systems for air combat and has improved its command and control system, which was found to be defective in the 1982 fighting.[24]

As already noted, the lag between deployment of a new technology by the United States and the Soviet Union and the introduction of this technology to the Middle East has been diminishing. For example, while the MiG-29 combat aircraft has only recently been deployed by Soviet forces, this system, according to a variety of published reports, is already in the pipeline to Syria.[25] The MiG-29 has a combat radius of 1,100 nautical miles and higher-performance look-down/shoot-down radar; it can be armed with short-range and over-the-horizon AA-9 and AA-10 missiles. This technology will increase the short-range combat payload of the Syrian Air Force by a factor of four or five.[26]

Egypt, Jordan, and Saudi Arabia are also acquiring new military technologies, which could alter the local balance of power. In the past few years, Egypt has purchased and started to receive M-60A3 tanks, TOW antitank weapons, mobile artillery, and the German-French Milan antitank missile.[27] It has sixty F-16s on order, as well as the Mirage 2000, CH-47C helicopter, and four E-2C Hawkeye airborne early warning systems. To improve its air defense, Egypt has added the Improved Hawk and Crotale SAM, and its navy is being modernized through the addition of new ships and Harpoon missiles.

By virtue of their financial resources, the Saudis are acquiring the largest arsenal of new military technology, including F-15 aircraft, AWACS, Tornado aircraft (configured both for air defense and interdiction and strike), and modern naval systems (from France). The deployment of AWACS places all Israeli airspace under constant surveillance and allows for early warning, targeting, electronic countermeasures (ECM) and electronic counter-counter measures (ECCM), as well as for jamming and interdiction. The F-15s and Tornados, armed with accompanying missiles, create the potential for air-to-air combat between Israel and Saudi Arabia. In addition, the Saudis have recently acquired a U.S.-made low-altitude surveillance system capable of detecting fighters at 200 feet and at ranges of 162 miles.[28]

Jordan, while currently perhaps militarily less significant, has also begun to acquire and deploy advanced military technology. The Hashemite Kingdom has acquired mobile SAM-8 batteries and ZSU-23 radar-directed antiaircraft guns from the Soviet Union. It also has purchased Mirage F-1 aircraft with inertial navigation and air-to-surface radar for ground attacks and interdiction missions.[29] Jordan has acquired advanced battlefield electronics systems from Britain and AH-1S Cobra helicopter gunships from the United States.[30] While this technology is not likely to affect the balance of power regarding Israel (or Syria), should King Hussein obtain the additional U.S. weapons he has been seeking, and should Jordan reenter a military coalition against Israel, the balance could change significantly. The improved mobile Hawks, with a range of 40 kilometers, would be able to support an attack and defend against Israeli counterattacks. Israeli aircraft deployed at the Ovda airfield would be vulnerable, while F-16s also would greatly improve Jordan's ability to interfere with Israeli air operations.[31]

It would seem, then, that the influx of new technology has changed the balance of power between Israel and the Arab states. Indeed, according to one prominent Israeli analyst, "Qualitative erosion is taking place at every level. Advances in air-to-air missile technology, for example, have nibbled at the superiority enjoyed by Israeli pilots."[32] Other technologies, such as over-the-horizon missiles, also have reduced the role of pilots. In the long term, the acquisition of standoff missiles capable of disabling runways and of chemical weapons that could also disrupt IAF operations could alter the balance of power.

Acquiring new weapons and technology largely to enhance prestige or for symbolic purposes might, however, lead to distortions in force structure and actually decrease capability. The Saudi acquisition of AWACS and some of the more advanced Soviet SAM systems deployed in Syria may provide examples of such distortion. These acquisitions force a redirection of resources, strategy, and tactics to fit the weapons rather than security requirements determining what kinds of weapons are acquired. As a result, the deployment of new technology by Israel or the Arab states will not necessarily lead to greater capabilities.

In addition, the gap has not closed entirely, and just as the United States still maintains a substantial edge over the Soviet Union in many technologies, so Israel continues to enjoy a qualitative lead over the Arab states. Israel has thousands of laser-guided and precision-guided munitions (such as Walleye, GBU-15, Maverick, Shrike, and Standard ARM), whereas most Arab air forces have none.[33] As a result, the IAF currently has a 2 to 1 advantage in air-to-surface ordnance-carrying capability over combined Arab forces and a 5 to 1 advantage in accuracy.[34] Furthermore, should the Lavi be deployed, it could increase the IAF's relative advantage. Optimized for a high sortie rate, maximum survivability (including low visual, IR and radar signatures, and active and passive ECM), the Lavi's proponents argue that it will provide a major improvement over the F-16.[35]

Operations, Maintenance, and Upgrades

The Israeli ability to operate, configure, and maintain the advanced weapons in its arsenal also continues to provide an important advantage. Modern, technologically sophisticated weapons require advanced skills for proper operation.[36] Both Iran and Iraq have been unable to use much of their costly and sophisticated arsenals, and during the Falklands/Malvinas conflict, even the British forces failed to exploit and operate the advanced technology at their disposal.[37]

In this area Israel has long held an advantage. Arab armies, reflecting their countries' social conditions, include a large complement of illiterate or marginally educated and semiskilled people. For instance, 75 percent of the inductees in the Egyptian military are illiterate.[38] In contrast, Israeli society is largely literate, and compulsory high school education provides the foundation necessary for advanced technical training. In addition, the country's technological infrastructure and university system is equivalent to that of the advanced industrialized states.

The results of this Israeli advantage in manpower and training are apparent in a number of areas. While the Arab states have generally been slow to integrate new weapons into battle and have had difficulty operating them in the field, the IDF has repeatedly shown that it can assimilate new weapons very rapidly. Even in 1948 the Israeli forces were able to make effective and immediate use of newly delivered weapons.

In addition, Israel has been able to maintain and operate even the most highly sophisticated weapons at full capacity during war. Indeed, while the increasing level of technological complexity of weapons such as the F-15 has led to difficulties and low readiness levels in U.S. and NATO forces, Israel, with the same weapons, has been able to maintain high levels of readiness. In the 1967, 1973, and 1982 wars, the sortie rate achieved by the IAF was far greater than that achieved by U.S. forces using the same or similar technology.[39] In a recent study Kenneth Brower calculated that Israel achieved a surge capacity of 4.5 sorties per day, versus 2.0 for Syria.[40]

Israeli technological skills also are apparent in the ability of the IDF and the local defense industry to adapt and improve advanced weapons. The bulk of the weapons used in the Arab-Israeli theater were designed for missions and theaters with quite different environments and requirements, such as the European central front. As a result, many of the weapons delivered to the Middle East are far from optimized for local conditions. Israel, however, has been able to make numerous adjustments and adaptations to improve the usefulness of these weapons. World War II vintage Sherman tanks received new guns and engines to become "Super-Shermans." Similarly, Israel Aircraft Industries (IAI) transformed the Fouga Magister trainer for use in attack and ground-support missions.[41] A number of Israeli innovations, particularly in the areas of avionics, electronics, and remotely piloted vehicles and decoys, also have been adopted by the U.S. military.[42]

In addition, Israel's flexible command system allows the IDF to make optimal use of its advanced technology. In contrast, the inelastic systems in Egypt and Syria, which are in large part the result of their forces' limited capabilities, prevent the full exploitation of their technology. To further improve the Israeli command structure and ability to employ and optimize its technological capabilities, the IDF created the Ground Forces Command to integrate tank, infantry, artillery, and engineering units. In the initial stages of the Yom Kippur War, the IDF's tanks faced large-scale antitank defenses without the support of artillery or infantry.

Therefore, as the level of technology continues to accelerate, Israel may actually increase its relative capability regarding the Arab confrontation states, despite the latter's acquisition of advanced technology. According to reports of U.S. advisors participating in joint military exercises in Egypt, the capabilities of the Egyptian military remain low, and similar problems are apparent in Syria and Saudi Arabia.[43] Jordan is an exception and seems to have developed the capability to maintain and use the technology at its disposal, which might explain some of Israel's concern with arms supplies to Jordan.[44]

Economic Impacts

If the rapid development of military technology has strained the U.S. and Soviet economies, the effect on their respective Middle Eastern clients has been far greater. While the F-4 Phantom cost $10 million, its replacement, the F-15, costs $30 million (measured in constant 1985 dollars).[45] The serious economic difficulties of Israel, Egypt, Syria, and Jordan can, to a major degree, be attributed to the ever-increasing costs of military technology. Israeli inflation (which exceeded 400 percent annually before recent emergency economic reforms) and a drastic decline in foreign currency reserves reflected the debt incurred in acquiring U.S. military technology. Syria and Egypt face similar problems. Even Jordan, which has acquired relatively older and less expensive technology, has had major problems. In 1983, when Jordan was in danger of defaulting on its U.S. Foreign Military Sales loans, it was rescued only by increased U.S. aid.[46]

As a result, the United States and the Soviet Union have been increasingly forced to absorb the costs of transferring new technology. For the United States this has amounted to a total of around $5 billion annually for Israel and Egypt. Reports from the Soviet Union also indicate increasing concern as to the costs of supplying advanced weapons to the Arab states.[47] During the 1970s Soviet military assistance to Egypt alone accounted for at least 7.5 percent of total Soviet conventional production. Arms transfers to Syria between 1982 and 1984 are reported to have exceeded $1.5 billion, although Saudi Arabia apparently paid for some of this.[48]

Some military analysts and theorists on development have argued that the importation of military technology creates a basis for the technical modernization of the civilian economy.[49] In many cases, electronics, computers, modern management techniques, advanced communications, and other technologies and skills are first introduced in the military sector. These are then transferred to the civilian sector and serve to promote general development.

While there is considerable evidence to support this model at the beginning of technological development, as military technology becomes highly specialized, it is no longer applicable to the civilian sector. Very small high-speed computers designed for missiles, for example, have limited, if any, nonmilitary applications. Indeed, at this level of technology, the military tends to compete with the civilian sector for scarce resources and trained manpower, and far from being a source of spin-offs, advanced military technology becomes a net drain on the system. With the level of technology currently being introduced into the Middle East, this stage appears to have been reached.[50]

The high costs associated with technological arms races have, in the past, been associated with a proclivity toward preemptive and preventive war. For example, prior to World War I, when Germany and Britain were engaged in a naval arms race, some German analysts feared that their country lacked the resources to compete with the British in building *Dreadnought* class battleships. This fear of potential vulnerability has been seen as one of the factors that led to German mobilization and the outbreak of the war.[51] As has been noted, Arab and Israeli short-term fears associated with the delivery of new weapons have contributed to several preemptive wars in the Middle East.

In addition, the continuing high costs of a conventional arms race also could lead to the adoption of an overt nuclear posture. The late Moshe Dayan argued that the costs of maintaining a technological lead would eventually begin to exceed Israeli resources and that in this situation, an openly declared nuclear deterrent would be preferable. Similar arguments have been made by Amos Rubin, an economist at the Bank of Israel, and by Shai Feldman of the Jaffee Center for Strategic Studies. Critics of this argument, including Yitzhak Rabin, argue that an overt nuclear deterrent would not lower conventional defense requirements.[52]

Production and Independence

In part to limit the costs of importing technology, and in part to reduce the degree of dependence on their superpower patrons, there have been efforts both on the Israeli and Arab sides to indigenously develop and produce advanced weapons. In the past decade firms such as Israel Aircraft Industries, Israel Military Industry (Ta'as), and the National Weapons Development Authority (Rafael) have produced a number of major weapons systems. These include the Kfir and Lavi combat aircraft, the Merkava main battle tank, RPVs, electronic systems, and a variety of air-to-air and sea-based missiles.[53]

Despite this effort and the tremendous investment that has accompanied it, Israel is likely to achieve only a limited level of independence. The Lavi, for example, will consume at least $20 billion (the equivalent of one year's gross national product) and will meet only a small percentage of the IAF's requirements for a limited time. Furthermore, while the design is local, much of the technology, including the engine, is based on U.S. licenses and components.

The Arab states also have sought to develop an indigenous weapons industry. Efforts to create an Egyptian arms industry can be traced to the 1950s, but until recently little was accomplished. Now, however, General Dynamics has contracted with Cairo to develop a tank production facility in Egypt. The first phase of Factory 200 is designed to assemble tanks, and the second phase calls for the complete production of 120 tanks per year. (Since there are no casting facilities in Egypt capable of producing turrets, the factory is likely to produce various European tank models based on fabricated turrets.)[54]

Prospects for Change

Since 1948 the level of superpower involvement in the transfer of advanced technology to Israel, Syria, Jordan, Egypt, and, more recently, Saudi Arabia has grown steadily. The level of technology, the rate at which it is transferred, and the costs of these weapons also have increased. As a result, the extent of direct superpower presence in the region has grown. Thousands of Soviet troops and technicians have been deployed to operate advanced systems, first in Egypt and later in Syria. Similarly, the presence and extent of U.S. involvement in Saudi Arabia is also growing. In addition, Soviet troops have been involved in direct clashes with Israel, and it is conceivable that American advisors and technicians in Saudi Arabia could be caught in similar incidents.

In the past the United States has made some effort to limit the level of technology that was introduced into the region. The unilateral initiatives of the Truman and Eisenhower administrations, and the multilateral effort during the Carter administration, to restrain arms exports met with little or no success.[55] Currently, the trend points in the opposite direction, with the most advanced technologies being transferred to the region with little or no restraint.

The particular dynamics of arms sales in the region also are likely to prevent effective limitations for the foreseeable future. Arms sales to Saudi Arabia and to countries receiving Saudi aid (including Jordan, Egypt, and Syria) have become profitable for both the United States and the Soviet Union and the most profitable sales involve the most advanced weapons, such as AWACS and F-15 fighters. In addition, in the face of congressionally imposed restraints on U.S. sales to Jordan, other suppliers, such as Britain, France, and West Germany, have been willing to fill the vacuum. As a result, externally imposed restraints on the level of technology transfer are unlikely to be effective.

There is also the cynical view that argues that both the United States and the Soviet Union use the Arab-Israeli theater as a means of testing new military technologies. Weapons capabilities, as well as flaws and limitations, have often been revealed through use in this region. The IDF, for example, was the first to use the F-15 and F-16 in combat. Modern American, Soviet, and European tank designs are based on the lessons derived from battles between Israel and the Arab states. Tactics, training, and deployments in other regions, including the European central front, also are influenced by the results of these wars. From this perspective, then, the superpowers could have an interest in continuing the current process and even encouraging frequent clashes.

The rates of technological development in the United States and the Soviet Union continue to accelerate, and in the absence of restraint, the importance and impact of this development in the Middle East will continue to increase. In the past few years this has led to greater instability and a premium on preemption and first strike. Furthermore, the transfer of advanced technology to Saudi Arabia has transformed that country into a likely Israeli target for preemption, placing it, for the first time, in the category of confrontation state.

At the same time, the new emphasis on defensive technology, particularly in the United States, has been felt in the Middle East. While Israel is unlikely to benefit directly from the Strategic Defense Initiative (SDI), this program includes an ATBM component. SDI-related research in which Israel is participating could in the long term increase stability by providing Isreal with a reliable defensive system and thus reduce Israeli fears of a surprise attack and its consequent emphasis on preemption.

This and other technologies, such as stealth capabilities, will increase the economic burden and degree of dependency of the local states on their superpower patrons. As technological complexity grows, the extent of superpower involvement and direct provision of troops and advisors, at least in the Arab states, also will increase. From the perspective of the United States and the Soviet Union, this is perhaps the greatest danger, as it increases the probability of direct U.S.-Soviet military clashes.

Notes

1. Although the United States operated AWACS aircraft in Saudi Arabia prior to 1982, beginning in October 1986, the Saudi military received its own AWACS system.

2. Andrew Pierre, ed., *The Conventional Defense of Europe: New Technologies and New Strategies* (New York: New York Council on Foreign Relations, 1986).

3. For a review of the role of technology during this period, see Chaim Herzog, *The Arab-israeli Wars* (New York: Random House, 1982); Dan Horowitz and Edward Luttwak, *The Israeli Army 1948–1973* (Cambridge, MA: Abt Books, 1983); and Zeev Schiff, *A History of the Israeli Army* (San Francisco: Straight Arrow Books, 1984).

4. Horowitz and Luttwak, *The Israeli Army*, p. viii.

5. Schiff, *A History of the Israeli Army*, p. 258. The US did agree to sell a few weapons earlier. In 1958 Isreal was allowed to purchase one hundred recoilless Browning rifles.

6. Herzog, *The Arab-Israeli Wars*, p. 218

7. Ibid., p. 229

8. Schiff, *A History of the Israeli Army*, p. 288

9. Herzog, *The Arab-Israeli Wars*, p. 309

10. Schiff, *A History of the Israeli Army*, p. 298

11. K. Bower, "The Middle East Military Balance", *International Defense Review*, July 1986, p. 911.

12. Benjamin S. Lambeth, *Moscow's Lessons from the 1982 Lebanon Air War*, The Rand Corporation, Report R-3000-AF, Santa Monica, CA, 1984.

13. Kenneth Hunt, "Strategy and Politics," in Louis Williams, ed., *Military Aspects of the Arab Israeli Conflict* (Tel Aviv: University Publishing Projects, 1975), p. 40.

14. Barbara Tuchman, *The Guns of August* (New York: Macmillan, 1962).

15. David Ben-Gurion, *Ma-arechet Sinai* (Tel Aviv: Am Oved, 1960), p. 232. See also Moshe Dayan, *Diary of the Sinai Campaign* (New York: Schoken, 1965), p. 4.

16. George Quester, *Offense and Defense in the International System* (New York: John Wiley, 1977); Robert Gilpin, *War and Change in International Politics* (Cambridge: Cambridge University Press, 1981); also B. H. Liddell Hart, "Aggression and the Problem of

Weapons," *English Review* 55 (1932), cited by Jack S. Levy, "The Offensive/Defensive Balance of Military Technology: A Theoretical and Historical Analysis," *International Studies Quarterly* 28 (June 1984), pp. 219–238.

17. Levy, "The Offensive/Defensive Balance of Military Technology," pp. 219–238.

18. Quincy Wright, *A Study of War* (Chicago: Chicago University Press, 1965).

19. Lambeth, *Moscow's Lessons.*

20. Changes in the relative technological capabilities of the U.S. and Soviet military forces are the subject of debate in the United States. See, for example, Seymour J. Deitchman, *New Technology and Military Power* (Boulder, CO: Westview Press, 1979), pp. 53–57.

21. Uzi Eilam, "Weapons Systems and Technologies—East and West," in Louis Williams, ed., *Military Aspects of the Israeli-Arab Conflict,* p. 23.

22. Michael Getler, "New Generation of Soviet Arms Seen Near Development," *Washington Post,* 11 October 1983, cited by Francis Fukuyama in chpater 10 of this book.

23. The gradual growth in sophistication of U.S. arms sales to Egypt and Saudi Arabia is traced by Steven L. Spiegel in *The Other Arab-Israeli Conflict* (Chicago: Chicago University Press, 1985).

24. Mark Heller, ed., *The Middle East Military Balance: 1984* (Boulder, CO: Westview Press, 1985), p. 211.

25. *Jane's Defence Weekly,* 19 August 1986. Also see Zeev Schiff, *Israel's Eroding Edge in the Middle East Military Balance,* Policy Paper No. 2, Washington Institute for Near East Policy, 1985; Hirsch Goodman, *Israel's Strategic Reality: The Impact of the Arms Race,* Policy Paper No. 4, Washington Institute for Near East Policy, 1985.

26. David M. North, "Soviet Advances Spurring Western Aircraft Upgrades," *Aviation Week and Space Technology,* 21 July 1986, p. 42.

27. Heller, *The Middle East Military Balance: 1984,* p. 87.

28. "Middle East Aerospace: Saudi Abaria," *Aviation Week and Space Technology,* 23 May 1983, pp. 42–97; "Saudis Agree to Trade Oil for Aircraft and Missiles," *Aviation Week and Space Technology,* 22 September 1985, p. 19; "Low-Altitude Surveillance System Readied for Shipment to Saudi Arabia," *Aviation Week and Space Technology,* 10 March 1986, p. 239.

29. "Middle East Aerospace: Jordan," *Aviation Week and Space Technology,* 27 June 1983, p. 38.

30. "UK Defense Package for Jordan," *International Defense Review,* October 1985, p. 1552.

31. Hirsh Goodman, "Arms for Peace," *Jerusalem Post International Edition,* 2 November 1985.

32. Ibid.

33. Kenneth S. Brower, "The Middle East Military Balance: Israel versus the Rest," *International Defense Review,* July 1986, p. 908. For an analysis of the impact of PGMs on conventional warfare, see Ivan Oelrich and Frederick Riddell, "Rational Performance Goals for Modern Munitions," *International Defense Review,* October 1985, pp. 1643–1646.

34. Ibid.

35. Peter Hellman, "The Fighter of the Future," *Discover,* July 1986; Germain Chambost, "Israel's Lavi," *International Defense Review,* July 1986, pp. 891–893.

36. Gerald Steinberg, "Israel's Advantage," *Military Logistics Forum,* March 1986, pp. 51–58.

37. "The Weakness of the Iraqi Air Force," *Ha'aretz* (Israel) 17 March 1986, (Hebrew).

38. Drew Middleton, "U.S. Aides Say Egypt Lacks Ability to Handle Weapons," *New York Times,* 21 February 1986.

39. Steinberg, "Israel's Advantage," pp. 51–58.

40. Brower, "The Middle East Military Balance, pp. 907–913.

41. Gerald Steinberg, "How Israel Recycles Weapons," *Technology Review,* April 1985, pp. 28–38.

42. See Gerald Steinberg and Steven Spiegel, "Israel and the Security of the West," *The Middle East in Global Strategy* (Boulder, CO: Westview Press, in press).

43. Middleton, "U.S. Aides Say Egypt Lacks Ability to Handle Weapons."

44. "Middle East Aerospace: Jordan," p. 38.

45. Goodman, "Arms for Peace."

46. "Middle East Aerospace: Jordan," p. 38.

47. *Military Aspects of the Israeli-Arab Conflict,* pp. 135–136. Also see Gur Ofer, "The Economic Burden of Soviet Involvement in the Middle East," *Soviet Studies,* January 1973, pp. 329–347.

48. See Francis Fukuyama, Chapter 10 of this book.

49. See, for example, Emile Benoit, *Defense and Economic Growth in Developing Countries* (Lexington, MA: D.C. Heath, 1973); Gavin Kennedy, *The Military in the Third World* (London: Duckworth, 1974).

50. See Gerald Steinberg, "Technology, Weapons, and Industrial Development: The Case of Israel," *Technology in Society* 7 (January 1986), pp. 387–398.

51. Many theories linking arms races and the outbreak of war have been proposed and debated. See, for example, Lewis Richardson, *Arms and Insecurity* (London: Stevens, 1960); Colin Gray, "The Arms Race Phenomenon," *World Politics,* October 1971, p. 39–79; Samuel Huntington, "Arms Races: Prerequisites and Results," in John E. Mueller, ed., *Approaches to Measurement in International Relations,* (New York: Appleton-Century-Crofts, 1969), pp. 15–33.

52. See Shai Feldman, *Israeli Nuclear Deterrence* (New York: Columbia University Press, 1982). For an alternative view, see Gerald Steinberg, "Deliberate Ambiguity: Evolution and Evaluation," in Louis Rene Beres, ed., *Security of Armegeddon: Israel's Nuclear Strategy* (Lexington, MA: Lexington Books, 1985), pp. 29–43.

53. Gerald Steinberg, "Israeli Military Technology," in Thomas Ohlson and Michael Brzoska, eds., *Arms Production in the Third World* (London: Taylor and Francis, 1986), pp. 163–192.

54. "Egyptian Tank Competition Hots Up," *International Defense Review,* August 1985, p. 1222; "Cap: Egypt May Coproduce M-1 Tank," *Defense Week,* 25 August 1986, p. 5.

55. For a history and analysis of such efforts prior to the Carter administration, see Yair Evron, *The Role of Arms Control in the Middle East,* Adelphi Paper No. 138, IISS, London, 1977. The Carter administration's policies are discussed by Andrew Pierre, *The Global Politics of Arms Sales* (Princeton, NJ: Princeton University Press, 1982).

6

Superpower
Nonproliferation Policies:
The Case of
the Middle East

Shai Feldman

The prospects of nuclear proliferation in the Middle East present separate challenges for the two superpowers, but both are likely to continue pursuing efforts to halt proliferation in the region, and in doing so, they may demonstrate cooperative behavior to a degree unknown in other areas of concern. Yet both superpowers also will continue to have other interests in the region competing for priority with their nonproliferation goals. Such competition has forced and will continue to force compromises in the modes and intensity of their efforts to halt proliferation.

U.S. Efforts to Halt Proliferation

Historically, the two superpowers have pursued quite different avenues with respect to nuclear nonproliferation. In general, U.S. policy on this issue has been considerably less consistent than that of the Soviets. At times, notably during President Dwight Eisenhower's Atoms for Peace program, the United States took a relatively generous attitude regarding the proliferation of nuclear know-how. Within the framework of the program, the United States installed 26 nuclear research reactors in other countries. Between 1954 and 1979, some 13,456 foreign researchers from non–Soviet bloc nations received training in the United States in the nuclear sciences. Of these, 3,532 were from nations that eventually did not sign the 1968 Nuclear Nonproliferation Treaty (NPT).[1]

At other times, notably from 1945 to 1952, and later during the Johnson and Carter administrations, the United States demonstrated a more restrictive nonproliferation policy. In 1946, in the form of the Baruch Plan, the United States envisaged the creation of an International Atomic Development Authority under U.N. supervision, which, in addition to controlling the world's nuclear raw materials, would have managerial control of all atomic energy activities considered potentially dangerous to world peace, as well as the power to inspect and license all atomic installations.[2] Later, the Johnson administration invested considerable energy in negotiating the Nuclear Nonproliferation Treaty. Finally, in the late 1970s, the Carter administration placed efforts to halt nuclear proliferation at the top of its foreign policy agenda.

The Carter years resulted in far-reaching antiproliferation legislation. The first was the 1978 Nuclear Nonproliferation Act, which forbade cooperation in nuclear matters and material with any country that did not place all its nuclear facilities under full-scope safeguards.[3] The second was the Glenn amendment to the 1977 International Security Assistance Act, which stipulated a cutoff of all economic and military aid to any country that conducted a nuclear detonation or imported or exported either a uranium enrichment or a plutonium reprocessing plant.[4]

The nonproliferation policy of the United States is propelled by a number of hypotheses: first, that nuclear proliferation increases the likelihood of nuclear war; second, that once nuclear weapons are used, such employment will acquire legitimacy and lead to further usage; third, that regional nuclear war may catalyze a superpower nuclear exchange; fourth, that the higher likelihood of nuclear war would require more frequent U.S. interventions in other regions, for the purpose of preventing local parties from escalating to nuclear war; fifth, that nuclear proliferation would decrease the superpowers' margin of power and hence would curtail their ability to influence developments in other regions; and sixth, that proliferation would increase the likelihood of nuclear terrorism. New nuclear states are assumed to be deficient in the realm of weapons control, hence the higher the odds that nuclear weapons will find their way into terrorist hands.

Yet, as observed earlier, U.S. efforts to stop proliferation have at times been inconsistent and almost always selective for three reasons. First of all, the United States is reluctant to invest in a product that others will enjoy free of charge. European unwillingness to invest in ensuring a less-proliferated world led to increasing U.S. reluctance to bear the costs on its own. Also, Washington's pessimistic assessments regarding the possibility of stopping proliferation contributed to reducing the government's willingness to invest in this objective. Such pessimism is based on the assessment that alternative nuclear suppliers are less willing to restrict themselves, while a highly determined small state, propelled by what it regards as supreme national interests, cannot be dissuaded from acquiring nuclear weapons. Finally, U.S. policy was influenced by the recognition that competing interests place limits on the extent to which nonproliferation goals can be pursued. For example, competition with the Soviet Union for influence in South Asia tamed Washington's reaction and subsequent policies with respect to India's nuclear program, and U.S.-Indian relations remained relatively unaffected by the 1974 Indian nuclear explosion. The United States did not even terminate its nuclear supply relationship with India, and shipments of enriched uranium to that country continued.[5]

U.S. Nonproliferation Policy

The equivocal nature of the U.S. nuclear nonproliferation policy is reflected in the Middle East as well. There, U.S. dilemmas have resulted primarily from the fact that the clearest case of proliferation in the region, namely Israel, also constitutes Washington's closest ally in the Middle East. There are a number of reasons why the United States found the Israeli case particularly troublesome. First, there is a widespread premise that once Israel goes nuclear overtly, many other states will follow, and the result will be a collapse of the NPT regime. Second, the intense involvement of both superpowers in the region has led to a U.S. concern that there is a higher danger in the Middle East than elsewhere that a local nuclear confrontation might escalate to a superpower nuclear exchange. In addition, the United States is particularly concerned that Israeli nuclearization will contribute to the deterioration of the United States' ability to influence her allies.

Yet close U.S.-Israeli relations have set clear limits to measures that might be taken to prevent Israeli nuclearization. Indeed, in the framework of its Atoms for Peace program, the United States itself aided Israel's nuclear program in the 1950s, providing it with a small, 5-megawatt (thermal) "swimming pool" reactor for the Soreq Research Center.[6]

The Eisenhower, Kennedy, and Johnson administrations made their opposition to Israeli acquisition of nuclear weapons crystal clear. Yet efforts by the Johnson administration to extract an Israeli commitment not to develop nuclear weapons as a condition for the supply of F-4 Phantom aircraft were called off in the face of congressional support for the arms sale. The Kennedy and Johnson administrations demanded that U.S. officials be allowed to inspect the Dimona reactor. Israel yielded, and a number of such inspections took place in the mid-1960s. These inspections were stopped by the Nixon and Ford administrations, which hardly ever raised the nuclear issue with Israel. In 1974, after Israel's President Ephraim Katzir stated that Israel had created a potential for nuclear arms, U.S. Secretary of State Henry Kissinger, after repeated attempts to evade the issue, merely remarked that he would have used a different formulation.[7]

The most conclusive evidence regarding Washington's equivocal approach to Israeli nuclearization is to be found in its lack of a forceful reaction despite mounting official assessments, leaks of these assessments, and other media revelations regarding Israel's nuclear program. Over the years neither the executive nor the legislative branch of the U.S. government has shown a propensity to take significant measures to halt this program. U.S.-Israel relations have not been affected negatively by these leaks, and U.S. economic and military aid to Israel has not been reduced.

Thus, the Johnson administration did not pursue a 1968 report issued by the CIA's Department of Science and Technology to the effect that Israel had nuclear weapons.[8] Neither did the Johnson or Nixon administrations pursue with Israel the latter's possible role in the disappearance of 100 kilograms of enriched uranium from the NUMEC nuclear plant in Apollo, Pennsylvania. The respective administrations refrained from taking up the issue with Jerusalem despite the reported availability to the FBI of some evidence linking a senior Israeli intelligence officer, Rafael Eitan, to the affair.[9]

Later, on July 7, 1970, during the Nixon administration, CIA Director Richard Helms briefed the Senate Foreign Relations Committee regarding the CIA's assessment of Israel's nuclear capability.[10] The administration and Congress both refused to take measures in response to this assessment. Nor did the Ford administration take any measures in response to a CIA report dated September 4, 1974, stating clearly its assessment that Israel had acquired nuclear weapons. The report cited Israeli purchases of large quantities of uranium, partly through covert methods, and "the peculiar nature of Israel's effort in the field of uranium enrichment as well as large investments in the development of a weapons system capable of delivering nuclear warheads."[11] In February 1976, still during the Ford administration, the CIA gave testimony to an interdepartmental coordinating committee on nuclear affairs regarding Israel's nuclear capability.[12] On March 11, 1976, a senior CIA official revealed at a private briefing that Israel was estimated to have ten to twenty nuclear weapons ready for use.[13] None of these reports elicited punitive action against Israel.

Similarly, both the Carter administration and Congress refrained from taking punitive measures against Israel when the existence of the aforementioned reports was made public in 1978. On the contrary, the leak regarding the 1974 report elicited the following response by Carter's White House Press Secretary Jody Powell: "The Israeli government has declared that Israel is not a nuclear power and will not be the first to introduce nuclear weapons into the area. We accept this as the official position of the government of Israel."[14] Equally evasive was a subsequent statement by President Carter himself. Speaking to newspaper editors, Carter said that the United States accepted Israeli statements with respect to its nuclear capability and added, "I don't have any independent sources of information beyond that."[15] Only years later did Carter reveal that he did indeed have independent sources of information. In a 1985 interview with NBC News, the former president said that Israel "either has nuclear weapons or the capacity of having them on very short notice."[16] Thus, competing U.S. interests caused President Carter and members of his administration to take measures skirting the issue of Israel's possible possession of nuclear weapons.

The Carter administration took a rather equivocal approach to Israel's nuclear capability despite its record as the postwar administration most committed to nonproliferation. In fact, one Carter administration official went so far as to hint that under specific conditions the administration would tolerate Israeli *use* of nuclear weapons. Testifying with respect to the proposed Glenn amendment, Undersecretary of State Lucy Benson asked that the president be granted the right, in specific circumstances, to suspend the amendment's implementation. Benson and Senator John Glenn exchanged the following observations:

Mrs. Benson: Without going into names of countries, I think that this is where it gets a little bit of a sticky wicket. If there was a Presidential waiver, then I think this would remove the problem, at least to a great degree.

There could easily be times when, regardless of what a country did, we might want to go ahead with military assistance for other quite separate reasons.

Senator Glenn: Do you mean even if it set off a nuclear explosion?

Mrs. Benson: Yes, I could see how that might happen. The President, I believe, would need the flexibility to declare that even if they did set off an explosion—you used an example yourself earlier in the hearing of supposing that a country which was at war set off a nuclear explosion in the middle of the desert to show its capability. That would be quite different from setting off an explosion in the middle of a city.

Senator Glenn: I am not against giving the President some flexibility in this, as I indicated earlier. I think that that might make this more acceptable to a lot of people in the Mideast situation, of course, which is the one that always comes up in any discussion as to what happens if Israel is being overrun. Senator Javits addressed it the other day when Mr. Warnke was here, I believe.

I think in a situation like that the President should have some flexibility, and I certainly would not object to it.[17]

This exchange is astonishing, not only as an illustration of the Carter administration's equivocal approach with regard to the Israeli case but also as a manifestation of the perception of Israel as a special case, adopted even by Senator Glenn, the strongest opponent of nuclear proliferation in the legislative branch. It is therefore hardly surprising that in June 1977 a distinguished U.S. Senate delegation recommended that the United States avoid conditioning the sale of nuclear power reactors to Israel on the latter's prior submission of its nuclear facilities to full-scope safeguards.[18] Equally consistent with such a special approach, the U.S. Senate in 1979 rejected by a margin of 76 to 7 an amendment offered by Senator Jesse Helms aimed at making the post–Israeli-Egyptian peace treaty's special aid package to Israel conditional on Israel's prior signature and ratification of the NPT.[19]

Likewise, the Carter administration avoided a possible collision with Israel over a reported nuclear test in the South Atlantic on September 22, 1979. According to press reports of questionable reliability, the CIA assessed the event as a 2- or 3-kiloton nuclear test conducted by Israel and South Africa (with Taiwan as a possible third partner).[20] Two months later, however, in November 1979, a Carter White House scientific panel maintained that the satellite sighting was not a nuclear explosion at all but some other occurrence, possibly a tiny piece of meteor striking the satellite.[21]

The pattern of compromising U.S. nonproliferation policy in Israel's case continued during President Ronald Reagan's first term, as well as during the first two years of his second term. When asked by a reporter whether Israel should sign the NPT, Reagan's response was ambiguous:

Q.: Mr. President, how appropriate do you believe is Israel's decision not to sign the Nuclear Non-Proliferation Treaty and not to submit to inspection by the International Atomic Energy Agency? And I have a follow-up.

The President: Well, I haven't given very much thought to that particular question there, the subject about them not signing that Treaty or, on the other hand, how many countries do we know that have signed it that very possibly are going ahead with nuclear weapons? It's, again, something that doesn't lend itself to verification.

It is difficult for me to envision Israel as being a threat to its neighbors. It is a Nation that from the very beginning has lived under the threat from neighbors that they did not recognize its right to exist as a Nation.

I'll have to think about that question you asked.[22]

Congress has taken a similar view of Israel during the Reagan years. Thus, no punitive action was taken against Israel, despite reported CIA testimony to the House Foreign Affairs Committee that Israel "was now believed to possess 10 to 20 nuclear weapons that could be delivered either by fighter-bombers or by Israel's domestically designed and built Jericho missile."[23] Later, the Reagan administration actually *averted* a move in the Congress that might have resulted in punitive action against Israel, its original purpose notwithstanding. In December 1981 two members of the House Foreign Affairs Committee, Congressmen Stephen J. Solarz and Jonathan B. Bingham, planned to introduce an amendment requiring a cutoff in U.S. aid to any country found to be developing nuclear weapons. They agreed to drop the provision after they were told, at a meeting with Under Secretary of State James L. Buckley, "that such a requirement might well trigger a finding by the administration that Israel has manufactured a bomb."[24]

The Reagan administration also abstained from action when learning, in mid-1985, of Israel's acquisition of 47 tons of depleted uranium in violation of International Atomic Energy Agency (IAEA) safeguards.[25] In response to an *Aerospace Daily* report to the effect that Israel had deployed nuclear-tipped Jericho II missiles in the Negev, a U.S. State Department deputy spokesman merely noted that the United States could not confirm the information.[26] The Reagan administration produced a similarly mild response upon learning in mid-1985 that krytrons (high-speed electronic switches that could be used to control the timing of nuclear detonations) were shipped to Israel in violation of U.S. export controls on sensitive technologies. The United States accepted Israel's explanation that the krytrons imported were used solely for nonnuclear research. The administration thus avoided making the affair an issue with the Israeli government, and State Department spokesman Edward Djerejian told reporters that "the government of Israel has been cooperative in our investigation." Reagan administration officials said the United States had not asked to inspect the sites where krytrons were in use, suggesting that such a request "could be construed by the Israelis as an affront to their national sovereignty." Israel did promise to return to the United States all unused krytrons and to certify that the remaining krytrons would not be used in nuclear-related projects.[27]

In late 1985 the Reagan administration also came to Israel's aid at the IAEA. In response to a draft resolution sanctioning Israel in connection with the 1981 bombing of Iraq's Osiraq reactor, Washington threatened to terminate its membership in the agency. Since the United States provides the largest financial contribution to the IAEA, the threat was sufficient to prevent adoption of the draft resolution, and a much more moderate formulation was adopted instead.[28]

A year later the London *Sunday Times* issued the most detailed and revealing report ever published about Israel's alleged nuclear weapons program. The report was based on testimony given and photographs taken by Mordechai Va'anunu, a former technician at the Dimona reactor.[29] The story received very little attention in the U.S. media, and the reaction of official Washington could only be described as a "nonresponse." Apparently, acceptance of Israel as a nuclear power is widespread; hence, Washington no longer regards the subject as news justifying a response. U.S. newspapers and television paid more attention to Va'anunu's reported disappearance from London following publication of the *Sunday Times* report. A kidnapping conducted by Israeli intelligence is a news story in Washington, D.C.; the alleged production of nuclear weapons is not.

When the Reagan administration learned in late 1984 of Israel's plans to purchase a nuclear power reactor from France, it moved to exert pressure on Paris to obstruct the sale. Prevented from selling such a reactor to Israel by the stipulations of the 1978 Nonproliferation Act and by Israel's refusal to sign the NPT and place its nuclear installations under full-scope safeguards, Washington was not about to permit implementation of the French sale. Even in this case, however, it is far from clear that the Reagan administration's response was determined primarily by nonproliferation concerns. More likely it resulted from the powerful reservations of Secretary of State George Shultz regarding the wisdom of a large Israeli financial investment in such a project at a time when dire economic conditions had forced Jerusalem to seek emergency aid from the United States. Also, Washington was not about to permit the French nuclear industry to acquire an edge in the Israeli market by pursuing a less restrictive nuclear policy.[30]

As noted earlier, competition with the Soviet Union for influence in the region has forced parallel compromises in U.S. nonproliferation policy at the eastern outskirts of the Mideast region, namely in the case of Pakistan. Close U.S.-Pakistani relations actually remained unaffected by President Ali Bhuto's 1974 statement to the effect that Pakistanis would, if necessary, "eat grass but produce the bomb." It was only later, in August 1976, that Secretary of State Henry Kissinger took action to dissuade Pakistan from purchasing a plutonium reprocessing plant from France. Kissinger warned that such a purchase would lead the United States to refuse to deliver the A-7 aircraft requested by Pakistan,[31] but he took no additional measures to halt the Pakistani program. Heavy pressure was not exerted on Pakistan or her European suppliers to halt the Pakistani effort.

Only later, during the Carter administration, did the United States succeed in persuading France not to complete the construction of the reprocessing plant it had sold to Pakistan.[32] Carter's unequivocal approach continued through 1979, when the administration employed the Glenn amendment, terminating U.S. military and economic aid to Pakistan. This was done following intelligence reports to the effect that the latter had bought components and begun construction of a uranium enrichment plant. Having invoked the Glenn amendment, however, only the $40 million of Agency for International Development (AID) funds for Pakistan were cancelled. The larger $80 million food grant program under Public Law 480 remained unaffected. This ambivalent message could hardly have elicited the desired Pakistani response.[33] Finally, in the wake of the December 1979 Soviet invasion of Afghanistan, President Carter asked Congress to lift the ban on aid to Pakistan; on December 30 his administration announced its intention to provide Pakistan with artillery, night vision devices, communications equipment, transport planes, and helicopters.[34]

President Reagan has proved at least as generous. Early in 1981 he approved a six-year, $3.2 billion economic and military aid package for Pakistan and a separate sale of forty F-16 fighter aircraft.[35] The administration on that occasion requested and received congressional consent to exempt Pakistan from the stipulations of the Glenn amendment. U.S. nonproliferation policy was compromised not only by the president's decision to waive the legislation's requirements but particularly by his decision to do so while failing to obtain a clear Pakistani commitment not to develop nuclear weapons in the face of mounting evidence that its efforts in the nuclear realm were continuing with great vigor.[36]

The compromise, which included the exemption for Pakistan from the Glenn amendment's sanctions against importing a uranium enrichment plant, did contain a stipulation of an automatic aid cutoff in the case of a nuclear detonation.[37] The net effect of Reagan's policy has thus been a tacit signal of the administration's willingness to tolerate Pakistan's development of a nuclear potential as long as the latter refrains from conducting a nuclear detonation test or from otherwise announcing its nuclear capability. Thus, for example, when in June 1984 U.S. law enforcement and legal authorities in Houston, Texas, caught and indicted a Pakistani national, Nazim Ahmed Vaid, for the illegal export of krytrons, the Reagan administration did not pursue the matter vigorously with Pakistan.[38] Most likely the administration was concerned that doing so might propel congressional opponents of proliferation to renew their demands that aid to Pakistan be suspended. Such a low-profile approach can hardly deter further proliferation, however, as potential suppliers and buyers could easily conclude that U.S. reactions to such conduct is tolerable.

By late 1984 the Reagan administration had become extremely concerned about the acceleration of the Pakistani program. Accordingly, it chose to abandon its low-key approach and issue some unequivocal warnings to Pakistani President Zia al-Haq.[39] With a view to avoiding a cutoff of U.S. aid, the Pakistanis are said to have slowed down their program.[40]

The conflicting influences on U.S. nonproliferation policy toward Pakistan were well illustrated in Washington's conduct during July 1986. Assessing that Pakistan remained "intensively involved in the development of atomic weapons," President Reagan warned Pakistani Prime Minister Mohammed Khan Junejo that "military and economic aid to Pakistan would be cut off if the country acquired nuclear arms."[41] At the same time, Washington concluded an agreement with Junejo for the supply of sensitive American technology to Pakistan.[42] Similarly, the State Department emphasized that Pakistan had not acquired nuclear weapons,[43] and when the Soviet Union issued a stern warning to Pakistan against pursuing its nuclear program, Washington issued a counterwarning, calling upon the Soviets to keep their hands off Pakistan.[44]

The Reagan administration's nonproliferation policy, particularly with respect to Pakistan, includes two additional efforts. The first is the application of quiet but very firm pressure on the suppliers of nuclear material and facilities in order to complicate the proliferation process. A significant intelligence effort was launched by the United States, particularly in Europe, to identify transactions containing potential contributions to proliferation. Following identification, diplomatic measures were used to undermine these transactions. Over the past six years, this policy has met with considerable success in slowing down the Pakistani program.

Simultaneously, the Reagan administration began to place increasing emphasis on proliferation management and employed various measures to reduce the risks and dangers inherent in nuclear proliferation. Thus, by the end of 1985 the Reagan administration was encouraging Pakistan and India to enter a dialogue aimed at reducing the odds that mutual misperceptions would lead to one or both parties employing nuclear weapons.[45] The purpose of the dialogue was to provide an opportunity for each party to explain its fears and concerns so that the other could learn what it should refrain from doing in order to prevent dangerous escalation.

To some extent, U.S. efforts at proliferation management inevitably undermine its nonproliferation policies. This is because sponsoring and encouraging strategic dialogue of the kind portrayed above imply recognition and acceptance of already developed nuclear capabilities. Additional potential proliferators may learn from this that instead of provoking far-reaching sanctions, nuclear programs are eventually granted legitimacy by the United States. This is sure to encourage potential proliferators by affecting their calculation of the costs entailed in developing nuclear weapons.

U.S. nuclear nonproliferation policy in the Middle East has thus proven to be rather equivocal and selective. While Washington continues to oppose proliferation to the region, two special cases prove its position to be less than firm. Except for some very brief periods, nonproliferation objectives have not been at the top of the United States' national agenda. Competing interests, as well as considerable pessimism regarding the ability to stop proliferation, have resulted in recurring compromises in U.S. nonproliferation policy. Short of a traumatic international event that would give proliferation top priority in Washington, this pattern is unlikely to change.

Soviet Nonproliferation Policy

The Soviet Union's nonproliferation policy has been both more consistent and less vocal than that pursued by the United States, and measures adopted by Moscow in this realm have been unlike those taken by Washington. Different relationships with respective potential proliferators, as well as differences in style between Moscow and Washington, account for their distinct nonproliferation policies.

There is little doubt that Moscow is genuinely concerned about the implications of nuclear proliferation. After Soviet nuclear assistance to China in the 1950s was redirected toward the construction of nuclear weapons, Moscow became determined to avoid a repetition of the experience. Indeed, the possibility that West Germany might develop a nuclear force evoked a terrifying nightmare in Moscow, possibly a causus belli. It was primarily the imperative of avoiding German nuclearization that led Moscow to cosponsor the 1968 Nuclear Nonproliferation Treaty and to lobby for its widest possible acceptance. Later, once it became clear that West Germany would not go nuclear, Soviet interest in nonproliferation diminished.[46]

That Moscow continues to be concerned about proliferation is hardly surprising. Most potential proliferators—Israel, Iraq, India, Pakistan, South Korea, and Taiwan—are located closer to Moscow than to Washington. In fact, give this strategic configuration, it is somewhat surprising that Moscow is not more assertive in pursuing nonproliferation.

The more inhibited Soviet approach to proliferation seems to be motivated by a number of important considerations. First, in the Kremlin's eyes further proliferation may be viewed as less than a revolutionary development. While the expansion of the nuclear club may mean that Washington might have a number of nuclear opponents instead of one, thus changing the world, from its perspective, from a bipolar to a multipolar system, for Moscow the change would be less dramatic. The Soviet Union already faces four separate nuclear opponents: the United States, Great Britain, France, and China. Current familiarity with a multipolar system may have diminished Soviet fears regarding proliferation.

Soviet nonproliferation policy is further affected by a shortage of means. Moscow enjoys very limited leverage over most potential proliferators—such as Israel, Pakistan, Brazil, Argentina, South Africa, South Korea, and Taiwan—for they have closer ties with the United States. Among all potential proliferators, only

Libya and Iraq enjoy closer ties to Moscow, while India holds the middle ground. Thus, with the possible and partial exception of Libya and Iraq, none of the potential proliferators is significantly dependent on the Soviet Union. This severely limits Moscow's ability to influence the choices made by these states.

The Soviet Union is also deficient in means with which to affect the choices of nuclear suppliers. Most of the suppliers—France, Germany, Canada, Italy, Great Britain, and Switzerland—belong de facto to the Western camp. Much irresponsible talk about the pending "Finlandization" of Western Europe notwithstanding, Moscow has little leverage over these states' policy choices.

Another consideration compromising Soviet nonproliferation policy is its desire to compete with the United States for influence on the Third World. This consideration led the Soviet Union to refrain from exerting pressure on India following the latter's 1974 nuclear explosion. In its aftermath, the Soviets retained both their formal and informal linkages to India. In fact, immediately following India's detonation, the Soviets moved quickly to replace Canada as India's primary supplier of heavy water.[47]

Elsewhere in the Third World, Soviet desires to gain influence have propelled it to label Washington's efforts to dissuade states from going nuclear as a form of imperialism.[48] In yet other areas, such as the Middle East, Moscow's attempts to increase regional dependencies has led it to publicize local nuclear activities. Scoring points in this manner has inevitably been at the expense of nonproliferation objectives; increasing the profile of nuclear activities increases the motivation of other states to do the same. In all cases, the desire to compete with the United States has prevented Moscow from taking drastic actions to limit proliferation. Its unwillingness to be portrayed as imperialist has resulted in Soviet reluctance to conduct military or clandestine operations aimed at subverting nuclear programs.

Yet Soviet interest in the Third world also provides most of the fuel for its genuine opposition to nuclear proliferation. Throughout the postwar era Moscow has done its best to avoid a redistribution of power to the superpowers' detriment. Moscow is probably also well aware that nuclear proliferation would entail a devolution of power: It would provide proliferators with a better ability to resist superpower influence, would make Third World regions more risky and hence more dangerous for the superpowers, and would therefore limit the superpowers' options and freedom of maneuver. Given their desire to avoid such outcomes, it is hardly surprising that the Soviets have opposed proliferation.

Moscow's approach to nuclear proliferation in the Middle East reflects the various aforementioned considerations. Their conduct in this realm proceeds along a number of different tracks. The first one steers clear of making any direct contribution to military nuclear programs in the region. Thus, the Soviets have refrained from supplying enrichment and reprocessing plants, power reactors that create a proliferation hazard, or even larger-scale research reactors of the type supplied by France to Iraq.

The Soviets have, however, supplied both Iraq and Egypt with basic knowledge in the nuclear sciences. During the 1960s Moscow provided both Cairo and Baghdad with nuclear research centers, including 2-megawatt reactors that were later expanded to 5-megawatt capacity. The Soviets thus have done the minimum required to maintain their political influence in the region. In part they have probably been propelled by the risk of losing influence to alternative suppliers of nuclear know-how.

In Egypt, and to a lesser extent in Iraq, Soviet nuclear aid resulted in the establishment of an impressive infrastructure in the nuclear field. In both cases, such Soviet assistance contained risks of proliferation. It is difficult to imagine Iraq launching its dedicated program in the mid-1970s without the infrastructure established years earlier with Soviet aid. It is equally clear that were Egypt to decide to embark upon a military nuclear program, the infrastructure established with Moscow's assistance will also prove critically important.

Similarly, in 1975 the Soviets agreed to supply Libya with a 440-megawatt, Luvissa-type dual-purpose nuclear reactor and a nuclear research complex.[49] True, in all cases the states provided with Soviet nuclear aid were signatories of the 1968 Nuclear Nonproliferation Treaty. Indeed, the Soviets have made their assistance conditional upon such a signature and the entailed willingness to place all supplied facilities under strict IAEA safeguards. Consistent with this policy, they refused to provide Libya with assistance in the nuclear field until the latter signed and ratified the NPT. Yet even with such strings attached, Soviet nuclear assistance implies compromising its nonproliferation objectives as it contributes to the creation of infrastructures in the nuclear field. Indeed, by 1982 Soviet-supplied 10-megawatt research reactor began operating in Libya, reportedly training one thousand Libyans in the nuclear sciences.[50]

By the mid-1980s the Soviet Union had accelerated its efforts to establish itself as a supplier of nuclear reactors to the Middle East. In 1984 it signed a contract with Iraq covering the initial planning for the construction of a 440-megawatt power reactor.[51] Later that year Moscow reportedly agreed to help Syria begin geological and geophysical studies at appropriate sites for the construction of Syria's first nuclear power station.[52]

The third element in the complex of Soviet nonproliferation policy in the Middle East is its public campaign regarding Israel's nuclear capability. The Soviet press, ever guided from above, refers quite often to Israel's nuclear capability. The purpose of these references might be to increase Arab dependence on the Soviet commitment to their security. Thus, for example, in late 1985 extensive reporting of Israeli nuclear weapons appeared in the Novosti press agency, in *Krasnaya Zvezda* (Red Star), in *Izvestia,* and in *Novoyo Vermia.*[53]

Still, the Soviets have refrained from exerting direct pressure on Israel in the nuclear realm. In contrast to the United States, Moscow has never warned Jerusalem against going nuclear. The Soviets also have abstained from subverting Israeli nuclear facilities by covert action. The Soviets thus signal their unwillingness to pay the costs involved in direct preventive action.

Likewise, until recently the Soviet Union refrained from exerting direct pressure on Pakistan. Moscow did not sound an alarm regarding the Pakistani nuclear program before early 1986, and only in July 1986 did it issue a stern warning to President Zia of the consequences of pursuing the nuclear option.[54]

A fourth element in the Soviets' Mideast nonproliferation policy is the possible provision of a nuclear umbrella for their closest ally in the region, Syria. A nuclear umbrella refers to the promise to counterdeter and thus neutralize an Israeli nuclear threat against Syria. Some sources have speculated that a secret appendix to the Soviet-Syrian Treaty of Friendship, Cooperation, and Mutual Assistance contains just such an understanding. On a number of occasions, Syrian Minister of Defense Mustafa Tlas has declared that the Soviets have provided Damascus with such a nuclear umbrella.[55] It is also noteworthy that thus far the Soviets have never issued an overt statement to the same effect, and yet in the absence of a Soviet denial of the assertions made by Tlas, it must be judged that to some extent such an umbrella already exists.

Providing a nuclear umbrella to a client state may serve two Soviet objectives. First, it increases Syria's dependence on the Soviet Union, thus increasing Moscow's influence in the region. Second, by countering the Israeli nuclear threat, the Soviet umbrella reduces Syria's incentives to seek an independent nuclear capability. Thus, the umbrella also meets the Soviets' nonproliferation objectives.

Yet the precise nature of the Soviet umbrella remains unclear. In the absence of evidence regarding its character, one can only speculate that it is probably defensive. In other words, it is possible that the Soviets promised Damascus to neutralize any Israeli attempt to use nuclear threats offensively—that is, for the purpose of compelling the Syrians to accept Israel-desired changes in the status quo. Given Soviet reluctance to assume excessive risks, it is unlikely that they provided Syria with a carte blanche promise to oppose any Israeli nuclear threats. Such a promise would imply Syrian freedom to launch a conventional war with the knowledge that Moscow would neutralize any Israeli attempt to deter such a war by nuclear threats. Damascus would thus be able to determine the agenda; the patron would be at the client's mercy. Moscow, however, has been reluctant to become involved in processes over which it does not enjoy complete control, and therefore it is unlikely to have provided Damascus with such an open ticket.

The final central element comprising the Soviet Union's nonproliferation policy in the Middle East and elsewhere is the continuous dialogue it conducts with the United States on this subject.[56] In fact, this dialogue continued even during periods when the superpowers found themselves unable to conduct a meaningful dialogue on any other subject. Little, however, is known about the content of these talks.

The U.S.-Soviet dialogue on nuclear proliferation raises the possibility that the two superpowers might reach some form of collusion concerning Mideast proliferation affairs. For example, analysts have referred to the possibility that the superpowers might intervene jointly against any nuclear state, such as Israel, that would threaten a nonnuclear state. The possibility exists, but its likelihood is low. First, the Middle East is an important arena for U.S.-Soviet competition, and neither Washington nor Moscow is likely to set this competition aside for the sake of nonproliferation. In more general terms, each of the superpowers has other interests in the region competing for primacy with their nonproliferation objectives. Each has a set of regional ties, some of which enjoy far greater salience than the interest in containing proliferation.

Given their competing interests and disparate ties in the Middle East, the United States and the Soviet Union are unlikely to collaborate against a regional nuclear program without a comprehensive agreement on the entire spectrum of issues that have led to the launching of this program. For example, given the generally intimate U.S.-Israel ties, a joint U.S.-Soviet move against Israel's nuclear capability would require that they also adopt a common approach regarding the conventional threat that led to the development of this capability. Syria's objectives in the Arab-Israeli conflict, however, and Moscow's ties to Damascus, would seem to preclude such an agreement.

During the past 12 years, the Soviet Union's influence in the Middle East has declined significantly. In 1972 Moscow enjoyed intimate ties with Egypt, Sudan, Iraq, Syria, and Libya. Today the Soviets enjoy close ties only with the latter two. Moscow is currently attempting to mend this situation, while Washington is trying to check the Soviet effort. A joint Mideast nonproliferation policy would, by definition, require Soviet participation on a coequal basis. Washington is unlikely to provide Moscow with such a status, and the Soviets, fearing a loss of their last remaining ties in the region, are unlikely to bargain with the United States over the conventional threat posed against Israel.

Notes

1. David Hoffman, "Aliens Gain U.S. Atomic Arms Lore," *Philadelphia Inquirer*, 19 May 1979. Cites a report by the U.S. Congress, General Accounting Office.

2. William Bader, *The United States and the Spread of Nuclear Weapons* (New York: Pegasus, 1968), p. 18.

3. U.S. Congress, Public Law 95-242, *The Nuclear Nonproliferation Act of 1978* (Washington: GPO, 10 March 1978.

4. U.S. Congress, Public Law 95-92, *International Security Assistance Act of 1977* (Washington: GPO, 10 August 1977).

5. Michael Nacht, "The United States in a World of Nuclear Powers," in Joseph I. Coffey, ed., *Nuclear Proliferation: Prospects, Problems, Proposals.* Annals of the American Academy of Political Science, no. 430 (March 1977), p. 163; Onkar Marwah, "India's Nuclear and Space Programs: Interest and Policy," *International Security,* Fall 1977, p. 118.

6. John K. Cooley, "Cairo Steers Clear of A-Race," *Christian Science Monitor,* 9 June 1969.

7. For further details, see Shai Feldman, *Israeli Nuclear Deterrence: A Strategy for the 1980s* (New York: Columbia University Press, 1982), pp. 210–211.

8. *Ma'ariv* (Israel), 2 March 1978.

9. *Ma'ariv,* 6 June 1986. Citing a report published in the *Washington Post.*

10. Hederick Smith, "The U.S. Assumes the Israelis Have A-Bomb or Its Parts," *New York Times,* 18 July 1970.

11. *Yediot Aharonot* (Israel), 27 January 1978.

12. *Ma'ariv,* 2 March 1978.

13. Arthur Kranish, "CIA: Israel Has 10–12 A Weapons," *Washington Post,* 15 March 1976.

14. *Ma'ariv,* 2 March 1978.

15. *Ma'ariv,* 9 April 1978.

16. *Jerusalem Post* (Israel), 2 June 1985.

17. U.S. Senate, Committee on Foreign Relations, *Hearings on S-1160* (Washington: GPO, April 21–22, 28, and May 2, 1977), pp. 234–235.

18. U.S. Senate, *Senate Delegation Report on American Foreign Policy and Non-Proliferation Interests in the Middle East* (Washington: GPO, 1977).

19. *The Congressional Record,* 14 May 1979, pp. S-5748 and S-5751.

20. Jack Anderson, "The United States Knew Israel and S. Africa Tested Nuke in '79," *Christian Science Monitor,* 26 April 1985.

21. *Ibid.*

22. President Ronald Reagan's Press Conference, 17 June 1981.

23. Judith Miller, "3 Nations Widening Nuclear Contacts," *New York Times,* 28 June 1981.

24. Judith Miller, "2 in House Withdraw Atom Curb," *New York Times,* 9 December 1981.

25. Steven J. Dryden, "Illegal Uranium Sales to Israel Discovered," *Washington Post,* 12 July 1985.

26. *Ha'aretz* (Israel), May 5, 1985; *Ma'ariv,* May 21, 1985.

27. Richard Holloran, "Israelis Illegally Got U.S. Devices Used in Making Nuclear Weapons," New York Times, 16 May 1985; *Ma'ariv,* 17 May 1985.

28. *Ha'aretz,* 29 September 1985.

29. *London Sunday Times,* 5 October 1986.

30. *Ma'ariv,* 13 December 1984; *Ha'aretz,* 13 December 1984; *Ma'ariv,* 31 January 1985; *Ha'aretz,* 10 February 1985.

31. Alan Cranston, "How Congress Can Shape Arms Control," in Alan Platt and Lawrence D. Weiler, eds., *Congress and Arms Control* (Boulder, CO: Westview Press, 1978), p. 208.

32. Jonathan Kandell, "France Cancels Contract on A-Plant for Pakistan," *International Herald Tribune,* 24 August 1978.

33. Associated Press release, from Karachi (Pakistan), 11 April 1979.

34. *International Herald Tribune,* 31 December 1979.

35. Edward A. Gargan, "U.S. Aide Defends Sale of F-16s to Pakistan," *New York Times,* 3 December 1981.

36. Judith Miller, "U.S. Aide Reports Pakistani Assurance of No Plans to Produce Nuclear Arms," *International Herald Tribune*, 26 June 1981; "Accounting Lapses Cited for Pakistani Plutonium," *International Herald Tribune*, 1 October 1981.

37. *Congressional Quarterly Almanac 1981* (Washington: Congressional Quarterly Service, 1982), p. 175.

38. John Goshko, "U.S. Seeks to Inspect Israeli Nuclear Sites to Verify Use of Prohibited Timing Device," *Washington Post*, 15 May 1985.

39. David Ignatius, "U.S. Pressuring Pakistan to Abandon Controversial Nuclear-Arms Program," *Wall Street Journal*, 24 October 1985; Simon Henderson, "U.S. Warns Pakistan on Enriching Uranium," *Financial Times*, 7 December 1984.

40. "Pakistan Goes Slow on the Bomb," *Foreign Report*, 21 March 1985.

41. Stuart Auerbach, "U.S. Expected to Agree with Junejo to Sell Sensitive Gear to Pakistan," *International Herald Tribune*, 17 July 1986.

42. *Ibid.*

43. *Ha'aretz*, 16 July 1986.

44. *Ma'ariv*, 16 July 1986.

45. Steven R. Weisman, "Visit by U.S. Officials Is Praised by Pakistan and Criticized by India," *International Herald Tribune*, 23 September 1985; Don Oberdorfer, "Gandhi, Zia Reported to Agree on Opening Nuclear Talks," *Washington Post*, 24 October 1985; "Straight Talk on the Bomb" (Editorial), *Hindustan Times*, 3 November 1985; *Ma'ariv*, 18 December 1985.

46. Benjamin S. Lambeth, "Nuclear Proliferation and Soviet Arms Control Policy," *ORBIS*, Summer 1970, pp. 312–313, 318.

47. Gloria C. Duffy, "Soviet Nuclear Exports, *International Security* (Summer 1978), p. 97.

48. The Soviet journal *Socialisticheskaya Industria* criticized U.S. pressure on Pakistan in such fashion. Cited by Shrin Tahir-Kheli, "Pakistan's Nuclear Option and U.S. Policy," *Orbis*, Summer 1978, pp. 363–364.

49. "Soviets Supply Plants, Labs, to Libya," *International Herald Tribune*, 4 October 1978.

50. *The Middle East*, September 1984. *Financial Times*, 10 June 1985.

51. *Financial Times*, 24 March 1984; *Ha'aretz*, 24 February 1986; *Ma'ariv*, 24 February 1986.

52. BBC, 18 December 1984, citing Syrian Arab News Agency (SANA), 10 December 1984.

53. *Krasnaya Zvezda*, 10 October 1985; *Novosti*, 21 November 1984; *Novoyo Vermia*, 20 December 1985; *Izvestia*, 4 July 1986.

54. *Izvestia*, cited by *Yediot Aharonot*, 21 January 1986; *Ma'ariv*, 16 July 1986.

55. Most recently in the ABC Special "The Fire Unleashed," cited in *New Outlook*, July 1985, p. 23. For further statements see Shai Feldman, *Israeli Nuclear Deterrence* (New York: Columbia University Press, 1982), pp. 182–184.

56. "U.S. and Russia to Hold Nonproliferation Talks," *International Herald Tribune*, 7 November 1984.

Part IV
Military Presence, Intervention, and Force Projection

7

Toward the Carter Doctrine: The Evolution of American Power Projection Policies in the Middle East, 1947–1980

Dore Gold

The study of U.S. power projection policies leading up to the Carter Doctrine requires more than a sketch of the emerging dilemmas for U.S. security planners looking at the Middle East in the late 1970s. It is impossible to judge whether the Carter Doctrine and the U.S. Rapid Deployment Forces to which it gave rise represented a continuation or a turning point in U.S. security policy toward the Middle East, without reviewing past U.S. military plans for the area. Unfortunately, while students of superpower involvement in the Middle East have written countless manuscripts on the respective policies of the United States and the Soviet Union in regard to the Arab-Israel conflict, insufficient attention has been devoted to the military-strategic dimension in their struggle for influence. Ironically, the paucity of studies on superpower military policies has been even worse in the case of the United States.

The purpose of this paper, therefore, is to put the U.S. power projection mission as developed by the Carter administration in a historical perspective. The main thesis presented here—in the starkest of terms—is that prior to the Carter Doctrine, the United States had not even begun to provide for a conventional ground deterrent or, if necessary, for a defense of the heartland of the Middle East against the Soviet Union. In addition, a review of declassified documents reveals that despite the repeated presidential doctrines directly related to the security of the Middle East—both the Truman and Eisenhower doctrines—the U.S. military establishment repeatedly advised that it was not prepared to assume the kinds of responsibilities for this region to which national security planners in the State Department and the White House were ready to commit. This interpretation of U.S. security interests in the Middle East is at variance with the common historical conception of Washington extending its Cold War hegemony over the area in the late 1940s and 1950s as part of its global containment policy against the Soviet Union.

These historical conclusions may have important implications for assessing future patterns of U.S. involvement in the Middle East and of superpower rivalry. If, in fact, the past record of U.S. interaction with the region was based on a background of relatively lower U.S. military interest in providing an effective defense against a direct Soviet intrusion, then the new U.S. military efforts of the 1980s made in response to the Carter Doctrine may vary possibly lead to very different patterns of U.S. policy.

How exactly this infusion of U.S. power and military interest will affect its positions on various Middle Eastern conflicts, as well as the struggle with the Soviets for influence in the area, will be briefly considered at the end of this chapter.

The Truman-Eisenhower Years

The position of the Middle East in U.S. strategic planning in the early Cold War years was derived from the inheritance left by Anglo-American planners from the Second World War. The latter, held during secret contingency planning discussions in March 1941, prior to Pearl Harbor, divided up the world into areas of military responsibility, according to which the United States was to serve as the senior military partner in the Pacific, while allied command was to be shared in the Atlantic area. Only in the region between the two—the Mediterranean, the Middle East, and the Indian Ocean—was primary strategic responsibility given to Great Britain. When British and U.S. chiefs of staff met six years later, in 1947 during the Pentagon Talks, this basic division of allied military responsibilities was renewed. The only exceptions to this reaffirmation of the British strategic position in the area were Greece and Turkey, where the United States was already being asked to move in.[1]

Only months prior to these discussions, in Truman's famous speech of March 12, 1947, before a joint session of Congress that became known as the Truman Doctrine, the United States had formally announced its readiness to meet the challenge of Soviet expansionism. The president declared that it was U.S. policy "to support Free peoples who are resisting attempted subjugation by armed minorities or by outside pressure." But what did *support* mean? Truman was appealing for $300 million for Greece and $100 million for Turkey, but was the United States ready to intervene militarily on behalf of those countries? Studies initiated by the Joint Chiefs of Staff (JCS) in late 1947 concluded that the United States was not capable of deploying sufficient armed forces in Greece to defeat a combined attack by Yugoslavia, Albania, and Bulgaria. In answer to an inquiry by Secretary of Defense James Forrestal concerning the use of U.S. forces in Greece, the JCS responded that "any additional deployment of United States armed forces to this area will, in view of our present extended position, automatically raise the question of the advisability of partial mobilization." Despite these warnings, the National

Security Council (NSC), with the full support of the Department of State, pushed for presidential approval of a policy paper on Greece that stated that the United States was ready to make full use of its "political, economic, and if necessary military power" to prevent Greece from falling under Soviet domination. The NSC did not accept the JCS view that deployment of more than token forces would require U.S. mobilization.[2]

In subsequent years the White House, the Department of State, and, in particular, its Near East, South Asia, and African Affairs (NEA) division increasingly pressured the U.S. military establishment to play a more prominent role in the security of the Middle East. In October 1950 President Truman provided the first presidential security guarantee to the king of Saudi Arabia, stating that "the United States is interested in the preservation of the independence of Saudi Arabia. No threat to your kingdom could occur which would *not* be a matter of immediate concern to the United States." In early 1951 NEA officials, in discussions with the JCS, explained that "the smaller states of the area [the Middle East] were becoming increasingly concerned about their future and want[ed] some assurances about their defense." Leading JCS reaction to the State Department initiative was the U.S. Army Chief of Staff, General J. Lawton Collins, who opposed even the dispatch of U.S. military missions to Saudi Arabia, Syria, Lebanon, and Israel. Collins concluded: "We are kidding ourselves and kidding them if we do anything which indicates that we are going to put forces in the area. The forces to do that are just not in sight. This is a UK responsibility."

In the end, presidential policy as expressed by NSC 47/5 was sympathetic with the JCS view. The NSC concluded in 1951 that "because of United States commitments in other areas it is United States' interest that the United Kingdom have primary responsibility for Israel and the Arab states."[3]

Whether the British were capable of assuming strategic responsibility for the Middle East was already doubtful in 1952. Strategic discussions between U.S. and British staffs indicated a wide gap between U.S. goals and British capabilities. The United States hoped that Britain could hold the defense of a strategic "outer ring" of the Middle East (including southern Turkey, the Levant, Iraq, and southern Iran). The British admitted that with current forces they could hold only a much smaller "inner ring," protecting the Suez Canal from positions in Lebanon and Israel. The defense of important U.S. interests, such as the oil-producing areas of the Arabian Peninsula, included in the outer ring, would definitely require U.S. ground and air forces in the Middle East. Otherwise, a two-division deficiency that existed at D-Day would increase to a nearly seven-division deficiency after 180 days of warfare. The JCS reminded the British chiefs that no U.S. forces were available for the assignment for at least two years in any future world war. JCS chairman General Omar Bradley summarized the JCS view as follows: "We just feel we cannot defend Europe and the Middle East at the same time—we could still win a war despite the loss of the Middle East, which would not be true of Europe."[4]

Would the United States be able to expand its responsibilities in the Middle East with the advent of the Eisenhower administration in 1953? Secretary of State John Foster Dulles's famous trip to the region in the early months of the new administration certainly indicated a greater U.S. desire for involvement. Perhaps the defense of the outer ring would become possible. In reality, however, defense planning in the Eisenhower Pentagon precluded such a possibility. Republican economic goals stressing a balanced budget with heavy defense cuts paved the way for the adoption of the "New Look" strategy. Rather than dividing U.S. defense efforts for several alternative threats, the Department of Defense now clearly focused on a general war scenario that involved reliance on U.S. nuclear air power to execute massive retaliation against worldwide Soviet aggression. Thus, Eisenhower budgets in the mid-1950s planned steady growth for the Strategic Air Command, while U.S. Army manpower was cut by one-third, as were the air force's troop carrier wings, which were necessary to deploy U.S. ground forces in "brushfire" wars. Thus, Anglo-American cooperation in the area, which stressed overall British responsibility, continued to underpin U.S. planning for the Middle East, although British military assets in the region began to be increasingly offset by the disadvantages of the United States being associated with a declining imperial power. This dilemma found expression in U.S. support for British-sponsored or -led regional command schemes for the Middle East, to which the United States resisted formal adherence.[5]

In light of the limited U.S. conventional capabilities in the Middle East, the declaration of the Eisenhower Doctrine in 1957 seems almost surprising. As is well known, that doctrine arose as part of an effort to fill the vacuum created by the British and French collapse at Suez. President Eisenhower, in an address before Congress on January 5, 1957, called for a joint resolution not only providing for military and economic assistance programs for the region but also authorizing the use of U.S. armed forces as the president deemed necessary "to protect the territorial integrity and political independence of any Middle Eastern state facing overt armed aggression from a country controlled by international Communism."

While the chairman of the JCS knew that a new Middle East policy was in the making, the JCS as a whole considered the Eisenhower Doctrine's military implications only after the president's speech before Congress. The first of the studies ordered by the JCS to examine the doctrine's military implications analyzed the prerequisites for its effective application in the Middle East. The study concluded, for example, that increased military planning with Middle Eastern countries was required, including planning through the British-led Baghdad Pact organization. In addition, the study recommended the establishment of a unified U.S. command for the Middle East, like other such U.S. commands for Europe and the Pacific. The study envisioned that adequate defense of the region would require the United States "to supplement limited indigenous forces—with the necessary U.S. atomic-capable and mobile land, sea an air forces." Force levels for the area, it was suggested, were dependent on a general U.S. defense plan for the region that Pentagon planners had not yet completed.[6]

The U.S. government initiated steps to implement most of these recommendations. First, on March 28, 1957, President Eisenhower announced U.S. membership in the Baghdad Pact military committee. Notably, for reasons that cannot be fully discussed here, the United States still resisted full membership in the pact, in contrast with its policy in its European and Far Eastern containment alliances, NATO and SEATO. Second, the Commander-in-Chief of the U.S. Naval Forces Eastern Atlantic and Mediterranean (CINCNELM)—who throughout most of the 1950s was both the naval component commander of the U.S. European command (EUCOM) and the commander of US Specified Command, Middle East (SPECOMME)—was now given broader responsibilities in the latter role. By order of the secretary of defense on Febraury 3, 1960, CINCNELM was directed to establish a unified multiservice staff for Middle Eastern planning separate from his exclusively naval staff for European responsibility. This arrangement, however, was described by the defense secretary's directive as only temporary, until a new Middle East unified command, MECOM, was established.[7]

Third, at the end of February 1958, the JCS completed their Middle East Emergency Defense Plan. As with planning done by CINCNELM, the JCS plan did not provide for the employment of substantial U.S. forces in the Middle East in case of a general war with the Soviet Union. The principal form of U.S. power projection against the Soviets consistent with New Look defense concepts was a strategic air attack from U.S. bases in Morocco and Libya against Soviet installations and troop concentrations adjacent to the Middle East, so that indigenous forces alone might hold back the Soviets. This primary reliance on indigenous forces for Middle Eastern defense—those belonging to the Baghdad Pact countries and its successor organization, CENTO—remained in the JCS Middle East Emergency Defense Plan for 1960 as well. JCS planners decided not to specify the role of U.S. forces in lesser contingencies against Soviet client states, leaving the choice of forces dependent on the situation. It was already recognized that existing joint plans could be modified on an ad hoc basis. Certainly, this was the case with the employment of the marines attached to the Sixth Fleet in Lebanon or with the marine units attached to the Seventh Fleet ships specially deployed at times of crisis in the Indian Ocean. Both constituted a U.S. limited power projection potential in lesser contingencies alone.[8]

The later Eisenhower years, in sum, entailed a further expansion of U.S. security commitments to the Middle East before the U.S. military establishment was prepared to meet them. While the Anglo-American global alliance that gave Britain primary responsibility for the Middle East was not entirely in a shambles after the Suez affair, Britain had by now clearly become the minor partner in the region, utilizing its remaining assets in Aden, East Africa, and the Persian Gulf to guard Western assets east of Suez. Given the limited conventional military forces that the United States could contribute in the fulfillment of its new position of Western leadership in the region, the projection of U.S. power at this time had to stress U.S. air power, including the use of U.S. nuclear weapons for the containment of the Soviets in the area.

Kennedy-Johnson-Nixon Years

President John F. Kennedy came into office in 1961, having been a strong critic of Eisenhower's New Look policy of massive retaliation that led to the U.S. conventional forces' poor state of affairs. Consequently, the Kennedy administration sought to substantially enlarge the size of U.S. Army forces based in the continental United States, as well as to double U.S. airlift capabilities by 1964. Organizationally, in October 1961 the Kennedy Pentagon created a new unified command, the U.S. Strike Command (STRICOM), to utilize the newly enlarged U.S.-based army forces for operation in the Third World. In December 1963 STRICOM took over from CINCNELM unified command responsibilities for the Middle East. It seemed as though the Kennedy administration was creating the forces and command arrangements to meet the responsibilities undertaken in the Eisenhower years.[9]

These military preparations may have already had some political implications for U.S. Middle East policy during these years. In December 1962 President Kennedy hosted Israeli Foreign Minister Golda Meir in Palm Beach, Florida, at which time he made an unprecedented oral U.S. commitment to Israel's security: "It is quite clear that in case of invasion of Israel, the United States would come to the support of Israel." His next sentence was of more interest in the context of this study: "We have the capacity and it is growing." It appears that Kennedy's awareness of the growing U.S. conventional capabilities for Middle East operations gave him the power and confidence to make an explicit security commitment that neither Truman nor Eisenhower would have felt comfortable uttering even if it were in line with their policies.[10]

A full U.S. regional command for the Middle East, however, did not emerge in the 1960s for several reasons. First, STRICOM, which brought together assets of the U.S. Army and Air Force, was unable to gain control of any naval units. Thus, contingencies requiring use of naval forces, even within STRICOM's area of responsibility, were delegated to the U.S. Sixth Fleet. For example, it was the Sixth Fleet, and not STRICOM, that handled the evacuation of U.S. citizens from Israel and the Arab states prior to the June 1967 war. Second, many of the enlarged U.S.-based conventional forces created by the Kennedy administration were increasingly assigned to the war in Vietnam in the 1960s.[11]

Another limit on the development in the 1960s of a U.S. intervention force for the Middle East was the loss of major U.S. air bases in the area that were an important source for pre-positioned manpower and logistical support. As U.S.

bombers reached intercontinental ranges (with the introduction of the B-52), justification for U.S. airfields in Morocco, Libya, and Saudi Arabia declined. On the other side of the Middle East, however, repeated crises on the Indian subcontinent increased the U.S. Navy's interest in expanding its power projection capabilities into the Indian Ocean, leading to negotiations with Great Britain over the lease of Diego Garcia in 1966. The full development of this facility would take at least a decade.

By the early 1970s the United States still had great difficulties in projecting conventional ground forces in the Middle East. Continuing U.S. commitments to Southeast Asia still consumed forces that might have been earmarked for Middle East contingencies. During the Jordanian civil war in 1970, Henry Kissinger detailed in his memoirs the limitations he discovered in using U.S. forces to defend King Hussein: The United States had only four brigades capable of reaching Jordan quickly; the operation, he estimated, would have used up the entire U.S. Army strategic reserve. Kissinger paid particular attention to the lack of adequate staging areas in the region for the effective use of even these U.S. forces. He explained that the constraints he discovered on using US forces in the crisis were to lead to his decision to coordinate with Israel and propose the use of Israeli power to aid Hussein. In the end, of course, Hussein managed to repulse the Syrian invasion to his kingdom by himself.[12]

This limitation on the projection of U.S. power in the Middle East was attested elsewhere by the application of the Nixon Doctrine to the Persian Gulf in the wake of Britain's withdrawal from its commitments east of the Suez. At least in the Middle East, the Nixon Doctrine was not revolutionary; rather it was more a frank admission of U.S. capabilities in the area. The idea that greater emphasis would in the future be placed on the use of *allied* instead of *American* ground forces in various regional conflicts had already been realized with regard to U.S. planning in the Middle East since the 1950s. What was new was that instead of a U.S. president declaring new U.S. responsibilities in light of Britain's last great imperial withdrawal from the area, Nixon simply and frankly admitted what had been true all along: that the projection of U.S. power would still depend on the use of air and naval power, while indigenous forces would conduct the ground war. To facilitate the job of the Shah in this division of responsibilities, the Nixon administration initiated arms transfers of unprecedented quality and quantity to both Iran and Saudi Arabia.

Finally, symbolizing the United States insufficient preparedness in projecting conventional power in the Middle East in the 1970s was the decision to formally put an end to the U.S. unified command that the Kennedy administration had established to intervene in Middle Eastern contingencies. On July 8, 1971, the Department of Defense announced that the U.S. Strike Command was to be dissolved and replaced by a new U.S. Readiness Command charged only with training responsibilities in the continental United States. STRICOM's responsibilities for the Middle East were transferred to the U.S. European Command, where they were to remain until the 1980s. A unified U.S. geographic command for the Middle East, which since the late 1950s had been identified by the JCS as one of the essential prerequisites for the effective projection of U.S. power to the area, would have to await the establishment of the U.S. Central Command (CENTCOM) in 1983.[13]

Toward the Carter Doctrine

The conceptual roots of the Carter Doctrine actually predate the principal event—the Soviet invasion of Afghanistan—generally attributed with having been its cause. In mid-1977 President Carter and his assistant for national security affairs, Zbigniew Brzezinski, ordered the NSC to review U.S. national security policy in light of changes in Soviet global strategy in an era of nuclear parity. Brzezinski was alarmed by improved Soviet conventional war–fighting capabilities as well as by Moscow's apparent drive for long-range deployment capabilities for intervention in the Third World. He also was concerned about Soviet nuclear policies. Presidential Directive (PD) 18, issued in August 1977, called for the creation of a light infantry force backed up by expanded air- and sealift capabilities. If U.S. power projection along the Soviet Union's Middle Eastern perimeter was in the past based on the threat to use U.S. air power and nuclear weapons, realities in the 1970s now called for a revision of that thinking.[14]

According to Brzezinski's memoirs, between 1977 and 1979 little progress on this light intervention force was made, despite presidential approval of the concept. The deteriorating security situation throughout 1979 in the area stretching from the Horn of Africa through Yemen and across the Arabian peninsula as far as Afghanistan led to Brzezinski's "arc of crisis" thesis that called for a reassertion of U.S. power throughout the area.

At the heart of this arc of crisis was the fall of the Shah of Iran in January 1979, whose removal undermined any continued application of the Nixon Doctrine in the Persian Gulf. The Iranian pillar had fallen, and the Saudi pillar was too weak to protect Western interest. In November 1979 Islamic militants seized the U.S. Embassy in Teheran, while fundamentalists in Saudi Arabia attacked the Great Mosque in Mecca. By December 4, 1979, President Carter, responding to the recommendations of the JCS, the Department of Defense, the CIA, and Brzezinski, approved plans for seeking military facilities in countries along the Indian Ocean to deal with contingencies that might require U.S. forces. This year-long process to develop a new policy for introducing a greater U.S. military presence in the Middle East was chiefly resisted by the Department of State, which adhered to earlier U.S. plans to seek a negotiated demilitarization of the Indian Ocean. This position, however, lost any chance of gaining further support with the Soviet invasion of Afghanistan.

President Carter's January 23, 1980, declaration that the United States would repel "by any means, including military forces" any attempt "to gain control of the Persian Gulf region" was thus aimed at a Washington bureaucracy that was already well at work on how to deal with the declining security situation in this sensitive area. The one exceptional element in this doctrine was an explicit reference to the forces that had to be developed in order to give the new policy credibility. In the longer written text of the president's statement, submitted two days earlier to Congress, Carter recommended that "our rapid deployment forces could be used in support of friendly governments in the Gulf and Southwest Asia region." In the cases of the Truman and Eisenhower doctrines, policy pronouncements preceded any full assessment of U.S. military capabilities. Carter, to his credit, initiated the creation of a force to back up his doctrine.

In January 1980 the United States was not any better prepared militarily than it had been in the past to resist Soviet expansion in the Middle East with U.S. conventional forces, but at least the Carter administration began planning the kinds of forces and facilities that would allow his successors to maintain the commitments he was undertaking. A Rapid Deployment Joint Task Force (RDJTF) for quick intervention in the Middle East and Persian Gulf area was established, at the president's order, between December 1979 and March 1980, when it first became operational. Military access agreements to facilities in Oman, Kenya, Somalia, and Egypt were negotiated. New strategic mobility programs aimed at increasing U.S. sealift in the area also were initiated. Whatever command and manpower problems emerged with the RDJTF and its successor organization, CENTCOM (most of its units continue to have responsibilities to other theaters as well), the United States had by the early 1980s established an institutionalized military interest in the Middle East that had not been previously developed to the same extent in the postwar era.

Conclusions

According to Brzezinski, the Carter Doctrine signified a formal recognition of the fact that the security of the United States "had become interdependent with the security of three central and inter-related strategic zones consisting of Western Europe, the Far East, and the Middle East–Persian Gulf area."[15] The above analysis has demonstrated that the Carter Doctrine appeared primarily to have led to an elevation of the latter strategic zone in U.S. security planning to a level of importance close to—although still not identical with—that of the former two. The historical record shows that since the Second World War the Middle East has been a problematic area for U.S. security policy. During the war it certainly was of tertiary interest to the United States after the more essential European and Pacific theaters. Allied command arrangements during the war and immediaely afterward assigned the region to Great Britain; as British power withered in and around the area—from Greece in 1947 to the Persian Gulf in 1968—an overburdened and overextended United States felt constrained to come up with a Middle East strategy that would contain Soviet penetration with a minimum of added force or expense. That strategy seemed to combine a firm U.S. declaratory policy (the Eisenhower Doctrine) with military planning involving the use of indigenous ground forces backed up by U.S. air (including nuclear) and naval power.

By the late 1970s this strategy appeared to have lost all credibility. Iran, the principal indigenous Middle Eastern power groomed by the United States, had collapsed, leaving doubts as to the advisability of relying on any other local state in a similar manner. Nuclear parity, achieved by the Soviet Union at the beginning of the decade, undermined any U.S. plan to make up for conventional force deficiencies with U.S. nuclear strength. At the same time, the dependence of the Western alliance on the oil-producing areas of the Middle East, especially the Persian Gulf, were underlined in 1973 and again in 1978 at a time when the deficiencies in Western strategy were becoming more apparent. These developments had as much influence on the Carter Doctrine as the Soviet invasion of Afghanistan in December 1979.

In sum, two conclusions emerge from the above analysis. First, the Middle East, from the standpoint of U.S. security policy, may not have been as important to the United States as American public concern over the Arab-Israel conflict appears to have indicated. Second, since the proclamation of the Carter Doctrine, the relative importance of the Middle East in relation to other global theaters has increased. Several questions from this study of the pre–Carter Doctrine period emerge for studies on the post–Carter Doctrine period. Will the elevated importance of the Middle East region continue even when the relative importance of Middle Eastern oil is in decline? How will the shift from primary reliance on proxies to the unilateral use of U.S. power affect U.S. policies—including arms sales policies—toward the states of the region? Finally, as U.S. military interest in the Middle East increases, will the United States seek to establish a more permanent regional strategic framework, short of an alliance system, that might serve the cause of peacemaking by restraining conflict between its local members? Whatever the answers to these questions, the pattern of future U.S. interaction with the area will undoubtedly be different from the pattern witnessed in the pre–Carter Doctrine period.

Notes

1. J. C. Hurewitz, *The Middle East and North Africa in World Politics: A Documentary Record*, vol. 2, *British-French Supremacy 1914-1945* (New Haven and London: Yale University Press, 1979), see analytic introduction to Document 142 pp. 609–610; Maurice Matloff and Edwin M. Snell, *Strategic Planning for Coalition Warfare 1941-1942* (Washington: Office of the Chief of Military History, Department of the Army, 1953), chapters 7, 11; "The British and American Positions," (undated) Memorandum, U.S. Department of

State Historical Office; *Foreign Relations of the United States, 1947*, vol. 3 (Washington: GPO), p. 514.

2. Joint Chiefs of Staff, RG 218, *The Joint Chiefs of Staff and National Policy, 1947–1949*, vol. 2, (Washington: National Archives, 1976), pp. 41–56.

3. Isadore Jay Gold, *The United States and Saudi Arabia 1933-1953: Post-Imperial Diplomacy and the Legacy of British Power*, Unpublished Dissertation, Columbia University, 1984, pp. 269–270; "State Department Draft Minutes of Discussions of the State-Joint Chiefs of Staff Meeting," 30 January 1951, in *Foreign Relations of the United States, 1951*, vol. 5 (Washington: GPO) p. 29.

4. Joint Chiefs of Staff, RG 218, *The Joint Chiefs of Staff and National Policy, 1950–1952*, vol. 4, (Washington: National Archives, 1979), pp. 331–378.

5. Glenn H. Snyder. "The New Look of 1953," in Warner Schilling, Paul Hammond, and Glenn Snyder, *Strategy, Politics and Defense Budgets* (New York: Columbia University Press, 1962), pp. 451–462.

6. *Military Aspects of the Proposed Joint Resolution for The General Area of the Middle East"* (JCS 1887/342), Report by the Joint Middle Eastern Planning Committee to the Joint Chiefs of Staff, RG 218/CCS 381 EMMEA (11-19-47), sect. 55, 20 February 1957. See also "The Eisenhower Doctrine and Middle East Plans," *The Joint Chiefs of Staff and National Policy 19-19*, pp. 391–396.

7. "The Lebanon Crisis and After," pp. 482–483.

8. "The Eisenhower Doctrine and Middle East Plans," pp. 415–417.

9. Robert P. Haffa, Jr., *The Half War: Planning US Rapid Deployment Forces to Meet a Limited Contingency, 1960-1983* (Boulder, CO: Westview Press, 1984), pp. 93–106.

10. Steven L. Spiegel, *The Other Arab-Israel Conflict: Making America's Middle East Policy, From Truman to Reagan* (Chicago: University of Chicago Press, 1985), pp. 106–107.

11. Haffa, *The Half War*, p. 102.

12. *Ibid.*, p. 48. See also, Henry Kissinger, *White House Years* (Boston: Little, Brown, 1979), p. 605.

13. General Bruce Palmer, Jr., *The 25-Year War: America's Military Role in Vietnam* (Lexington, KY: The University Press of Kentucky, 1984), p. 137.

14. Zbigniew Brzezinski, *Power and Principle: Memoirs of the National Security Adviser 1977-1981* (New York: Farrar, Straus, Giroux, 1983), pp. 443–448, 454–456.

15. *Ibid.*, p. 443.

8

The "Reagan Doctrine" and U.S. Policy in the Middle East

Sanford Lakoff

A t least to some degree, the Reagan administration's approach to the Middle East bears the imprint of a general strategy in foreign policy that has been called the "Reagan Doctrine" and is said to have emerged in clearest outline during the administration's second term.[1] Inasmuch as this administration is the most overtly ideological since the Wilson administration during the Progressive era, it is hardly surprising that such a perspective should inform its foreign policy, but the degree to which this perspective has shaped U.S. policies in the Middle East since 1980 is not as well appreciated. These policies have in fact been influenced by the administration's ideological commitments, although not so strongly as to override pragmatic considerations or as to diverge fundamentally from established patterns of U.S. behavior in the region.

Origins and Character of the Reagan Doctrine

The Reagan administration took office convinced that Soviet leadership had taken advantage of the timorousness of previous U.S. administrations, especially of an unwillingness to resist Soviet expansion arising out of the Vietnam syndrome. The Soviet Union had embarked on a major military buildup, the president and his advisors argued, in order to achieve military superiority over the United States and to extend its power in the Third World, directly or indirectly, most notably in Afghanistan, Angola, Ethiopia, and Nicaragua. By raising defense spending and reviving military programs cancelled by the previous administration, the new administration sought to redress the perceived military imbalance. Intermediate missiles were installed in Europe, despite Soviet efforts to divide the Western alliance over the issue, while the Strategic Defense Initiative (SDI) was introduced in the hope of finding an alternative to deterrence by the threat of retaliation. The president has persisted with SDI, despite warnings that it will lead to the end of arms control, in the belief that the Soviets will be deterred most reliably, with or without arms control, by U.S. offensive and defensive preparedness.

The Reagan Doctrine is said to have emerged out of the formulation of policy regarding competition with the Soviet Union for influence in developing countries. Although the president himself has never used the term, others, including champions of the administration line such as Jeane Kirkpatrick, have attributed it to him, and they cite Reagan's State of the Union message of February 6, 1985, as the basic text for this doctrine. In this speech the president asserted that freedom was not simply an American value but a universal birthright. Peace and prosperity, he suggested, come only where "people live by laws that ensure free press, free speech and freedom to worship, vote and create wealth." In what amounts to a mirror image of the Soviet Marxist notion that the world can truly be at peace and on the path to prosperity only when socialism is the universal condition, the president pressed the case for a kind of liberal, anticommunist alternative. The American "mission," he said, " is to nourish and defend freedom and democracy and to communicate these ideals everywhere we can." This was not just a matter of preaching values but of taking action in support of them. Thus, "we must stand by all our democratic allies. And we must not break faith with those who are risking their lives on every continent, from Afghanistan to Nicaragua, to defy Soviet-supported aggression and secure rights which have been ours from birth."[2]

This pledge of support for opponents of Soviet expansion has been celebrated by its backers as a return to the vigorous championing of freedom, coupled with a sense of mission, which was the hallmark of the American past, and a turning away from the defeatism and appeasement supposedly characteristic of the Carter years. Administration policy has been consistent with this statement of doctrine in certain respects. Its spokesmen have openly called for the support of insurgents fighting communist or procommunist regimes, such as the contras in Nicaragua, instead of seeking, as the Carter administration did in Angola with the help of the Clark amendment, to protect American economic interests by making an accomodation with a Marxist government.

Rather than reject alliances with right-wing regimes accused of violating human rights, as the Carter administration sometimes did, the Reagan administration has openly declared its willingness to make common cause with anticommunist authoritarian regimes on the grounds that they can be reformed and are preferable to the communist systems that threaten to replace them. Therefore, instead of opposing the South African regime outright, lest the country fall into pro-Soviet hands, the Reagan administration opted for a policy of "constructive engagement," in which efforts were to be made to persuade Pretoria to abandon apartheid and to move toward power-sharing. It has also sought congressional support for aid to the mujahidin in Afghanistan and to the contras in Nicaragua, in what is perhaps the most distinctive aspect of the Reagan Doctrine: the support of insurgency movements against established communist, procommunist, or simply anti-Western regimes. In addition, and most recently, the administration has embarked on a policy of responding to terrorism, especially state-sponsored terrorism, wherever feasible.

Critics have charged that the departure from a less aggressive, more pragmatic approach to foreign policy actually represents a resurgence of narrow American nationalism, with its penchant for frontier vigilantism. The Reagan Doctrine, it is said, rests on the dangerous illusion that, in a nuclear world, strategic superiority is both possible and desirable, even if it threatens the prospects for managing global conflict. Critics also warn that in pursuing a policy of supporting insurgencies and threatening direct U.S. involvement in the Third World, the United States risks escalating such conflicts into superpower confrontations.[3]

Whatever may be said for and against it, this effort to formulate and implement a new doctrine caught the imagination of the American people and moved the lines of debate to the right of center. During Reagan's first term, Congress was willing to incur unprecedented federal deficits in order to oblige the president's increased military budget. Despite the debacle in Lebanon and the gambles he took in other uses of U.S. force, the president's popularity rose.[4]

The Doctrine and the Middle East

It would be surprising if the Reagan Doctrine should have had no bearing on U.S. policy in the Middle East, especially inasmuch as previous similar doctrines were either designed to suit the Middle East or else had considerable relevance to the region. The Truman Doctrine was tailored to apply to Turkey and Iran as well as Greece. The Eisenhower Doctrine led to the first dispatch of U.S. marines to Lebanon, though it was intended to indicate U.S. support for those nations prepared to take their own initiative in order to resist the encroachment of Soviet communism. The Nixon Doctrine led the United States to rely on Iran to be the policeman of the Persian Gulf and, to a lesser extent, on Israel as a stabilizing force in the area to the west of the Gulf. The Carter Doctrine, declared in response to the Soviet invasion of Afghanistan and to the overthrow of the Shah in Iran, announced a resolve to protect vital interests in the Gulf by any means necessary, including military force. Although the Reagan Doctrine is at once more sweeping and less specific than any of these predecessors, it too carries implications for the Middle East.

In assessing these implications, certain obvious caveats must be kept in mind. All such doctrines need to be both broad enough to achieve consensus and flexible enough to allow for diverse interpretations and tactical maneuvering. In the case of policies toward the Middle East, domestic factions, bureaucratic interests, and administrative officials have been free to interpret the doctrine more or less as they choose until some major decision point or crisis occurs, forcing the president to decide which interpretation will carry the day. Nor is the United States able to carry out its objectives without taking account of constraints upon its capacities. It is one thing to decide to destroy a communist regime in a small country like Grenada before it can take root and another to consider mounting an attack against a well-entrenched regime like that of Cuba's Fidel Castro, where the Soviet Union stands as guarantor. Similarly, it is easier to decide to retaliate against an international pariah like Qaddafi than against Syria, which enjoys a Soviet promise of protection made tangible by the presence of several thousand Soviet advisors. To suppose that any doctrine—whether some operational code of the Politburo or some less formally binding presidential flight of rhetoric—will fully account for every aspect of policy and conduct would be to commit the rationalist fallacy in its worst form. Tactical considerations alone will dictate flexibility, and concessions designed to achieve particular objectives will sometimes be made even though they deviate from doctrinal guidelines. The much-criticized decision to provide arms to Iran covertly in contravention of a declared embargo is a glaring case in point.

The Reagan Doctrine, moreover, represents no fundamental departure from the pattern of postwar U.S. policy. Basically, the various doctrines that have been identified with this and previous administrations are all variations on a common Cold War theme. Since World War II U.S. foreign policy has been based on the axiom of competition with the Soviet Union, with the aim of detering a Soviet attack on the United States and its allies and of containing Soviet expansion. These doctrines have all dealt with the problem of how this strategy could be pursued in regions where the United States does not have the benefit of strong alliances. Just as the Monroe Doctrine asserted a U.S. policy with respect to the Western Hemisphere at a time when the United States had only tenuous relations with other American states, subsequent doctrines have all asserted policy for regions not adequately protected by treaty arrangements. The Eisenhower Doctrine was promulgated in January 1957 to prevent the dissolution of the Baghdad Pact in the face of an attempt by Nasser's Egypt, backed by the Soviet Union, to achieve regional hegemony. The Nixon Doctrine was designed to deal with a situation in which, despite the existence of a treaty organization (SEATO), the United States had found itself drawn into the quagmire of Vietnam.

In general, these various doctrines pull in two directions: the Truman, Eisenhower, and Nixon doctrines assert the need to support friendly regimes so that they can defend themselves; the Carter and Reagan doctrines assert both the need to support local allies and the readiness to intervene directly. (Not that there is any necessary link between doctrine and action. President Kennedy sanctioned the Bay of Pigs invasion even though no "Kennedy Doctrine" controlled such involvements; the Truman Doctrine called for aid but not for the kind of intervention he ordered in Korea. Similarly, the Reagan Doctrine called for active resistance to state-sponsored terrorism, not the trading of arms for hostages that the president apparently approved in connection with a covert approach to Iran.)

Elements of the Doctrine
Applied to the Middle East

With these qualifications, the Reagan Doctrine can be described as a restatement of conventional U.S. Cold War strategy, which emphasizes a general commitment to resist the spread of Soviet influence and power by a variety of means. These include the buildup of U.S. forces to prevent political blackmail or compellance; the delivery of aid to allies, both formal and de facto, who promote regional stability; support for insurgent groups fighting regimes either under Soviet control or hostile to Western interests; and, most recently, a vigorous response to state-sponsored terrorism. Inevitably, such an ambitious agenda can be carried out only selectively, sometimes even only symbolically. The administration has decided, for example, that Cambodia is worth no more than token support, that Syria is too important in the Arab world and too closely tied to the Soviet Union to attack except under the most blatant provocation, and that it may make sense to seek improved relations with the revolutionary fundamentalist regime in Iran in view of the potential threat that regime poses to Western interests and the opportunities offered by its fear of the Soviet Union.

Nevertheless, the Reagan Doctrine is reflected in a set of active policies for the Middle East, in particular:

1. A commitment to Israel's security and to cooperation with Israel for the sake of common interests in regional stability.

2. Support for and cooperation with pro-Western or moderate Arab states, chiefly Egypt, Saudi Arabia, and Jordan, for the sake of maintaining ties to the Arab world and of preventing the internal subversion or external overthrow of these regimes, and in the expectation that these states will play some role in protecting Western access to oil and cooperate with the United States in the event of an emergency requiring direct U.S. intervention.

3. Readiness to mediate in the Arab-Israeli conflict, in the belief that amelioration of the Palestinan issue would greatly improve Arab attitudes toward the United States.

4. Readiness to interject U.S. forces in order to safeguard Western access to Middle East oil.

5. Readiness to use diplomatic pressure and force (where it is not counterproductive) against terrorism on the understanding that terrorism is a form of low-intensity warfare directed against Western interests by hostile states, with indirect assistance from the Soviet Union.

A brief review of each of these aspects of policy will indicate that despite the twists and turns on particular issues, and despite the play of personalities, these underlying applications of the Reagan Doctrine help account for the general pattern of the administration's Middle East policies since taking office.

Commitment to Israel's Security

During both terms of the Reagan administration, U.S. support for Israel's security has been reaffirmed by verbal commitments and, even more importantly, by tangible actions. As a presidential candidate, Ronald Reagan declared that after the fall of the Shah, Israel remained the one regional ally on which the United States could still count. He even went so far as to support Israel's claim to a unified Jerusalem and to argue that Israeli settlements on the West Bank were not illegal—positions from which he retreated once in office. Although relations were badly strained early in the administration's first term by the efforts of the Begin government and its U.S. supporters to prevent the 1981 sale of AWACS aircraft to Saudi Arabia, by subsequent Israeli military strikes against the Iraqi nuclear reactor and Palestine Liberation Organization (PLO) bases in Beirut, and by Israel's virtual annexation of the Golan Heights, the United States did not deprive Israel of vital military supplies, economic assistance, or political support. Shipments of F-16 aircraft, frozen after the attack on the Iraqi reactor, were resumed shortly therafter, and the Reagan administration instructed its U.N. representative to veto a proposed Security Council resolution condemning Israel for the raid and threatening sanctions. Although the siege of Beirut during Israel's 1982 incursion into Lebanon brought the relationship to its lowest point, Israel was not explicitly threatened with withdrawal of assistance at any time during its campaign, and in the aftermath of the war, not only has U.S. aid to Israel reached an all-time high, but the two nations have entered into a security cooperation agreement that ensures close military coordination.

The Lebanon war tested the limits of U.S. willingness to align itself with Israel at the cost of its relations to pro-Western Arab regimes. Reagan had previously agreed with his first secretary of state, Alexander Haig, that the best policy for the United States was to encourage its friends in the region to recognize their common interests as partners in a "strategic consensus." Haig has argued that this policy reflected the regional fear of terrorism, Islamic fundamentalism, and the Soviet Union, all of which boiled down to "one consolidated fear: that terrorism and fundamentalism would so destablize the region that the Soviets could either subvert the Islamic movement of their own purposes or seize control of Iran and possibly the whole Gulf in a second revolution after the Iranian revolution collapsed under the political and economic weight of its own excesses."[5] From this perspective, Lebanon in itself was of only marginal concern. The administration feared that Israel might become embroiled in a war with Syria in Lebanon that in turn would prevent the return of the entire Sinai to Egypt in April 1982 and thus destabilize the Mubarak regime in Egypt and cause difficulties between the United States and its Arab allies.

When the Begin government kept its word and returned the Sinai to Egypt, Secretary Haig responded by expressing understanding for Israel's oft-repeated intention to react strongly against PLO violations of the ceasefire worked out by Ambassador Philip Habib. Begin and his closest advisors felt that with Haig in charge of the State Department, they could take a militant position against Syria and against terrorism initiated from Lebanon.[6] Habib had been unable to secure Syrian withdrawal of its SAMs from the Bekaa Valley, and Haig made it clear that in his view the Syrians were becoming virtual Soviet puppets. While General Ariel Sharon elaborated plans for a military assault on the PLO in Lebanon, the Begin government undertook a campaign to win U.S. approval for such an offensive. This campaign began with a conversation between Begin and Haig at Sadat's funeral in October 1981 and reached its climax first with the visit in February 1982 of the chief of military intelligence, General Yehoshuah Saguy, to Haig in the United States, and then with that of General Sharon himself in May. Sharon understood Haig's response to mean that the United States would not object strongly if Israel responded to PLO provocation by attacking its bases in Lebanon. For his part Haig reiterated in a letter to Begin on May 28 U.S. concern for Israeli restraint. The reportedly "mild tone" and "indulgent language" of the letter were interpreted by the Israeli cabinet as an indication of U.S. desires to put its formal reservations on record in case the operation jeopardized U.S. interests.[7] Haig has insisted that his letter was actually intended to call on Israel to exercise "complete restraint" and to warn, as he had for months, that any retaliation should be in response to clear and internationally recognized PLO provocation.[8]

Whether or not he can be said to have encouraged the Israeli operation, it is clear by his own admission that Haig wanted the United States to capitalize on what he saw as the "historic opportunity"[9] opened by the outcome of Israel's military operation in Lebanon. He argued that the United States should seize the chance to reconstitute an independent Lebanon under a friendly government and to encourage Jordanian entry into the peace process begun at Camp David. Although Haig was dismissed before he could implement this policy, his successor, George Shultz, did not essentially deviate from it. With U.S. mediation and the dispatch of a multinational peacekeeping force, the PLO agreed to leave Beirut. After the Sabra and Shatila massacres, the peacekeeping force returned to enable a new Lebanese government to gain control.

Meanwhile, Shultz and Habib tried to negotiate the withdrawal of both Israeli and Syrian forces, and Shultz sought to win support for the new Reagan Plan of September 1982 aimed at reinvigorating Arab-Israeli peace negotiations over the future of the West Bank and Gaza. When Syria refused to comply with the terms of the pact negotiated by the United States between Lebanon and Israel, and when terrorist car bombings inflicted major casualties on U.S. and French peacekeeping forces, Washington decided to cut its losses and withdraw. In the end, both Israel and the United States decided independently that they could not afford to persevere in Lebanon, and the United States did not pursue the Reagan Plan with much vigor. In the aftermath U.S.-Israeli relations have steadily improved.

Although at the time Haig's departure was interpreted as a victory for forces within the administration less sympathetic to Israel, forces led by Secretary of Defense Caspar Weinberger and National Security Adviser William Clark, subsequent events hardly show a decline in U.S. support for Israeli security. Secretary Shultz, who was reportedly passed over in favor of Haig in 1980 because of a supposedly pro-Arab bias, has turned out to have no less concern for Israel's security than his predecessor, and Secretary Weinberger's irritation with the Begin govenment's behavior has not prevented him from supporting the creation of a strategic cooperation agreement whose secret terms reportedly include close cooperation on the sharing of advanced technology and intelligence. This agreement, coupled with U.S. support of Israel's development of the Lavi fighter aircraft and the negotiation of a free trade agreement, has cemented relations more strongly than under any previous administration. However misguided the administration's covert dealings with Iran in 1985–1986 may have been, the fact that they were carried out in close cooperation with Israel is an indication of the strength of the relationship.

Ties to Pro-Western Arab States

The Reagan administration's readiness to develop and maintain good relations with friendly Arab states is signaled both by what it has done and by what it has not done. It has, for example, continued the military aid and cooperation program with Egypt initiated under the Carter administration in accordance with commitments made in connection with the Camp David agreements, and the latest U.S. joint Bright Star exercise with Egypt involved more U.S. troops in Africa than at any times since World War II.

Ties to Saudi Arabia have been buttressed by a willingness to overcome domestic opposition to arms sales, which resulted in a $7 billion sale of AWACS aircraft, the largest-ever arms sale to an Arab country. In this deal, domestic motives were combined with foreign policy goals. Large sales add to the purchasing power of U.S. defense outlays by lowering unit costs, and the big orders helped U.S. defense contractors during a period of economic recession. The sale also served the foreign policy objective of assisting the major Gulf state in deterring an Iranian attack and in demonstrating U.S. readiness to protect the West's oil suppliers by strengthening Saudi armed forces and those of the Gulf Cooperation Council. In seeking Saudi cooperation, the Reagan administration has had to recognize that the Saudis will make diplomatic moves only when they know there is a strong consensus within the Arab world, but that with respect to their own security and that of the Gulf, they are ready to play a more positive role. The

Saudis' use of American weapons to repel an attack by Iranian aircraft in the Spring of 1984 has been cited as evidence of the success of the U.S. policy of providing the Saudis with the weapons they need to defend themselves.[10]

Support for Jordan has faltered lately, but the administration may well have calculated that in not attempting to override congressional resistance, the United States has signaled to pro-Western Arab leaders that they cannot take U.S. support for granted without at the same time inflicting a serious blow on the strength of the Jordanian armed forces.

Just as significantly, the administration has resisted suggestions for an oil import tax to break the back of OPEC once and for all, partly on the ground that they represent a protectionist departure from laissez-faire economic principles, partly in fear that they would stimulate domestic inflation, and partly in order to maintain good relations with the Saudis.

Efforts to Mediate the Arab-Israeli Conflict

The most forthright move made by the Reagan administration to resolve the Arab-Israeli conflict was the Reagan peace initiative of September 1982. In his statement, made at the urging of Secretary Shultz and discussed beforehand with King Hussein, the president called for direct negotiations between Israel and a Jordanian delegation that would include Palestinian representatives to conclude a peace treaty on the principle of an exchange of territory for peace. The president made clear that in his view such an arrangement would require the return to Arab sovereignty of virtually all the territories on the West Bank and in Gaza, which had come under Israeli control in 1967. The negotiations might entail minor border rectifications but no substantive changes, except for the status of Jerusalem, concerning which the president indicated that the city's unity should be maintained but that the question of sovereignty and control should be left to negotiations. This speech was plainly designed to alter the U.S. stance from what it had been as a result of the Camp David accords to make it more acceptable to the Jordanian and Saudi rulers, even though the new position was certain to arouse Israeli and PLO hostility.

It is unlikely that the administration made this move in the serious expectation that it would bring the parties immediately to the negotiating table. The Begin government's rejection of the proposal, for example, must surely have been anticipated. The administration's position went well beyond the Camp David formula, which left open the final status of the territories until after the envisaged period of transition, and the president added a call for a freeze on Israeli settlements on the West Bank. There has been some speculation that the proposal was made in the expectation that Arab acceptance would provoke a political crisis in Israel, resulting in a Labor-dominated cabinet willing to negotiate a return of the territories. There has also been speculation that the administration did not anticipate a total Israeli return of the territories but was laying the groundwork for negotiations in which Israel could expect to receive certain concessions. Israeli opponents charged that the plan was drawn up with the collusion of Labor party leaders, a number of whom took a more conciliatory line toward the Reagan Plan than did Prime Minister Begin and his supporters.

More likely, the Reagan administration was eager to respond to Saudi and Jordanian pleas that the United States send some positive signal to the Palestinians. Even if negotiations did not result, Washington would have made a gesture of support for the Palestinians, which might counterbalance growing resentment of the United States for its alleged complicity in the invasion of Lebanon. Thanks to the timing of the president's speech, the Saudis could go to the Arab summit without the fear that they would be denounced as U.S. lackeys. Instead, the Saudi representative posed with PLO leader Yasser Arafat as he gave the victory sign. If Reagan and Shultz expected that the two key moderate Arab states would accept the Reagan proposal shortly, however, they were disappointed. Conceivably, the proposal was made in the hope that it might lead to an eventual negotiation. The Fahd Plan, even though it differed considerably from the Reagan proposal in calling for the creation of a Palestinian state with its capital in Jerusalem and in not explicitly conceding Israel's right to exist or calling for direct negotiations with Israel, has been interpreted by administration spokesmen, such as Ambassador Richard Murphy, as showing movement toward conciliatory positions by the Arabs.[11] Even without such movement, the plan had the political benefit of distancing the United States from the policies of the Begin government and, for that matter, from the policies of the Haig period. It therefore served the purpose of shoring up U.S.-Saudi and U.S.-Jordanian relations, regardless of whether it had any chance of succeeding in moving the Arab-Israeli conflict closer to resolution.

Since that effort, the administration has claimed to be continuing to pursue the president's initiative and has conducted discussions with the leaders of Egypt, Jordan, and Israel in the hope of encouraging negotiations. Reportedly, U.S. mediation helped facilitate the 1986 meeting in Ifrane, Morocco, between Prime Minister Shimon Peres and Morocco's King Hassan II. On the surface, the major obstacle has been the general Arab insistence on the Rabat formula, according to which the PLO is considered the sole representative of the Palestinians, and the unwillingness or inability of Yasser Arafat to agree to the Jordanian terms for participation in joint negotiations, which would require the PLO to accept U.N. Resolutions 242 and 338, conceding Israel's right to exist. In view of the divisons within the PLO and within the overall Arab camp, it seems highly unlikely that a breakthrough can be anticipated, but the diplomatic effort costs the United States nothing, while demonstrating good intentions toward the Arab world.

The Rapid Deployment Force

The Reagan administration is implementing a Carter administration plan to equip a U.S. force for possible use in the defense of the West's vital interest in the

Persian Gulf oil resources. No less than its predecessor, the administration recognizes that the Western alliance, especially the European nations and Japan, depends heavily on oil imported from the Gulf, where the world's largest reserves are located. As the leader of the alliance, the United States has accepted the responsibility of protecting access to these supplies. The failure of the policy of depending on the Shah left Washington no choice but to continue to count to some extent on the Saudis for deterring regional attacks, but the United States must rely on its own resources to deter the Soviet Union or to prevent disruption of oil shipments.

The major change made in the Carter program has been to convert the Rapid Deployment Joint Task Force into a separate command, Central Command. The main reason for this was to overcome the lack of coordination and the interservice rivalry that have plagued U.S. operations in recent years, even including the disastrous 1980 Iran rescue mission. Otherwise, the Rapid Deployment Force (RDF) has been provided with fourteen pre-positioned ships and with new air transports designed to enable the immediate dispatch of a blocking force that would take control of the southern oil fields in the event of an emergency. The military strategy behind this effort recognizes that the Soviets enjoy an important tactical advantage in their proximity to the region but attempts to deter any adventurism on their part by forcing them to take into account the likelihood that they would be opposed by a U.S. force.

Whether this force is in fact a credible deterrent is a subject of considerable dispute among students of strategy,[12] but its political significance lies in the fact that it represents a more credible alternative than the immediate resort to nuclear weapons, the only other means by which this declared vital interest can presumably be defended. At the same time, it sends a strong signal to the Soviets and the Iranians that the United States would not permit a hostile takeover of the oil resources.

In June 1987 the Reagan administration announced that the United States would re-flag Kuwaiti oil tankers operating in the Gulf and provide them with naval and air defense. This decision was criticized by Democrats in Congress as well as by some military officers, who warned that by abandoning its neutrality in the Iran-Iraq war and tilting toward Iraq, the United States was inviting Iranian attack without due consideration of the full chain of consequences that might result. The president replied that he had acted to forestall the Soviets from filling a vacuum and to deter an Iranian attack. In its willingness to risk the use of force, this decision bears the stamp of the Reagan Doctrine, adding a degree of activism to the Carter Doctrine's declaration of intent that some critics complain is unnecessarily provocative and adventurous.

Resistance to Terrorism

The destruction of the U.S. Marine barracks in Lebanon by a car bomb, a deed perpetrated by shadowy terrorist forces thought to have been directed by Syrian intelligence, followed by a succession of terrorist attacks on U.S. installations and civilian and military personnel, perpetrated or guided by radical Middle Eastern movements and regimes, inspired strong statements by administration spokesmen. These warnings culminated in the air attack on Libya in April 1986 and in the steps taken to coordinate Western antiterrorism measures at the subsequent Tokyo summit. At the urging of Secretary of State Shultz, the Reagan administration has taken the view that terrorism represents a form of low-level warfare practiced not only by radical political movements but also by hostile regimes, notably Libya, often with the support of the Soviet Union. In responding to such efforts, the administration argues, it is taking the lead in sponsoring better adherence to legal norms and at the same time protecting legitimate national interests in an increasingly anarchic world system. This policy has aligned the United States much more closely than previously with Israel, which has been largely alone in advancing this argument as a rationale for striking back.

U.S. policy has had a considerable political impact. In acting decisively to intercept an Egyptian airliner carrying the hijackers of the Italian cruiseship Achille Lauro to safety and to force it to land in Italy, the administration made clear that it expected better cooperation from its allies in fighting terrorism. The Italian courts subsequently tried and convicted several of the hijackers. The terrorist actions were no doubt intended to punish the United States for supporting Israel and to reinforce the position of those in the United States and Europe who have argued that only by acknowledging the grievances of those whom the terrorists claim to represent—that is, by getting to the "root causes" of terrorism—can Americans and Europeans avoid the fate of Israel and become victims of an endless spiral of violence. This strategy had backfired. American revulsion against attacks on innocent civilians in no way responsible for government policies, coupled with anger at the attacks and humiliations inflicted on U.S. armed forces and diplomats, has led to widespread support for antiterrorist measures. At the same time, U.S. counterterror efforts have had the effect of pointedly compelling the Europeans to recognize that by seeking to conciliate Arab radicals for the sake of preserving commercial interests in the Arab world (even at the expense of breaking ranks with the United States), they risk forcing the United States to take steps that will endanger them even more and will have economic repercussions, if only in tourist revenues.

The Reagan administration has sought to capitalize on this broad hostility toward terrorism by arguing that support for the contras in Nicaragua is tantamount to resisting the spread of terrorism, because Nicaragua is likely to become the Libya of Central America. However farfetched the analogy, and however obviously contrived it is to win support for the administration's policies in Central America, it suggests a perception of affinity between the opposition to terror and a more general defense of Western interests against hostile forces, especially those supported by the Soviet Union. Again, the Reagan Doctrine's influence is not hard to discern. The fact that funds acquired by the sale of arms to Iran should have been diverted in support of the contras is another indication of the role of the Reagan Doctrine in integrating the administration's efforts in otherwise separate arenas.

The Reagan Doctrine and the Danger
of Superpower Conflict
in the Middle East

Inasmuch as the Reagan Doctrine, as it is applied to the Middle East, continues a fairly well-established pattern, it has not introduced any new and particularly unsettling or incalculable elements into the already volatile politics of the area. The Middle East has long been an arena of Cold War conflict, and it remains relatively less settled than the main arena in Europe. Both superpowers confront difficult realities in the region, which serve to inhibit or constrain their ability to manipulate conditions to their liking.

One of the realities that the United States must take into account is the obvious Soviet interest in the region. What the United States defines as the Middle East and Southwest Asia is to the Soviet Union its hinterland. Russian rulers have historically been anxious to maintain a belt of weak states in this peripheral area, and this interest is now all the more intense in view of Soviet fears of NATO at one end and of the Chinese at the other. In addition, the Soviets have reason to be concerned about the subversive impact of an upsurge of Islamic identity from Iran and Afghanistan on their own considerable Muslim populations. The possibility that another Khomeini-style regime might arise in Afghanistan, or at least one that was not prepared to take orders from Moscow, undoubtedly had much to do with the Soviet decision to occupy the country and to persist in its war against insurgent Muslims, even though the war has dragged on and inflicted considerable costs. The Soviets have a political interest is not being shut out of the politics of the area because their ability to play a major role in the Middle East is symbolic of their superpower status and their claim to parity with the United States. They have more tangible economic interests as well. As the Middle Eastern countries have modernized, they might have been Soviet customers were it not for the backwardness of the Soviet economy. If the Soviets should indeed become net oil importers, as the CIA has predicted they would as early as the 1980s, the Soviets will have an interest in preferential access to Gulf oil. Strategically, the Soviets have an interest in exerting influence in the area, if only because the area is so vital to the West. In time of conflict, they could hope to weaken the West's ability to fight a war by denying Gulf oil and interfering with the West's lines of communication.

Already the Soviets have made considerable strides in achieving their strategic objectives. The West is now at a serious logistical disadvantage due to the loss of bases in the region, whereas the Soviets have access to facilities in South Yemen,

Syria, Afghanistan, and Libya. The Soviets have considerably enhanced their naval presence near the Mediterranean and in the Indian Ocean (making use of their newly acquired base in Vietnam), they deploy naval aviation forces that could threaten Western RDF supply ships, and they also benefit strategically from the collapse of the pro-Western regime in Tehran, which has removed Iran as a potential ally of the West.

Nevertheless, the Soviets are not an overpowering threat in the region because of offsetting disadvantages. One of these is the fact that except for Syria, their allies in the region are militarily weak. Another is that the Soviets are separated from religious and nationalistic Arabs and fundamentalist Iranians by a considerable ideological chasm. Their potential role in the region is further diminished by the strong Arab desire to remain free of Soviet dictation, as is evident both in the case of Egypt and of Iraq, even though Iraq remains dependent on the Soviets. That relative weakness, coupled with the military strength of Israel and the economic strength of the pro-Western regimes in the area, makes the Soviet threat remote for the time being.

Possibilities exist, however, for the Soviets to expand their influence and control. In the event that the present Iranian regime should disintegrate, it is possible the Soviets will be tempted to invoke their 1921 treaty with Iran that gives them the right to intervene if their security is threatened.[13] Should the Tudeh forces attempt to gain power in the central and southern regions of the country, the Soviets might effectively annex northern Iran, as they tried to do immediately after World War II, and to send "volunteers" to assist farther south. A different possibility might arise if the fighting in Afghanistan should escalate and the Soviets decide to deal with it by extending the war into the Baluchistan district of Pakistan, perhaps by encouraging a separatist movement in that region. A less likely danger is that the Soviets might provide enough military aid and guarantees of protection to encourage Syria to provoke a war with Israel, in the expectation that U.S. intervention on the side of Israel would rekindle anti-Western feelings in the Arab world, especially in Egypt.

Otherwise, the major problem for the United States is the possibility that Iran will succeed in its war with Iraq, either to the extent of seizing control over the southern part of the country or in its larger ambition of toppling the regime of Saddam Hussein and replacing it with a Shiite counterpart of its own Islamic republic. In either event, Kuwait and Saudi Arabia would be seriously threatened, not necessarily by the danger of an outright invasion by Iranian forces but by efforts to foment subversive uprisings among other Islamic fundamentalists and the Shiite minorities in these countries, perhaps coupled with the sabotage of oil installations and transportation. If the Gulf Cooperation Council is unable to control these threats, either alone or with the help of Egypt and Jordan, the United States may be forced to intervene directly, in conditions that would not agree so much with the primary rationale of the RDF (that is, a Soviet invasion) but would resemble the interethnic strife of Lebanon. If the United States intervenes, the

Soviets might decide to play a more active role as well, and the possibility of a superpower confrontation in the region would emerge in the Gulf as it has in the Arab-Israeli conflict.

The danger that the superpowers could be drawn into a Middle East conflict will persist as long as their de facto allies are in conflict with each other and as long as internal instabilities encourage the superpowers to fish in troubled waters. There are further ramifications. A superpower conflict in the Middle East may not necessarily be confined to this region. Most scenarios envision one side or the other attempting a diversionary strike elsewhere, including the European theater. Nor is it certain that the conflict could be kept from escalating to a nuclear level. Both sides would be deploying dual-capable forces, and the United States in particular might have no choice but to strike at Soviet launch platforms and facilities that carry nuclear as well as conventional weapons, for in the fog or war, it would be impossible to be certain that capabilities available and deployed by both sides would not be used.

Any U.S. administration, and for that matter any Soviet government, is bound to tread warily before involving itself in the region to such an extent that it might become involved in direct combat with its primary antagonist. Nor is the motivation on either side for such an engagement so strong that it is inevitable. The Soviets support Syria, but they have shown no enthusiasm for being dragged into Syria's regional conflicts. Given their difficulties in Afghanistan, and the embarrassment of their expulsion from Egypt, they may well have second thoughts about absorbing more Muslims into the Soviet empire or about how easy the passage is from national liberation to socialism.

The Reagan administration's military buildup, and its readiness to use force against lesser targets and to intervene in Lebanon, if only in a very limited way, can be read by the Soviets, the Iranians, and the Syrians only as an indication that any attempt to threaten vital Western interests would not be met with appeasement. President Carter's accommodationist policies—including his reported veto of Sadat's plan to attack Qaddafi[14]—may have left U.S. enemies in more doubt. The rhetoric of the Reagan administration and its actual behavior suggest that the Reagan Doctrine applies to the Middle East as it does elsewhere.

Doctrine and Flexibility

The Reagan administration has thus followed in the footsteps of its predecessors, if with a somewhat bolder stride. Even if President Reagan took more risks in Lebanon than his predecessor might have, the U.S. commitment was still quite circumscribed and hardly an illustration of the cowboy or Rambo style his critics have often decried. Only in its use of force against Libya, as a response to state-sponsored terrorism, has this administration taken an unprecedented course. In the past, however, terrorism against U.S. interests was more sporadic and less clearly state sponsored. These policies have been carried out in ways that reflect the particular stamp of the Reagan administration, with its overriding concern with the Soviet challenge, its readiness to use force in defense of Western interests and principles (as defined by American conservatives), and its willingness to support states and insurgent movements whose aims are compatible with those of the United States. The unsuccessful arms-for-hostages negotiation with Iranian officials was not an application of the Reagan Doctrine. As the Tower Commission noted, it "ran directly counter to the Administration's own policies . . . " and resulted from inconsistency in policy and the president's delegation of authority to subordinates who were left free to operate without proper supervision or review.[15]

So long as the Soviet war in Afghanistan grinds on, as the Iran-Iraq conflict persists without decisive results, and as OPEC is unable to inflict severe economic hardships on the West, the United States can be content with the status quo in the region. The real test of whether the Reagan Doctrine makes a major difference would come only if the present uneasy balance were to be violently disrupted in such a way that would jeopardize the U.S. and Western position in the region. So far, however, U.S. policy in the region under Reagan has been to avoid committing U.S. forces in combat roles while signalling a clear resolve to do so if necessary. Doctrinal commitments have been tempered by pragmatism so as to minimize the likelihood of crises that would require costly and dangerous action in support of these commitments. The intervention in Lebanon was nearly one in which ideology triumphed over caution, but in the end caution prevailed. The overture to Iran was a botched effort to put pragmatic considerations ahead of principles.

Despite a tendency to weave between dogmatic statements of doctrine and more erratic behavior in practice, the Reagan administration's policies in the Middle East are less inconsistent and muddled than they may appear to critics.[16] They reflect a recognition that U.S. interests in the region are multiple and best served by policies that are bound to appear inconsistent. The charge of inconsistency, it is worth remembering, has also been directed at previous administration.s[17] Too much consistency should not be expected of any U.S. administration operating in this volatile region. Although the Middle East's energy resources are vital to the security of the West, and although the region's trouble spots are potential flashpoints for conflict with the Soviet Union, the area has not yet acquired the same saliency for U.S. policy as Europe has had since the end of World War II. In the Middle East spheres of influence between East and West are not as well defined as they are in Europe, and both superpowers, far from being as committed to defending their allies as they are in Europe, are wary of being drawn into local conflicts by client states whose interests they do not fully share. The very diversity of U.S. interests in the region is in itself enough to guarantee the appearance of inconsistency. There especially, as Abba Eban has perceptively noted, U.S. diplomacy "recoils from sharp, exclusive alignments and thus ends up distributing displeasure across a broad field."[18]

Domestic considerations also contribute to the appearance of inconsistency.

Differences of perspective arise within any U.S. administration due to conflicting bureaucratic responsibilities and interests. Clashes between the State and Defense departments, between the NSC and the departments, or between career diplomats with ties to the Middle East and political appointees more attuned to domestic sentiment are endemic. Since discipline in the executive branch is traditionally lax, these differences are apt to be magnified by the media until events compel some action by the president to end the confusion for the time being. Because of the constitutional separation of powers, any administration must anticipate congressional reactions and trim its sails accordingly. Under these circumstances, a perfect consistency would be an altogether unrealistic expectation.[19]

Judged by a more tolerant and realistic standard, the Reagan administration's policies toward the Middle East are well within the parameters of what can be expected. They follow a by now well-established pattern that reflects a broad consensus of U.S. interests and values, but with an edge and coloration stamped with the ideological conceptions of the president and his closest advisors. If these policies have not always been implemented successfully, it is in part because conditions in this conflict-ridden region rarely provide neat opportunities for the pursuit of underlying interests and values. In addition, the relative marginality of the conflicts to the central concerns of U.S. foreign policy has made both the administration and Congress reluctant to commit the resources that would make greater control possible but that would also require deeper involvement. In contrast with Central America and arms control negotiations with the Soviet Union, the Reagan administration in the Middle East has been able to live up to its ideological commitments without rupturing the domestic bipartisan consensus in foreign policy because it has chosen to act firmly, but with restraint, in defense of generally acknowledged national interests. Except for the abortive attempt to stabilize Lebanon, it has been content to maintain the status quo in the region by making clear its intention of supporting its allies and intervening directly if necessary against Soviet threats. This administration has broken with precedent by speaking loudly and carrying a big stick, but so far it has refrained from using the stick indiscriminately.

Notes

1. The term is used and examined in Stephen S. Rosenfeld, "The Guns of July," *Foreign Affairs* (Spring 1986), pp. 698–714; Jeane J. Kirkpatrick, "The Reagan Doctrine and U.S. Foreign Policy" (Washington: The Heritage Foundation, 1985), and "Implementing the Reagan Doctrine," National Security Record No. 82 (Washington: The Heritage Foundation, August 1985); and Robert W. Tucker, "Intervention and the Reagan Doctrine" (New York: The Council on Religion and International Affairs, 1985).

2. Quoted in Rosenfeld, "The Guns of July," p. 702.

3. See *Ibid., passim.*

4. In January 1982 public approval of President Reagan's performance in office, as measured by a Gallup Poll, was lower than that of his six most immediate predecessors at a comparable period in office (49 percent approve, 40 percent disapprove). In October 1982, during the Lebanon crisis, 40 percent of those polled disapproved of his handling of the "Middle East problem," while 36 percent approved and 24 percent expressed no opinion. By January 1986 ratings of his performance in office had risen: 64 percent approved and 27 percent disapproved. The retaliatory air attack on Lybia in April 1986 was approved by 71 percent and disapproved by 21 percent. Sources: *The Gallup Report*, No. 203 (August 1982), p. 23; No. 207 (December 1982), p. 26; Nos. 244–245 (January–February 1986), p. 22; No. 247 (April 1986), p. 3.

5. Alexander M. Haig, Jr., *Caveat: Realism, Reagan and Foreign Policy* (New York: Macmillan, 1984), p. 170.

6. Ze'ev Schiff and Ehud Ya'ari, *Israel's Lebanon War*, trans. Ina Friedman (New York: Simon and Schuster, 1984), p. 31.

7. *Ibid.*, p. 75.

8. Haig, *Caveat*, p. 317.

9. *Ibid.*, p. 342.

10. Richard W. Murphy, "Arms Sales Policies Toward the Middle East," Current Policy No. 822 (Washington: Department of State Bureau of Public Affairs, 1986), p. 2.

11. *Ibid.*, p. 3.

12. For critiques of the concept, see Jeffrey Record, *The Rapid Deployment Force and U.S. Military Intervention in the Persian Gulf* (Cambridge, MA, and Washington: Institute for Foreign Policy Analysis, 1981); "The RDF: Is the Pentagon Kidding?" *Washington Quarterly*, Spring 1981, pp. 41–51; and Joshua M. Epstein, "Soviet Vulnerabilities in Iran and the RDF Deterrent," *International Security* 6 (Fall 1981), pp. 126–158. For a balanced and comprehensive assessment, see Thomas L. McNaugher, *Arms and Oil: U.S. Military Strategy and the Persian Gulf* (Washington: Brookings Institution, 1985). See also Kenneth N. Waltz, "A Strategy for the Rapid Deployment Force," *International Security* 5 (Spring 1981), pp. 69–73; Albert Wohlstetter, "Half-Wars and Half-Policies in the Persian Gulf," in W. Scott Thompson, ed., *National Security in the 1980s: From Weakness to Strength* (New Brunswick and London: Transaction Books, 1980), pp. 123–171; and Sanford Lakoff, "Power and Limit: U.S. Strategic Doctrine in the Middle East," in Aurel Braun, ed., *The Superpower Conflict in the Middle East* (Boulder, Co: Westview Press, 1987).

13. See Shahram Chubin, "L'Union Sovietique et le Golfe: une Stratégie indirecte," in B. Kodmani, ed., *Quelle Sécurité pour le Golfe?* (Paris: Institut Français des Relations Internationales, 1984), p. 157.

14. See Michael Ledeen, "Fighting Back," *Commentary* 80 (August 1985), p. 29.

15. John Tower, Edmund Muskie, and Brent Scowcroft, *The Tower Commission Report* (New York: Bantam Books, 1987), p. 62.

16. See especially Steven L. Spiegel, *The Other Arab-Israeli Conflict: Making America's Middle East Policy from Truman to Reagan* (Chicago and London: University of Chicago Press, 1985), pp. 428–429.

17. See Mark Heller, ed., *The Middle East Military Balance 1984* (Tel Aviv: Tel Aviv University, Jaffee Center for Strategic Studies, 1984), p. 24.

18. Abba Eban, *The New Diplomacy: International Affairs in the Modern Age* (New York: Random House, 1983), p. 215. Eban adds, "On the face of it, this seems to add up to vagueness and irresolution. On deeper analysis, these versatile attitudes reflect a desire

to be universally present across the entire range of Middle Eastern realities and interests. America seeks a relationship not with a part of the Middle East but with the whole of it. Nothing is completely written off" (p. 216).

19. For a similar conclusion, see Richard Rosecrance, "Objectives of U.S. Middle East Policy," in Haim Shaked and Itamar Rabinovitch, eds., *The Middle East and the United States: Perceptions and Policies* (New Brunswick and London: Transaction Books, 1980), pp. 31–52.

9

Peacetime Presence and Wartime Engagement: The Soviet Case

Efraim Karsh

T his chapter seeks to analyze the essence of Soviet military support as a foreign policy instrument in the Middle East and to determine its components and principal features. It does not address the overall political considerations that dictate the timing and scope of military support or its relative position regarding other foreign policy instruments, such as economic aid. Instead it purports to define the two components of military support, peacetime presence and wartime engagnement, as well as to examine the interrelationships between them and to forecast some future trends.

Military Engagement: Definition and Characteristics

Soviet peacetime military presence in the Third World can be manifested either in the deployment of advisory missions within the local armed forces or in the maintenance of independent units within the respective client states (or alternatively, in international waters).

The first type of presence constitutes an integral part of the Soviet Union's military aid programs to its local clients and has nothing to do with direct Soviet military objectives. Arms deals between the Soviet Union and its Third World clients account not only for the supply of arms and military equipment but also for the provision of technical and advisory services to facilitate the absorption of weapons systems. Since the sole objective of the advisory mission is to bridge the gap between the sophistication of the systems supplied and the technological level of the local armed forces, it is only natural that the magnitude of this mission is a function of the size of the local army, the quantities of weapons it absorbs, and its operative and technological level. The larger an army, the more weapons it

The Author would like to thank Professor Yaacov Ro'i, who read an earlier draft, for his helpful comments.

procures; the lower its operative level, the more extensive the technical and advisory aid it requires. Consent on the part of a client to accept a vast Soviet military advisory system extending down to the lower ranks is clearly the result of political considerations. Once such political readiness is expressed, however, the size of the relevant advisory mission is determined solely by the aforementioned variables rather than by politically motivated factors.

The peacetime presence of independent Soviet units in a local state may often be one of the benefits that the Soviet Union derives by supplying military aid—a gain in the superpower competition for assets in the Third World. Even in those few cases where such a presence was, most uncharacteristically, intended primarily to aid the client state (for instance, Egypt in 1970–1972, when it was by and large an extension of Soviet intervention during the War of Attrition), it served the strategic needs of the Soviet Union as well. The Soviets had maintenance installations at Port Said and Alexandria for their Mediterranean Squadron, as well as twenty aircraft (*Tupolov*-16s and *Ilyushim*-28s), developed in Egypt which carried out surveillance flights over the U.S. Sixth Fleet. To these may be added some Soviet-piloted MiG-25 aircraft for Soviet surveillance and aerial photography missions.

Both forms of peacetime presence may be exploited for military support during wartime. For the purposes of this paper, all the kinds of military support furnished to regional clients by Soviet advisory missions deployed in the local armed forces will be defined as *military involvement*. *Military intervention*, both actual and demonstrative,[1] refers to armed activities performed by independent Soviet units on behalf of a local client. Military intervention can be manifested in a wide spectrum of activities, ranging from shows of force designed to fulfill deterrent functions, through defensive/supportive missions such as intelligence gathering and electronic warfare activities, to active engagement in the fighting (such as defense of naval routes or a naval blockade).

Needless to say, military intervention indicates a higher degree of willingness on the part of the Soviet Union to support the local state. The existence of an advisory mission in the local army and its participation in the fighting is a relatively subtle means of support and does not imply a direct Soviet engagement in the military and strategic affairs of the particular region. By contrast, a peacetime independent presence and, much more so, wartime intervention create a direct confrontation between Soviet regular units and a Third World state; as such, at both the regional and global levels, they have far greater political and strategic implications than military involvement.

Soviet Peacetime Presence in the Middle East

The peacetime presence of Soviet military advisors in the postwar Middle East predates the positioning of independent units in the area. Since this form of military presence is directly related to arms supplies, it was only natural that the establishment of procurement relations with Middle Eastern countries would be followed by the provision of advisory support. Indeed, the 1955 Czech-Egyptian arms deal (known as the Czechoslovak Deal, since Czechoslovakia was the official cosignatory to this agreement) led to the establishment of a modest, yet permanent, Soviet advisory mission (totaling some three hundred personnel) within the Egyptian armed forces. Similarly, arms deals between the Soviets and a number of Arab countries (Syria, Algeria, Yemen, and post-1958 Iraq) in the late 1950s and early 1960s were followed by the provision of advisory support.

Until the 1967 Six Day War, as the Arab armed forces remained relatively small, the size of Soviet advisory missions deployed within the respective client states was rather modest and on average did not exceed a few hundred. The seriousness of the 1967 Arab defeat and the consequent acceleration of the arms race in the Middle East considerably increased Arab military dependence on the Soviet Union and enabled the latter to deepen its military presence in the local armies. A Soviet advisory mission stationed in Egypt, for example, grew from a few hundred advisors in mid–1967 to approximately 2,500 by 1968. This mission permeated all branches of the Egyptian armed forces, operating at every air and naval base and every training installation. Soviet advisors were attached to Egyptian commanders, from the highest echelons (personal advisors to the defense minister and the chief of staff) down to batalion commanders. Soviet advisory missions in Syria, Libya, and Iraq underwent a similar expansion during the 1970s.

To date permanent Soviet independent presence in the Middle East has been confined to the naval field. To be sure, there was an independent presence in both Egypt and Syria that had little or nothing to do with Soviet naval affairs; but this presence was temporary, on an ad hoc basis, and directly related to a regional crisis. Once the crisis had abated, it was removed.

Since 1964 the Soviet Union has maintained a permanent naval presence in the Mediterranean. Until the Six Day War, however, Soviet naval strength in the area reained relatively limited and averaged some eight vessels. Afterward, the size of the Soviet Mediterranean Squadron (Fifth Eskadra) grew steadily until there were at least thirty-five vessels in the Mediterranean: ten to fifteen warships (cruisers, destroyers, frigates, and escort ships), two to three amphibious ships, eight to nine submarines, and ten to fifteen auxiliary vessels. Until March 1976 Egypt provided the main Soviet foothold in the Mediterranean, offering the Soviets repair, replenishment, and maintenance facilities for their vessels and a base for conducting maritime patrol missions against the Sixth Fleet. After President Anwar Sadat unilaterally ordered the Soviets out of Egyptian ports, they were forced to look for adequate substitutes. This search was only partially successful, and new Soviet port services in other countries (such as Syria and Yugoslavia) are extremely limited and in no way compare to those the Soviets enjoyed in Egypt.

It is noteworthy in this connection that the establishment of a Soviet naval presence in the Mediterranean was not a new phenomenon. Control of the Dardanelles in order to provide an outlet for naval activities in the rest of the world, as well as to block the passage of European warships into the Black Sea, was a long-standing Russian strategic interest in the Middle East, and it led to the establishment of a naval presence in the Mediterranean in the late eighteenth century. The Russians also fought naval battles in the Ionian Sea (1798–1799) and near Mount Athos (1807) and participated in the Battle of Navarino in 1827. After the Bolshevik Revolution, Soviet vessels used to pay regular calls at Turkish, Greek, and Italian ports, and during the 1950s, until the break in Soviet-Albanian relations, Soviet submarines were stationed in Albania.

Nonetheless, the Soviet naval presence in the Mediterranean since the mid-1960s has been different from previous naval activities in that it has been permanent and has reflected an overall politico-strategic design. Since the early 1960s the Soviet navy, under the command of Admiral Sergei Gorshkov, has strived to maintain a worldwide peacetime naval deployment that would enable it to respond quickly, at least demonstratively, to global or regional crisis situations in any part of the world. According to Gorshkov's philosophy, the main advantage of the navy over the other Soviet armed services as an instrument of foreign policy lies in the fact that its peacetime presence is in international waters, whereas any ground, aerial, or air defense presence must, by its very nature, be physically manifested on foreign soil. As he put it:

> Thus, the fleet has always been an instrument of the policy of states, an important aid to diplomacy in peacetime. To this corresponded the very nature of a navy, the properties peculiar to it, namely—high combat readiness, mobility and ability in short time to concentrate its forces in selected areas of the ocean. In addition, the neutrality of the waters of the World Ocean means that the forces of fleets can be moved forward and concentrated without violating the principles of international law, and without providing the other side with formal grounds for protest or other forms of counteraction.[2]

Soviet Engagement in Middle Eastern Wars

The transformation of the Soviet Navy into an ocean-going fleet coincided with a growing Soviet willingness to expand its military commitments to belligerent Third World clients. Until the mid-1960s the Soviets did not regard military involvement and intervention in local wars as a viable foreign policy instrument and viewed such wars as conflicts that only the imperialists engaged in, in pursuit of their strategic goals. In the late Stalin era the avoidance of Soviet participation in local wars reflected the "two camps" doctrine, which rejected military support for nonsocialist regimes. During the Khrushchev and the early Brezhnev eras, this abstention resulted from the Soviet belief that such military intervention would inevitably escalate into a world war.

After 1966 the Soviet doctrinal posture regarding local wars underwent a profound, though not precipitous, change. Soviet military thought gradually leaned toward increased acceptance of the risks of local wars. The American experience in Vietnam, coupled with the Soviet attainment of nuclear strategic parity in the late 1960s and early 1970s, greatly increased Soviet self-confidence and decreased Soviet fears of the escalatory potential of local wars. The inherent dangers of local wars seemed less menacing, since the considerable growth in Soviet military power on the one hand and a perceived reduced inclination on the part of the United States to become emgaged in local wars on the other hand were believed to prevent such wars from turning into a world war.[3]

This conceptual shift found its first operational expression in the 1967 Six Day War. Indeed, this war was a landmark in the evolution of Soviet military intervention in local wars, as it was the first time the Soviets employed their independent peacetime presence on behalf of a belligerent Third World client, mainly in naval and ground demonstrative activities. In the naval sphere, the Soviets augmented their Mediterranean deployment and increased their surveillance activities against U.S. naval forces. Soviet ground intervention manifested itself in messages delivered to the Israeli and U.S. administration threatening necessary action, including military, unless Israel halted its advance into Syria. The Soviet threat was taken seriously by the United States, which responded by sending a naval force to the Syrian coast and, simultaneously, by pressing the Israelis to halt their military operations immediately.

Three years later, during the Egyptian-Israeli War of Attrition, Soviet interventionary policy took another step when, for the first time, Soviet troops participated in significant numbers in a Third World interstate war. Following a series of Israeli raids against military targets deep in Egyptian territory, President Nasser paid a secret visit to Moscow in January 1970 and obtained a Soviet commitment to defend Egypt's airspace, which was put into service later that year. The Soviet buildup in Egypt, which consisted of some 15,000 troops manning 75 to 85 independent surface-to-air missile sites and about 150 Soviet-piloted MiG-21s, played an important role in the course of the war. On April 6, 1970, Israel halted its deep strikes, and on 7 August, a ceasefire went into effect—although not before Israeli combat aircraft had shot down four Soviet-piloted warplanes.

Soviet military support during the War of Attrition was not restricted to aerial and air defense intervention but also included arms shipments, participation of Soviet advisors in combat, and a naval presence in Alexandria and Port Said, designed to deter Israeli air raids on these ports.

Once the precedent was set, the Soviet Union did not find it too difficult to repeat it in future wars. Indeed, the 1973 October war precipitated the first massive Soviet resupply effort to a Third World belligerent in the course of full hostilities. By and large, Soviet military engagement during this war resembled the Soviet engagement in the War of Attrition and comprised both military involvement and military intervention, including the participation of Soviet advisors in the fighting, demonstrative activities by the Soviet Mediterranean Squadron, and the dispatch of air defense units to Syria (which were quietly withdrawn soon after the war). In addition, the Soviets placed their airborne units on alert and threatened to dispatch fighting units to the Egyptian front if Israel did not immediately halt its advance.

This interventionary mode was repeated in a milder form during the 1982 Lebanon war. At that time the Soviet Union warned Israel that the Middle East "is an area lying in close proximity to the southern borders of the Soviet Union, and that developments there cannot help affecting the interests of the USSR." Therefore, the Soviet Union was determined to support its Arab clients "in deeds rather than words." This warning was accompanied by the movement of a considerable naval task force off the Lebanese and Syrian coasts and the partial alert of the airborne divisions in the Soviet Union.[5] Moreover, in an attempt to restore the credibility of its air defense weaponry, which had been seriously tarnished by the Israeli Air Force (IAF) during the war, the Soviets deployed two SAM–5 brigades in Syria in late 1982.

Cautious Wartime Support

The growing scope and intensity of Soviet wartime military engagements in Third World wars in general and in Middle Eastern wars in particular led many analysts to conclude that "the Soviet Union generally has proved a reliable, effective patron-protector," demonstrating "an impressive capability and relentless determination to intervene on behalf of clients who request assistance."[6] This relentless determination was expressed in Soviet preparedness "to commit whatever forces are necessary to save a client from defeat . . . regardless of the possibility of confrontation with the United States.[7]

The historical record can hardly support such a view. Although rising steadily since the late 1960s, Soviet military engagements in Middle Eastern wars proved to be reactive and defensive rather than aggressive and offensive, cautious and incremental rather than forceful and relentless. Even in those cases where the Soviet Union decided to throw its military support behind a belligerent client, it nonetheless revealed an unequivocal reluctance to risk a direct confrontation with any regional forces, let alone the United States. Indeed, the American factor has always played a crucial role in Soviet calculations. By postulating that military intervention in local wars does not necessarily lead to world war, Soviet military thinking still did not preclude such an outcome, and a direct superpower clash was the type of conflict that the Soviet Union was eager to avoid.

The influence that an anticipated U.S. response had on Soviet restraint is perhaps best illustrated by the Soviet Union's decision to introduce air defense units into Egypt during the War of Attrition. According to Egyptian sources, the initiative for the unprecedented nature and scale of this Soviet intervention emanated not from the Soviets but from President Nasser, who during his secret visit to Moscow, confronted the Soviet leaders with the unexpected demand that they take responsibility for the air defense of Egypt.

The immediate Soviet reaction was negative. Brezhnev pointed out that the placing of independent Soviet units in Egypt "would be a step with serious international implications. . . . It would provide all the makings of a crisis between the Soviet Union and the United States, and I don't know if we are justified in taking it."[8]

The Egyptian president remained unimpressed. "As far as I can see," he said, "you are not prepared to help us in the way that America helps Israel. This means that there is only one course open to me: I shall go back to Egypt and I shall tell the people . . . that the time has come for me to step down and hand over to a pro-American President. If I cannot save them, somebody else will have to do it."[9]

Having realized Nasser's uncompromising posture, the Politburo convened for a special session and eventually decided to dispatch air defense units to Egypt. It was still not eager to do so, however, and Brezhnev made certain that the Egyptian leader understood the gravity of the decision: "Comrade Nasser," he said, "the Soviet Union has today taken a decision fraught with grave consequences. It is a decision *unlike any we have ever taken before.* It will need your help in carrying it, and it will call for restraint on your part."[10]

Soviet actions during the October 1973 war provide another vivid illustration of their awareness of the connection between Soviet Middle Eastern policy and the state of Soviet-American relations. Not only was the Soviet Union not prepared to "jeopardize détente with the United States if need be in order to safeguard a prized Third World client,"[11] but its behavior prior to and during the war reflected an unequivocal desire to avoid any escalation that could lead to a superpower confrontation. Hence, the Soviet Union took considerable pains to prevent the Arabs (particularly Egypt) from going to war.

As early as 1971 the Soviets had manipulated arms supplies to Egypt with the aim of disrupting Egyptian war preparations. Ultimately, in July 1972, this caused an open rift between the two countries, when President Sadat unilaterally expelled fifteen thousand Soviet military personnel who had been sent to Egypt during the War of Attrition. Having learned that withholding supplies was a double-edged sword, the Soviets abandoned this tactic in favor of diplomatic means. They employed a variety of mechanisms to prevent the eruption of hostilities in the Middle East[12]—from attempts at persuading their Arab allies to discreet and public warnings to the U.S. administration of the impending war.

Once the October war did break out, the Soviet Union, to its dismay, found it had no other choice but to throw its unequivocal support behind its Arab clients. Yet Soviet military engagement in that war— one of the more prominent examples of wide-scale Soviet wartime efforts—was cautious and incremental. The initial Soviet reaction to the outbreak of hostilities was purely demonstrative, consisting of the augmentation of the Mediterranean Squadron and the concentration of naval power in the eastern Mediterranean. When the initial Arab offensive was checked by the Israeli Defense Force (IDF), with the attacking forces suffering heavy material losses, the Soviets initiated a massive airlift on their behalf.[13] Only after the Syrian air defense system faced serious operational difficulties did the Soviet Union dispatch regular air defense units to the Latakia and Damascus areas. Finally, when Israel continued to advance despite a cease-fire agreement and the Egyptian Third Army was on the verge of surrender, Moscow threatened to send airborne units to the Egyptian battle zone. Indeed, this threat is commonly regarded as a major indication of the Soviet Union's willingness to "commit whatever forces are necessary" to save a client from defeat.

Such a belief, nevertheless, fails to take a note of two fundamental facts. First, it was only after the U.S. administration had categorically rejected an Egyptian appeal to send a joint U.S.-Soviet task force to police the cease-fire that Brezhnev dispatched a very urgent message to President Nixon, in which he implied the possibility of a unilateral Soviet intervention. Moreover, even this message reflected a clear Soviet preference for joint superpower action, as it urged the United States to join the Soviet Union in the dispatch of contingents to Egypt. It is conceivable, therefore, that had the United States accepted the Soviet offer of a joint action—a step that probably would have halted the Israeli advance—the Soviets might have foregone their threat.

Second, it seems most unlikely that the Soviets seriously entertained the idea of sending airborne units to Egypt, since doctrinally and operationally such airborne units were not fitted to this sort of combat role. According to Soviet military doctrine, the primary mission of airborne units is to "solve operational-tactical problems in enemy rear areas and assure continuous action throughout the entire depth of the enemy defense." In order to accomplish this, these divisions must "perform independently such missions as capture and retention or destruction of nuclear missiles, air force and naval bases, and other important objectives deep within the theaters of military operations."[14] These units are not intended for front-line combat and certainly not for fighting independently and without the support of armored and mechanized units. Airborne landings, in the Soviet view, are useful supplements to existing military operations but cannot be regarded as an independent form of operation. In addition, if one considers the battlefield conditions during the October war, particularly total Israeli air superiority, it is almost impossible to imagine the dispatch of airborne units to the front.

From an operational point of view, the Soviets also must have been well aware that the firepower of their airborne units (each of which includes only ninety BMD armored personnel carriers) was considerably inferior to the IDFs armored and mechanized divisions (each of which comprises some three hundred tanks).

Obviously, should the Soviets ever decide to dispatch ground forces to a combat zone in order to make a military impact on a local war fought between large modern armies, they would not send airborne but rather mechanized or armored units. Given this fact, the implied Soviet threats to employ their airborne units on behalf of their Arab clients in the 1967 and 1973 wars should be viewed as a skillful manipulation of the U.S. administration. In both cases, the Soviet threats generated the desired U.S. response without challenging their credibility. The United States acted to head off the possibility of Soviet military intervention, while at the same time it applied pressure on Israel to stop fighting. Hence, the Soviet Union was able to appear a reliable patron and influence the course of two local wars through purely demonstrative means when real intervention was clearly beyond its reach.

The preceding discussion clearly indicates that the Soviet Union is far from willing to "commit whatever forces are necessary" to save a client from defeat. Not only has the Soviet Union always refrained from sending ground forces to participate in a Middle Eastern war (or in any Third World interstate conflict), but this reluctance has repeatedly prompted the Soviets to act to prevent their local clients from resorting to armed force. As already indicated, the Soviets tried to prevent the outbreak of the October war by manipulating arms supplies to Egypt and Syria; similarly, it has coercively employed its peacetime military support to check both the growing direct Syrian intervention in Lebanon in mid-1976, and the Iraqi invasion of Iran in September 1980.

Once hostilities broke out, however, the Soviet Union has found it hard, if not impossible, to remain passive and watch its client suffer a military defeat. At the same time, Soviet wartime support has so far been very cautious and incremental, and the Soviets have been very careful to avoid any intervention before they have utilized their peacetime military presence—that is, advisory missions deployed in the Arab armies and the Fifth Eskadra. Soviet military intervention, with the exception of the naval sphere, has never occurred unless the local client was on the verge of a major defeat or the local regime was in imminent danger. Hence, Soviet military intervention in the Egyptian-Israeli War of Attrition did not take place until Nasser was on the verge of resignation; similarly, Soviet air defense units were sent to Syria during the October war and after the 1982 Lebanon war only after the incompetence of the Syrian air defense system had been unequivocally exposed.

Even the commitment of naval forces and advisory missions has been carried out in a most circumspect manner, reflecting a desire to help the local client cut its losses and hold back (or deter) the opposing forces rather than go on the offensive. First, one can detect a clear Soviet preference for demonstrative over actual intervention. Since the Soviet Union first committed its navy to demonstrative activities in the Six Day War, Soviet naval forces have intervened demonstratively in six out of eight Middle Eastern wars, compared with three instances of actual intervention.

Second, the Soviets took care to avoid involving their advisors in frontline fighting. During the October war, for example, Soviet advisors and technicians helped the Syrian Army by repairing military equipment damaged in the fighting, by driving tanks from Latakia and Tartus to Damascus, and by advising Syrian commanders in rear headquarters and at its air defense units. Soviet advisors in frontline units were withdrawn.

Finally, Soviet advisors have never been involved in war operations outside the local client's territory. During the 1970 Syrian-Jordanian war, for example, the Soviets hurried to withdraw their advisors from the Syrian armored units that had invaded Jordan and made sure that the United States was well aware of this fact. This same scenario has repeated itself in all Middle Eastern wars initiated by Soviet clients during the 1970s and the early 1980s. Soviet advisors did not accompany the Egyptian and Syrian units that attacked Israel in October 1973 (despite the fact that the fighting took place in Syrian and Egyptian territories that had been occupied in 1967); neither did they accompany the South Yemeni units that invaded North Yemen in 1979 or the Iraqi forces invading Iran. The Soviet Union also has refrained from any involvement in the Syrian military intervention in Lebanon. Soviet advisors did not accompany Syrian units that invaded Lebanon in June 1976, and the Soviet Union has strictly avoided any permanent presence of its advisors in Lebanon. Consequently, no Soviet advisors were involved in combat during the 1982 Lebanon war.

Future Trends

What does this state of affairs indicate about possible Soviet engagement in future Middle Eastern wars? As most types of military involvement and intervention have already been attempted in previous Middle Eastern conflicts and have not proved to be too costly, either regionally or globally, and as there is in principle a doctrinal willingness to accept the risks of local wars, these patterns might well be repeated (though not too enthusiastically), depending on the specific operational requirements. Hence, the Soviets can be expected to employ their peacetime military presence on behalf of their clients in a variety of cases:

1. Soviet advisors deployed within the local armed forces will probably continue to support regular operational activities, such as the reassembly of aerial and air defense weapons systems delivered to the local army or the operation of control and communications equipment, and air defense systems. It can be assumed, however, that since the Soviets are unwilling to see their advisors taken prisoner, those advisors attached to ground formations would, in wartime, be withdrawn from their units, except perhaps for senior officers who would not participate in frontline activities.

2. The Fifth Eskadra will continue to arrange demonstrative (and, if necessary, limited actual) activities on behalf of its local clients. Such activities might include the securing of sea routes from the Black Sea to the respective client states; the maintenance of a demonstrative presence within the combat zone to counterba-

lance possible U.S. shows of force and to limit the maneuvering range of local opposing forces; and the performance of intelligence-gathering and electronic countermeasures (ECM) activities.

3. The Soviet Union might supply its clients with all necessary arms and war materiel, as well as dispatch Soviet air defense, electronic warfare, and perhaps even aerial units to the battle zone if needed. But it is doubtful the Soviets would be willing to send ground units to participate in such a war. Not only could such a step—which would constitute a major turning point in Soviet strategic conceptions and actual conduct—be perceived by the United States as a deviation from the accepted rules of the game, but it also would involve serious logistical and operational problems. As shown earlier, it is only through the dispatch of armored or mechanized (but not airborne) units to the combat zone that the Soviet Union can hope to have a real military impact on the course of a war. It would, nevertheless, take between one and three months for such units to reach full strength in the area, depending on their envisaged mission (that is, offensive or defensive). This time period would increase significantly if the Soviets were simultaneously occupied with delivering large quantities of military equipment to the local client and if the opposing forces were attempting to hinder this delivery. Given the relatively short duration of most Middle Eastern wars of movement[15]—the only time ground intervention would be relevant—it is likely that hostilities would be over long before the Soviet emplacements could be completed.

Hence, even in the most extreme circumstance, where the Soviet Union might see no alternative to rescuing its client regime save sending ground forces to the combat zone, it will still strive to limit this type of intervention to the lowest possible level and to avoid any direct confrontation with the local opposing forces. A token force of up to a division is the most far-reaching undertaking the Soviet Union is likely to commit in a Middle Eastern war.

Summary and Conclusions

Interestingly enough, despite their insufficient means for projecting significant armed, particularly ground, forces across long distances within a short period of time (even the 1970 deployment of the Soviet air defense division in Egypt took approximately three months), the Soviets have not been eager to establish a permanent independent peacetime presence in client states that could significantly facilitate wartime intervention. Instead, the Soviet Union has consistently sought to limit such a presence to the barest minimum. Thus, for example, as long as the Soviet Union could rely on naval and aerial facilities in Egypt, it did not seek to construct and obtain additional complexes in the Mediterranean. Only when they were denied access to these facilities did the Soviets initiate an extensive search for adequate substitutes.

This circumscribed approach casts some doubt on the belief that the Soviet Union has persistently sought—at least since the late 1960s—to maximize its peacetime presence in the Middle East. If anything, it reflects an underlying Soviet skepticism regarding the value of an independent peacetime presence. On the one hand, the Soviet Union appears to have been fully aware of the fact that "an extensive presence is no assurance of influence. . . . A presence is important in assuring access to decision-makers, but access, taken by itself, is no guarantee of influence."[16] Apart from its awareness of the limited value of peacetime presence as a tool of influence, Moscow has not failed to recognize the potentially adverse consequences of such a presence. The existence of an advisory mission within a local army has more than once become a major source of friction between the Soviet Union and the respective Arab client state; the presence of independent Soviet units on local soil, moreover, has given rise to feelings of hostility and frustration among local circles who felt that their country's sovereignty had been compromised. Furthermore, by deploying independent units in a Middle Eastern country, the Soviet Union runs the risk of becoming a direct party in a regional conflict, thus pressuring the United States to respond in kind, especially if one of its allies is threatened by Soviet intervention. Such a development would undoubtedly "provide all the makings of a superpower crisis," to use Brezhnev's words, and it would be the Soviets' least desired outcome.

This explains Soviet reluctance to install air defense units in Egypt in 1970, as well as Soviet uneasiness about keeping them in place once the War of Attrition ended. Had it not been for the public humiliation attending Sadat's unilateral expulsion of Soviet personnel from Egypt in July 1972, Moscow would have been relieved to avoid the perils of keeping these units in Egypt. Indeed, Soviet air defense units that appeared in Syria during the October war and after the 1982 Lebanon war were quickly and quietly withdrawn, after having handed control over to the Syrians.

The only exception to this rule has been the naval presence in the Mediterranean, which, being deployed in international waters, has not involved a presence on sovereign territory. To be sure, the maintenance of a peacetime naval deployment necessitates some access to onshore support facilities and, at time, even military bases. The political cost of such bases, however, is far less than that of any other type of independent presence in a client state. Soviet naval facilities do not constitute the fighting element of their naval presence, which is concentrated at sea, but rather its logistical and supportive component. As such they do not pose any direct threat to either regional or U.S. forces.

Yet despite the institutionalization of onshore facilities as an accepted behavior within the superpower rules of the game, the Soviet Union has not only tended to limit this type of presence to the lowest possible level but has occasionally mooted the idea of a nuclear free zone in the Mediterranean and the withdrawal of foreign fleets from the area (this last suggestion having been made in March 1986, in light of the U.S.-Libyan clashes). Notwithstanding the extreme unlikelihood that the Soviet Union would abandon its historical ambitions in the Mediterranean and would leave Western naval presence there uncontested, the Soviet proposals seem to reflect the essentially defensive nature of the Fifth Eskadra. In these circumstances some U.S. recognition of traditional Russian/Soviet fears concerning the security of its southern borders could provide an adequate basis for reducing the level of superpower naval presence in the Mediterranean.

Notes

1. *Actual engagement* refers to tangible engagement in the war operations, either through involvement or the dispatch of independent units to the battle zone. *Demonstrative engagement* implies military moves not directly connected to the war operations and designed to fulfill deterrent functions by illustrating Soviet support for the local states. In many cases, demonstrative activities are not directed against the opposing local belligerent but rather against its allies, especially the United States. Demonstrative support might include naval shows of force, physical changes in the disposition of Soviet units in the Soviet Union and other Soviet bloc countries, and even the dispatch of symbolic independent units to the theater of operations, without their being deployed in the actual battle zone.

2. S.G. Gorshkov, *The Sea Power of the State* (New York: Pergamon, 1979), p. 248.

3. For a detailed discussion of the evolution of Soviet military doctrine regarding engagement in local wars, see M. Katz, *The Third World in Soviet Military Thought* (London: Croom Helm, 1982).

4. Soviet Government Statement, TASS (in English), 14 June 1982, brought by *Foreign Broadcast Information Service, Soviet Union*, 15 June 1982, p. H1.

5. *Ma'ariv*, 15 June 1982, 8 April 1983; *Ha'aretz*, 16, 23 June 1982 (Hebrew).

6. A.Z. Rubinstein, "Soviet Intervention in the Third World," in J.H. Maurer and R.H. Porth, eds., *Military Intervention in the Third World* (New York: Praeger, 1984), pp. 28–29.

7. *Ibid.*, p. 24.

8. M. Heikal, *The Road to Ramadan* (London: Collins, 1975), p. 86.

9. *Ibid.*, p. 87.

10. *Ibid.*, p. 89. [Emphasis added].

11. Rubinstein, "Soviet Intervention," p. 24.

12. For a detailed analysis of Soviet behavior prior to the October 1973 war, see Efraim Karsh, "Moscow and the Yom Kippur War: A Reappraisal, *Soviet Jewish Affairs* (1986), pp. 3–19.

13. The Soviet airlift to Syria began on 10 October, and the airlift to Egypt began a day later. The sealift had already begun on October 7, when the first Soviet ships left the Black Sea port, arriving in Syria and Egypt on October 10 and 11, respectively.

14. V.D. Sokolovskiy, *Soviet Military Strategy*, 3rd ed. (New York: Crane & Russak, 1975), pp. 135, 250.

15. A war of movement is a war in which at least one side tries to conduct maneuver operations designed to occupy areas and destroy opposing forces. A static war (or a war of attrition) aims at wearing down the enemy by gradual and prolonged application of pressure.

16. A. Rubinstein, *Red Star on the Nile* (Princeton, NJ: Princeton University Press, 1977), pp. 335–336.

10

Soviet Military Power in the Middle East; or, Whatever Became of Power Projection?

Francis Fukuyama

I n the immediate aftermath of the Soviet invasion of Afghanistan in December 1979, the prognosis of most Western observers was very pessimistic as to the likelihood of growing Soviet use of military power in pursuit of its interests in the Third World generally and in the Middle East in particular. This conclusion was quite understandable given the trends of the past two decades. From a small coastal force, the Soviets had built and deployed a bluewater surface navy, stationing a permanent squadron in the Mediterranean for the first time in 1964 and using it as an instrument of "coercive diplomacy in Middle East conflicts in 1967, 1970, and 1973, as well as in connection with the Indo-Pakistani war in 1971.

The Soviets established and then broke a sequence of precedents in the quantity and character of their force deployments in support of Third World allies. They moved from the arms supply/advisor deals typical of the 1950s and 1960s to the dispatch of pilots to South Yemen in 1969 and twenty thousand air defense troops to Egypt in 1970. The Soviets threatened intervention during the October 1973 war, then began a qualitatively new phase by staging a joint intervention with Havana on behalf of the (Popular Movement for the Liberation of Angola) in Angola in 1975, followed by a second joint intervention in the Horn of Africa in 1977–1978 and threatening moves along the Sino-Soviet frontier at the time of China's attack on Vietnam in 1979. This sequence culminated in the invasion of Afghanistan, the first time large numbers of Soviet ground forces had been used outside the Warsaw Pact area.

Western analysts watching this behavior, the present writer included, saw a monotonically increasing Soviet willingness to use military force, accompanied by what some observers called an "interventionary doctrine," which formalized the status of Third World power projection in Soviet military theory and practice.[1]

The views expressed in this paper do not necessarily represent those of the RAND Corporation or its sponsors.

The consequence of the changed correlation of forces, proclaimed by many Soviet spokesmen, was thought to be a greater freedom of action in the pursuit of Soviet interests in the developing world. Many in the West feared even more direct and daring applications of power in response to future opportunities. Indeed, anxieties that the Soviets would exploit instability in the Persian Gulf by intervening in places such as northern Iran were the basis for major policy initiatives, including the Carter administration's investment in the Rapid Deployment Force (now Central Command, or CENTCOM) and associated military programs to meet Third World contingencies, actions continued by the Reagan administration.

From the perspective of the mid-1980s, Soviet behavior does not look nearly as threatening as it did at the end of the 1970s, for it seems reasonably clear that the apparent trend of ever-increasing Soviet willingness to use force has at least suffered an interruption and may not get back on track for some time to come. This statement should not be misconstrued. Soviet military activities in the Middle East continue to pose enormous problems for pro-American states in the region, including Israel and the conservative Gulf monarchies. The Soviets have remained stiff competitors, providing SA-5 missiles to Syria and Libya, intervening in the January 1986 civil war in the People's Democratic Republic of South Yemen (PDRY), and conducting offensives of ever-mounting intensity in Afghanistan.[2]

But these actions, while involving a certain level of risk, all fall within the boundaries of familiar Soviet behavior established by the early 1970s. One can argue that Soviet involvement in the first half of the 1980s has had a markedly different character from that of the mid- to late 1970s, being aimed primarily at consolidating Soviet influence in certain important existing client states rather than searching for new opportunities to expand the overseas empire. The Soviets have not fulfilled the worst fears of Western statesmen and specialists by intervening in the Persian Gulf, nor have they undertaken activities on the more modest scale of their earlier interventions in Angola, Ethiopia, and Afghanistan. Indeed, levels of economic assistance have lagged seriously, leading to the defection of certain states, such as Mozambique, from the Soviet camp, and the Soviets have deemphasized their navy, both in terms of shipbuilding programs and deployment patterns.

Drawing conclusions about Soviet failures to act is always tricky, of course, since inaction may have resulted from the absence of opportunities rather than from conscious decisions.[3] What is more impressive and perhaps most significant for the future is evidence of a downgrading of the priority of the power projection mission within the Soviet military from the early to mid-1970s, and beyond that a broad-ranging reassessment of the Third World within the political leadership. These shifts in official attitudes have been accompanied by changes in institutional structure and personnel within the major Soviet bureaucracies that handle Third World policy, changes suggesting that the Soviets are not seeking new ways to use their military forces in the Middle East and other peripheral theaters.

This chapter begins by tracing the growth and subsequent decline of the So-

viet military's interest in the power projection mission over the two previous decades and how it was reflected in external behavior. It will then touch briefly on
how the views of the professional military paralleled those of the political leadership over the same period. Finally, the chapter discusses how these broad tendencies were reflected in actual Soviet policy toward several key Middle Eastern countries and concludes with some speculations on future behavior trends.

The Soviet Military and the Development of the Power Projection Mission

Within the Soviet military, the most consistent advocate of power projection into
Third World theaters such as the Middle East has been the navy. While there was
some military interest in adjacent regions such as the Northern Tier during the
1940s and 1950s, and the deployment of a cruiser to Syria during the 1957 Syrian-
Turkish crisis, serious interest in distant power projection did not begin until the
navy began searching for basing facilities around the Mediterranean littoral in the
1960s. This interest was prompted by three developments: the Soviet expulsion
from their base in Vlona, Albania, in 1962 as a result of the rift with Tirana;
the development of missile-carrying submarines (SSBNs) and submarine-launched
ballistic missiles (SLBMs), which drew the Soviet Navy into the business of offensive and defensive strategic antisubmarine warfare (ASW); and the Soviet Navy's
desire (carried over from the previous decade) of countering U.S. forward-based
aircraft carriers armed with nuclear weapons. The primary mission of the Fifth
Eskadra, stationed permanently in the Mediterranean after 1964, was to neutralize
American seaborne nuclear systems, including aircraft carrier battle groups and
the early-generation Polaris SSBNs patrolling there.

Gorshkov and Naval Presence Projection

The navy's active role in promoting Soviet involvement in the Middle East is
evident from Admiral Sergey Gorshkov's four visits to Egypt during the 1960s (in
1961, 1965, 1966, and 1967). Gorshkov pressed Egyptian President Nasser for
access to naval facilities in his country, a relatively more urgent requirement for
Soviet ships due to their relative lack of nuclear propulsion, carrier-based aircraft,
and underway replenishment. Nasser did not agree to Gorshkov's requests until
after his defeat by Israel in the wake of the June 1967 war, when he permitted
Soviet ships to dock for rest and replenishment as Sollum, Alexandria, Mersa
Matruh (on the Red Sea coast), and other ports. The quest for naval access also
explains the strength of Soviet interest in other countries around the Middle East;
Soviet ships could anchor at Tartus and Latakia in Syria and in Algeria, and the
Soviets developed a large missile-handling facility at Berbera, Somalia.

It was during the early 1970s that Soviet navalism became most fully articulated and that the Soviet surface navy came to be used with some regularity as an instrument of crisis diplomacy. February 1972 saw the beginning of the publication of an eleven-part series of articles by Admiral Gorshkov, titled "Navies in War and Peace," in the navy's journal, *Morskoy Sbornik*. Much of this material was incorporated into Gorshkov's much longer 1976 book, *The Sea Power of the State*, which came out in a second edition in 1979.

A number of Western observers have argued convincingly that "Navies in War and Peace" and the two editions of the book were not pronouncements of established naval doctrine so much as naval advocacy in what were presumed to be the ongoing battles over naval roles, missions, and budget shares in the early to mid-1970s.[4]

If this interpretation is correct, the substance of Gorshkov's writings concern not so much the contemporary navy as the kinds of missions Gorshkov would like to see the navy perform in the future and the forces needed to carry them out. Gorshkov's book is justly famous in the West for the attention he pays to the mission of peacetime power projection and the use of navies to support allies in the Third World. Gorshkov is commonly credited not only with being the father of the modern Soviet bluewater navy but with defining that navy's role in terms of global power projection and with formulating a kind of Soviet navalist doctrine to support Third World intervention.

Nonetheless, Gorshkov's writings and the modern Soviet navy itself have been subject to a certain degree of misinterpretation. While the Third World power projection mission is undeniably part of Gorshkov's vision, it has always been of secondary importance to the navy's primary strategic missions, both in practice and in theory. What Gorshkov is arguing for above all is a larger surface navy, whose chief purpose would be bastion defense of the new Delta-class SSBNs from hostile ASW in areas, such as the Sea of Okhotsk and the Barents Sea. The capital ship of modern navies is the nuclear missile-carrying submarine. Power projection, according to Gorshkov, is something like icing on the cake, which the Soviet Union will get if it spends the money to procure more surface ships.

Gorshkov, in writing about the peacetime role of the navy, stops just short of developing an actual doctrine of intervention. What he does instead is to argue in favor of the navy's positive demonstration value in situations short of actual combat.[5] According to him, navies are impressive symbols of the might and technological prowess of the states that wield them and act as mobile representatives of the Soviet people; moreover, their appearance during crisis situations may have the effect of deterring the imperialists from taking military action against Soviet clients. In other words, he elaborates what might be called a doctrine for the projection of presence rather than the projection of power.

These theoretical arguments are consistent with actual Soviet shipbuilding programs and deployments during this period. The major new classes of large Soviet surface combatants designed and launched during the 1970s, such as the Kiev-class VTOL carrier, the Udaloy- and Sovremenny-class destroyers, or the

Kirov-class crusier, while frequently portrayed as power projection ships, were in fact designed primarily to work together in surface action groups tasked with SSBN bastion defense.[6] Obviously, combatants such as the Kiev and the Kirov can be used for Third World power projection, but their weapons load and deployment indicates a rather different primary mission.

Actual Soviet employment of the navy in this period corresponds quite well with Gorshkov's description of its purpose. Repeatedly, in Middle East crises following the June war the Soviets sent anticarrier task forces into the eastern Mediterranean and assigned "tattletales" to shadow U.S. ships. The Soviet navy was used to signal diplomatic interest to the other superpower and to demonstrate political support for the local client; in the case of Soviet combatants docking in Alexandria harbor during the War of Attrition, the navy performed a quasimilitary deterrent function. There was never any indication, however, that Soviet forces had a serious intention of engaging U.S. forces or even of providing direct military assistance (other than through protection of arms supply lines) to local allies.

Grechko and the Liberating Mission of the Armed Forces

Gorshkov's navalist views broadened into a general doctrine of power projection within the Soviet military through the personality of Andrey Grechko, the Soviet defense minister from 1966 to 1976. Grechko himself seems to have taken a particular interest in allies such as Egypt and in the use of the Soviet armed forces to support national liberation movements in the Third World.[7] There is a certain amount of evidence to suggest, for example, that at the height of the War of Attrition in January 1970, Grechko and other senior commanders went to the political leadership and explained that if something more was not done to support Egypt militarily, Nasser was likely to suffer defeat. The result was the well-known decision to deploy approximately twenty thousand Soviet air defense forces, manning SA-2 and SA-3 missile sites and flying interceptors over the interior of Egypt.[8]

Shortly after the deployment of forces to Egypt, a number of statements were made by senior military figures suggesting that the Soviet military was developing a new mission in support of national liberation movements and other Third World clients. The most common formulation was to speak of a historical "liberating mission" of the Soviet armed forces. This thesis was delineated at length by General Yepishev, chief of the Main Political Administration of the armed forces, in his 1972 book, *Mighty Weapon of the Army*. The same theme was taken up by Grechko in 1974, when he explained that the Soviet army initially had both an internal and an external mission at the time of the foundation of the Soviet state but that the former had fallen away in subsequent years with the consolidation of Soviet power throughout the Soviet Union. He first defines the external mission to include the defense of the socialist fatherland (the Soviet Union) and the other countries of the socialist commonwealth. Then, in a frequently quoted passage, he states:

At the present stage the historic function of the Soviet armed forces is not restricted merely to their function in defending our motherland and the other socialist countries. In its foreign policy activity the Soviet state actively and purposefully opposes the export of counterrevolution and the policy of oppression, supports the national liberation struggle, and resolutely resists imperialist aggression in whatever distant region of our planet it may appear. The party and Soviet government rely on the country's economic and defense might in fulfilling these tasks. The working people of the whole world and all progressive mankind see in the economic and defense might of the USSR and the other socialist countries a reliable bulwark in the struggle for freedom and independence, the people's security, and social progress.[9]

This argument is repeated in Grechko's book, *The Armed Forces of the Soviet State,* also published in the spring of 1974.

There is good reason to think that Grechko and Gorshkov were allies in promoting the power projection mission and that the defense minister was the main avenue through which Gorshkov's navalist theories found broader acceptance within the General Staff and the political leadership as a whole. It was during the latter half of Grechko's tenure that the navy's influence reached a peak, whereas this service suffered a number of setbacks after his death in 1976. Grechko and Gorshkov were old comrades-in-arms, the latter having been Grechko's deputy for naval affairs in the Caucasus in 1942, and it appears that this close personal relationship continued into the early 1970s.

Thus, by the mid-1970s the Soviet military had developed what was beginning to look like a doctrine of power projection, which established the latter as a distinct mission for the Soviet armed forces.[10] The Soviets had in the meantime developed a bluewater navy, airborn forces, and military transport aviation (VTA), which, while intended primarily for other uses,[11] gave them the capability to project power into noncontiguous regions such as the Middle East. These developments then set the stage for the series of Third World adventures of the mid- to late 1970s.

The Decline of Power Projection

Just at the moment when the Soviets were poised to undertake ever more ambitious interventions in the Third World, a number of changes occurred, which had the effect of undercutting support for the power projection mission within the military. In the first place, there was a change in the senior military leadership in 1976, with Defense Minister Grechko being replaced by Dmitriy Ustinov and Viktor Kulikov being succeeded as chief of the General Staff by Marshal Nikolay Ogarkov. Second, the party leadership decided to cut the rate of growth in the Soviet defense budget from the 4 to 5 percent annual growth that had been characteristic since 1964 to approximately 2 to 3 percent in the Tenth Five-Year Plan, with the weapons procurement budget being essentially frozen. Taken together, these developments had the effect of shifting the military's policies and priorities in a variety of areas, including power projection.[12]

The most important of these changes was the replacement of the military's top leadership. A survey of the writings and actions of both the new defense minister and chief of staff indicate a much lower level of interest in Third World issues than was true for Grechko. For example, Ustinov's references to the Soviet armed forces "liberating mission" only occur in the historical past tense. While warning frequently of the aggressiveness of imperialism in Third World situations, and in particular of the threat posed by the American Rapid Deployment Force to Persian Gulf security, he never went on to define a role for the military in defending revolutionary regimes or in providing support to national liberation movements. Hie exclusion of the power projection mission was perhaps most pointed in a speech that was published in Vietnam in 1982, when he explained that:

> The Constitution of the Soviet Union states clearly that the defense of the socialist homeland is the most important function of the state and an undertaking of all the people, that *the Soviet armed forces were formed to defend the accomplishments of socialism, the peaceful labor of the Soviet people, and the sovereignty and territorial integrity of the Soviet Union.*[13]

Whereas Grechko had explicitly stated that the external function of the military extended beyond defense of the Soviet homeland and the other developed socialist countries, Ustinov saw fit to deliver to the Vietnamese a short dissertation on Soviet constitutional law underlining the fact that the Soviet armed forces were intended for the defense of the Soviet Union only.

Similar kinds of Kremlinological evidence can be adduced to indicate that Ogarkov too was not particularly interested in the power projection mission. Like Ustinov, Ogarkov talked very little about the Middle East, the Third World, the liberating mission of the armed forces, or any related topic.[14] Indeed, Ogarkov asserted once again that local wars were dangerous because of the possibility that they would escalate into global ones involving the two superpowers.[15] He thereby reversed the trend set by other, less authoritative Soviet military writers in the late 1960s and early 1970s, who had maintained that local wars did not risk escalation and that the Soviet Union could presumably exercise a freer hand in support of its Third World clients.[16]

Ogarkov's relative lack of interest in power projection can be explained by his belief that there were other, more pressing priorities. Ogarkov's central objective while chief of staff was to modernize the two major theaters in Europe and the Far East. Almost all the major innovations from his tenure in office, such as the establishment of the Far East High Command, the reorganization of the military districts and the reassignment of PVO Strahy (air defense) assets to theater commanders, the creation of the operational maneuver group, and the emphasis on high-tech conventional weapons can be seen as directed toward this end. Given the fact that the party apparatus had begun to squeeze the military budget in 1975 (a trend continued in the 1980–1985 Eleventh Five-Year Plan), it was natural that Ogarkov should regard power projection as peripheral to his principal objectives and not want to devote more than minimal resources to it.

Indeed, there is some reason to believe that the entire Grechko-Gorshkov emphasis on power projection and the navy was more of a passing episode than a permanent direction for Soviet military policy. The Soviet military has always had a strong ground forces orientation, directed primarily toward the European theater but with increasing emphasis on the Far East, following the rift with China. Within the Soviet system as a whole, the principal advocates of support for Middle Eastern and other Third World clients have been the civilian bureaucracies charged with foreign affairs, primarily the Central Committee's International Department and the Foreign Ministry, and, within the military, the navy. It should not be surprising that, in the absence of a defense minister with strong personal interest in the Third World (as we are hypothesizing Grechko had), the "natural" orientation of the military toward the major theaters should reassert itself. This appears to be what in fact happened after 1976. As confirmation of this hypothesis, we can look at what happened to the Soviet Navy in this period.

De-emphasis of the Navy

There is considerable textual evidence suggesting a downgrading of the role of the navy. Beginning after Grechko's death in 1976, a number of documents appeared whose overall theme was that there was no such thing as an independent navalism, naval science, or doctrine of the sea power of the state independent of the overall teachings of Marxism-Leninism on war and the army—that is, a direct attack on the central thesis of Gorshkov's articles and book from earlier in the decade. The first instance of this was found in the second edition of *The Sea Power of the State* itself, which appeared in 1979. The principal change between the editions was the addition of a new section affirming that there was only one overarching military strategy, which could not be divided into separate naval and land components.[17]

While Gorshkov was formally the author of the revised version, this section was probably added under duress. The striking feature of his earlier writings, after all, had been the unadorned thesis that, historically, naval power was in itself a major factor in the power of states, independent of ideology or class, and that implicitly criticized the postwar Soviet party leadership for being negligent in not developing naval power. Gorshkov was in essence forced to retract this assertion in the second edition of his book.

A similar theme is present in the so-called Stalbo debate that took place in the pages of *Morskoy Sbornik* between April 1981 and July 1983. A central point raised by all the participants was an admission that there was only one unified military science and no independent science or doctrine of the navy. Admiral Chernavin, the man who would eventually succeed Gorshkov as head of the Soviet Navy, wrote: "Victory is achieved by coordinated efforts, and this gives rise to the necessity of integrating all knowledge about warfare within the framework and limits of a single, unified military science."[18]

The Stalbo debate confirmed that by early 1980, the navy had come to accept the downgrading in its status; the purpose of the debate was to define the structure and limits of naval theory as opposed to naval science. Advocacy of a strong navy, with its associated power projection mission, had come under attack in the late 1970s or had at least lost some of the support it had had during the publication of "Navies in War and Peace" and the first edition of *The Sea Power of the State.* Indeed, one might speculate that Gorshkov's views had received strong endorsement from Defense Minister Grechko, but that with his death in 1976, the ground forces–oriented general staff reasserted its dominance and forced the navy to drop its pretensions to having its own science and a special role in supporting the interests of the Soviet state.[19]

This view is supported by a shift in the Soviet Navy's deployment patterns that took place in the late 1970s, which suggested a downgrading in the Soviet Navy's role as an instrument of coercive diplomacy. Soviet naval activity in the Mediterranean peaked in 1973 with the October war in the Middle East. After that point, the number of ship days spent on forward deployment declined by about one-fifth by 1977 and leveled off subsequently. After 1980 the number of amphibious and mine warfare forces kept on-station declined, and no effort was made to station strike aircraft abroad in places such as Syria or Libya. Most importantly, the Soviets did not surge ships into the eastern Mediterranean in response to the Lebanon crisis of 1982. During the Lebanon war, when the United States had concentrated four aircraft carriers within striking distance of the Soviet Union, Moscow failed to augment the Fifth Eskadra to anything approaching the level of October 1973. The Soviets had expanded their fleet during crises in 1967, 1970, 1971, and 1973; the contrast to Lebanon is striking and indicates a reduced interest in using the navy as an instrument of crisis diplomacy.[20]

The downgrading of the navy in the late 1970s also was apparent in building programs. Only the lead ship in the *Berezina*-class underway replenishment group was constructed, and only two *Ivan Rogov*-class high-speed, long-range lift ships were built at a five-year interval. In addition, the 50 percent increase in allocations for naval nuclear reactors achieved in the early 1970s was apparently rescinded.[21] The Soviet Navy has never been strong on underway replenishment; had the General Staff been serious about developing a distant power projection capability, it would have invested much more heavily in logistics and supply ships, as well as in amphibious and heavy-lift vessels, which would permit the projection of forces ashore. While much was made of the *Ivan Rogov* in the West, it and its sister ship do not constitute a credible armed landing capability.

The 1986 launching of the lead ship in a class of 60,000-ton large-deck carriers has been interpreted as an indication of Soviet interest in moving in the direction of American-style power projection. There is no question that this kind of ship could be very useful in projecting presence in Third World contingencies. Gorshkov's writings have hinted at this type of application.[22] It is not clear, however, that the aircraft carrier's primary role in Soviet eyes is power projection rather than the more traditional one of bastion defense and sea control. Just like the *Kiev* or the *Kirov*, the large-deck carrier can serve as the command-and-control ship of a modern surface action group whose primary mission is strategic ASW, particularly in remote polar regions where U.S. and Soviet submarines increasingly operate.[23]

This deemphasis of the navy under the Ustinov-Ogarkov tenure reflects a reassertion of the natural biases of the ground forces–oriented Soviet General Staff toward land warfare in the major theaters. It is the product not only of decreasing interest in power projection in the narrow sense but also of technological changes that have lowered the requirements for overseas facilities in the Middle East and other areas on the southern periphery of the Soviet Union. With the deployment of the latest generation of SSBNs, the Soviet Typhoon-class and the American Ohio-class, submarine patrol areas have moved much closer to the home waters of both superpowers.[24] The decline in the number of Soviet ship days spent in the Mediterranean reflects the fact that the Soviet Navy no longer has to track Polaris submarines patrolling there. The same is true of the Indian Ocean, which is not a desirable patrol area due to its distance from the superpowers' home ports.

Retrospective and Future Prospects

All these developments taken together suggest that the senior leadership of the Soviet military in power during the crucial decade between 1976 and the mid-1980s emphasized modernization of the central theaters and lowered the priority of the power projection mission from the status it was given by Andrey Grechko. This is particularly ironic since two major interventions, in the Horn of Africa and in Afghanistan, as well as the Soviet buildup in Vietnam, were undertaken during the Ustinov-Ogarkov tenure. One way of explaining this anomaly is that within the Soviet system, the chief organs responsible for making decisions on Third World intervention are civilian, above all the Politburo and the International Department, and their attitudes on the desirability of power projection did not begin to turn around until the early 1980s. Furthermore, the building programs and doctrine that Grechko had espoused probably acquired a certain amount of momentum within the military and took a few years to be turned around.[25] By the time Ogarkov was removed and Ustinov died in 1984, however, the Soviet military, while still heavily involved in supporting existing clients, had fallen off the trend line of ever-broadening application of military power around the world.

It does not seem likely that the military's new leadership—Marshal Akhromeev, who replaced Ogarkov as chief of staff, and Marshal Sokolov, who succeeded Ustinov as defense minister—will restore power projection anytime soon to the level it had under Grechko.* Neither one has given any evidence of strong interest in the power projection mission during the time they have been in office, being preoccupied above all with arms control and strategic issues such as the Strategic Defense Initiative (SDI). Sokolov was, of course, the commander of Soviet forces in Afghanistan in 1980 and therefore has Third World experience, but it is very difficult to say whether this makes him more or less an advocate of future interventions. Sokolov was in any case appointed at a late stage in his career and will be a transitional figure. Whatever his personal opinions, Brezhnev's successors have sharply curtailed the influence of the professional military, ousting Marshal Ogarkov and downgrading the defense minister to candidate member of the Politburo. Given continuing budget stringencies, it does not seem likely that power projection will receive high priority anytime in the near future.

The military's declining interest in power projection paralleled and was supported by a similar turnaround in the views of the political leadership toward the Third World. While space constraints prevent a more extensive discussion, there is by now considerable evidence that particularly after the death of Leonid Brezhnev, the entire late 1970s legacy of activism in the Third World came under increasing attack within the Soviet leadership, with both Andropov and Gorbachev taking strong verbal stands against further exposure to Third World commitments.[26] Reasons for this reassessment included the increasing economic burden of support for Third World clients at a time of increasing economic stringency, the negative effects of Third World activism on the central U.S.-Soviet relationship, and the relatively poor performance of the Marxist-Leninist states such as Afghanistan, Ethiopia, South Yemen, and Angola set up by the Soviets in the mid- to late 1970s.

Mikhail Gorbachev's first year in office also saw a number of personnel changes, which suggest a lower level of institutional support for Third World activism in the future. The most important is the replacement of Boris Ponomarev as head of the International Department by Anatoliy Dobrynin, the longtime Soviet ambassador to the United States. In addition, Georgiy Kornienko, the former first deputy foreign minister, has become a second chief deputy of the International Department next to Ponomarev's assistant, Vadim Zagladin, and Karen Brutents has taken over responsibilities for the Third World as a whole from Rostislav Ul'yanovskiy. The International Department has been the traditional home of the heavily ideological advocates of strong Soviet support for the worldwide revolutionary process, and in the 1970s it was frequently at odds with the Foreign Ministry over initiatives that the latter thought might damage U.S.-Soviet relations.[27] One assumes that Dobrynin, by contrast, will be relatively more sensitive to the negative effects of Third World behavior on U.S.-Soviet relations than his predecessor was. This may lead to no more than a cosmetic change in Soviet rhetoric

---

*This chapter was written before Marshal Sokolov's replacement by Marshal Yazov in mid-1987.

on this score, but given the other bureaucratic shifts that have occurred, one can predict more careful policies as well.

Thus, on both the military and political sides there have been shifts in attitude and institutional changes within the bureaucracies that determine Soviet policy toward the Third World, all of which suggest a more selective Soviet involvement in local conflicts. None of this should suggest that Moscow has in any way given up on critical regions such as the Middle East, of course. Indeed, one of the particularly thorny problems for contemporary Soviet policymakers is how to translate the general perspectives and inclinations toward a reduced Third World role into actual practice, given the credibility and great power concerns that the Soviet Union faces in the real world. How this translation has been made in the Middle East is the subject of the following section.

The Soviet Military in the Middle East

In another context I have characterized Soviet policy toward the Third World in the years since the Afghanistan intervention as a period of muscular retrenchment or consolidation.[28] That is, the Soviet Union has decided to avoid taking on new commitments and to minimize wherever possible the overall costs of the empire, while concentrating on the consolidation of the Soviet position in a number of existing client states. It is a bit ironic to preface a discussion of Soviet military policy toward the Middle East with a long dissertation on the decline of power projection, since the Middle East is the area where the Soviet retrenchment has been the most muscular. Nonetheless, Moscow's recent behavior in this region fits the overall pattern: The Soviets have gone to considerable lengths to protect their relationships with traditional friends, Syria most of all, but also Libya, Iraq, and South Yemen. At the same time, Moscow has not changed its level of commitment qualitatively from that established by the early 1970s, and it has not been particularly active in seeking an expanded role for its own military forces.

Syria

Since the departure of Egypt from the Soviet camp and the unfolding of the Camp David process, Syria has been the single most important Soviet client in the Middle East—arguably, in the Third World as a whole. In fact, the durability of this tie in spite of numerous vicissitudes is testimony to the mutuality of interest between the two countries and the doggedness of Soviet pursuit of a regional Middle East role.

Nonetheless, the nature of Soviet interests in Syria has shifted slightly over the years, with a decline in the importance of the military component. Moscow supported Damascus during the 1960s primarily for two reasons: first, because the latter represented a brand of radical pan-Arab nationalism that was strongly anti-imperialist and posed an ideological threat to Western positions throughout the

Middle East; and second, because the Soviets needed base facilities in Syria, which would support naval deployments in the eastern Mediterranean.

Since that time, the basing requirement has become less pressing for the reasons outlined in the previous section. Soviet ships still dock in Syrian ports (particularly after the loss of access to Alexandria and other Egyptian harbors), but there are fewer of them and their strategic role is less critical. From a Soviet point of view, the political rationale has probably changed somewhat as well. From being a weak and unstable bastion of pan-Arab ideological purity, Damascus's hardheaded pursuit of power has made it a much more formidable actor than it was in the 1960s or 1970s.[29] Indeed, its quest for strategic parity with Israel in recent years has made it the most militarily capable country in the Arab world, with the ability to block U.S. initiatives in Lebanon and the Arab-Israeli conflict. After the loss of Egypt, there could be no question but that Moscow would continue its support of Damascus if it was to remain a player in the Arab-Israeli theater.

The Soviet military's role with respect to Syria is an instrumental one, providing the cement that holds together an essentially political relationship. Over the years the relationship has been maintained within strictly defined limits. The Soviets, for their part,

supply Damascus with large quantities of relatively modern weapons;

do not interfere in internal Syrian domestic politics or try to shape its internal evolution in the direction of vanguard parties, Marxism-Leninism, and the like;

do not demand across-the-board Syrian cooperation in foreign policy (hence, they do not let areas of disagreement, such as policy toward the Palestine Liberation Organization (PLO), damage the overall relationship).

On the other hand, the Syrians

follow a generally confrontational anti-imperialist line against Israel and the United States, while avoiding overt resort to arms;

defer to Soviet wishes on secondary issues such as Afghanistan or Soviet participation in an international Middle East peace conference;

do not expect the Soviets to provide them with economic assistance and pay for the bulk of their weapons in hard currency;

do not expect the Soviets to back them up in a conflict with Israel or the United States through direct military intervention.

Over the years, the Soviets would have liked greater Syrian tractability and cooperation on a variety of issues (such as Lebanon), while Damascus has consistently hoped for overt Soviet guarantees and higher levels of direct military involvement.[30] Neither party, however, has been willing to pay much of a price in terms of its half of the bargain to get these things, so the relationship has remained at arm's length—a fact that has not prevented it from being very profitable to both parties.

None of the military initiatives that the Soviets have undertaken with Damascus during the 1980s have violated the norms of their earlier relationship. The decade began with the signing of the Syrian-Soviet Treaty of Friendship and Cooperation on October 8, 1980, an agreement that was very similar to those the Soviets signed with Iraq, India, and, at one time, Somalia and Egypt. The document, for which the Soviets had pressed for more than a decade, was signed by Syrian President Assad only in response to his internal difficulties with the Sunni fundamentalist opposition. The fact that it did not signify a higher level of support on the part of Moscow was made abundantly clear when Israel invaded Lebanon in June 1982 and the Soviets failed to provide Syria with even minimal verbal support, much less threats of intervention as in earlier crises. This passivity was perfectly in keeping with previous Soviet behavior. In the past the Soviets had threatened intervention only when the territory and political existence of a client regime was at stake, and even then the threats were made too late to have any effect. In Lebanon the chief object of attack was a nonstate actor, the PLO, and the Israelis never attacked Syrian forces on their own territory.

The weakness of Soviet support during the Lebanon war was the target of considerable criticism in the Arab world, which probably explains the major military initiative undertaken by Moscow in the 1980s—the delivery in January 1983 of SA-5 air defense missiles to Syria, together with six thousand to eight thousand Soviet personnel to man them. The Soviet decision was not the routine act of resupply that it is sometimes made out to be[31] but involved considerable risk of entangling Moscow in a messy confrontation with Israel. The decision to deploy the missiles was probably made in September or October 1982, partly in response to President Reagan's September 1 peace initiative. At that time, Ariel Sharon was still Israel's defense minister, and Israeli and Syrian troops were confronting each other in the Bekaa Valley. When the decision was made, the Soviets ran a real risk of being caught up in a renewal of hostilities that may have led to Israeli attacks on their missile sites, which would have presented them with the embarrassing dilemma of either upping the ante or losing credibility with the Syrians. The Soviets were rescued from this no-win situation only by Sharon's removal in the wake of the Kahan Commission report and the turn in Israeli public attitudes against the war in the winter of 1982–1983.

It does not seem to have been the Soviet intention to use the SA-5 deployments to create a permanent military presence in Syria, since the Soviet troops were gradually withdrawn over the following year and operational control of the missiles was turned over to Syria. While the initial use of Soviet personnel may have been due to the lack of Syrian technicians capable of operating the missiles effectively, the slowness with which the transfer was completed suggests that the Soviets were hoping for a deterrent effect as well.[32]

The decision to provide the SA-5 missiles was only the most visible component of a larger decision to support the Syrian buildup after the Lebanon war. Between 1982 and 1984 the Soviets were reported to have transferred between $1.5 and $2 billion worth of arms, including T-72 and T-74 tanks, MiG-25 and MiG-27 aircraft, Mi-8 and Mi-24 helicopters, TU-126 early-warning aircraft, and, in September 1983, SS-21 surface-to-surface missiles, which were a follow-on to the Frog missile already in the Syrian inventory.[33] With the SA-5 and SS-21, the Soviets again gave Syria weapons not generally provided to Moscow's Warsaw Pact allies, the SS-21 having previously been deployed only in East Germany.[34] The Soviets have thus given de facto support to the Syrian quest for strategic superiority—in large measure, one imagines, because the Syrians pay cash and because such sales are an important component of Soviet hard currency earnings. This does not mean that the Soviets would support the actual use of these weapons, however. Even after the post-Lebanon buildup, it is not clear how Syria would fare in a war with Israel, and the Soviets would not like to be put in the uncomfortable position of supporting the losing side again.

The subsequent turns in Soviet policy have reflected the tactical situation rather than shifts in the Soviet evaluation of Syria's strategic significance or their level of overall commitment to Damascus. As it became clear that public pressure to withdraw was growing in Israel, the Soviets became increasingly bold in their verbal support of Syria. When, in the course of 1983, the United States became more heavily involved in Lebanon, with naval units engaging Syrian forces on behalf of the government of Amin Gemayel, the Soviets played down their support for Syria and actively distanced themselves after the bombing of the U.S. Marine compound in Beirut.[35]

Recent trends in Soviet military support for Syria indicate two things. The first is that the Soviet military's declining interest in power projection and the reassessment of the Third World by the political leadership does not imply that Moscow will be any less competitive in critical theaters such as the Arab-Israeli conflict. Through their military support of Syria, the Soviets have been highly successful in derailing U.S. efforts at a Lebanon settlement and a settlement, via Jordan, of the Arab-Israeli conflict. This is to be explained largely by great power considerations of prestige and geostrategic position and in part by the fact that Syria does not cost the Soviets anything in economic terms—indeed, it is a major source of hard currency.

The second trend is that the bounds of U.S.-Soviet competition are likely to remain the familiar ones of arms transfers and training. The Soviet military commitment to Syria, even in the event of threats to its territory, remains limited, as does the Soviet force presence in the country. The deployment of Soviet combat forces in Syria in the aftermath of the Lebanon war was an expedient meant to meet a short-term political need and did not reflect a higher level of commitment. While risky, the level of this risk was no higher than others the Soviets have tolerated on behalf of their Arab clients in the past, such as when they passed on warnings of an imminent Israeli attack in May 1967 that played a role in triggering the Six Day War, or when they deployed combat forces to Egypt during the War of Attrition. Subsequently, the Soviets could have taken a number of steps to bind themselves more closely to the Syrians, for examples, by making the troop presence larger and more permanent or by taking on further combat roles, but instead Moscow phased out these forces and took some pains to distance itself from Damascus when it looked like there was a risk of direct U.S.-Syrian confrontation.

Libya

Moscow's stake in Libya is considerably smaller than it is in Syria, and it is therefore willing to do even less in the way of direct military support. While many observers were surprised by the Soviet decision in December 1985 to provide SA-5 missiles to Colonel Qaddafi just as Libya was about to embark on another round of confrontation with the United States, Moscow's subsequent behavior confirmed the narrow limits of its military commitment to Tripoli.

While Soviet ships have docked in Libyan ports, and while reconnaissance aircraft have flown from bases in Libya, the Soviet military has evidently hoped for a larger and more permanent arrangement there in order to keep better track of developments in the western Mediterranean. Facilities in Libya have been sought not so much as a strategic necessity as a convenience, but the Libyans have evidently turned them down. Once again, as in the case of Syria, the Soviet interest is primarily political, and the Soviet military has played more of an instrumental than a directing role, providing enormous quantities of modern weapons.

There are numberous reasons for the lower Soviet stake in Libya. Moscow has tended to regard Qaddafi as somewhat of a reckless adventurist in his support for innumerable subversive and terrorist groups around the world. While these activities are almost universally anti-Western and therefore serve Soviet interests, they are also a potential source of embarrassment, and for this reason Moscow would like to avoid too close an association. Unlike Moscow's other Marxist-Leninist clients of the 1970s, Qaddafi has ideological pretensions in his espousal of the Third International Way in his *Green Book*, which any self-respecting Soviet must find at once childish and pretentious.[36] Finally, Libya is militarily weaker, more exposed to Western power, and even farther from the sources of Soviet military strength than Syria. For all of these reasons any Soviet leader would be foolish to extend any degree of military protection to Qaddafi's regime, and none have done so to date.

Apart from this support of a variety of subversive activities, Moscow's other chief interest in Libya is the mercenary one of hard currency earnings from weapons sales. Over the years, Qaddafi spent more than $20 billion in Soviet weapons he manifestly does not need and cannot use.[37] Indeed, the fact that the Libyan military could operate only a small proportion of the equipment it has acquired has led to theories in the West that the Soviets are stockpiling materiel that could be used by Soviet forces during a crisis (much like the forward-deployed POMCUS stocks in NATO). While equipment has certainly been transferred out of Libyan inventories to Lebanon, Iran, and other countries, the theory itself is implausible: The level of maintenance is so low that most of the equipment would be unusable in a real emergency, and it is, moreover, hard to come up with scenarios in which the Soviets would suddenly want to man three thousand tanks in the middle of the Libyan desert, with little or no supporting infrastructure.

The Soviet transfer of SA-5s at the end of 1985 raises several interesting questions regarding the level of Soviet commitment. Were Soviet technicians or troops at the controls when these missiles were launched at Sixth Fleet ships exercising in the Gulf of Sidra in April 1986, and were they still there when the Americans returned fire? Were any Soviets killed in the U.S. response, either during the Gulf of Sidra incident or in the bombing raid later that month? Did the Soviets provide Libya with tactical information or advice during the latter event? A positive answer to any of these questions would suggest an atypical and unexpectedly high degree of Soviet military support, but the apparent answer is *no* in all cases.

The Soviets did station a number of naval combatants in the Mediterranean in January 1986 in connection with their deployment of SA-5s, forming an electronic picket line from just off Tripoli to the coast of Syria and increasing the level of their surveillance of U.S. military activity.[38] However, these moves were evidently a bluff. Unlike the Syrian case, the SA-5 missiles were turned over to Libyan control very shortly after their arrival, so the decision to launch them in April was (as one would otherwise imagine) a Libyan one. The fact that the missiles were turned over so quickly suggests that the Soviets were concerned about the possibility of getting involved in such a confrontation. When the actual shooting began, the three hundred advisors in the area reportedly refused to leave their underground bunkers despite Libyan appeals for assistance.[39] The Soviets also were slow in providing parts for the missiles, to the point where the Libyans were forced to turn to British and French experts to repair their radars.[40] At the time of the U.S. bombing attack, Soviet ships reportedly moved out of port and did not pass on any intelligence information warning of the attack. All these details suggest that the Soviets were aware of the risks they were taking in supplying the SA-5s and were determined to get out of harm's way. Indeed, this lack of support led to Libyan recriminations, despite efforts to pretend that there was full solidarity.[41] When Qaddafi's associate Jalloud visited Moscow in late May 1986, the joint communiqué stressed the importance of "strengthening [Libya's] defense capability" but also condemned "those pretexts that the imperialists use" in attacking countries like Libya.[42]

Thus, Gorbachev and the Soviet leadership felt the need to demonstrate a certain level of support for Libya, not only in response to U.S. pressure against Qaddafi but also perhaps as a signal intended to be read more broadly—that the Soviet Union would not remain passive in the face of the U.S. offensive against Soviet positions around the Third World, embodied in the unofficial Reagan Doctrine. At the same time, the Soviets were not prepared to increase their level of military support to the point where it would risk a direct military confrontation with the United States.

South Yemen

Moscow's relationship with the People's Democratic Republic of Yemen (PDRY) is qualitatively different from its relations with Syria, Libya, or any other Arab country. South Yemen falls into the group of countries with a socialist orientation, including Angola, Mozambique, Ethiopia, Cambodia, Afghanistan, and Nicaragua, most of which came to power during the 1970s with Soviet bloc assistance. All these states are ruled by overtly Marxist-Leninist regimes and were encouraged by the Soviets to establish formal vanguard parties modeled on the Soviet Communist party.[43]

As was characteristic for the other states in this group, the Soviets played a much more intimate role in the shaping of domestic policies and institutions in the PDRY than they did in any of their older Arab nationalist clients. Soviets, Cubans, and East Germans were crucial in shaping the ruling Yemeni Socialist party (or YSP, founded in 1978), writing the country's constitution, collectivizing agriculture, creating a popular militia, and particularly building an internal security apparatus. In contrast to Syria, the Soviets went to considerable lengths to control the internal factional politics of the leadership of the YSP.

Moscow's military relationship with the PDRY has always been much closer than with other Arab nationalist states. The South Yemenis permitted the Soviets to build an extensive complex of naval and air facilities in Aden and Mukhalla and on Socotra and Perim islands. These bases support the Soviet presence in the Indian Ocean and Persian Gulf and, in the event of a war with China, would be very important in maintaining the sea line of communication between European Russia and the Soviet Far East. The PDRY became much more important after the break with Somalia in 1977 and the loss of Berbera. The Soviets used South Yemen as an entrepôt for supporting other clients in the region, such as Ethiopia during the 1977–1978 war with Somalia. In part because they have had other sources of leverage over South Yemen, Soviet military assistance has always been relatively small and in most years was exceeded by the aid given to rival North Yemen.

The South Yemenis made it much easier for the Soviets to interfere in their internal affairs by practicing a particularly vicious kind of factionalism, first Qahtan al-Shaabi against Selim Rubai Ali, then Rubai Ali against Abd al-Fattah Ismail, then Ismail against Ali Nasser Mohammed. All these leaders were basically pro-Soviet, but some tended to be more receptive than others to normal relations with the PDRY's neighbors and other pro-Western states. The Soviets from time to time saw their interests lying with one or another of the factions, and in June 1978 they apparently participated in the coup that removed Rubai Ali from power. Rubai Ali had been practicing an evenhanded diplomacy for some months before the coup, trying to build relations with the conservative Gulf states, and the Soviets evidently feared that he might become another Sadat if not stopped. East German internal security advisors and Cuban troops based in Ethiopia were apparently used to help bring the hard-line Abd al-Fattach Ismail to power in his place.

The events of January 1986 show both the depth of Soviet involvement in internal PDRY politics and the limits of their influence.[44] As a result of a factional fight, Ismail was ousted by Ali Nasser Mohammed in 1980 and sent into exile in Moscow until the spring of 1985, when he returned to South Yemen. The Soviets do not seem to have been engineering a comeback by Ismail, since their current policy in the Gulf at the time was much more akin to Ali Nasser Mohammed's conciliatory approach than to Ismail's isolationism. They were evidently taken by surprise when Ali Nasser Mohammed attempted to assassinate his rivals in the YSP Politburo and eliminate the Ismail faction physically, and their initial reaction was to seek intervention by some Arab group that would bring an end to the fighting and then to seek Soviet mediation between the two groups. After January 17 they gave up on the idea of outside intervention, probably fearing a move by North Yemen, and shifted to open support of the rebel (Ismail) side. In the course of the next days' fighting, there were reports that Soviet pilots had flown sorties on behalf of the Ismail forces and that Soviet ships had jammed Ali Nasser Mohammed's appeals for Yemeni Navy ships at Perim Island to come to his assistance. The shift to the rebel cause seemed to have been an entirely tactical decision based on the fact that Ismail was winning, as both sides were pro-Soviet.

The January civil war in South Yemen presents a mixed picture for the Soviets. On the one hand, they effectively employed their military power in the fighting and retained their position in that country. On the other hand, events in South Yemen clearly surprised them and got out of control. Neither the Ismail comeback nor the Mohammed coup was neatly stage-managed the way the Rubai Ali overthrow had been, and the East German, Cuban, and Soviet forces on the scene played only an auxiliary role in the conflict. The YSP was wrecked as a result of the fighting (with some twelve thousand reported casualties and the city of Aden in ruins), and it showed the tribal mentality underlying the veneer of Marxist-Leninist institutions and rhetoric. Moreover, the civil war was a setback to Soviet and South Yemeni hopes to show a more moderate and accommodating face to the pro-Western nations of the Persian Gulf.

Iraq

The final important Soviet client in the Middle East is Iraq. Historically, Iraq's military importance to Moscow was a negative one: The Soviets disliked the Iraqi monarchy's role as founding member of the Baghdad Pact in the mid-1950s because this led to the stationing of U.S. strategic forces on Iraqui territory. This concern, however, was diminished in 1958 when the Hashemite monarchy was overthrown by Brigadier Abal al-Karim Kassem, and since that time Iraq's significance has been more political than military. The Soviets have never been granted basing rights (other than overflight) or other military privileges in Iraq.

The Soviet-Iraqi relationship, like the one with Syria, has increasingly evolved in the direction of a hardheaded marriage of convenience, based on an exchange of weapons for influence. When Moscow began cultivating Baghdad after 1958, and particularly in the early 1970s, Iraq was seen as a source of anti-imperialist radicalism whose activities might undermine Western positions throughout the Middle East and Persian Gulf. The friendship treaty was signed in 1972 to shield Baghdad from Western retaliation when it nationalized foreign oil assets, and the Soviets played a major role in developing Iraq's oil industry. To an even greater degree than Syria, however, Iraq was determined to follow its own national interests, which did not necessarily correspond with those of the Soviet Union. The most important divergence was the invasion of Iran in September 1980, which the Soviets opposed because they entertained hopes of cultivating closer relations with Teheran. To pressure the Iraqis, the Soviets imposed an arms embargo from September 1980 to May 1982 and shifted back to more extensive military support only after the Iranians turned the tables and invaded Iraq in the summer of 1982. Between the end of the embargo and 1984, the Soviets shipped some $5 billion in military hardware, including T-72 tanks, SS-21 surface-to-surface missiles, and MiG-23, MiG-25, and MiG-27 aircraft.[45]

Whereas the Soviets may have believed in the early 1970s that they were supporting a country at the vanguard of radical Arab nationalism, they now undoubtedly understand that their relationship rests on a much more narrow and cynically pragmatic base. The Iraqis defer to Soviet wishes because of their heavy dependence on Soviet weapons to continue the war with Iran, but they felt betrayed in some measure by the Soviet embargo and have shown themselves willing not only to mute their radicalism but to deal with countries such as France and the United States when it was believed they could be of help. The Soviets probably have few illusions about Iraqi reliability at this point but feel content to maintain the relationship because Baghdad, like Syria and Libya, pays cash for its weapons. It is doubtful that the Soviet arming of Iraq will go beyond quantitative increases in weapons to anything like security guarantees or the stationing of Soviet forces there, even to the extent that exists in Syria. Whereas the major constraint on the Soviet presence in Syria is the risk of Israeli and U.S. reaction, the constraint in Iraq is the potential backlash from Iran. While Soviet-Iranian relations have fallen into open hostility and polemics following the 1983 crackdown on the Tudeh party, the Soviets still have residual concerns that Iran might tilt back to the West (toward Western Europe, if not the United States) and do not want to burn all their bridges.

Conclusions

- The trend toward the ever-expanding Soviet use of power projection forces around the Third World suffered an interruption in the early 1980s, after having reached a peak in the mid- to late 1970s. The institutional forces that supported a broader application of Soviet power in peripheral theaters during this period, both in the civilian party apparatus and within the military, were replaced by other actors with a different set of priorities.

- The specific strategic requirements (primarily ASW) that drive Soviet interest in overseas basing in the 1960s and that made Middle Eastern countries such as Syria and Egypt of particular value have become less salient in the 1980s due to technological changes.

- The Soviets, in the meantime, have been in a phase of consolidation and have concentrated their military assets in support of the key constituent members of their empire (Angola, Afghanistan, Syria, Libya, and so on). In this respect, they remain just as competitive and prone to taking risks as they were in the 1970s.

- Soviet behavior in Syria, Libya, South Yemen, and Iraq shows them continuing to transfer resources at a high rate to preserve their position of influence. At the same time, all these countries (with the exception of the PDRY) are able to pay their own way so that the economic constraints that have hampered the Soviets' relationships with other Third World clients do not apply here. Indeed, continuing high levels of arms sales will be all the more important with the decline in prices for Soviet oil and the concomitant loss of hard currency revenues.

- The main effect of the downgrading of the power projection mission institutionally is that the Soviet leadership is not likely to seek new and creative uses for Soviet military power and will probably not break precedents in the use of force the way it did from 1964 to 1979. In fact, in areas such as naval diplomacy the Soviets are already less active than they were a decade ago.

- It seems rather unlikely that the Soviets will commit themselves to building qualitatively new capabilities for Third World intervention— for example, something that would allow them to project power into the eastern Mediterranean/Arab-Israeli theater more effectively than is possible at present. An interesting test case will be their use of the new large-deck carrier.[46]

Notes

1. This term was used by Carl Jacobsen, who stated, "It has been established that the early 1970s saw the emergence and evolution of what can only be called a Soviet 'doctrine of intervention.'" *Soviet Strategic Initiatives* (New York: Praeger, 1979), p. 26.

2. If one looks beyond the Middle East/Persian Gulf area, one can multiply examples of Soviet military activism in the early 1980s to include arms to Nicaragua, Cuba, and North Korea, the direction of the MPLA offensive against UNITA in Angola, and the deployment of aircraft and ships to Cam Ranh Bay in Vietnam.

3. Nonetheless, it is possible to make the argument that the Soviets *did* have opportunities to take a more risk-prone or activist posture in the Irana-Iraq war and with regard to Pakistan.

4. See, for example, Michael MccGwire, *Military Objectives in Soviet Foreign Policy* (Washington, DC: Brookings Institution, 1987), appendix C, "The Debate over Naval Roles and Missions."

5. The argument has been made that contemporary Soviet surface combatants were "intended to provide forces able to engage a carrier battle group far from the Soviet Union, and so of shielding an insurgency from Western intervention." (Norman Friedman, "The Soviet Fleet in Transition," *US Naval Institute Proceedings/Naval Review* (1983), p. 163). Aside from the fact that Gorshkov never states this as his intention, the notion that the Soviets were contemplating combat operations against U.S. carrier battle groups is highly implausible. Moscow has demonstrated in a variety of ways that its stake in even as important a Middle Eastern client as Egypt is sufficiently low as to be not worth the risk of direct conflict with the United States.

6. Development of large antisubmarine ships to protect SSBNs started considerably earlier, with the *Kashin* and *Kresta I* classes. See Robert G. Weinland, "The Evolution of Soviet Requirements for Naval Forces: Solving the Problems of the Early 1960s," *Survival* 26 (January-February, 1984), p. 23.

7. Evidence from this comes partly from Mohammed Haykal. According to him, Grechko told the Egyptian defense minister on the eve of the June War to "stand firm. Whatever you have to face, you will find us with you. Don't let yourself be blackmailed by the Americans or anyone else." Haykal, *The Sphinx and the Commissar* (New York: Harper and Row, 1978), pp. 179–180.

8. See Uri Ra'anan, "Soviet Decision-Making in the Middle East, 1969–73," in Michael MccGwire et al., eds., *Soviet Naval Policy: Objectives and Constraints* (New York: Praeger, 1975).

9. Marshal Andrey Grechko, "The Leading Role of the CPSU in Building the Army of a Developed Socialist Society," *Voprosy Istorii KPSS,* April 1974. (Emphasis added.)

10. This mission was given further theoretical elaboration by any number of other Soviet military writers from the early 1970s on. Much of this material is discussed in Mark N. Katz, *The Third World in Soviet Military Thought* (Baltimore: Johns Hopkins University Press, 1982).

11. Strategic ASW in the case of the navy, and combined arms operations on the central front in the cases of the airborne forces and VTA.

12. For an extended discussion of these changes, see Jeremy Azrael, *The Soviet Civilian Leadership and the High Command: 1976-1986* (Santa Monica, CA: The RAND Corporation, R–3521-HF, 1987).

13. Italics added. Dmitriy Ustinov, "Strengthening the National Defense Capability of the Soviet Union," *Tap chi quan doi nhan dan* (Hanoi), November 1982.

14. For more documentation of this and other points, see F. Fukuyama, *Soviet Civil*

Military Relations and the Power Projection Mission (Santa Monica, CA: The RAND Corporation, R-3504-AF, 1987).

15. Marshal Ogarkov, *Soviet Military Encyclopedia,* September 1979.

16. See Katz, *The Third World in Soviet Military Thought,* pp. 18–21, 38–39.

17. See MccGwire, *Soviet Military Objectives,* appendix C, p. 33; Bruce Watson, "Gorshkov's Views on a Unified Military Strategy and Its Implications for the Soviet Navy," *Soviet Union/Union Sovietique 9* (1982), p. 228; Charles Peterson, *The 'Stalbo' Debates: Their Point of Departure,* CNA Professional Paper No. 404, January 1984, pp. 3–4.

18. Admiral V. Chernavin, "Naval Theory," *Morskoy Sbornik* 1 (1982).

19. The first edition of *The Sea Power of the State* was signed to press in November 1975 and therefore presumably had Grechko's approval.

20. Bradford Dismukes and Kenneth G. Weiss, *Mare Mosso: The Mediterranean Theater,* Center for Naval Analyses, Professional Paper No. 423, Alexandria, VA, November 1984, pp. 2–8. It cannot be argued that the Lebanon crisis was less important than either the Jordanian crisis of 1970 or the Indo-Pakistani crisis of 1971, particularly in light of the U.S. show of force off the coast of Lebanon.

21. MccGwire, *Soviet Military Objectives,* p. 444ff.

22. For example, see Gorshkov's article "U.S. Aircraft Carriers—An Instrument of Expansion," *Krasnaya Zvezda,* 1983.

23. Plans for this class of carrier were laid in the 1970s and originally called for catapults, arresting gear, and other equipment that for the first time would give the Soviet Navy the capability of launching high-performance aircraft. These have subsequently been scaled back, and the lead ship will employ VTOL aircraft like the *Kiev.*

24. Indeed, with the 5000+ nm ranges of the latest Soviet and U.S. SLBMs, many targets can be hit while the submarine is still in port.

5. The second edition of *The Sea Power of the State* did not appear until 1979, and the Stalbo debate did not occur until the 1980s.

26. For a detailed description of this debate, see F. Fukuyama, *Moscow's Post-Brezhnev Reassessment of the Third World* (Santa Monica, CA: The RAND Corporation, 1986; and Francis Fukuyana, "Gorbachev and the Third World," *Foreign Affairs,* Spring 1986.

27. Arkady Shevchenko gives several examples of this in *Breaking with Moscow.* (New York: Knopf, 1985).

28. See Fukayama, "Gorbachev and the Third World."

29. Syria's radical credentials and pan- Arabist ideological purity have been tarnished considerably by its totally cynical pursuit of power politics—that is, supporting the Lebanese Christians against the PLO in 1976, backing Iran against Iraq after the outbreak of the Gulf war in 1980, and crushing the Arafat faction of the PLO in Tripoli in 1984, while the narrowly sectarian basis of the Assad regime was demonstrated by the ongoing war it has been waging against Sunni fundamentalists. Syria's brand of pan-Arabism itself has been overtaken by a more recent and fashionable ideological trend, Islamic fundamentalism, so that Syria can no longer be said to represent an "idea" of any great consequence in the Muslim world.

30. The persistent rumors in the Arab world that Moscow extended security guarantees to Syria have inevitably been the product of wishful thinking outright disinformation on the part of Damascus.

31. For an example of this line of argument, see Cynthia Roberts, "Soviet Arms Trnasfer Policy and the Decision to Upgrade Syrian Air Defences," *Survey* 25 (July-August 1983).

32. This becomes more evident in light of the transfer of SA-5s to Libya, discussed later in this chapter.

33. Judith Miller, "Syrian Fear: Soviet Shift," *New York Times,* 14 February 1984; Judith Miller, "Israelis Reporting a Soviet Buildup," *New York Times,* 29 April 1983.

34. Michael Getler, "New Generation of Soviet Arms Seen Near Deployment," *Washington Post,* 11 October 1983.

35. Dennis Ross, "Changing Soviet Behavior: Soviet Responses to the Lebanon and Iran-Iraq Conflicts," Unpublished Paper, May 1986, pp. 23–24.

36. See Lisa Anderson, "Qaddafi and the Kremlin," *Problems of Communism,* 34 (September-October 1985), pp. 29, 33ff.

37. *Ibid.*

38. Bill Keller, "Soviet Expands Surveillance Off Libya, Weinberger Says," *New York Times,* 14 January 1986; George C. Wilson, "Soviets Send Flagship to Libya Port," *Washington Post,* 15 January 1986.

39. "Libya Is Reported to Find Soviet Help Insufficient," *New York Times,* 14 April 1986.

40. *Ibid.*

41. Ihsan A. Hijazi, "Libya-Soviet Ties Reported Strained," *New York Times,* 6 May 1986.

42. Foreign Broadcast Information Service, Soviet Union *Daily Report,* 28 May 1986, p. H1; Celestine Bohlen, "Soviet Cautions Libyan on Terror," *Washington Post,* 28 May 1986.

43. For more on this phenomenon, see F. Fukuyama, "The Rise and Fall of the Marxist-Leninist Vanguard Party," *Survey,* May-June 1985, pp. 116–135.

44. For much of the following section, I am relying on personal comments from Professor Stephen Page.

45. *International Defense—DMS Intelligence,* 7 February 1983; *Defense and Economy,* 23 April 1984; International Institute for Strategic Studies, *Military Balance, 1983–84,* London, 1984.

46. My prediction is that they will be reluctant to deploy this ship in a future Middle East crisis because its superior capabilities mean it may have to be used.

11

The American Response
to State-Sponsored Terrorism

Brian M. Jenkins

On April 14, 1986, U.S. aircraft bombed selected targets in Libya. Although the United States in 1980 had attempted the rescue of American hostages held in Teheran and in 1985 had deployed fighters to persuade the pilot of an Egyptian plane carrying terrorist passengers to land at a U.S. base in Italy, this was the first time the United States had used military force in response to terrorism. The attack came approximately two and half years after terrorists detonated a huge truck bomb at the headquarters of the U.S. Marines in Lebanon, killing 241 marines and for all intents and purposes destroying the multinational peacekeeping force of which they were a part. Libya was not blamed for the attack. Intelligence officials believed, but could never prove, that Iran and Syria were behind the operation. The attack in Lebanon and the U.S. bombing of Libya, however, were linked, as we shall see. They embrace a period during which U.S. policy toward international terrorism, and specifically state-sponsored terrorism, was defined and ultimately implemented.

Although Americans were the number one targets of terrorist attacks abroad, for most Americans in the early 1980s terrorism remained a distant threat. In addition, government interest tended to be spasmodic. Terrorist attacks provoked occasional outrage, but between episodes the problem of terrorism tended to sink on the agenda. That began to change after the seizure of the U.S. embassy in Teheran. The protracted spectacle of blindfolded Americans paraded daily before Iranian mobs aroused strong emotional reactions. It spelled political disaster for President Jimmy Carter, whose defeat in the 1984 presidential election was directly attributed to his inability to free the hostages. And although the U.S. rescue attempt failed, it made the use of military force seem less reprehensible than it had become during the Vietnam War. The release of the hostages in January 1981 relieved the political crisis but left a residue of anger reflected in President Ronald Reagan's warning that terrorists who attacked Americans in the future would be met with "swift retribution."

In combating abroad, the United States faced a twofold problem. On the one hand, it had to protect Americans abroad against what had by the 1980s become almost routine terrorism. Diverse groups espousing a variety of causes had attacked American citizens and facilities in seventy-two countries. In responding to this threat, the U.S. posture was primarily a defensive one, which relied on physical security measures and generally cooperative local governments to protect U.S. citizens and pursue local terrorists.

Acts of terrorism that were instigated and supported by state sponsors posed a different sort of problem—one that seemed to be growing in the early 1980s, even though state sponsors never numbered more than a few. Nevertheless, state sponsorship of terrorism had serious consequences. It put more resources into the hands of the terrorists, permitting them to carry out more ambitious operations. Protection by government patrons also made them more difficult to combat.

State sponsorship also changed the equation of success and failure. Although the use of terrorist tactics had brought publicity, provoked alarm, and won occasional concessions, few terrorist groups could boast of having achieved any of their stated long-range goals. In that sense terrorism had failed, but the ruthless use of terrorism as an instrument to achieve certain national objectives could still impose costs, divert resources, encourage passivity, and alter policies.

The simultaneous terrorist attacks directed against the U.S. marines and French soldiers in Beiruit offer such an example. Despite the brave words of leaders who vowed that the attacks would have no effect on their policies, the bombings in fact demonstrated that the multinational peacekeeping force could not even protect itself, let alone maintain order in Lebanon. Its days were numbered, and without the multinational force the weak Lebanese government had no choice but to seek an accommodation with other forces in the region, including the Syrians, who were suspected of involvement in the terrorist attacks. Terrorism for the sake of influencing policy posed a more serious threat. Washington feared that other aggressive nations might be encouraged to adopt terrorism as a mode of surrogate warfare, against which it seemed the United States was ill prepared to defend itself.

The suicide attack on the U.S. marines in Beirut set off an intense debate in Washington. How should the United States respond to such acts of terrorism? Secretary of State George Shultz advocated a forceful response. In a speech to members of the Trilateral Commission, he spoke of the gray area between major war and millennial peace and of the contemporary weapons of state-sponsored terrorism. He said it was increasingly doubtful that a purely passive strategy could even begin to cope with the problem. The United States could not simply stand there and take terrorist punches. It needed an *active defense* (he underlined these words), which meant the use of military force. While the secretary of state did not rule out diplomacy as a means of dealing with terrorism, he rejected the separation between military options and diplomatic alternatives, pointing out that diplomatic success often rests on perceptions of military power.

The leaders of the U.S. military establishment took a different view. The soldiers were generally against the use of military force to combat terrorism, for both good and bad reasons. Warfare in the gray area, as the secretary of state had put it, was not the preferred mission of most military men. The use of military force, in their view, should be reserved for threats of the greatest consequence—war with the Soviet Union, for example—not some putative war against terrorists.

It was not simply that fighting terrorists was not the "big war" the military was trained for and equipped to fight. The soldiers' reluctance had a lot to do with their reading of American attitudes. A military campaign against terrorism seemed filled with the perils of imprecise missions, political constraints, and uncertain measures of success. It disturbingly resembled the problem of fighting insurgencies, and the U.S. military had had its fill of that in Southeast Asia. It had taken nearly 10 years for the military to recover from the disaster of Vietnam, and military leaders were fearful that military action against terrorists, with the potential risks of highly visible failure, civilian casualties, and a lack of results, would squander the goodwill and support that it had only recently regained. That, in turn, would imperil congressional support for the major weapons systems the military felt were essential to meet a major threat. Thus, trying to fight terrorists with military force could jeopardize U.S. defenses.

In response to the secretary of state's arguments, the Pentagon offered a list of conditions to be met before military force could be used against terrorists:

The United States must possess adequate intelligence to identify targets and to justify the use of military force, and it must be prepared to divulge that intelligence.

The military action contemplated must be legal.

It must be timely and appropriate in terms of the scale of operations.

There must be little risk of civilian casualties.

It must have a good chance of success.

It must have public support.

While one cannot argue with any of these considerations individually, collectively they make the chances of getting a green light for any operation very slim—which may have been their intended purpose.

The debate swirled on inside the government from October 1983 to April 1984. Then, on April 3, 1984, two things happened: The secretary of state made his first major public speech on terrorism, in which he argued that if the United States was to combat state-sponsored terrorism effectively, it must be prepared to use force; and the president signed a new National Security Directive on terrorism stating that military force henceforth would be an option in this battle. Together, the directive and the speech constituted a declaration of war against terrorists. It was, to be sure, a curious declaration against an unspecified terrorist foe, to be fought at an unknown place and time, with weapons yet to be chosen, but it was a declaration nonetheless. The advocates of force had won the first round. It was one thing to declare war, however, and quite another to fight it.

First of all, what would be the objectives of using military force? The first would be to reduce the terrorists' or their state sponsors' capabilities to continue their terrorist campaigns, but this is very difficult to do. Terrorist operations require only a handful of people recruited from a large reservoir, and they do not need much in the way of infrastructure. To destroy a state's capabilities to wage a war of terrorism would require more damage than the United States might be willing to inflict.

Can the United States persuade state sponsors of terrorism to desist? Given the fanatical leadership in Teheran, U.S. frustration in dealing with the Iranian government during the embassy hostage episode, and the unpredictability of Libya's Qaddafi, it is doubtful that the United States can persuade the sponsoring countries in the Middle East to do or not to do anything.

By demonstrating that sponsoring terrorism will invoke a U.S. military reprisal, can the United States discourage other states from adopting terrorism as a mode of conflict? Possibly. Can the United States demonstrate that it is not impotent? Probably. Can the United States satisfy domestic demand for action? Certainly, but while public support may be a prerequisite for military action, satisfying domestic opinion should not suffice as the objective of such action. Continued acts of provocation without any U.S. response, however, could make public pressure irresistible, even if military responses were ill considered.

If the United States decides to use military force in response to state-sponsored terrorism, whom does it hit? The terrorist group? The principal advantage of directing operations against the terrorists is the direct connection. If they attack you, you attack them. That is easy to justify. In addition, fewer political liabilities, and probably fewer allied objections, are involved in attacking terrorist groups than in attacking governments.

The principal disadvantages of going after a terrorist group are the paucity of significant targets (those that are destroyed can be easily reconstituted); the high risk of visible failure and, consequently, the risk of U.S. military casualties or prisoners; the risk of civilian casualties; and the possibility that the action may have little effect on the state sponsors.

Military operations against state sponsors present a different array of advantages and disadvantages. On the positive side, states offer a wider range of vulnerable targets. In attacking these targets, the United States could more easily avoid civilian casualties than it could in going after terrorist groups, and it could impose costs that would be more likely to affect decision making. On the negative side, some proof of the connection between the terrorist perpetrator and the state sponsor is needed to justify the operation. In addition, attacking states incurs greater political liabilities, and there is the risk of escalation. Finally, if the United States were to attack a state sponsor of terrorism, which one should it attack?

A country-by-country look at the problem, focusing on the three countries most frequently mentioned as sponsors of terrorism, revealed an array of risks. The principal risk of military action against Syria is that country's defenses and the resulting high risk of U.S. casualties and POWs—a risk that was clearly illustrated in November 1983 when a U.S. Navy flyer was shot down and captured.

Iran, weakened by war, presents less formidable defenses, but it is more difficult for the United States to reach targets throughout the country with air power. In addition, as we know now, beginning in the summer of 1985 the United States engaged in secret negotiations with Iran in an attempt to free American hostages in Lebanon and develop closer relations with Iranian moderates. That provided Iran with immunity against U.S. military action despite its designation by the U.S. government as a leading state sponsor of terrorism.

In Libya the principal problem was the presence of American and friendly nationals, which could cause U.S. allies to oppose or denounce military operations there. Qaddafi had already demonstrated his willingness to create hostage situations in his dealings with West Germany and the United Kindgom.

Until April 1986 international terrorism continued to pose a challenge, but no military option seemed relevant or appropriate. The United States did not respond with force when a suicide driver crashed a truck loaded with explosives into the U.S. embassy annex in East Beirut in September 1984. There was no military response to the terrorist attacks on U.S. servicemen in Western Europe. Military force was not used in dealing with the kidnapping of U.S. citizens in Lebanon. Nor did military retaliation seem applicable to the airline hijackings in which U.S. citizens were singled out and killed.

But public pressure for some kind of action was building. It was not simply that international terrorism was increasing; statistics merely reinforced what people saw on their television sets. And it was not simply that U.S. citizens continued to be targets of terrorists abroad; they always had been. Most terrorist violence had focused on specific target groups: U.S. diplomats, servicemen, or businessmen. This did not make terrorism any more tolerable, but somehow these were seen as occupations that entailed risks, including terrorism.

Beginning with the hijacking of TWA Flight 847 in June 1985, however, this perception began to change. The passengers aboard this plane were not only diplomats, servicemen, and businessmen, they were also ordinary Americans on vacation or visiting relatives in Europe, and that made terrorism more frightening. The news media also played a tremendous role in this particular episode, and for its duration, the TWA hijacking was perhaps the most intensely covered hostage incident in history.

The TWA hijacking was followed in October 1985 by the hijacking of a Mediterranean cruise ship, the *Achille Lauro*. In the hijacking of Flight 847, the terrorists had beaten and murdered a young U.S. serviceman. In the *Achille Lauro* hijacking, they murdered a 72-year-old American invalid.

The *Achille Lauro* hijacking provided the U.S. government with its first opportunity to take direct action. Having learned that the hijackers had been released by Egypt and were flying across the Mediterranean in an Egyptian airliner, the president ordered U.S. fighter aircraft to intercept the flight and force it to land at a U.S. base in Italy, where the hijackers were taken into custody by Italian authorities.

In November 1985 terrorists hijacked an Egyptian airliner. Once again, they singled out American hostages. Two women and one man were ordered to stand in the doorway of the aircraft, where they were shot in the back. Two of the victims survived, but the third died. The episode ended in further tragedy when Egyptian commandos attempted to storm the aircraft. In the ensuing gun battle and fire, fifty-four of the remaining hostages died.

After the Egyptian hijacking came the terrorist assaults at the Rome and Vienna airports in December 1985, when Palestinian terrorists loyal to Abu Nidal opened fire on passengers, killing sixteen and wounding ninety-nine at Rome, and killing three and wounding thirty-nine at Vienna. Five Americans died in the two attacks, including a twelve-year-old girl.

In April 1986 terrorists planted a bomb aboard TWA Flight 840 to Athens. The bomb detonated while the plane was in midair, blasting a hole in the side of the fuselage and hurling four passengers, all Americans, including a mother and her infant child, to their deaths.

These five episodes, each a deliberate demonstration of brutality against persons guilty of nothing except being in the wrong place at the wrong time, alarmed and angered Americans. American tourist traffic to Europe plummeted. Asked whether fear of terrorism had caused them or would cause them to alter their travel plans abroad, two out of three Americans said yes. Nor did Americans feel safe at home; according to one opinion poll, a majority of Americans expressed the belief that terrorists from abroad would soon carry out attacks in the United States. Fear congealed to anger. Americans felt that European governments were not doing enough to combat terrorism. They felt that the U.S. government should do more, too. It mattered little to the American public whether Pentagon planners thought terrorism was a threat to national security—an overwhelming majority of American citizens already felt so. They saw terrorism as a form of warfare that had to be countered like any other form of warfare, and that meant the use of military force. Again, by a margin of better than 2 to 1, Americans thought that the United States should use military force against terrorists and their state sponsors, even if doing so would inevitably cause civilian casualties.

In retrospect, we might ask whether public pressure forced the government to take military action or whether the government fanned public anger to gain support for action it wanted to take anyway. This is a fair question. The view herein is that while government officials sustained a generally bellicose rhetoric throughout the period dating from the Beirut attack on the U.S. marines to the air attack on Libya, the terrorist incidents of 1985—their quality more than their number or scale—were the catalyst that stoked public wrath. During the 30-month period preceding the bombing of Libya, the government on several occasions could have responded militarily and with popular support, had it chosen to do so; but it did not, sometimes with political embarrassment. Whether their government wanted them to be or not, Americans were mad as hell!

The question of whether the U.S. government directed public wrath against Libya rather than Iran or Syria, regardless of their comparative roles in sponsoring terrorism, is more complex. Libya was certainly no innocent party. Although U.S. government figures credit Iran and Syria with sponsoring more incidents, Libya is clearly one of the principal state sponsors of terrorist attacks. In addition, although Libya had no apparent role in the hijacking of TWA Flight 847 and had at most an indirect role in the hijacking of the *Achille Lauro*, Abu Nidal's group, which was blamed for the Egyptian hijacking and the attacks at the Rome and Vienna airports, draws support from both Libya and Syria; moreover, U.S. officials blamed Libya for the April 5, 1986 bombing of the LaBelle Discotheque in West Berlin, which was cited as the principal provocation for the U.S. bombing of Libya. And while Libyan leader Qaddafi argued about the definition of terrorism, he seldom denied Libya's role in the assassinations of his foes abroad or in supporting the most violent factions of the Palestinian movement. Instead (and in marked contrast to Iranian officials and Syria's Assad, both of whom operated with some discretion), Qaddafi, for his own political purposes, boasted of his role as the United States' principal antagonist. Responsible or not, he publicly rejoiced in American casualties and warned of more to come. This boasting was principally intended for his radical Arab audience, but his remarks were reported internationally and provoked growing outrage in the United States.

Accurately reflecting the United States' belligerent mood, President Reagan picked up the gauntlet and hurled back his own warnings to Qaddafi. The verbal duel between the two leaders began to resemble the menacing hype that precedes a professional wrestling match. Qaddafi became the center of attention, which he probably found both emotionally satisfying and politically useful. On the U.S. side, fear and anger focused on a single villain. For the American people, the complex issue of international terrorism was reduced to a personal matter: something had to be done about Qaddafi.

There may have been an element of deliberate provocation in the words and actions of the U.S. government. The president could have ignored Qaddafi's extravagant remarks, although to have done so would have put him out of tune with the American people, with whom, as an extremely successful and popular politician, he had a very close rapport. Therefore, the maneuvers of the U.S. Sixth Fleet and the deliberate challenge to Libya's claim of sovereignty over what the United States and others regarded as international waters could be seen in three lights: (1) as goading Qaddafi into some ill-considered action; (2) as part of a long-established U.S. practice of vigorously challenging all such threats to open seas (as administration officials argue); or (3) as an attempt to deter Qaddafi from further action by demonstrating overwhelmingly superior military power.

If the objective was to deter further terrorist action, it failed. On April 5, a terrorist bomb exploded at the LaBelle Discotheque in West Berlin, killing 3 and injuring 196. According to U.S. intelligence, the attack had been instigated by Libya and was part of a campaign of terrorist actions about to be carried out against U.S. personnel throughout Europe and the Middle East.

The Berlin bombing tipped the decision for military action. It was felt that something had to be done to persuade Libya to halt its terrorist operatives. From the longer-range perspective offered by Secretary of State Shultz, the United States had to demonstrate that it could and would use military force in response to state-sponsored terrorism. In addition, the American public was demanding some visible action.

The American attack on Libya was successful in the strictest military sense. A complex military operation had been carried out with precision and with minimal losses. It was marred, however, by the accidental bombing of a residential quarter in Tripoli, resulting in the death of thrity-seven civilians.

It is more difficult to measure the effectiveness of the U.S. attack as a deterrent to state-sponsored terrorism. It produced no apparent diminution of international terrorism. Terrorist operations carried out by Middle Eastern groups in Western Europe did decline, but the apparent lull may simply have been the result of the extraordinary security measures taken by European authorities who fully expected Libya to retaliate for the U.S. attack. Qaddafi himself dropped from sight for a while, and when he reappeared, he did seem more subdued. Some attributed this to deep depression; an adopted daughter had been killed in the U.S. attack. Some believed his political authority had been reduced.

The lull lasted until September, when terrorists believed to be connected with Abu Nidal hijacked a Pan American airliner in Karachi and attacked a synagogue in Istanbul. Twenty-two died in the Istanbul attack, while in Karachi terrorists aboard the plane, possibly fearing a commando assault, opened fire on the hostages, leaving nineteen dead. Initial intelligence reports indicated that Libya played a role in the Pan American attack.

As a deterrent to other state sponsors of terrorism, the bombing of Libya failed. Iran and Syria continue to operate, although perhaps with greater attention to covering their tracks. Nonetheless, the American people saw the attack as a great success. Qaddafi had been dealt a blow and had less to say in public. Terrorism, for a spell, was out of the headlines.

12

Soviet Attitudes toward Middle Eastern Terrorism

Ariel Merari

Several studies have been published in recent years on the issue of Soviet support of terrorism.[1] The cumulative body of evidence leaves no doubt about the Soviet support of terrorist groups. Even an author such as Galia Golan, who stresses the Soviet preference for political means over armed struggle as the recipe for national liberation movements, concludes:

> It would appear, then, that given the Soviet attitude towards the use of terror, its policies are connected with the realities of the present situation. That is, without necessarily preferring or even condoning it, the phenomenon of the use of terror may be exploitable for ends beneficial to the Soviet Union. At the very least it should be prevented from working against Soviet interests. For these objectives the Soviets have sought to contact and penetrate, if possible manipulate and exploit such groups.[2]

Indeed, the Soviet approach to terrorism is exploitative rather than initiating. The Soviet Union has directly and indirectly supported existing terrorist groups, but it has not created them.

Without attempting to reconcile the disparity between official Soviet writings on terrorism as a mode of warfare and indisputable Soviet behavior in actuality, it is important to indicate the main features of Soviet sponsorship for terrorism. The most important of these features is pragmatism: The manner and scope of Soviet support of terrorist groups is dictated by profit and loss considerations much more than by ideology. Thus, the Soviet Union supports terrorist groups in Third World countries more directly and more readily than in Western countries, not only because insurgent groups in the Third World better fit their definition of national liberation movements but because such support is considerably less risky in terms of political price in the international arena.

Pragmatism and political convenience are also expressed in the Soviets' general preference for channeling their support for insurgent movements through intermediaries. Direct Soviet assistance to a group that systematically uses terrorist tactics is rarely given, such as when the group in question has acquired a considerable degree of international legitimacy not only in the Eastern Bloc and the Third

World but in the West as well. The two typical movements in this category are the Palestine Liberation Organization (PLO) and the African National Congress (ANC). The closest example in Latin America is the Salvadoran Farabundo Marti National Liberation Front (FMNLF). In contrast to the PLO and the ANC, however, Soviet support for the FMNLF is mostly political, and the practical aspects of assistance are left to its satellites, mainly Cuba and Nicaragua. In the great majority of the cases in Latin America, as well as in other regions of the world, the Soviet Union does not even openly condone the terrorist group, let alone grant it direct assistance.

It should therefore be emphasized that the term *Soviet support* is rather general and inaccurate. In most cases the Soviet Union itself does not directly assist terrorist groups. This task is usually the domain of Soviet satellites, and Soviet support is implied on the basis of the assumption that these satellites' actions are not only condoned by the Soviet Union but could not have been carried out without its permission. While this assumption is plausible enough in the case of Warsaw Pact countries, it cannot be taken for granted regarding Cuba and Nicaragua, for instance, and even less so concerning other Soviet clients, such as Syria and Libya. A safer, albeit more vague, wording would, therefore, refer to the Soviet *bloc* support of terrorist groups. This distinction has particular importance in the context of this paper. In the Middle Eastern arena, more than in other regions such as Latin America and Western Europe, the Soviet Union's attitude toward terrorism is influenced and sometimes obscured by its relations with client states. It should be understood that Soviet influence over its Middle Eastern clients is not uniform. Moreover, Soviet clients in the Middle East have a record of supporting and even creating terrorist groups for their own needs with no direct connection to Soviet interests.

In the context of this chapter, the term *Soviet bloc* includes Soviet allies such as Libya, Syria, and the PLO. Although these Soviet clients cannot be described as Soviet puppets, the Soviet Union has considerable leverage over them and could presumably exert significant influence over their attitudes toward terrorism. For one, Libya (and even more so Syria) relies on the Soviet Union to deter large-scale American punitive attacks on them in retaliation for their sponsorship of anti-American terrorist activity.

It is therefore necessary to distinguish between several facets of Soviet policy concerning Middle Eastern terrorism. The remainder of this chapter examines several angles of the Soviet Union's attitude toward Middle Eastern terrorism.

The People's Democratic Republic of Yemen (PDRY)

Special interest in the PDRY stems from the fact that in the Arab world the PDRY is closest to the concept of a Soviet satellite. In no other Middle Eastern country are Soviet influence and presence as significant as in the PDRY. Furthermore, unlike Libya, the PDRY does not espouse a spirit of international revolutionary fervor, and unlike Syria, it has no direct interests and relatively little involvement in Palestinian issues. It is therefore possible to assume that the PDRY's involvement in international terrorism beyond the Arab peninsula serves Soviet bloc interests.

There is sufficient evidence to conclude that members of several European terrorist groups have been trained in the PDRY since the mid-1970s.[3] Nevertheless, evidence based on the generally reliable testimony of captured or repented terrorists has indicated that such training has taken place in the camps of the Wadi Haddad Faction. Allegations of direct Soviet involvement in training have so far remained unsubstantiated.[4] One may, therefore, claim that the PDRY is merely serving as a host for radical Palestinian terrorists, who in turn train foreign terrorists for their own reasons, without direct involvement or encouragement on the part of the South Yemeni government.

Still, although existing evidence does not allow drawing firm conclusions about active Soviet bloc participation in the sponsorship of foreign terrorists' training on PDRY soil, it is reasonable to assume that this kind of sponsorship could not have occurred without the PDRY's full knowledge and consent and, in view of the Soviets' status and role in the PDRY, is also condoned by the Soviet Union.

The PLO

The Soviet Union's relations with the PLO and its attitude toward the PLO's activities go beyond the question of using terrorism in the service of Soviet interests. For one thing, the Soviets truly regard the PLO as a genuine movement for national liberation. Moreover, they consider the PLO as an influential entity in Middle Eastern politics and as a stable rather than an ephemeral phenomenon that is worth a long-range investment. These basic constituents of the Soviet attitude toward the PLO have received overt expressions such as the granting of full diplomatic status to PLO representatives in Moscow and in other Soviet bloc countries, official visits of PLO leaders to Moscow, and an undenied assistance in training and arms.

Ever since 1970 the Soviets have regarded the official leadership of the PLO as the genuine representatives of the Palestinian national movement. Soviet relations with the movement were channeled through the PLO bureaucracy, although this bureaucracy was dominated by Fatah, which could not be described as a communist movement by any stretch of the imagination. Arrangements for training Palestinians in Soviet and other Warsaw Pact countries' camps, for instance, were not made through the Marxist Democratic Front for the Liberation of Palestine (DELP) but through PLO functionaries who allocated places in the training groups to the various member organizations.

The PLO's misadventures after the 1982 war have obfuscated the Soviet position. Not only has Yasser Arafat's leadership been seriously challanged by the majority of the organizations that comprise the PLO,[5] but a major rift has formed between Arafat and Syria, the most important Soviet client in the Middle East. Arafat's accord with Jordan and his passes at the United States have not endeared him to the Soviets. Under these conditions, the Soviet refusal to side with the rejectionist groups (the organizations that seceded from Arafat's PLO and founded the Salvation Front) has been truly remarkable. Although they have refused to invite Arafat to Moscow (a symbol of support he very much wants), other Fatah leaders, especially Farouk Kadoumi and Salah Khalaf, who have rightly been considered as a brake to Arafat's Jordanian orientation, have, unlike Fatah rebel leaders, (such as Abu Musa), been welcome guests in the Soviet Union. The fact that the Soviets did not dump Arafat and put their weight on the side of the rejectionists—whose pure anti-American position might guarantee the Soviets relatively headache-free relations—indicates that the Soviets place a high value on the extent of popular support that an insurgent movement enjoys. Presumably, in the Soviet view, the one factor in Arafat's favor is that most of the Palestinian people are behind him, and this single fact seems to outweigh his many disadvantages: ideological impurity (from a Marxist point of view), flirting with the United States and its allies in the region, and the animosity between him and Syria. Despite strong Syrian pressure, the Soviet Union continues to regard the PLO as the legitimate representative of the Palestinian people. The Soviets also seem to use their influence on the secessionist groups to persuade them to reunite the PLO. Their effort has borne fruit, at least in the case of the DFLP, the closest ideologically to Moscow among the various Palestinian groups, which is striving to achieve a compromise between Arafat and the rejectionists.

Soviet support of the PLO needs no proof. In the narrower context of this chapter, however, a more specific question concerns the Soviet Union's attitude toward the PLO's terrorist activity. In this regard, differentiation must be made between terrorist attacks in Israel and in the administered territories and Palestinian terrorist activity abroad. The Soviets clearly approve of, even praise, the former. An article that appeared in the Soviet press conveys this view:

> The term "terrorism" should be clarified. Only those with malicious intentions regard the Arab struggle of liberation from the Israeli occupiers as terrorism. . . . General Ehud Barak, the Director of Israel's Military Intelligence, admitted in mid-October, 1985 that in three quarters of this year Palestinian partisans carried out 660 operations—almost twice as many as in the same period last year. Eighty were killed and tens of Israeli soldiers were wounded. It should be emphasized that these were soldiers, because the Palestinian leaders consistently stress that their attacks are directed against military targets, not against civilians, as Israel does.[6]

In Soviet terminology, the derogatory word for political terrorists is *bandits*, whereas the word *partisans* carries a positive meaning. The emphasis that the attacks were directed against soldiers (in reality most of the casualties have been civilians) is also meant to justify this kind of terrorist activity. This justification is apparently important for Palestinian terrorist activity to be officially admissible by the Soviets, since in the case of particularly appalling attacks on civilians (such as the hijacking of a bus in March 1978, which resulted in thirty-five fatalities), Soviet announcements did not hesitate to make crude distortions of the truth by describing the victims as soldiers.

The Soviet position regarding the PLO's international terrorist attacks is more complex. Traditionally, the Soviet Union has officially opposed this kind of activity. The formula for settling the disparity between Soviet backing of the PLO and the fact that this organization is involved in international terrorism has been as follows:

1. Condemning the terrorist act itself.
2. Saying that the perpetrators' motivation is nevertheless understandable.
3. Denying the PLO's responsibility.
4. Blaming Israel and the United States for sponsoring and using terrorism themselves.

A typical example is the description of the seizure of an Israeli yacht in Larnaca on September 25, 1985, by Fatah members, in which a woman and two men were murdered in cold blood:

> In September, in the port of Larnaca in Cyprus, three bodies of Israeli tourists were found. Information leaked that these were not only tourists, but agents of the Mossad, led by a certain lady known under three different family names. Who murdered and for what purpose—this question remained unsolved. But it became known soon who wants to utilize this murder. Israel started blaming the PLO for the murder, and although this organization strongly denied any connection with this act, Israeli air force carried out a "retaliation attack" on its base in Tunisia.[7]

A similar response appeared following the hijacking of the *Achille Lauro* on October 7, 1985, by the Abu al-Abbas faction of the Palestine Liberation Front (PLF), a group closely linked to Arafat's PLO. On that occasion, Leonid Ponomarev wrote:

> Well, the anger and indignation of the Americans at the misdeed which was committed on board of the cruise ship by aggressors is understandable and just. The crimes of terrorists, wherever they are committed, should be punished with all the severity of the law, and this severity must be observed rigorously with respect to all persons who commit such acts. In connection with this, one cannot fail to recall the no less malicious criminal hijackers of a Soviet plane, the father and son Brazinskas, who have settled down on a lasting basis and without punishment in the United States.[8]

Izvestiya, commenting on the U.S. interception of the Egyptian plane that carried the *Achille Lauro* hijackers, went even further in condemning the United States and almost expressing sympathy for the terrorists:

> Prime Minister Craxi showed a principled and strong position in refusing to extradite the four Palestinians to the United States, declaring that Italy had no jurisdictional basis justifying the arrest of the other two Arabs.
>
> An event celebrated in the United States as a victory has turned out to be another link in a chain of acts of repression and terrorism. When a power such as the United States joins the terrorists' circle, it is ten times more dangerous and irresponsible for the whole world, not only for a handful of passengers.[9]

As in the case of international terrorists training in the PDRY, it is highly unlikely that the Soviets are unaware of the PLO's direct responsibility for international terrorist attacks. That does not necessarily mean that they support such attacks, but at the very least they have been uncooperative in efforts to combat them.

Libya and Syria: Troublesome Partners

Libya and Syria are the Soviet Union's two most valuable clients and allies in the region. Both of them have an undeniable record of sponsoring and using international terrorism for purposes that are at least partly overlapping with those of the Soviet Union. In late 1985 and early 1986 both Libya and Syria were involved in a wave of international terrorist attacks on U.S. and Israeli targets. In at least some of these attacks their involvement took an active operational form, such as giving a ready-made explosive device to the perpetrator at a Libyan or Syrian embassy shortly before the operation.

Basically, Soviet attitudes toward Libyan- and Syrian-sponsored terrorism has been similar to its attitude toward the PLO: condemnation of the act while denying the perpetrating state's responsibility. For example, following the bombing of the West Berlin discotheque in which two persons were killed and nearly two hundred were wounded, Vladimir Lomeiko, the Soviet foreign ministry's spokesman, responded: "The Soviet Union condemns all terrorist acts . . . [but] it rejects any attempt to place responsibility on states that have absolutely nothing to do with them, including the Libyan authorities who have stated that they had nothing to do with this [Berlin] action."[10]

One aspect of Soviet attitude merits special mention with regard to Libyan and Syrian terrorism: the response to U.S. threats to punish state sponsors of terrorism and, eventually, to the United States' punitive raid on Libya. In early 1986, when tension mounted following an increased level of terrorist activity and

growing U.S. warnings were directed at Libya, the Soviets issued general statements of support for Libya against "U.S. state terrorism."[11] Nevertheless, they
were careful enough to refrain from any clear commitment of military involvement
in case U.S. threats materialized.

Soviet condemnations of the April 15 American raid on Libya were not surprising. More interesting are the reports that, following the raid, Soviet leaders
exerted pressure on Libya and Syria to halt their international terrorist activity.[12]
Apparently, in the Soviet view terrorism becomes too dangerous when it forces
them to choose between a superpower confrontation and the loss of face involved
in deserting a client in trouble.

Being on the Wrong Side of the Barrel

In September 1985 Syrian troops were closing in on the last strongholds of the
Islamic Unification (Tawhid) Movement in Tripoli, Lebanon. The Tawhid is a
militia of a fundamentalist Sunni movement led by Sheikh Sa'id Sha'aban. They
had been longtime foes of Syria and fought alongside Arafat's forces against Syria
and the Palestinian rejectionist groups in the battle that preceded the evacuation
of PLO forces from Tripoli in December 1983. On September 30, 1985, when
the fate of Sheikh Sha'aban's militiamen seemed to be sealed, four Soviet diplomats were kidnapped in Beirut. Responsibility for the kidnapping was claimed by
the shadowy Shiite Islamic Jihad and by the previously unheard of Islamic Liberation Organization. While these names were not sufficient to identify the perpetrating organization with reasonable certainty, the kidnappers' demand was quite
clear: the removal of the Syrian siege from around Tripoli. A couple of days later
the abductors murdered Arkadi Katakov, one of the kidnapped diplomats, and a
caller claiming to be a member of the Islamic Jihad later threatened to blow up
the Soviet embassy in Beirut and demanded that all Soviets leave Beirut.

Rarely have the Soviets found themselves on the receiving end of international
terrorist attacks. Moreover, this has been the only incident, so far, in which the
Soviet Union has faced extortionate terrorism. The Soviet response in the aforementioned case was, therefore, of considerable interest, and to many observers
their overt reaction to the crisis was quite unexpected: the hasty evacuation of
more than half of their 150-odd diplomatic personnel from Beirut, without any
attempt to conceal what might be interpreted as a sign of weakness. More significant was the direct pressure exerted by the Soviets on Syria to concede to the
terrorists' demand to terminate the Tripoli siege on the Tawhid. A meeting between Syrian President Assad and Sheikh Sha'aban was arranged in Damascus on
October 3, 1985, only three days after the kidnapping. Yuri Suslikov, the Soviet
chargé d'affaires in Damascus, admitted that the Syrians agreed to hold the meeting only under severe Soviet pressure.[13] A cease-fire agreement was reached, and
the Syrian siege of Tripoli was lifted.

Another facet of the Soviet Union's response involved its behavior in the United Nations in the wake of the kidnapping. It is not surprising that Soviet organs condemned the abduction as an "ultra-right criminal act" and expressed vague threats that "violence against Soviet citizens will further aggravate the guilt of all those who have anything to do with the matter."[14] This time, however, the Soviet Union extended its standard condemnation of anti-Soviet activities to the phenomenon of terrorism in general. In the months that followed the kidnapping, Soviet delegates supported U.N. motions against terrorism in an unprecedented manner. In December 1985, after more than a decade of debate, the U.N. General Assembly unanimously adopted a resolution condemning all acts of terrorism as criminal. Later that month the Soviet Union unprecedently supported a Security Council condemnation of Abu Nidal's attacks on the Rome and Vienna airports (albeit without naming the perpetrating organization or its sponsors). Both decisions had no practical significance, but they marked a change in the Soviet Union's traditional position concerning international terrorism. Although the Soviet Union voted for U.N. decisions condemning terrorism as early as 1970, it had always insisted that these condemnations also include state terrorism, referring to various forms of "imperialistic aggression." What was so special about the Soviet attitude in late 1985 was that it constituted an unconditional condemnation of terrorist activity as such. In the past similar single-mindedness was exhibited by the Soviets only concerning hijacking; of all types of terrorist offenses, this was the one the Soviet Union condemned without any reservations, and this unequivocal position did not appear until October 15, 1970, when two Latvians hijacked a Soviet airplane to Turkey and requested political asylum. It seems more than likely that the recent sudden shift in the formal Soviet position on terrorism reflected another adaptation to the role of the victim of terrorism.

Altogether, Soviet behavior in what could be viewed as a test case of the Soviets' response under the pressure of extortionate terrorism was both concessionary and panicky. Nevertheless, it is too early to generalize on the basis of this single incident concerning future Soviet behavior under similar circumstances. Presumably, at least part of the Soviet behavior in October 1985 could be attributed to the fact that this kind of experience was new for the Soviet Union. At least the panicky nature of the response, if not the political decision to concede to terrorist pressure, may have resulted from the lack of Soviet contingency plans for events of this sort. Possibly the Beirut kidnapping prompted the Soviets to develop such plans. The extent of their willingness to bend under terrorist pressure in the future remains to be seen. Still, it can be assumed with reasonable certainty that Soviet willingness to cooperate with the West in efforts to combat terrorism will increase as a result of anti-Soviet terrorism. Hypothetically, therefore, a wave of anti-Soviet terrorist attacks might contribute more than any other factor to increased international cooperation in combating terrorism, since the main sponsors of terrorism are states over which the Soviet Union wields a considerable degree of influence.

In an unconfirmed story, after the 1979 takeover of the U.S. embassy in Teheran, a Soviet diplomat was asked how the Soviet Union would have responded to the same situation. Allegedly, the Soviet diplomat's answer was: in two hours there would be no Iran. The 1985 experience, however different from the Iranian affair, was a far cry from this story, although there may have been another, more shadowy aspect to it. A rumor has persisted that, their concessions to the kidnappers' demands notwithstanding, the Soviets sent a special KGB team to Beirut, which captured and killed a relative of the kidnappers' team and sent his mutilated body to the kidnappers, threatening to continue this kind of retaliation if any remaining hostages were hurt.[15]

Whether or not this particular story is true, Soviet willingness to resort to such cloak and dagger methods in the face of a direct terrorist threat should be taken into account. Furthermore, it can be assumed that their willingness to use such methods would be a positive function of their perception of the severity and persistence of the threat.

Notes

1. Academic works on this subject include Ray Cline and Yonah Alexander, *Terrorism: The Soviet Connection* (New York: Crane Russak, 1984); Shlomi Elad and Ariel Merari, *The Soviet Bloc and World Terrorism* (Tel Aviv: The Jaffee Center for Strategic Studies, Paper No. 26, 1984); Roberta Goren, *The Soviet Union and Terrorism* (London: George Allen and Unwin, 1984); and Samuel Francis *The Soviet Strategy of Terror* (Washington, DC: The Heritage Foundation, 1985). For an extensive study of Soviet relations with the PLO, see Galia Golan, *The Soviet Union and the Palestine Liberation Organization* (New York: Praeger, 1980). A more popular and controversial work is Claire Sterling's *The Terror Network* (New York: Holt, Rinehart and Winston, 1981). Many other articles on this subject have appeared in academic journals as well as in the popular press.

2. Galia Golan, "The Soviet Attitude toward the Use of Terror," in Anat Kurz, ed., *Contemporary Trends in World Terrorism* (New York: Praeger Greenwood, forthcoming).

3. For a summary of the evidence, see Elad and Merari, *The Soviet Bloc and World Terrorism*, p. 17.

4. For example, Wilkinson estimated that about fifteen hundred Soviets, seven hundred Cubans, and one hundred East Germans were involved in training terrorists in the PDRY (P. Wilkinson, "Uncomfortable Truths about International Terrorism," *Across the Board,* January 1982, pp. 78–84).

5. The organizations that have challenged Arafat's leadership include Fatah rebels, the PFLP, PFLP-GC, PPSF, Saiqa, and two of the three splinter groups of the PLF. The DFLP has vascillated between Arafat and pro-Syrian groups, trying to achieve reunification based on compromise.

6. D. Volskey, *Novoye Vremya,* 25 October 1985.

7. *Ibid.*

8. TASS International Service (in Russian), 11 October 1985.

9. *Izvestiya,* 18 October 1985.

10. Reuters, 8 April 1986.

11. For example, Soviet Deputy Foreign Minister Mikhail Kapitsa's announcement, Reuters, 9 January 1986.

12. For example, *Ma'ariv* (Israel), 29 May 1986.

13. *Ha'aretz* (Israel), 4 October 1985.

14. *Ha'aretz*, 2 October 1985; *Newsweek*, 14 October 1985.

15. See, for example, *Ma'ariv*, 27 February 1986.

Part V
The
Economic
Dimension

13

U.S. Economic Interests in the Middle East

Eliyahu Kanovsky

U nited States interest in the Middle East is long-standing, extending beyond the economic dimension. The oil crises of the 1970s and early
1980s, however, greatly intensified U.S. interest, especially since the almost unanimous view of the "experts" was that U.S. and Western dependence on
Middle East oil would continue to grow, at least until the end of this century,
accompanied by an inexorable rise in (real) oil prices and a massive accumulation
of financial (petrodollar) surpluses. The widely publicized 1977 CIA report that
projected a substantial decline in Soviet oil production, transforming the Soviet
Union from a net oil exporter to a net oil importer, greatly enhanced the importance of Middle Eastern oil supplies. The rapid growth in U.S. oil imports from
the Middle East until the late 1970s, and the projections of the oil experts, had a
powerful impact on U.S. interests and policies in the Middle East.

The trends in U.S. trade with the Middle East also are important indicators
of U.S. economic interests. It is important, however, to distinguish between trade
with the major Middle Eastern oil-exporting countries and trade with other countries in the region, primarily those that are recipients of large-scale U.S. aid,
mainly Israel, Egypt, Turkey, and Jordan. U.S. arms shipments to the region are
other important indicators of U.S. interest. The flood of oil revenues enabled the
oil-exporting countries to increase their imports, both civilian and military,
sharply, including purchases from the United States. These countries also financed, in part, arms imports on the part of some other Arab countries. Increased
U.S. aid to a number of countries in the region financed civilian and military
shipments. The determinants of U.S. aid are far more complex, but there is little
doubt that its magnitude stems, in part, from a perception that a deterioration in
the Arab-Israeli conflict may adversely affect the flow of oil.

Middle East Oil and U.S. Dependence

Measured in terms of volume, U.S. oil imports from the Middle East (defined as the Arab members of OPEC plus Iran) rose steadily in the 1960s and even more sharply in the 1970s, reaching a peak in 1977. The rise in U.S. oil imports, especially from the Middle East, between 1970 and 1977 was due to a number of factors:

1. Domestic controls on oil prices in the United States led to a marked shift in the basket of energy supplies in favor of oil. Following the 1973–1974 oil shock, other major Western industrialized countries permitted domestic prices of oil products to rise, and inevitably, there was a shift away from oil in favor of coal and other energy sources, which reduced overall oil consumption in these countries. In the United States this shift was delayed until the gradual decontrol of oil prices beginning in 1978. The move away from oil was greatly accelerated with the complete abolition of price controls by the Reagan administration in January 1981.

2. Imposition of price controls on natural gas in the United States led to shortages, and electric utilities and other users of natural gas were compelled to switch to oil. The subsequent gradual decontrol of natural gas prices has, more recently, led to abundant supplies.

3. Venezuelan oil production, an important source of U.S. oil supplies, reached a peak in 1970. Similarly, Canadian oil production, another important source of oil, peaked in 1973.

U.S. oil consumption continued to rise after 1973, albeit at a far slower pace, reaching a peak of 18.8 million barrels per day (mbd) in 1978 (see table 13–1). Oil imports peaked in 1977 at 8.8 mbd, accounting for 48 percent of U.S. oil supplies. Imports from the Middle East also were at an all-time high that year, 3.7 mbd, accounting for one-fifth of U.S. oil consumption. Although U.S. consumption rose in 1978, imports declined, mainly because Alaskan oil began to flow in mid-1977. Subsequently, there was a sharp drop in consumption from 18.8 mbd in 1978 to 15.7 mbd in 1985, and oil imports dropped to 5.1 mbd, 32 percent of consumption. Imports from the Middle East, however, had dropped precipitously to 0.5 mbd, or 3 percent of total U.S. oil supplies.

This change was precisely the opposite of what had been projected by the large majority of oil specialists in the 1970s. Rising dependence on Middle East oil had been replaced by a very low level of dependence. Oil exporters, Middle Eastern and others, were competing for markets, including the United States, which remained the world's largest oil importer. The change was due to a number of factors: to a minor extent, the small rise in U.S. production after 1976; to a greater extent, the drop (by one-sixth) in U.S. oil consumption between 1978 and 1985; and mainly, the far greater diversification of imports, with Mexico, Canada, Venezuela, and the United Kingdom becoming the major sources of supply (see table 13–1).

Table 13-1
U.S. Oil Production, Consumption, and Imports
(thousands of barrels per day)

	1973	1974	1975	1976	1977	1978	1979	1980	1981	1982	1983	1984	1985
Total Production	10950	10485	10010	9735	9865	10275	10135	10170	10180	10200	10245	10505	10540
Total Consumption	17308	16653	16322	17461	18431	18847	18513	17056	16058	15296	15231	15726	15726
Total Imports	6256	6112	6056	7313	8807	8363	8456	6909	5996	5113	5051	5437	5067
From Arab	915	752	1383	2424	3185	2963	3056	2551	1848	854	632	819	472
OPEC:													
Saudi Arabia	486	461	715	1230	1380	1144	1356	1261	1129	552	337	325	168
Algeria	136	190	282	432	559	649	636	488	311	170	240	323	187
United Arab Emirates	71	74	117	254	335	385	281	172	81	92	30	117	45
Libya	164	4	232	453	723	654	658	554	319	26	0	1	4
Total Non-Arab imports	5341	5360	4673	4889	5622	5400	5400	4358	4148	4259	4419	4618	4595
From:													
Iran	223	469	280	298	535	555	304	9	0	35	48	10	27
Nigeria	459	713	762	1025	1143	919	1080	857	620	514	302	216	293
Venezuela	1135	979	702	700	690	645	690	481	406	412	422	548	605
Canada	1325	1070	846	599	517	467	538	455	447	482	547	630	770
Mexico	16	8	71	87	179	318	439	533	522	685	826	748	816
Total Imports from OPEC	2993	3280	3601	5066	6193	5751	5637	4300	3323	2146	1862	2049	1830

Sources: British Petroleum Company, *BP Statistical Review of World Energy* (London) 1986 and earlier issues; U.S. Department of Energy, *Monthly Energy Review*, various issues.

Notes: Production and consumption figures include natural gas liquids (NGLs). Import figures include both crude and products.

The oil shock of 1973–1974 set into motion powerful economic forces unforeseen by the large majority of oil analysts. The second oil shock of 1979–1980 strongly reinforced these trends, which included the following:

1. A trend toward rising energy efficiency—that is, more tons of steel, more heating, more air conditioning, and so on, produced per unit of energy (from all sources); more miles per gallon of gasoline or diesel fuel; and so on. It is interesting to note that the *real* gross national product (GNP) in the United States rose by more than one-third between 1973 and 1985, while energy consumption remained unchanged. During the decades preceding 1973, the real GNP and energy usage rose at about the same rate. In Japan and in a number of other industrialized countries, the improvement in energy efficiency was even more marked.

2. Following the decontrol of oil prices in the United States in the late 1970s, the move away from oil assumed major dimensions. Oil's share of U.S. energy usage, which had peaked at 47 percent in 1978, dropped to about 40 percent in 1985. As noted earlier, this trend had begun earlier in most other industrialized countries following the 1973–1974 oil shock. When the United States, which alone accounts for more than one-fourth of world oil usage (or one-third, excluding the communist countries) joined this trend, world oil consumption declined sharply.

3. Non-OPEC noncommunist oil production, which had been stagnant between 1970 and 1976 at around 16 to 17 mbd, rose sharply to 25 mbd by 1985, as higher oil prices stimulated worldwide exploration. The bulk of this increase was concentrated in Mexico and the United Kingdom, as well as in a large number of smaller producers.

4. The flood of oil revenues accruing to oil-exporting countries was soon followed by a massive growth in government expenditures and imports, both in small- and large-population oil countries. This was in sharp contrast with the projections of the large majority of oil analysts, who had assumed that the small-population Middle Eastern oil-exporting countries would be low absorbers of revenues and would therefore accumulate huge and growing financial surpluses. This development has profound implications for stability in these countries; for trade, foreign aid, and the arms race; and for world oil markets.

Revenues and Expenditures in the Mideast Oil-Exporting Countries

The wholly unexpected massive increase in revenues was followed, in a relatively short time, by an inordinate acceleration in military, development, and various civilian expenditures. Space does not permit a country-by-country review of the developments in all the Mideast oil-exporting countries. We shall, therefore, confine ourselves to Saudi Arabia, the leading oil exporter. The first oil shock raised

Saudi government revenues from less than $4 billion in fiscal year 1972/73 to more than $28 billion in fiscal year 1974/75. Expenditures rose rapidly but could not close the gap initially, and huge financial surpluses emerged. Subsequently, revenues continued to rise, but spending rose far more rapidly, and already in fiscal year 1977/78 the Saudis experienced a budgetary deficit of $4 billion, followed by an even larger deficit the following year.[1] Inevitably, trends in the balance of payments were similar, and the current accounts balance skyrocketed from a $2 billion surplus in 1972 to $23 billion in 1974, followed by a steady decline and a deficit of more than $2 billion in 1978.

These deficits were short-lived. The Iranian revolution of 1978–1979 sharply reduced both oil production and exports from that country, and the fear that the Islamic Revolution would spread to neighboring Arab countries stimulated a speculative fever without parallel in recent history. Prices rose from $11 to $12 per barrel in 1978 to $34 to $40 per barrel in early 1981. Saudi government revenues rose from $38 billion in 1977/78 to a peak of $108 billion in 1981/82. Despite forecasts that this time Saudi Arabia and other oil exporters would be far more moderate with respect to spending, the record shows that until 1982–1983, they repeated their experiences of the latter half of the 1970s. Initially, there were large Saudi financial surpluses, reaching a peak of $36 billion in 1980/81, followed by a smaller surplus of $30 billion in 1981/82. Saudi expenditures rose from $30 billion in fiscal year 1976/77 and $42 billion in the following year to a peak of $79 billion in 1981/82. The 1980–1985 Development Plan, issued in 1980, called for total spending of $390 billion, and in 1981 the deputy minister of planning stated that expenditures would probably reach $450 billion over the five-year period. In other words, spending would continue to rise at a rapid pace.

Although the demand for oil and prices began to decline after 1981, the preponderant view of oil specialists was that this was a temporary phenomenon due mainly to recessions in the industrialized countries as well as to the utilization of stockpiles accumulated by the oil buyers in 1979–1981. The Saudis and other oil-exporting countries made little effort to curb spending. As it became increasingly clear that the oil glut was long-term and that oil revenues were plummeting, a greater effort was made to restrain expenditures. But while it was very easy for governments to raise spending, it was correspondingly difficult to implement strong cutbacks, no matter what the absolute level of outlays. In a sense, public spending takes on a life of its own, especially if it affects the local population. The bulk of cutbacks actually implemented were foreign aid outlays and new construction projects. Foreign aid, as reported in the budget, was curtailed from a high of more than $7 billion in 1980/81 and in 1981/82 to only $3 billion in 1985/86. The projects budget, mainly devoted to new construction, was cut from $43 billion in 1981/82 to $21 billion in 1985/86.

The main impact has been on contractors, mainly foreign, as well as foreign workers, as few Saudis are employed in construction. Nonetheless, these cutbacks have had a serious recessionary impact on the economy as a whole, and on the local population. The wide range of subsidies—for electricity, water, education, health services, and so on—have, however, been left largely untouched, for fear of the social and political consequences of such actions. Similarly, producer subsidies have been maintained or moderately curbed.

Saudi government revenues, which reached $108 billion in 1981/82, were down to $30 billion in 1985/86.[2] Expenditures declined far more moderately, from a high of $79 billion in 1981/82 to $53 billion in 1985/86. These figures exaggerate the magnitude of the decline in spending, since the finance ministry had accumulated debts to contractors and suppliers unofficially estimated at more than $10 billion.

What emerges from these figures is that the financial needs of Saudi Arabia, and of most other Middle Eastern oil-exporting countries, have been raised to far higher levels. At the same time, U.S. and Western dependence on Middle Eastern oil has noticeably diminished. The Saudi ability to curb output over longer periods and thereby maintain high OPEC prices is ephemeral at best, and the abandonment of its role as swing producer since the fall of 1985 was determined solely or overwhelmingly by its deteriorating financial position. Huge budgetary surpluses had turned into growing deficits, reaching $24 billion or more in 1985/86. Official foreign assets declined from almost $150 billion to about $60 billion in early 1986.[3]

The fact that U.S. oil imports from Saudi Arabia and other Middle Eastern producers rose strongly in 1986 is no indication of rising U.S. dependence on Middle Eastern oil. Quite the contrary, it stems from a desperate struggle by oil exporters for market shares. Developments in world oil markets as a consequence of the two oil shocks and the far higher level of financial needs of Mideast oil exporters have weakened the stability of these countries and have greatly enhanced the ability of the United States to shape its Mideast policies with far less concern for its oil needs. The United States continues to have an interest in the stability of the region, but the degree of concern and the vitality of its interest have diminished.

The Oil Crash and Its Impact on Other Middle Eastern Countries

The sharp drop in both oil prices and in the volume of oil exports has had pervasive effects throughout the region. The deepening recession has affected even the strongest, including Kuwait, and bankruptcies have been widespread. The construction industry has suffered the greatest decline, but various service industries, including banking, trade, and others, also have been affected. Moreover, the effects of the recession in the major Middle Eastern oil-exporting countries have been regional.

Egypt

Egypt, which had become an important oil producer, has been severely affected not only by the sharp drop in prices but by the return of hundreds of thousands of Egyptian nationals who had lost their relatively lucrative jobs in the major oil-exporting countries. In the early 1980s oil exports had exceeded $3 billion per year, puny by comparison with Saudi Arabia and other large oil exporters but of crucial importance to Egypt's economy. By comparison, all other commodity exports, including cotton, were only $1 to $1.5 billion per year.

Suez Canal revenues also benefited from the oil boom in the Persian Gulf region. This has occurred directly in terms of transit dues collected from oil tankers to and from the Gulf region and indirectly in terms of freighters from Europe and North America using the canal to reach the rapidly growing markets in the Gulf region, thanks to rising oil revenues. Transit dues approached $1 billion per year in the early 1980s, but the end of the oil boom has meant virtual stagnancy in transit dues since 1982.

The tourist industry also has expanded, due in no small measure to the influx of rich Arabs from the Gulf states. Moreover, some of these rich Arabs invested in real estate and some other ventures in Egypt. The end of the oil boom, as well as widely publicized terrorist incidents, have had an adverse effect on tourism, and private Arab investments in Egypt also appear to have diminished.

The single most important development in Egypt was the migration of millions of Egyptians to work in the Gulf region and in Libya. According to some estimates, as much as one-sixth of the Egyptian labor force was employed in these countries. The impact on the Egyptian economy was massive: Unemployment levels, both overt and hidden, were lowered; returning migrants and their families enjoyed far higher standards of living and, in some cases, invested in the modernization of their farms and in trade and industry; and the remittances of these workers to their families reached $3 to $4 billion per year, according to official accounts (unofficial estimates are that possibly an equal amount of money entered through unreported channels). Within the context of a gross domestic product of possibly $30 billion, the impact of remittances, oil exports, tourist revenues, and so on, was nothing less than overwhelming.

The end of the oil boom has sharply reversed these trends. The Egyptian economy is again dependent on its traditional main sectors, agriculture and manufacturing, and these are severely hobbled by the inefficiency of the nationalized industries, bureaucractic controls, adverse policies with respect to agriculture, and the legacy of huge consumer and producer subsidies. So long as the state was enjoying expanding revenues engendered by the oil boom, it was able to finance large-scale subsidies, and the poor performances of the traditional sectors was masked by the boom in other sectors. All this changed rather abruptly, and the resulting recession threatens the stability of the regime, which in turn has increasingly concerned Washington.[4] U.S. economic and military aid have been steadily increased to almost $3 billion annually. The economic aid program is designed, in part, to bring about more fundamental changes in the economy. Internal resistance to far-reaching changes is powerful, however, and the leverage exercised by U.S. aid in bringing about such changes has been very limited.[5]

Syria

The Syrian economy also has been adversely affected by the oil bust, although on a smaller scale than Egypt's. Syrian oil production peaked in 1976 at 10 million tons, about 200,000 barrels per day. During the first half of the 1980s, this had declined to about 8.5 million tons annually. Rising domestic consumption, as well as the drop in output, eliminated a small export surplus. Since its 1982 agreement with Iran, however, Syria has been receiving large shipments of superior quality oil, partly as a grant and partly on easy credit terms and discounted prices, as compensation for Syria's agreement to close the pipeline from Iraq. In reality, Syria has paid Iran very little for its oil, enabling it to export most of its own oil and to utilize Iranian oil for domestic consumption.

Since 1974 oil has been the dominant commodity export, accounting for some three-fourths of total exports in the early 1980s. The sharp decline in oil prices since 1982 has, therefore, had a strongly negative impact on the country's balance of payments. Grants from the rich Arab states grew to major dimensions in the early 1980s, reaching $1.8 billion in 1981, and commodity exports—overwhelmingly oil—reached $2.2 billion in 1981. By 1984 total grants had been reduced to about $1.3 billion, about $1 billion from Arab states and the balance from Iran in the form of the oil grant. In addition to reported grants, the rich Arab states also provided concessional loans and partly financed Soviet arms shipments to Syria.[6]

The Syrian economy also benefited from job opportunities and remittances from its approximately 400,000 nationals working in the rich Arab oil states. If these figures are accurate, it means that during the peak years in the early 1980s, possibly one-sixth of the Syrian labor force was employed in these countries. At the same time, reported remittances declined almost steadily, from $901 million in 1979 to $327 million in 1984. This was mainly a reflection of the widening gap between official and free market exchange rates, as a growing proportion of remittances flowed into the black market, financing large-scale smuggling from Lebanon into Syria. In any case, the end of the oil boom has seriously affected the Syrian economy, and there are persistent news reports of unrest in Syria aggravated by the economic difficulties.

Jordan

Although Jordan's oil production is minuscule, it was strongly affected by the oil boom. Reported Arab grants reached $1.2 billion in 1980 and 1981, equivalent to almost 30 percent of the country's GNP and almost double its commodity exports.

In addition, the rich Arab states provided concessionary loans and made payments to arms suppliers for shipments to Jordan. During the early 1980s some 250,000 to 300,000 Jordanians were working in the Arab oil states, equal to about one-third of the labor force. Moreover, on average, the skill and professional level of Jordanian workers were higher than those of workers from other Arab states (with the possible exception of Lebanon), and their earnings and remittances were correspondingly greater. Reported remittances in the early 1980s were estimated at about $1 billion a year, and estimates of remittances entering the country through unofficial channels added another $500 million to $1 billion. Jordan also took advantage of its geographic location to expand its exports to the growing markets in the Arab oil states, and it also benefited from some private Arab investments and tourism from these countries. All in all, Jordan acquired many of the attributes of an oil state, despite the absence of local oil production.

The end of the oil boom had a strong impact on the Jordanian economy. Arab grants in 1984 were half their 1980–1981 level. Reports published in 1985 and 1986 indicated that many Jordanians were returning from the Gulf countries and that unemployment was becoming a serious problem. Gross domestic product, which had been expanding by 7 to 8 percent per year in real terms between 1972 and 1982, has been stagnant or declining (in per capita terms) since 1983. The United States, which has long maintained an interest in Jordan, has recently expanded its aid program, compensating in part for the drop in Arab aid.[7] Barring external or internal severe political shocks, however, Jordan's prospects of emerging from the current recession are far better than those of Egypt or Syria.

Israel

The oil shocks added immensely to Israel's economic problems. In fact, the near-stagnancy of its economy (on a per capita basis) since 1974 stemmed in no small measure from the escalating cost of imported oil. Fuel imports rose from less than $100 million in 1972 to $775 million in 1978. The balance of payments (current account) deficit has risen sharply, and inflationary pressures have intensified. Israel's withdrawal from the Sinai Peninsula oil field in 1979, under the terms of the Camp David accords, was concurrent with the second oil shock. Payments for fuel imports skyrocketed to $2 billion per year in 1980–1982. To put these figures into perspective, one might note that U.S. military and civilian grants during this period averaged $1.4 billion per year. Alternatively, one might note that direct military imports (excluding the importation of machinery, spare parts, and raw materials for Israel's military industries) were $1.8 billion per year. The result was a sharp increase in the balance of payments deficit, an escalation in foreign indebtedness, and runaway inflation. The oil shocks were not the only factor, but they added enormously to the economic malaise already aggravated by the high levels of military expenditures since the 1973 war.

The steady decline in oil prices has been of the greatest importance for Israel.

In 1985 fuel imports were down to $1.5 billion, $600 million less than in 1980. Provisional estimates indicate that this figure dropped to some $750 to $850 million in 1986. The new economic policy adopted in mid-1985, designed mainly to battle runaway inflation, owed much of its success to lower oil prices. Inflation, which peaked at about 400 percent in 1984, declined to less than 20 percent in 1986.

U.S. economic aid began shortly after Israel's independence in 1948. In the 1960s and early 1970s, however, aid began to diminish and came mainly in the form of loans to finance food and other imports from the United States. The massive military shipments from the United States to Israel since the Yom Kippur War have been financed, directly and indirectly, by higher levels of U.S. aid. Between 1973 and 1984 U.S. grants (for both civilian and military purposes) averaged $1.3 billion, while U.S. loans (net of repayments) averaged $400 million per year. Since 1985 all U.S. aid has been in the form of grants (as is the case for Egypt) and presently totals $3.9 billion. During the period following the Camp David agreements of 1979, however, U.S. loans were given at very high interest rates that were fixed for the period of the loans (ranging usually from 10 to 20 years). Thus, in 1985 loan repayments to the U.S. government totaled $1,056 million, of which $946 million was interest and only $110 million principal.[8]

U.S. Trade with the Middle East

In analyzing U.S. trade with the Middle East, it is important to distinguish between the major oil-exporting countries and other states in the region. U.S. aid to a number of countries in the region, in particular Israel, Egypt, Jordan, and Turkey, is largely tied to the purchase of U.S. products. U.S. imports from the Middle East, other than oil and, to a small extent, other raw materials, is a function of economic development and the ability of the exporting country to compete in international markets in terms of price and quality, particularly with respect to manufactured goods.

As noted earlier, total U.S. oil imports peaked in 1977 at 8.8 mbd, of which 3.7 mbd was from Middle East OPEC members. By 1980 total U.S. oil imports had dropped to 6.9 mbd, of which 2.6 mbd came from the Middle East. In terms of dollar outlays on oil imports, however, there was a sharp rise from $26 billion in 1974 to a peak of $82 billion in 1980, accounting for one-third of all U.S. imports, of which 40 percent was from the Middle East. Subsequently, there was a continued decline in the overall volume of U.S. oil imports as well as a significant drop in prices. By 1985, total U.S. imports from the Middle East OPEC nations were down to $6.4 billion, less than 2 percent of total American merchandise imports, as compared with 14 percent in 1980.

U.S. merchandise exports to the Middle East OPEC countries also declined, but far less steeply. While U.S. imports from these countries fell by 81 percent between 1980 and 1985, exports fell by less than one-half from their peak in 1982. This reflects the relative inflexibility of government expenditures, discussed earlier, which has a powerful impact on imports. Moreover, overall imports of the Middle East OPEC countries fell far below that indicated from an examination of U.S. exports to these countries. Total Saudi merchandise imports, for example, fell by less than one-third between 1982 (the peak year) and 1985. During the same period Saudi imports from the United States fell by one-half. Between 1980 and 1985, the U.S. dollar was rising in value against the currencies of other major industrialized countries, adversely affecting U.S. exports. Foreigners, including the Middle East OPEC nations, were diverting their purchases to other countries. At their peak in 1982, U.S. exports to Mideast OPEC nations accounted for 5.9 percent of total sales abroad, declining to 3.2 percent in 1985.

With respect to the major Middle Eastern recipients of U.S. aid, the story is different, since aid is mostly tied to purchase of U.S. products. U.S. exports to Israel ranged from $2 billion in 1980 to $2.5 billion in 1985. Exports to Egypt were close to the same range, with wider annual fluctuations mainly reflecting changes in food import prices. Exports to Turkey rose from more than $500 million in 1980 to $1.3 billion in 1985.

With respect to U.S. imports from these countries, there are much greater differences. Israel's exports to the United States greatly exceed those of other non-oil-producing countries in the region, reflecting its far more developed and diversified manufacturing sector. Israel's exports to the United States rose from less than $1 billion in 1980 to $2.1 billion in 1985. Turkish exports rose more rapidly, from less than $200 million in 1980 to $600 million in 1985. This reflects the rapid expansion of its industry and the overall advance of its economy during this period. As noted earlier, Egyptian commodity exports are dominated by oil, followed by cotton, textiles, and other agricultural products. It has little to sell to the United States, other than oil, and petroleum exports to the United States dwindled rapidly, from more than $500 million in 1980 to less than $100 million in 1985 (see table 13–2).[9]

The United States and Middle East Arms Imports

Many or most Middle Eastern countries reveal little with respect to their military budgets in general and their arms imports in particular. There are strong indications that the latter are excluded, largely or wholly, from the published budgets and balance of payments of Jordan, Syria, Egypt, and others.[10]

International tension and conflict is not uncommon in other parts of the world, but there is little doubt that the massive inflow of oil revenues in the 1970s and early 1980s permitted a number of countries to spend huge sums on building up their military forces. In many countries the armed forces are dominant and the

Table 13-2
U.S. Merchandise Trade with the Middle East
(millions of dollars)

	Exports 1980	Imports 1980	Exports 1981	Imports 1981	Exports 1982	Imports 1982	Exports 1983	Imports 1983	Exports 1984	Imports 1984	Exports 1985	Imports 1985
Algeria	542	6881	717	5208	909	2673	594	3551	520	3638	430	2333
Egypt	1873	572	2146	412	2875	547	2813	302	2700	169	2317	79
Iraq	724	482	913	167	511	39	512	59	663	124	426	474
Jordan	407	3	716	2	618	7	430	5	298	4	377	14
Kuwait	886	521	929	91	941	40	741	130	602	260	542	184
Libya	509	8905	811	5476	301	512	191	1	200	9	310	44
Saudi Arabia	5769	13468	7123	15237	8830	7443	7906	3627	5445	3741	4359	1907
Syria	239	28	143	87	138	10	112	8	104	2	106	19
UAE	998	3164	1057	2102	1085	2032	856	510	684	1187	592	671
Israel	2045	978	2426	1280	2171	1164	2016	1255	2145	1750	2509	2123
Turkey	540	187	771	276	866	274	783	320	1245	433	1289	602
Iran	23	478	300	66	121	585	190	1130	162	700	74	725
Total Middle East OPEC	9451	33899	11850	20347	12698	13324	10990	9008	8276	9659	6733	6338
Share of Above in Total U.S. Trade (%)	4.3	13.8	5.1	7.8	5.9	5.5	5.5	3.5	3.8	3.0	3.2	1.8
Total Middle East	15952	36462	19752	31011	20931	15925	18867	11390	16600	12402	14419	9408
Middle East Share of Total U.S. Trade (%)	7.2	14.9	8.5	11.9	9.9	6.5	9.4	4.4	7.6	3.8	6.8	2.7

Source: U.S. Department of Agriculture, *Middle East and North Africa: Outlook and Situation Report*, various issues.

Notes: "Middle East OPEC" includes Algeria, Iraq, Kuwait, Libya, Saudi Arabia, United Arab Emirates, Qatar, and Iran.

"Total Middle East" includes Morocco, Tunisia, Bahrain, Cyprus, Lebanon, Oman, North and South Yemen, and Qatar, in addition to those listed in the table.

expansion of military power serves as a means of coping with possible domestic opposition as well as external threats, real or otherwise. Between 1972 and 1983 the Arab members of OPEC increased their annual arms purchases from less than $500 million to more than $11 billion. Even when measured in constant dollars, Arab OPEC arms purchases increased at least 500 percent during this period, and their share of total international arms transfers rose from 4 percent in 1972 to 30 percent in 1983. In addition, during the 1970s the rich Arab states partially financed arms purchases of other Arab countries, including Jordan, Syria, and Egypt. The total Arab share of world arms imports rose from 15 percent in 1972 to more than 50 percent in 1983. Iran under the Shah was also a major importer of sophisticated and expensive military equipment (see table 13–3).

For the five-year period 1979 to 1983, the U.S. Arms Control and Disarmament Agency provides the following estimates of arms imports and their suppliers:

Iraq: $17.6 billion—57 percent from the Soviet Union and other communist countries, with the balance from France and other Western countries.

Saudi Arabia: $12.1 billion—42 percent from the United States, with most of the balance from France, the United Kingdom, and other Western suppliers.

Libya: $12.1 billion—60 percent from the Soviet Union and other communist countries, with the balance from Western European sources.

Syria: $10.5 billion—93 percent from the Soviet Union and other communist countries, with most of the balance from Western Europe.

Egypt: $5.6 billion—43 percent from the United States, with most of the balance from Western Europe.

Iran: $5.4 billion—22 percent from the United States, presumably within the context of orders placed by the Shah prior to his downfall in February 1979, 18 percent from the Soviet Union, and the balance from various suppliers.

Israel: $3.8 billion—almost solely from the United States.

Algeria: $3.6 billion—87 percent from the Soviet Union, with the balance from Western Europe.

Jordan: $3.4 billion—28 percent from the United States, 7 percent from the Soviet Union, and almost all the balance from the United Kingdom and France.

North Yemen: $2.4 billion—one-half from the Soviet Union, 8 percent from the United States, and the balance from a variety of sources.

Turkey: $1.9 billion—40 percent from the United States, 46 percent from West Germany, and the balance from Italy and other sources.

Table 13-3
Middle Eastern Arms Imports
(millions of dollars, unless otherwise stated)

	1972	1973	1974	1975	1976	1977	1978	1979	1980	1981	1982	1983
Saudi Arabia	100	80	340	250	440	875	1300	1200	1800	2900	3100	3300
Kuwait	5	–	–	50	80	310	300	60	40	120	130	100
UAE	10	10	50	30	100	130	50	150	170	230	30	40
Iraq	140	625	625	675	1000	1500	1600	2300	1900	3700	4300	5100
Libya	160	180	330	550	1000	1200	2000	2500	2200	2500	2900	1900
Qatar	–	–	–	10	–	40	20	20	90	150	270	230
Algeria	10	40	20	90	320	480	725	450	525	1200	1100	350
Total Arab Members of OPEC	425	935	1365	1655	2940	4535	5995	6680	6725	10800	11830	11020
Share of World Arms Imports (%)	4.1	6.8	11.1	13.0	17.6	23.1	25.8	24.2	22.7	29.7	30.8	30.1
Other Arab Countries:												
Egypt	550	850	230	350	150	250	400	625	550	575	2100	1700
Syria	280	1300	825	380	625	650	900	2100	2700	2100	1900	1700
Oman	5	10	10	40	10	50	270	30	100	60	90	290
Jordan	30	50	80	80	140	120	170	100	260	1100	850	1100
Total Arms Imports of Arab Countries	1290	3145	2510	2505	3865	5605	7735	9535	10335	14635	16770	15810
Arms Imports of Arab Countries: Share of World (%)	12.4	23.0	20.5	19.7	23.1	28.5	33.3	34.6	34.9	40.2	43.6	43.2
Iran	525	525	1000	1200	2000	2500	2200	1600	400	1000	1500	750
Israel	300	230	975	725	975	1100	900	490	800	1200	950	370

Source: U.S. Arms Control and Disarmament Agency, *World Military Expenditures and Arms Transfers 1985* and earlier issues.

Notes: I have not taken into account (in the listing of Arab countries) the following: Bahrain, Lebanon, Sudan, North Yemen, South Yemen, Morocco, and Tunisia. Their inclusion would not alter the trends or conclusions in any significant manner. I have included Kuwait, Qatar, and the United Arab Emirates, despite the fact that they are relatively small buyers of arms. According to many reports, they have, however, provided financing, together with Saudi Arabia, for the arms purchases of Egypt (until 1979), Jordan, Syria, and others.

The U.S. Arms Control and Disarmament Agency also makes estimates in constant dollars. U.S. prices in 1983 were about two and a half times those prevailing in 1972.

Morocco: $1.8 billion—24 percent from the United States, 53 percent from France, and the balance from a variety of sources.

South Yemen: $1.5 billion—almost solely from the Soviet Union. Arms imports of other countries in the region were by comparison small, amounting to less than $1 billion over the five-year period.

What emerges from these figures is that burgeoning oil revenues financed massive military spending not only by the major oil-exporting countries but, indirectly and in part, by Syria, Jordan, Egypt, and others. Although the Arab oil states cut off financial aid to Egypt following the Camp David agreement in 1979, shipments to Egypt during this period were, in part, a consequence of commitments made earlier. Leaving aside Iraq and Iran, locked in a protracted war, one can project that declining oil revenues since 1982, and rising deficits, should de-escalate the regional arms race. This assumes that the major arms suppliers will not increase their financing of arms purchases. The Saudi military budget, which includes both local expenditures and arms purchases, which had averaged about $19 billion annually in 1981/82 to 1984/85—huge even by comparison with other Middle Eastern countries—was reduced to $16.6 billion in 1985/86. (By comparison Israel's military budget is about $5 billion.) This may be a precursor of things to come.

Conclusions

U.S. economic interests in the Middle East were strongly reinforced as a consequence of the oil shocks of the 1970s and early 1980s. These interests expressed themselves in vastly increased outlays for oil imports from the major oil exporters in the region. The massive oil revenues were soon followed by escalating imports, some of which were from the United States. The U.S. trade balance with respect to these countries was largely unfavorable during this period. U.S. arms exports to a number of Middle Eastern oil-exporting countries during the 1970s also expanded rapidly, especially to Saudi Arabia and Iran. The Soviet Union and some Eastern European countries, however, dominated arms supplies to other large Middle Eastern oil-exporting countries, in particular Iraq, Libya, and Algeria. The Soviet Union also dominated arms supplies to Syria, financed in part by Saudi Arabia and other Arab oil exporters. U.S. arms supplies to Israel, Turkey, and Egypt since the late 1970s were financed by U.S. aid.

U.S. policies in the Middle East were strongly influenced by the projections of the large majority of analysts that oil prices would continue to rise, even in real terms, and that U.S. and Western dependence on Middle East oil would grow, at least until the end of the century. The decline in oil prices since 1981 and subsequent diminishing petroleum imports, especially from the Middle East, have sharply reversed the earlier trends. The unprecedented escalation in expenditures during the heyday of the oil boom has underscored far higher levels of revenue needs on the part of the oil-exporting countries, and the limited ability of the Middle Eastern oil exporters to restrict spending, combined with the drastic decline in oil revenues, resulted in persistent deficits in Saudi Arabia, Libya, and a number of other Middle Eastern oil-exporting countries. The U.S. trade deficit with respect to the Middle Eastern OPEC countries has been reversed. These countries may well be compelled to reduce their outlays for arms, but the record shows that this will affect the Soviet Union and some Western European countries far more than the United States.

The economic trends that have emerged since 1982 should strengthen the United States' position in its competition with the Soviet Union for influence in the Middle East. The Arab states more closely aligned with either the United States or the Soviet Union have become more susceptible to U.S. influence, especially because of continuing Soviet economic problems and in part on account of the decline in oil prices. At the same time, the leverage that the Arab oil producers had with the United States has diminished as their economic problems have increased. By contrast, the positions of the area's major oil importers, Israel and Turkey, have been enhanced as a result of the oil crash. These radical economic changes have greatly altered the parameters of Soviet-American competition in the Middle East.

Notes

1. See my study, "Saudi Arabia's Dismal Economic Future: Regional and Global Implications," The Dayan Center for Middle Eastern Studies, Tel Aviv University, April 1986. The figures used in this chapter in reference to more recent years are based on revised data available following the completion of my study.

2. The official figures show that revenues were $36 billion in 1985/86, but this includes more than $6 billion that the finance ministry transferred from Aramco and Petromin. The $11 billion transferred from Aramco and Petromin in 1984/85 and in 1985/86 almost exhausted the funds set aside by the two state-owned companies for investment.

3. The latter figure excludes so-called loans to Iraq and other loans of dubious value.

4. For sources and details, see my study, "Mubarak's Inheritance: Egypt's Troubled Economy," in *Middle East Contemporary Survey*, 6 (1984). Data for more recent years are from the International Monetary Fund's *International Financial Statistics* (various issues) and from National Bank of Egypt's *Economic Bulletin* (various issues).

5. See M.G. Weinbaum, "Dependent Development and United States Economic Aid to Egypt," *International Journal of Middle East Studies*, May 1986, pp. 119–133.

6. For sources and more details, see my study, "What's Behind Syria's Current Economic Problems?," The Dayan Center for Middle Eastern Studies, Tel Aviv University, May 1985.

7. For sources and details, see my study, "Jordan's Decade of Prosperity: Will It Persist?," in *Middle East Contemporary Survey* 7 (1985).

8. All data are from the Bank of Israel's *Annual Reports*.

9. Also see *Middle East Economic Digest* (London), various issues.

10. *World Military Expenditures and Arms Transfers 1985* provides data only up to 1983. At this writing, December 1986, no later data are available.

14
Soviet Economic Interests in the Middle East

Gur Ofer
Joseph Pelzman

T he Egyptian-Czechoslovakian arms deal of 1955 and the Soviet-Egyptian agreement to build the Aswan Dam in 1956 are the equivalents in Soviet–Third World relations of Sputnik in the sphere of great power strategic competition. In both cases they were signals of the emerging of the Soviet Union as a world power across a full range of activities.

Evaluating the Soviet record as a world power 30 years later bears mixed observations. Nevertheless, there is no question that the overall record is one of net success, both on the global and Third World levels. On both levels the Soviet Union advanced itself to a position near par with the United States, managing to reach this status by relying on an economic base that is, at best, only half of that available to the West. (The cost of this effort was paid by the Soviet people, of course). In the Third World the Soviet Union has a number of important strongholds and allies, ranging from Cuba to Syria to Vietnam, some of which follow versions of the socialist system. The Soviet Union is widely recognized as the other major power to be taken into account in any regional dispute or strategic consideration.

But just as Sputnik did not signify rapid technological superiority, military advantage, or economic catching up, so also the arms deal and the Aswan Dam portended higher expectations in some quarters and more fears in others than were actually warranted. While Soviet penetration into the Third World is a basic reality today, the record is much more mixed. The Middle East, the cradle of the Soviet thrust, has witnessed some of the peaks, as well as the very low points, of this experience. The Middle East was the setting for virtually the entire range of Soviet involvement with the Third World and a major area for its competition with the United States. Even to a higher degree than on the global level, the Soviet Union found its competition with the United States in the Middle East more costly, more hazardous, and less rewarding than initially anticipated.

This chapter concentrates on the economic aspects of Soviet involvement in the Middle East within the context of big power competition. It is only appropriate, when dealing with economic aspects, to use a rational, cost-benefit framework of analysis. While the analysis presented in this chapter is of an ex-post-facto nature, we work with the hypothesis that the relevant Soviet decision-making authorities also make decisions on the Middle East with an equally rational decision-making process. Since most decisions involve allocation of resources, or at least have such consequences, and since Soviet decision makers always operate under tight budgetary constraints, such as approach should not be considered unreasonable.[1]

This does not preclude the possibility of Soviet miscalculations and errors. Considering the inexperience of the Soviet Union in its initial relations with the Third World, and in the Middle East in particular, such mistakes should be expected and have indeed occurred. Furthermore, allowances must be made for a delay in the response of political bodies to changes in circumstances and the resultant delay in the materialization of needed policy changes. In many cases, such changes involve other changes that may delay decisions even further.[2]

In a cost-benefit model of big power regional involvement, economic considerations may enter into the situation in a number of ways. First, there may be direct economic interests in a region with a concentration of an essential raw material, such as oil, or concern over potential markets for particular products. In exchange for these quantifiable economic benefits, there are economic expenditures, which together produce net economic benefits or costs. Furthermore, a more comprehensive accounting of expected benefits and costs involves the inclusion into the analysis of strategic, political, and ideological benefits that big powers seek in exchange for payments in the form of economic, military, or political support for regional clients. While, in principle, noneconomic benefits can, and indeed do, move in both ways, the typical current situation in big power–client relations involves the net outflow of economic payments from big powers in exchange for (net) noneconomic concessions to them. This is what was labeled by Wolf and others as "the cost of empire."[3]

The estimate of such costs can be used as an indicator of the intensity and importance of the strategic and other noneconomic benefits for the big power. In this context, the net economic investment that the Soviet Union is willing to put into the region, or a specific country, measures the expected benefits it is hoping to receive in exchange. The mirror image, from the point of view of the client state, is that the higher the economic benefit, the higher the amount of concession it will be expected to grant. The granting of military aid, free of charge, will usually buy back more noneconomic benefits than the selling of military equipment for hard currency, which has been the Soviet practice since the Energy crisis of 1973.

This chapter takes the more general approach of the economic aspects, reviews the history of Soviet involvement in the Middle East, and speculates on its future prospect by evaluating and disucssing strategic, political, and economic interests through the prism of Soviet economic commitments to the region.

A cost-benefit framework of analysis for Soviet involvement includes a list of expected benefits and a counterlist of costs. It includes a discussion of shifts in their respective importance, both over time and across geographic regions. The test of this approach is to what extent the pattern of actual net economic commitment corresponds closely to the changing configurations of expected benefits and costs. A list of the main groups of Soviet interest in the Middle East might include the following:

1. Strategic interests of the first degree. These occur when the region becomes an integral part of the nuclear strategic world balance. An example is the positioning by the United States of nuclear submarines (Polaris) in the Mediterranean.

2. Strategic interests of the second degree. These reflect the proximity of the region to the Soviet Union and include the Soviet determination not to be threatened from the region and to have some influence regarding major military and political changes. This is probably the most permanent Soviet interest in the region.

3. The region as a vital source of energy to the West. In a framework of big power competition, a vital interest of the other power can be considered a strategic interest of the third degree for the Soviet Union. It presents a potential opportunity to interfere or gain control over energy supplies. For reasons that are explained below, we do not believe that the energy resources of the Middle East constitute a vital need of the Soviet Union or the Soviet bloc.

4. The Middle East as part of the Soviet effort to gain political, ideological, economic, and military influence in the Third World. This is part of the Soviet ideological mission and part of the big power competition over global influence.

5. Other specific economic interests. The chief direct Soviet economic interest in the region is the region's ability to pay with hard currency for Soviet industrial goods, both military and civilian. The potential opportunities for such transactions were dramatically enhanced following the energy crises of 1973 and 1979 but have been declining recently in line with oil prices. High oil prices, the source of Middle Eastern affluence, also benefit the Soviet Union directly by enhancing its hard currency proceeds from export of energy products. To the extent that such high prices are connected with tensions in the region, such tensions benefit the Soviet Union.

    The Soviet Union is much less interested in Middle Eastern oil for its own use. Self-sufficiency in energy is a prime Soviet interest, and unless prices fall sharply, the Soviet Union will hesitate to depend on outside sources. If the prices fall to very low levels, importing oil turns into a favor to the producers rather than an economic requirement.

The above list of interests are to a considerable degree interactive, which makes the analysis more complex. On the cost side, and in the context of big power competition, the crucial long-term factor is the Soviet Union's smaller economic base from which it can grant aid. If the Soviet equivalent of one American dollar has equal purchasing power, then in order to stay in the game, the Soviet Union has to make a sacrifice twice as large as the corresponding one by the United States. Such a sacrifice may be warranted for a power climbing uphill to catch up. In the case of the Soviet Union, however, one can hypothesize that it would look for opportunities where its rubles buy more clout than an equivalent U.S. effort.

The Soviet Union may enjoy such a comparative advantage if clients seeking assistance believe that the Soviet Union demands fewer political concessions or if behaving better than the traditional colonial powers, or if they believe that Soviet aid, due to the Soviet model of growth, type of technology, and economic system can provide more development per unit of aid or even more power and prestige to the central government. In the early stages of penetration, Soviet policymakers may have assumed that if developing countries follow the Soviet model of growth, they may be able to develop successfully with less external aid and more self-reliance, just as some people in the 1950s believed the Soviet Union had managed to do.

One of the main vehicles of big power penetration is regional conflict. In this context, costs for the big power are calculated by comparing the needs and abilities of its client state relative to those of the opposing state, such that a balance or even an advantage may be achieved. Indeed, in many cases the Soviet Union penetrated through the support of the underdog so that, compared with the United States, it had to invest more in aid and accept a greater risk of getting directly involved in hostilities or of losing face as a result of its client's defeat. Nevertheless, it is true that in some cases readiness to support an underdog may bring higher benefits in exchange for higher investments.

Finally, economic costs of penetration also depend on support for client states from third parties not directly involved in big power competition.

Following rapid penetration and considerable initial successes up to the late 1960s, the second half witnessed a reduced level of net investment by the Soviet Union in the region, accompanied by a geographical shift in the direction of oil countries, the Persian Gulf and the Red Sea, and Afghanistan, and a shift toward poorer and non-Arab countries.

The major changes responsible for this trend consisted of changes both in the relative importance of relevant interests and in the various cost elements. On the interest side we find:

1. A secular decline in the intensity and importance of strategic interests of the first degree in the Eastern Mediterranean.

2. An increased strategic interest in the Persian Gulf and Northern Tier countries (Afghanistan, Iran, and Turkey).

3. A growing direct economic interest in the oil revenues of the region as a major provider of badly needed hard currency.

On the cost side, there was a steep rise in cost per "unit of concession" or "unit of influence" due to the following:

1. A realization by both the Soviet Union and its clients that the comparative advantage of Soviet economic aid is much lower than anticipated. The sums needed for economic aid are astronomical by Soviet (and not only Soviet) capabilities.
2. A rapid rise in costs of military support and of military risks in regional conflicts.
3. The emergence of strong local economic and political powers with the ability to compete with the Soviet Union and replace it.
4. A rise in the intensity of U.S. interests in the region, followed by a corresponding rise in the level of its commitments.
5. A development of a comparative U.S. advantage in the region in a number of respects, in particular with respect to the peace process.

The rise in oil revenues of regional countries is a major factor contributing to the continuous compensating increase in the volume of Soviet goods, especially military, entering the area. It obscures the fact that net economic investment is declining. Indeed, since 1974 and up to 1984, there was probably a net flow of economic benefits to the Soviet Union from the region.

In view of this, it is intneresting to analyze and speculate on the prospects for future Soviet involvement in the new environment of much lower oil revenues and the region's reduced purchasing and financing capabilities, combined with direct Soviet losses of oil export revenues for the same reasons.

Despite all the aforementioned factors calling for a decline in Soviet interests and in (net) investment in the region, one should keep in mind that the basic Soviet interests in the region are important and permanent and that they exclude the option or prospect of deserting their client states or of ceasing to invest in their defense or preservation.

Following is a brief review of the basic data on Soviet economic involvement in the region, an elaboration of the main points listed above with the use of data, and a discussion of options and constraints in a regime of low energy prices.

Pattern of Aid and Triad

In determining the value of aid flowing from a donor country to a recipient, one would like to have an entire set of balance of payment data evaluated at relevant market prices. In our case, we have only partial and imperfect information with respect to both quantity and prices. Based on this set of limited information, we will outline the pattern of Soviet aid and trade to the Middle East since 1955.

The bulk of the available aid data is presented in tables 14–1 and 14–2. Table 14–1 includes data on Soviet military deliveries, and table 14–2 presents data on economic aid disbursements. Soviet trade data with the region are presented in tables 14–3 through 14–5. It should be pointed out that Soviet export data exclude military deliveries to the region but include economic aid flows as defined here. All the data are presented in constant 1984 dollars. Military delivery data are based on Arms Control Disarmament Agency (ACDM) current dollar figures converted to 1984 dollars using the U.S. gross national product (GNP) price deflator. The ACDA data are considered by some to understate the true volume of military deliveries. We decided to use the data because the ACDA is the only source that presents an up-to-date consistent aid breakdown by country over the entire period.[4]

The series on economic aid and trade are taken from Soviet foreign trade yearbooks. Economic aid deliveries are assumed to consist of reported exports of equipment and materials delivered for projects being constructed with Soviet aid. The current ruble figures were transformed into constant 1984 dollars in two stages. We assumed a constant 2 percent rate of inflation for transactions in rubles over the entire period and converted the current ruble series into constant 1984 rubles.[5] We then used the official 1984 dollar/ruble exchange rate (0.816) to convert the series into constant 1984 dollars.[6]

The data cover all noncommunist less-developed countries (LCDs).[7] We consider in detail a broad region ranging from Afghanistan in the northeast to Morocco in North African to the two Yemens. India is not part of this region but is included as a separate observation in the tables as a reference. The countries included form the broadest possible definition of the Middle East and the Arab world. The data are grouped into three subperiods: the initial decade of Soviet activity up to the Six Day War; the era of the two major Arab-Israeli wars; and the period of high oil revenues. This reflects the most significant structural shifts in Soviet involvement in this region.

One can observe a number of trends in the aid and trade data. First, there is a secular increase over time in all aid and trade series to the region. The average annual level of militry deliveries increased from $726 million over the 1955–1966 period to $6,903 million over the 1982–1983 period (an annual increase of 10.3 percent). Annual economic aid flows rose from an annual average of $111 million to $618 million (an annual increase of 7.4 percent). The overall growth advantage of military aid is even more pronounced in the period since 1973, while in the pre-1973 period economic aid grew faster than military aid. In correlation with aid, the volume of trade in general also has increased rapidly. Export to the region increased at an annual rate of 9.7 percent, while imports from the region increased at an annual rate of 10.9 percent.

Table 14-1
Military Deliveries
(millions of 1984 dollars)

	1955–1966	1967–1973	1974–1983	1982–1983	Annual Growth (percent) 55/66–82/83	67/73–82/83
Total	15,722	9,296	70,497	15,759	0.0	4.1
Total Annual Avg.	1,310	1,328	7,050	7,879	8.1	14.7
Egypt	423	537	78	14	−13.7	−24.3
Syria	109	122	1,518	1,670	12.6	22.3
Iraq	131	111	1,452	2,034	12.7	25.1
Iran	4	99	237	218	18.6	6.3
Libya	1	27	1,245	1,226	34.6	33.9
O.N. Africa	43	46	553	679	12.7	23.1
Red Sea	15	21	840	778	18.9	31.9
Afghanistan	0	53	265	284	NA	13.8
Turkey	0	0	0	0	NA	NA
India	252	269	653	906	5.7	9.8
Oil Countries	136	237	2,934	3,478	15.1	22.9
Northern Tier	4	152	501	502	23.0	9.6
Region	726	1,017	6,188	6,903	10.3	15.9

Percent Distribution

	1955–1966	1967–1973	1974–1983	1982–1983		
Region as percent of total	55	77	88	88		
Country as percent of region						
Egypt	58.3	52.8	1.3	0.2		
Syria	15.0	12.0	24.5	24.2		
Iraq	18.0	10.9	23.5	29.5		
Iran	0.6	9.7	3.8	3.2		
Libya	0.2	2.7	20.1	17.8		
O.N. Africa	6.0	4.5	8.9	9.8		
Red Sea	2.0	2.1	13.6	11.3		
Afghanistan	0.0	5.2	4.3	4.1		
Turkey	0.0	0.0	0.0	0.0		
India	34.6	26.5	10.6	13.1		
Oil Countries	18.8	23.3	47.4	50.4		
Northern Tier	0.6	14.9	8.1	7.3		
Region	100.0	100.0	100.0	100.0		

Source: 1955–1966—ACDA and CIA; all other years ACDA.

O.N. Africa = Algeria, Tunisia, Morocco.
Oil Countries = Libya, Iran, Iraq.
Northern Tier = Afghanistan, Iran, Turkey.
Red Sea = Ethiopia, Somalia, S. Yemen, Yemen.
Region = All listed countries except India.
For 1955–1966, figure for India includes Afghanistan.

Table 14-2
Soviet Economic Aid Disbursements
(millions of 1984 dollars)

	1955–1966	1967–1973	1974–1984	1982–1984	Annual Growth (percent) 55/66–82/84	67/73–82/84
Total	2,804	3,696	9,855	3,354	0.7	−0.7
Total Annual Avg.	234	528	896	1,118	6.7	5.9
Annual Average						
Egypt	54	99	48	24	−3.2	−10.3
Syria	4	35	35	36	9.6	0.3
Iraq	15	20	113	60	6.1	8.6
Iran	1	102	142	131	24.9	1.9
Libya	0	0	57	72	NA	
O.N. Africa	2	29	62	85	16.6	8.6
Red Sea	5	7	46	88	12.7	21.3
Afghanistan	30	28	63	87	4.5	9.1
Turkey	1	62	43	36	16.0	−4.1
India	97	106	92	120	0.9	0.9
Oil Countries	15	123	312	263	12.6	6.0
Northern Tier	31	193	249	253	9.1	2.1
Region	111	383	610	618	7.4	3.8
Percent Distribution						
Region as Percent of Total	47	73	68	55		
Country as Percent of Region						
Egypt	48.5	26.0	7.9	3.9		
Syria	3.6	9.0	5.7	5.8		
Iraq	13.1	5.3	18.5	9.7		
Iran	0.6	26.7	23.4	21.2		
Libya	0.0	0.0	9.4	11.6		
O.N. Africa	1.9	7.6	10.2	13.7		
Red Sea	4.5	1.9	7.5	14.3		
Afghanistan	26.8	7.3	10.4	14.0		
Turkey	0.9	16.2	7.1	5.8		
India	87.5	27.7	15.0	19.4		
Oil Countries	13.7	32.0	51.2	42.5		
Northern Tier	28.3	50.3	40.8	40.9		
Region	100.0	100.0	100.0	100.0		

Source: Vneshnyaya Torgovlia, SSSR.

O.N. Africa = Algeria, Tunisia, Morocco.
Oil Countries = Libya, Iran, Iraq.
Northern Tier = Afghanistan, Iran, Turkey.
Red Sea = Ethiopia, Somalia, S. Yemen, N. Yemen.
Region = All listed countries except India.

Table 14–3
Soviet Exports
(millions of 1984 dollars)

	1955–1966	1967–1973	1974–1984	1982–1984	Annual Growth (percent)	
					55/66–82/84	67/73–82/84
Total	9,837	11,879	52,575	20,091	3.0	4.1
Total Annual Avg.	820	1,697	4,780	6,697	9.1	11.1
Annual Average						
Egypt	182	428	297	312	2.3	−2.4
Syria	19	77	215	277	11.9	10.4
Iraq	38	120	681	681	12.7	14.3
Iran	39	189	481	577	11.9	9.0
Libya	3	14	150	261	21.0	25.1
O.N. Africa	22	129	285	356	12.3	8.1
Red Sea	13	30	230	397	15.4	21.9
Afghanistan	61	65	313	585	9.9	18.4
Turkey	17	99	203	175	10.2	4.5
India	207	246	933	1,600	8.9	15.5
Oil Contries	80	324	1,312	1,519	13.1	12.6
Northern Tier	117	352	997	1,337	10.7	10.8
Region	393	1,151	2,856	3,622	9.7	9.2
Percent Distribution						
Region as Percent of Total	41	64	53	54		
Country as Percent of Region						
Egypt	54.9	39.4	11.7	8.6		
Syria	5.6	7.1	8.5	7.6		
Iraq	11.5	11.1	26.8	18.8		
Iran	11.6	17.4	18.9	15.9		
Libya	0.8	1.3	5.9	7.2		
O.N. Africa	6.6	11.9	11.2	9.8		
Red Sea	3.8	2.8	9.1	11.0		
Afghanistan	18.4	6.0	12.3	16.2		
Turkey	5.1	9.1	8.0	4.8		
India	62.3	22.6	36.7	44.2		
Oil Countries	23.9	29.8	51.6	41.9		
Northern Tier	35.1	32.5	39.2	36.9		
Region	100.0	100.0	100.0	100.0		

Source: Vneshnyaya Torgovlia, SSSR.

O.N. Africa = Algeria, Tunisia, Morocco.
Oil Countries = Libya, Iran, Iraq.
Northern Tier = Afghanistan, Iran, Turkey.
Red Sea = Ethiopia, Somalia, S. Yemen, Yemen.
Region = All listed countries except India.

Table 14–4
Soviet Imports
(millions of 1984 dollars)

	1955–1966	1967–1973	1974–1984	1982–1984	Annual Growth (percent 55/66–82/84	67/73–82/84
Total	10,90	12,433	64,054	25,113	3.5	5.6
Total Annual Avg.	908	1,776	5,823	8,371	9.7	12.7
Annual Average						
Egypt	176	362	410	387	3.3	0.5
Syria	18	49	208	342	13.1	16.2
Iraq	4	60	413	440	21.5	16.5
Iran	33	125	331	336	10.1	7.9
Libya	1	13	507	1,364	38.0	42.8
O.N. Africa	14	113	176	144	10.2	1.9
Red Sea	4	7	21	28	8.2	11.4
Afghanistan	32	47	228	357	10.6	16.8
Turkey	15	49	114	125	9.3	7.5
India	142	391	1,030	1,584	10.6	11.4
Oil Countries	38	198	1,251	2,141	18.3	20.1
Northern Tier	80	221	673	818	10.2	10.6
Region	297	825	2,408	3,524	10.9	11.8
Region as Percent of Total	33	46	41	42		
Country as Percent of Region						
Egypt	59.4	43.9	17.0	11.0		
Syria	6.0	5.9	8.6	9.7		
Iraq	1.4	7.3	17.2	12.5		
Iran	11.3	15.1	13.7	9.5		
Libya	0.2	1.6	21.1	38.7		
O.N. Africa	4.7	13.7	7.3	4.1		
Red Sea	1.4	0.8	0.9	0.8		
Afghanistan	10.7	5.8	9.5	10.1		
Turkey	5.0	5.9	4.7	3.5		
India	47.8	47.3	42.8	44.9		
Oil Countries	12.9	24.0	52.0	60.7		
Northern Tier	26.9	26.8	27.9	23.2		
Region	100.0	100.0	100.0	100.0		

Source: Vneshnyaya Torgovlia, SSSR.

O.N. Africa = Algeria, Tunisia, Morocco.
Oil Countries = Libya, Iran, Iraq.
Northern Tier = Afghanistan, Iran, Turkey.
Red Sea = Ethiopia, Somalia, S. Yemen, Yemen.
Region = All listed countries except India.

Table 14–5
Soviet Trade Balance
(millions of 1984 dollars)

	1955–1966	1967–1973	1974–1984	1982–1984	1982–1983
Total	(1,063)	(554)	(11,479)	(5,022)	
Total Annual Avg.	(89)	(79)	(1,044)	(1,674)	
Annual Average					
Egypt	6	66	(113)	(75)	
Syria	1	28	7	(66)	
Iraq	34	60	267	241	
Iran	5	64	150	241	
Libya	2	1	(357)	(1,103)	
O.N. Africa	8	16	109	212	
Red Sea	9	23	210	369	
Afghanistan	29	17	85	229	
Turkey	2	50	89	50	
India	65	(145)	(97)	16	
Oil Countries	41	125	61	(621)	
Northern Tier	37	132	325	519	
Percent Distribution					
Region as Percent of Total	−109	−411	−43	−6	−64
Country as Percent of Region					
Egypt	6.2	20.2	−25.2	−77.2	−8.5
Syria	0.7	8.7	1.5	−67.4	3.4
Iraq	35.4	18.4	59.6	247.2	45.0
Iran	5.3	19.8	33.6	247.2	25.9
Libya	2.1	0.3	−79.5	−1132.4	−46.5
O.N. Africa	8.5	4.8	24.4	217.9	16.8
Red Sea	8.9	7.2	46.7	379.0	30.7
Afghanistan	30.5	5.4	19.1	234.7	16.9
Turkey	2.3	15.3	19.8	51.0	16.2
India	67.2	−44.6	−21.6	−16.6	−15.6
Oil Countries	42.9	38.5	13.6	−638.1	24.5
Northern Tier	38.1	40.4	72.5	532.8	59.0
Region	100.0	100.0	100.0	100.0	100.0

Source: Vneshnyaya Torgovlia, SSSR.

O.N. Africa = Algeria, Tunisia, Morocco.
Oil Countries = Libya, Iran, Iraq.
Northern Tier = Afghanistan, Iran, Turkey.
Red Sea = Ethiopia, Somalia, S. Yemen, Yemen.
Region = All listed countries except India.

Second, despite the fact that there is an increasing trend in all the series, as shown above, this is not always the case when we consider changes in shares of Soviet trade and aid to the region relative to their corresponding volumes to all LDCs. While the share of military deliveries to the region increased monotonically from 55 percent in the first periof to 88 percent in recent years, the share of economic aid peaked during 1967–1973 and has declined ever since. The share of Soviet exports demonstrates the same pattern as economic aid, while that of Soviet imports increased until 1967–1973 and stagnated with a downward tendency after that.

Third, until the 1973 Arab-Israeli conflict, Soviet military deliveries were primarily directed to those countries active in the conflict. The share of military deliveries to Egypt and Syria declined from 65–75 percent of the regional total up to the 1973 Arab-Israeli war to less then 25 percent since then. The share of the oil countries, however, increased from less than 25 percent to more then 50 percent over the same period.[8] The principal element in this shift is the transfer of military deliveries from Egypt to Libya. The same driving force probably explains the sharp rise in military deliveries to Iraq and even the increased flow to Syria, which clearly remains a conflict country. A similar trend is observed for economic aid and trade flow.

Fourth, one observes over time a growing emphasis on an increased flow of military deliveries and economic aid to Soviet client states in the Red Sea region. Military deliveries to Somalia, and later to Ethiopia and the Yemens, increased from 2 to more than 10 percent, and economic aid rose from less than 5 to more than 14 percent. The relatively low absolute levels of aid to these countries are attributed to their small size and economic backwardness.

In the Northern Tier no one trend is apparent. In Turkey intensive Soviet participation in economic aid have tapered off since the mid-1970s. In the case of Iran the flow of economic aid persists despite the Khomeini revolution and strained Soviet-Iranian relations. Soviet interest to raise its level of influence in Iran has not materialized thus far. In Afghanistan the data fail to show the high cost involved in the direct Soviet military intervention in that country. Wolf et al.[9] estimate the direct cost of Soviet intervention in Afghanistan at between $500 million and $1.8 billion a year in the early 1980s.

The major trends noted above reflect the resulting shift in Soviet aims in view of their reevaluation of the earlier record and of new opportunities and constraints in the region. These trends will be discussed in the next section.

Economic Costs and Benefits

If we interpet the increasing trend in gross Soviet aid and trade flows, as noted in tables 14–1 through 14–5, as an indicator of rising Soviet economic investment in the region, this would lead us to conclude that Soviet noneconomic interests in the region rose at a high enough rate to justify these large Soviet economic costs. Before reaching such a conclusion, one has to calculate the net Soviet economic commitment to the region. This involves subtracting the economic benefits to the Soviet Union, most of which are not included in the tables.

The major economic event in this region over the period examined was the oil crisis of 1973. This crisis brought large economic benefits to the Soviet Union and caused enormous economic damage to the West. To the extent that Soviet activity in the Middle East prior to this crisis contributed to it, the rate of return on Soviet investment in the region was clearly very high. The same is true concerning the possible Soviet role in prolonging the oil crisis since 1974. If such a scenario is correct, then the magnitude of Soviet gains from oil sales to the West and the economic burden imposed on the West dominates any economic measure of costs and benefits in this region. In light of this, let us consider the energy crisis as an exogenous event to the big powers and return to the regional economic cost-benefit analysis.

The elements of a cost-benefit analysis, in addition to Soviet investment shown in the tables, include the flow of repayments for economic aid, the flow of repayments for military supply, and the benefits of balanced civilian trade. In the post-1973 period we observe a worsening in the terms of credits to client states.[10] The observed increase in the proporation of military deliveries to economic aid have a similar effect, since the terms of repayment on military deliveries are more severe than on economic aid. The annual flow of repayment on present and past economic loans could easily exceed the annual flow of new economic aid. In the case of the extended Middle East region, this assumption leads at most to a net annual Soviet outlay of $300 million (in 1984 dollars).[11]

These figures are very small compared to the repayment on Soviet military deliveries. The increase in military supplies after 1973 represent, at least in part, the Soviet desire to earn hard currency from oil revenues accruing to Arab countries. It is difficult to imagine the volume of Soviet military deliveries at these levels without this financial consideration, which is demonstrated by the fact that despite the political stakes in Syria, the Soviet Union insisted on payment in hard currency for most of its military aid to that country.

In Libya, where the political stakes are much less important, the Soviets were ready to sell huge numbers of weapons solely for hard currency. One may argue that in this case the Soviet Union may not mind if those weapons rust in the desert. This, in effect, may reduce the risk of arming Libya.

Just as data on Soviet arms sales are not included in Soviet trade data, so are most payments for these arms excluded unless they are made in the from of exports to the Soviet Union. The existence of such payments is evident in the trade tables presented here in the form of import surplus that the Soviet Union enjoyed with a number of countries during the 1970s. Thus, the large import surplus with

Libya reflects Soviet imports of oil, mostly in payment for arms (see table 14–5). Similarly, the import surplus shown for Egypt represents repayment of past debts with goods.

Most arms payments, however, are made in hard currency and are not shown in the trade data. Although no hard evidence is available in open sources on such flows, it is generally agreed that the bulk of the arms shipments to Libya, Iraq, Iran, Syria, and Algeria since the mid-1970s were paid for in hard currency or equivalent goods, such as oil, upon delivery or under short-term credit arrangements. Zoeter, for example, presents CIA data, according to which up to 90 percent of all Soviet military supplies to LDCs are for hard currency.[12] The actual figures presented by Zoeter for the late 1970s and early 1980s total around $4 billion a year, and even as such they consist of about 85 percent of all military supplies to the extended Middle Eastern region as reported in table 14–1.[13] Wolf et al.[14] quote Soviet hard military sales to LDCs as equal to $5.5 billion and $6.2 billion for 1982 and 1983, respectively.

It is reasonable to assume that most of the hard currency arms deals are made with Middle Eastern countries. Even if such cash deals do not cover the full extent of Soviet arms supplies to the region, however, and even if there are some softer agreements with larger grant elements, it is our claim that the hard currency revenues earned on the bulk of the arms deals is worth much more to the Soviet Union than the true ruble costs of the arms supplied. For example, from Treml and Kostinsky[15] one can conclude that the value of a dollar to the Soviets, in terms of its purchasing power, is approximately double the official exchange rate. Even if the true degree of overvaluation is smaller, this will still preserve a net Soviet benefit from its military transactions with the region.

Finally, it may be assumed that the observed rise in the volume of Soviet trade with the area throughout the period also reflects a growing flow of economic benefits to the Soviet Union. A full analysis of the content of this trade cannot be offered here, but it seems safe to assume that at least part of the trade consists of the sale of Soviet "soft" industrial goods, which cannot be sold in the West, in exchange for "hard" goods.

It should be clear from this discussion that the gross figures on economic aid and military deliveries largely overstate the true economic costs to the Soviet Union of its relations with the region. The net costs, if positive, are very likely to be small; in fact, it is possible that during the late 1970s and early 1980s they became net benefits.

If our assessment that during the late 1970s and early 1980s there was little or no net Soviet economic support to the region is correct, then one should not expect the Soviet Union to acquire large gains in military, ideological, or political spheres. What forces brought the Soviet Union into such a position? In the wake of the energy crisis, the region became more important to the United States and the West in general. Consequently, the United States was willing to raise the level of its economic and military commitment to the region. At the same time, however, the Soviet Union was in the process of scaling down its previously extensive naval expansion in the Mediterranean and elsewhere. Furthermore, the Soviet perception of the U.S. nuclear strategic threat in the Mediterranean was also being reduced.[16]

The energy crisis also facilitated the emergence of local powers such as Saudi Arabia, which also competed for influence. These new competitors dramatically raised the market price of influence. In addition, in the 1960s the Soviet Union suffered from a less than successful record with its aid program in the region, and it was at a political disadvantage when the Arab-Israeli conflict entered peace negotiations. The Soviet Union did not find its interests in the region to be sufficiently essential to warrant the much larger expenditure necessary to meet the challenge of the increased regional competition. It is also doubtful that the Soviet Union had sufficient resources to meet such a challenge.

One can argue that the Soviet Union's shift from Egypt to Libya is consistent with the above considerations.[17] Due to the peace process, Syria remained the last Soviet ally in the conflict, a fact that justified a much larger Soviet commitment to Syria. Even so, the Soviets found it advisable and possible to demand payment for supplied arms and not to commit themselves to underwrite Syria's economic development. This relatively limited commitment to Syria may be explained by Syria's weakened position in the Arab world, its deteriorating economy, and the increased need for arms to supports its extreme position. Under these circumstances the provision of advanced arms, even for full payment, carried with it significant Soviet leverage, but the relative limited Soviet commitment to Assad still leaves him with a significant degree of independence.[18]

The United States, in line with its interests, dramatically increased its level of aid to the area in the late 1970s and early 1980s. It took an expenditure of tens of billions of dollars in military and economic aid to Israel, Egypt, and other countries to establish itself as a dominant power in the area. This achievement was bought at a price much above the capability of the Soviet Union.

Around the Red Sea the Soviet Union succeeded in positioning itself in small countries where there is limited potential for economic development. In South Yemen and Ethiopia the Soviet Union has the advantage of good relations with Marxist governments, a fact that confines the threat to outside competition. In Iran the Soviet Union is reaping a windfall from the expulsion of the United States, but although it should be willing to commit substantial resources to gain influence in that country, political developments in Iran have not been conducive to Soviet intentions.

The above picture of Soviet behavior in the post-1973 period is in contrast to its conduct before the October war. Before 1973 the Soviets were more ready to commit substantial resources to establish and protect a solid foothold in the region.[19]

Soviet Prospects When Oil Revenues Decline

In view of our discussion thus far, one may deduce the following options, problems, and prospects for continued Soviet involvement in the region. The basic premise of this discussion is that for the next decade oil prices will remain at their current low levels. This reduced oil wealth will diminish the level of competition over influence. On the supply side of aid, reduced intensity of U.S. interest may lower its willingness to compete for influence in the region and thereby lower the level of its support. Second, the ability of local financial powers to buy influence will be reduced as the flow of funds is reduced. Third, even some of the oil exporters themselves will develop economic crises. On the demand side for aid, we will find an increase in demand for economic assistance by the former aid recipients. In addition to the decline in outright aid, they will also suffer from a sharp decline in incomes formerly derived from migrant workers, oil transportation services, and other spin-offs of the oil boom. The decline in oil revenues also will drastically reduce the ability of the region to finance the purchase of weapons as well as civilian equipment for development purposes.

What are the Soviet options in such a new environment? It is very clear that, in the near future, the flow of hard currency earned from Soviet arms sales will significantly be reduced. This decline is especially harmful to the Soviet Union when combined with a paralled decline in their oil revenues. The regional environment, where there is increased demand for aid and possibly less stiff competition may open some new opportunities for the Soviet Union. Nevertheless, these aid requirements are substantially higher compared to what the Soviet Union was ready to grant in the past. Moreover, it comes at a time when the Soviet economic situation can ill afford increased aid to the region. This constraint is recognized by Soviet policymakers and in official pronouncements, and it is being internalized into a new official policy toward the Third World.[20]

This new environment presents the Soviet Union with a serious dilemma: to substantially increase aid in order to take advantage of the new opportunities or to risk losing its present level of influence by refusing to do so. As we have seen in the previous section, maintaining the former level of gross deliveries requires a substantial increase in net Soviet commitments. This reality exacerbates the dilemma even more.

The aid recipients, also facing economic difficulties, will have to weigh the granting of greater concessions to the Soviets in exchange for a limited amount of additional aid. Given the new dilemma and constraints on both sides, one should expect a period of hard bargaining and increased tension between the Soviet Union and its traditional clients in the region.

Notes

1. There is ample support for such considerations in official Soviet pronouncements. See Abraham S. Becker, "The Soviet Union and the Third World: The Economic Dimension," paper presented at a conference titled "The Soviet Union and the Third World: The Last Three Decades," Bellagio, Italy, November, 1985; Francis Fukuyama, "Gorbachev and the Third World," *Foreign Affairs* 64 (Spring 1986), pp 715–731; Francis Fukuyama, "Soviet Military Power in the Middle East; or, Whatever Became of Power Projection?," Chapter 10 in this book; Elizabeth K. Valkenier, *The Soviet Union and the Third World: An Economic Bind* (New York: Praeger, 1983).

2. Fukuyama ("Soviet Military Power in the Middle East") attributes shifts in policies to personal changes in the relevant decision-making bodies. One should be aware of the fact that changing circumstances may determine the choice of people for particular positions and also help shape their own minds as to the appropriate policy.

3. Charles Wolf, Jr., K.C. Yeh, E. Brunner, Jr., et al., *The Costs of the Soviet Empire*, Rand Report No. R–3073/1-NA, Spetember 1983.

4. See Moshe Efrat, "The Economics of Soviet Arms Transfers to the Third World," in Peter Wiles and Moshe Efrat, *The Economics of Soviet Arms* (London: Suntory-Toyota Centre for Economics and Related Disciplines, London School of Economics and Political Science, 1985); and "The Soviet Union and the Third World."

5. Given available evidence on Soviet machinery prices, an average annual rate of inflation of 2 percent was assumed for the entire period. This rate of inflation should be viewed as a conservative measure. See U.S. Congress, Joint Economic Committee, *USSR: Measures of Economic Growth and Development, 1950-80*, September 1985, pp. 169–244.

6. The official dollar/ruble exchange rate was used for both imports and exports. No attempt was made to correct terms of trade effects. Such corrections would only distort the data.

7. We excluded data on Nicaragua and Angola from the total.

8. The shift in shares is even more pronounced when he considers Algeria as an oil country.

9. Charles Wolf, Jr., K. Crane, K.C. Yet, et al., *The Costs and Benefits of the Soviet Empire 1981-1983*, Rand Report No. R–3419-NA, August 1986, pp. 28–30.

10. Elizabeth K. Valkenier, *The Soviet Union and the Third World*, chap. 1.

11. Based on methodology presented in Joan P. Zoeter, "U.S.S.R.: Hard Currency Trade and Payments," in U.S. Congress, Joint Economic Committee, *Soviet Economy in the 1980s: Problems and Prospects*, part 2, 1982, p. 489; Valkenier, *The Soviet Union and the Third World*; and Wolf, *The Costs and Benefits of the Soviet Empire 1981-1983*.

12. Zoeter, "U.S.S.R.: Hard Currency Trade and Payments," pp. 488–489, 503–504.

13. The figure of $6.2 billion given in table 14–1 as an annual average for 1974–1984 is in 1984 dollars, which is equivalent to about $5 billion in current 1980 prices.

14. Wolf et al., *The Costs and Benefits of the Soviet Empire 1981–1983,* p. 28.

15. V. Treml and B. Kostinsky, "Domestic Value of Soviet Foreign Trade: Exports and Imports in the 1972 Input-Output Table," in U.S. Department of Commerce, Bureau of the Census, Foreign Economic Report No. 20, p. 15.

16. Fukuyama, "Soviet Military Power in the Middle East."

17. Gur Ofer, "Soviet Military Aid to the Middle East—An Economic Balance Sheet," in U.S. Congress, Joint Economic Committee, *Soviet Economy in a New Perspective,* 1976, pp. 216–239.

18. Itamar Rabinovich, *The Soviet Union and Syria in the 1970s* (New York: Praeger, 1982); Fukuyama, "Soviet Military Power in the Middle East."

19. A detailed analysis of Soviet behavior during 1955–1973, along similar lines, is presented in Gur Ofer, "The Economic Burden of Soviet Involvement in the Middle East," *Soviet Studies* 24 (January 1973), pp. 329–347; and Ofer, "Soviet Military Aid to the Middle East."

20. Fukuyama, "Gorbachev and the Third World."

Part VI
The
Political-Diplomatic
Context

15

The Soviet and U.S. Record on Arab-Israeli Wars

Barry Rubin

In theory, superpowers control the direction of international events and determine the actions of client states through military and economic aid (or the threat to withhold such aid), diplomatic and strategic backing, and direct intervention. There has always been—to borrow a phrase from mathematics—a cummutative principle in regard to influence between a superpower and client in three respects.

First, the smaller power can act on its own, retaining a large degree of independence, particularly when it considers essential interests to be at stake.

Second, superpower rivalry gives the client nation leverage of its own, since it can threaten to change sides, improve relations with its sponsor's rival, or cease aiding its ally. As Henry Kissinger noted, "In contemporary international affairs a country suffers fewer disadvantages from being neutral and may gain some international stature through the competition of the major powers for its allegiance. . . . Neutrality then becomes an invitation to be wooed."[1]

Third, one of the most important indexes of superpower competition is the great power's willingness and ability to help its own allies. Thus, Soviet inability to prevent the defeat of its Arab allies in three Middle East wars undermined Moscow's attraction as an ally for these states and damaged Soviet credibility among outside observers. The same situation occurred when the United States was unable to help allied governments in Iran and Lebanon. Of course, the damage is cushioned by the superpower's individual strength, which client states need to rebuild or to face the resulting, more threatening state of affairs.

These considerations are amply demonstrated in the history of the Arab-Israeli wars of June 1967, October 1973, and June 1982. But there is another, countervailing series of factors as well. Since the U.S.-Soviet rivalry is global and involves the potential use of nuclear weapons, both sides seek to contain friction and avoid direct confrontation. And since the Middle East is an area where regional conflict may most likely escalate, the superpowers are especially careful to circumscribe local tensions in that region. As U.S. Under Secretary of State Nicholas Katzenbach commented in November 1967, "We shall find outselves often, as we have in the Middle East crisis, with a shifting mixture of shared and rival interests."[2]

Thus, superpower interests in supporting allies is matched by the need to restrain these same allies. The presence of superpower guarantees can make a client state more confident, even adventurous, in pursuing its own interests. The three Mideast crises discussed in this chapter reveal that restraint is often the principal aspect of superpower intervention. Still, while there may occur a balance between superpower encouragement and restraint of an ally, Middle East wars have shown that the latter effort comes into play only after the former effort has helped set off a local confrontation. As Kissinger argued, superpower competition creates "a new element of volatility" because its umbrella allows smaller powers to "feel free to practice vis-à-vis their own neighbors the kind of power politics which they urge the great powers to abjure."[3] They ignored injunctions for caution when they felt, rightly or wrongly, that essential interests, ambitions, and concerns were at stake.

Differing Demands on U.S. and Soviet Middle East Strategy

Differing societies, assets, geopolitical positions, and alliance patterns require major divergences in the strategies of Washington and Moscow, despite their common superpower status.

In the Middle East the Soviet Union's alliance relationships have been with radical Arab states, where the Soviet Union has had the advantage of being the sole large-scale arms supplier but, alternatively, has been unable to win for these states a peaceful diplomatic settlement (in the event of conflicts) or supply them with sizable economic aid and modern technology. When the Soviets could not supply Egypt with these requirements, for example, President Anwar Sadat broke with Moscow.

Further complicating the Soviet position is the need to go along with their allies' militancy, including their professed eagerness to fight Israel, while Moscow's interest required restraining these extremist enthusiasms. Thus, while the Soviet Union has to support radicalism— to preserve its bilateral advantage, to stir up anti-Americanism, and to weaken relatively moderate forces—it also has shied away from the prospect of war. An Arab-Israeli conflict would, after all, create a situation in which Soviet clients could (and did) lose and in which prospects for U.S.-Soviet conflict were heightened. Moscow believed it would benefit from the rhetorical radicalism of Egypt, Syria, Libya, and Iraq, but adventurous radicalism was seen to be extremely dangerous. Thus, while Moscow might have helped create the conditions leading to war, it also sought to prevent an outbreak of actual fighting.

In the past, once a conflict began, the Soviet Union could only accelerate arms supplies to allies, try to limit the fighting, and seek to end it on the most favorable terms. These efforts did not prevent an Arab perception during Mideast crises that the Soviets had let them down. Egypt and Syria found it convenient to blame their defeat in 1967 on a lack of Soviet assistance; Cairo was dissatisfied with Soviet diplomatic efforts and military aid prior to the 1973 war; and Syria found the Soviets sluggish in responding to its plight in 1982. Moreover, Iraq reached a similar conclusion concerning the Soviet failure to help it in its war against Iran. The Soviets have paid a price for their attempts to curb Arab adventurism and their inability to deliver benefits to clients states, resulting in a general decline in Soviet regional influence. One result was that Damascus ignored Moscow's opposition to its invasion of Lebanon and its efforts to split the Palestine Liberation Organization (PLO). At the same time, however, alignment with the Soviet Union has remained important for Syria and Libya.

The United States has a different set of considerations. It maintains good relations with elements on both sides of the Arab-Israeli conflict and has been able to combine a special relationship with Israel with close ties with the more moderate Arab regimes. While Israel's military successes have benefited U.S. interests, however, they also have created potential friction with the United States' Arab friends. Hence, the United States has an incentive to avoid regional confrontations that create contradictions among its relationships. By the same token, U.S. contacts with both sides give it an advantage as mediator of disputes, while allowing the deployment of the United States' other assets over the Soviets: its ability to provide aid (but not military equipment to those fighting Israel) and development assistance.

In short, while the Soviets have some stake in the preconditions for war, the United States has a greater stake in avoiding military conflict. Nevertheless, war brings with it the possibility of superpower confrontation, encouraging both Washington and Moscow to limit and quickly terminate the fighting. Moreover, while both sides share an advantage in restraining their respective allies, the United States has been able to do so without causing significant damage to its bilateral relationships.

The 1967 War

In 1967 the Soviets followed the aforementioned pattern of restraint and encouragement. They did not want to promote an Arab-Israeli war, but maintaining their valuable link with Egypt and Syria required actions that led to confrontation. As Nadav Safran commented, "By some reasoning that is not very clear, the Russians somehow trusted that they could handle things so as to have it both ways: to get all the benefits accruing from supporting the Arabs politically and militarily on an issue these people considered vital, without actually producing the armed clash they wished to avoid."[4]

There has been speculation that Moscow's efforts at avoiding war were based on either wishful thinking, a misunderstanding of Arab politics, or a mistaken belief that Israel would back down or be restrained by the United States. This miscalculation was based on a strategy with a minimal aim of aiding Salah Jadid's radical regime in Syria and a maximal objective of uniting the Arab states under Soviet protection.

These developments arose out of events starting in April 1967. On April 21 Moscow ingenuously warned Israel that "serious consequouces" would result if it "threatened" Syria. To show its own value as the Arab world's ally, the Soviets spread false rumors about Israeli troop concentrations on the Syrian border as part of a plan to attack Syria: Moscow could then claim to have prevented the attack while Nasser could be brought in to support Damascus, thus forging a pro-Soviet, anti-U.S. Arab alliance and ending intra-Arab bickering. Soviet officials told Egyptian leaders that an invasion of Syria was about to take place. In addition, the Soviet ambassador to Israel refused an Israeli offer to visit the site and satisfy himself that no troop concentrations existed.

Faced with the taunts of fellow Arab leaders, Soviet warnings, and an alleged threat by Israel, on May 14 Egyptian President Gamal Abdel Nasser placed his army on high alert and then demanded the removal of the United Nations Emergency Force on the Israeli-Egypt border. On May 22 Nasser announced a blockade of the Gulf of Aqaba, amid a series of bellicose statements threatening Israel. While this escalation worried both U.S. and Soviet leaders, Moscow's behavior, as Safran points out, "amounted in fact to an invitation to [Nasser] to take some substantial military measures against Israel that he could not resist."[5]

While the Soviets may have sought to cool the crisis, their actions actually inflamed it. A formal Soviet government statement May 23 warned that "should anyone try to unleash aggression in the Near East, he would be met not only with the united strength of Arab countries but also with strong opposition to aggression from the Soviet Union and all peace-loving countries."[6] While this was worded as a deterrent to war, Arabs could only interpret it as a pledge of strong support and a warning to the United States. Similarly, according to Heikal, Kosygin told Egyptian Minister of War Shams Badran, "We are going to back you. But you have . . . won a political victory. So it is time now to compromise, to work politically."[7] Again, Badran and Nasser saw this as a promise of support. Indeeed, in a May 29 speech threatening to destroy Israel, Nasser cited Kosygin as saying "that the Soviet Union stands with us in this battle and will never allow any state to intervene. . . . "[8] The Arabs never expected Soviet military intervention on their behalf, but they did believe Moscow would neutralize the United States, a belief reinforced by a Soviet naval buildup in the Mediterranean. In this situation, Arab leaders believed they could destroy Israel.

If the first phase of the crisis was characterized by destabilizing Soviet disinformation sparking Nasser's escalation, the second phase saw a U.S. effort to defuse the threat of war. On May 22 President Lyndon Johnson wrote Kosygin: "Your and our ties to nations of the area could bring us into difficulties which I am confident neither of us seeks. It would appear a time for each of us to use our influence to the full in the cause of moderation."⁹ The Soviets urged Egypt not to initiate hostilities, while Johnson contacted Nasser directly to say the transcendent objective was to prevent hostilities or to stop any war quickly should one break out. He publicly condemned the Egyptian blockade, promised Israeli Foreign Minister Abba Eban that the United States would act on the straits of Tiran, proposed a multinational fleet to convoy ships, and asked Israel to abstain from military action for two weeks to give diplomacy a chance to resolve the issue.

From Washington's viewpoint, these actions—coupled with parallel Soviet steps—defused the crisis. There was, however, no visible progress, and the United States' European allies hesitated to endorse Johnson's plan. Nasser could well conclude that Israel was isolated from effective Western assistance. In contrast to the rosy U.S. view, Israel saw only Egyptian forces getting stronger daily and Iraq and Jordan joining the Egypt-Syria alliance, coupled with U.S. passivity. The situation was becoming increasingly threatening to Israel's survival.

Contacts between the superpowers made clear that neither would intervene in a war, but far from making regional conflict less likely, this stance emboldened Egypt and made Israel more determined to act unilaterally to defend its security. Israel would not be alone unless it decided to go alone, Johnson told Eban, but this prospect was less worrisome when Israel considered the alternative. While Johnson's reassurance was focused on the symbolic but strategically marginal blockade, Jerusalem was more worried about a direct Arab atack. Given Washington's reluctance (and Western Europe's passivity) to act decisively on the straits, Israel could hardly feel secure in pinning all its hopes on U.S. support.

Thus, Israel launched its successful preemptive attack on June 5. Superpower coordination, which had been unable to avoid regional war, proved to be more effective in limiting the conflict. The U.S.-Soviet hot line was used for the first time as both sides assured each other they had no intention of becoming militarily involved and attempted to work together to work out a cease-fire. The United States stressed its neutrality and asked all parties to support U.N. efforts for an immediate cease-fire. The Soviet Union generally followed a similar course, refusing to resupply Arab armies during the fighting lest this bring a U.S. counteraction.

Moscow's original proposal blamed Israel for its aggressiveness and demanded a return to prewar lines. As the United States insisted on an unconditional cease-fire, however, and as it became clear that Soviet allies were being severely beaten, Moscow accepted the U.S. draft proposal, and the resolution, adopted on June 6, came into effect after six days of fighting ended in a decisive Israeli victory.

This war, whose conditions were initiated by the Soviets and Arabs, was a disaster for both. The events of June 1967 began a process that eroded Soviet influence, eventually alienated Cairo from Moscow, strengthened Israel, and allowed the United States to emerge as the major Middle East mediator. As Jon Glassman concluded, "In the weeks before the Six-Day War Soviet diplomacy had played a dangerous game that had backfired. . . . The Soviets contributed, perhaps decisively, to the political atmosphere that engendered the Six-Day War. They did, however, engage in substantial efforts to seek to avert the war."[10]

This argument is generally accepted. Less appreciated, though, is that the "substantial efforts" to resolve the crisis actually made the conflict more likely. Moscow attempted to have its cake and eat it too by encouraging the Arabs to believe they enjoyed Soviet support. Washington did not act swiftly or surely enough to assure Israel of U.S. protection in light of the greatest threat it had ever faced. Avoiding trouble seemed a higher priority for the United States than protecting its client.

The Political War of 1973

In 1973, as in 1967, the ambiguity of Soviet interests led it to both seek to constrain its Arab clients and to play a central role in their decision to go to war. This time, however, the order of dominance was reversed: Moscow's initial reluctance to support Arab military action later swung to a willingness to back an Arab attack in order to safeguard its own influence.

While ultimately supporting Israel, U.S. behavior was also conditioned by a concern to maintain and, where possible, increase its influence in the Arab world. During 1969–1973, two distinct U.S. strategies arose in this regard. One, represented by Secretary of State William Rogers and the State Department, narrowly focused on the Arabs, stressing the urgency of a quick resolution of the Middle East conflict via concessions to them. The other, represented by National Security Advisor (and later Secretary of State) Henry Kissinger, was predicated on the objective of reducing Soviet influence and the assumption that the Arabs were not yet ready to make peace on any reasonable terms. The Kissinger approach, which was adopted by President Richard Nixon, was to show the Arabs that radicalism and a Soviet alignment would not allow them to attain their objectives. Only moderation toward the United States and a serious commitment to peace with Israel could enable them to regain the occupied territories and realize regional stability. Ironically, although the 1973 war could be said to have arisen from a flaw in Kissinger's conception, the events of the 1970s demonstrated the correctness and ultimately the relative success of his approach.

As in 1967, the Soviet-Egyptian relationship played a key role in the causes of the 1973 war. Moscow had ample evidence of its tenuous hold on Cairo: Nasser's death in September 1970 was followed by purge of pro-Soviet leaders in May 1971. While President Sadat agreed to consult Moscow before taking military action, his evident eagerness to go to war was inconsistent with Soviet desires. Not only were the Soviets concerned as to the effect a new conflict would have on détente with the United States, but they were not eager to risk the consequences of another Arab defeat and doubted whether Egypt could find an alternative to dependence on Soviet aid.

In October 1971 and again in February and April 1972, Sadat asked for more offensive weapons, while the Soviets attempted to discourage any attack on Israel, labeling it as dangerous and disadvantageous to the Arabs. Soviet leader Leonid Brezhnev promised to highlight the Middle East in his May 1972 meeting with Nixon, but nothing came of it. In regard to that summit, Ismail Fahmy wrote that Egypt could not indefinitely accept the prevailing "no war, no peace" stalemate. "Whereas the Soviet's policy objective was intentionally to limit the Egyption military option . . . they grossly miscalculated the effect that policy had in discrediting them with the Egyptians and thereby the negative impact it had on their interests in the region."[11] This led to Egypt's decision in July 1972 to expel Soviet military advisors and remove Soviet military installations.

Sadat's actions shocked the Soviets into relenting somewhat and resigning themselves to the possibility of another war, so long as they could minimize their own risks. Although friction between the two countries remained, by March 1973 Sadat was talking about good Soviet-Egyptian relations due to new arms deliveries, including MiG-21s and T-62 tanks. At the same time, restrictions on the use of Soviet weapons were removed and similar buildup was taking place in Syria. In September 1973 Moscow was informed of Arab plans to attack Israel, although it was not provided with exact dates or further details.

Jon Glassman concludes that "Russian policy toward the Middle East during the 1971–1973 period can thus be understood as a continuing series of capitulations in the face of Egyptian insistence on the renewal of the war with Israel."[12] In addition, Moscow was influenced by other signs of its declining influence, such as the failure of a communist-backed coup in Sudan and the fall of the Jadid regime in Syria. Having abandoned its opposition to an Arab attack, Moscow sought to integrate this course into its traditional strategy of seeking an anti-American, anti-Israeli united front under the Soviet umbrella. Once again, the Soviet Union could demonstrate its own militancy, pressure Arab moderates, and seek gains for its clients. The feeling that U.S. support for Israel was equivocal also might have encouraged this political line. Ironically, while the Soviets acceded to Sadat's demands in order to prevent a loss of their foothold in Egypt, Sadat's overall strategy of using the war as a springboard for a U.S.-mediated diplomatic effort inevitably doomed Moscow's previous relationship with Cairo.

This was apparent even before the 1973 war. Hafez Ismail met Kissinger in February 1973 and again in May, and a back channel was opened through Saudi Arabia. The United States, however, still awaited an Arab diplomatic breakthrough. Kissinger either missed the significance of Sadat's expulsion of the Soviets or, as he put it, encountered continued Egyptian reluctance to negotiate seriously. Given Israel's strategic and regional importance, especially in light of continued Arab radicalism, the U.S.-Israeli relationship warmed considerably during 1967–1973 and resulted in the start of U.S. arms shipments to Tel Aviv.

The United States failed to anticipate the Yom Kippur War, however, because, like the Soviets and Israelis, it interpreted the political-military situation in a traditional manner. If the Arabs knew they would lose a war, Washington, Moscow, and Jerusalem reasoned, then they would not start one. Sadat, however, was not trying to attain military victory in the usual sense of the word but rather was seeking a disruption of the status quo that would require the superpowers to press for a solution and establish the necessary preconditions for Egypt to negotiate with Israel. In addition, Kissinger was surprised by the war because he believed the Soviets would continue to discourage an Arab offensive in order to preserve détente.

Once the war began, the Soviets' principal objective was to demonstrate support for the Arabs without going so far as to blunder into a confrontation with the United States. The United States' major goal was to establish a situation in which it could become the postwar mediator, and to this end, the United States urged Israel not to stage a preemptive attack and refuse to make an issue of the fact that the Arab states had started the war.

Nixon and Kissinger thus walked a thin line. They were determined to show support for Israel within the framework of superpower competition, but they also wanted a certain balance to emerge so as to encourage the Arabs to seek negotiations. In addition, Kissinger feared that the Soviets might intervene if their allies appeared to be near collapse. One effect of this strategy was to move the Sixth Fleet into the area as a demonstration of U.S. power and to discourage Soviet intervention. But U.S. actions were also restrained in order to avoid sending a wrong signal to Moscow. On October 7 Nixon sent Brezhnev a letter urging mutual restraint, to which the Soviet leader gave an encouragingly conciliatory reply. The U.S. expectation was optimistic: The Arabs would accept a cease-fire as soon as the tide began to turn in Israel's favor; the United States would then be able to show an evenhanded approach.

Consequently, Nixon and Kissinger took their time in resupplying Israel, blaming the delay on the Defense Department. When a large-scale Soviet airlift to Egypt and Syria began on October 10, however, the United States responded by making a parallel effort on Israel's behalf a few days later.

Despite détente, the superpowers' diplomatic efforts were also more at odds than in 1967. Washington quickly called for a cease-fire, but Sadat was in no hurry to end the fighting. Moscow, concluding that its Arab friends were doing well, also opposed a quick cease-fire. Its next step, however, cost the Soviets much of the Egyptian goodwill they had previously earned. While Egyptian forces were able to hold captured ground in the western Sinai, the Syrians were quickly stopped and pushed back. Syrian President Assad asked Moscow to seek a cease-fire, and Moscow quickly relayed the request to Sadat. This angered Egypt, particularly when Assad later denied that he had made the request, reinforcing Egypt's suspicion that Moscow placed Cairo's interests far below superpower relations.

Nonetheless, the Soviets were caught short when Israel began to pull ahead. Brezhnev then urged that troops from both superpowers, or Soviet soldiers alone, be sent to stop the fighting. The U.S. response was a worldwide military alert called on October 25. Superpower conflict, while still remote, now seemed closer than before. "Everyone felt the crisis would be crucial for U.S.-Soviet relations," William Quandt writes. "If collaboration worked, détente would take on real meaning."[13] But, the 1973 Middle East war marked the beginning of the end for détente. This was due not only to the Soviet desire to use regional wars to gain strategic advantages over the United States but also to the U.S. ability to use diplomacy as a means to undermine Soviet regional influence. The United States eventually triumphed by saving the Egyptian Third Army, rebuilding relations with Cairo, negotiating disengagement agreements, and ultimately serving as broker in the 1979 Camp David accords.

The 1982 Lebanon Crisis:
Soviet Weakness vs. U.S. Opportunity

The 1982 Lebanon crisis confirmed this development of growing U.S. strength and Soviet weakness. Once again, Moscow was powerless to affect events, while the United States was thinking ahead to the diplomatic implications of military developments. And, once again, superpower cooperation was adequate to prevent any widening of the conflict, but the Soviet Union was forced to relinquish the political lead to Washington. The United States continued to hold center stage in Middle East diplomatic efforts, while the Soviets were largely shut out from playing any mediating role.

Brezhnev's ill health and the jockeying for succession further weakened the Soviet position. Syria was its sole remaining ally in the Middle East, but Syrian-Soviet relations brought as many problems as benefits. The Soviets rightly considered the Syrian leadership as adventurous, and while Syria's isolation in the Arab world increased Damascus's dependence on Moscow, it also lessened the relationship's value. Furthermore, Soviet support for the ambitions of an unpopular Syrian regime hardly helped Moscow's regional position.

The Soviets did not support Syria's invasion and occupation of Lebanon, drawing a clear line between support for Syrian security and a willingness to defend Damascus's position in Lebanon. Assad appeared to have consulted Moscow before he moved SAM missiles into Lebanon in 1981. To make matters worse, despite its massive aid, the Soviet Union still felt insecure in regard to its position with Syria. After all, it had lost Egypt under similar conditions. Washington's immense diplomatic assets, and its collusion with the rich, anti-Soviet Arab oil producers, threatened to woo away Syria or even the PLO. As Robert Freedman notes, "It was a badly disunited Arab world—whose pro-Soviet members were isolated and whose centrist states were gradually moving toward a reconciliation with Egypt—which faced Soviet policymakers on the eve of the Israeli invasion of Lebanon."[14]

Washington, of course, was experiencing its own difficulties in the Middle

East. The Camp David peace process was at a dead end, and events in Iran and Afghanistan constituted major setbacks. In this context, in 1981–1982 the Reagan administration shifted its emphasis to security in the Persian Gulf and the need to strengthen U.S. capabilities to deal directly with contingencies in that region. Strategic consensus—the unification of all possible regional forces under the U.S. umbrella—was Washington's version of Moscow's anti-American Arab front.

Events of 1981, including the PLO-Israel artillery war along the Israeli-Lebanese border and the deployment of Syrian SAM missiles in Lebanon, highlighted the Arab-Israeli conflict. There was, however, no promising option nor likely success for U.S. diplomacy on that front.

As for Lebanon, Washington had never opposed a Syrian presence per se. U.S. calls for respecting Lebanese sovereignty and for ending the civil war did not conceal the fact that there was nothing Washington could do about the situation. Only some effort to break the regional logjam would motivate the United States or offer a prospect for progress.

Washington was well aware of Israel's concern over the threat on its northern border. The Regan administration had discouraged Israeli military action during the SAM missile crisis but could not fulfill its promise to have the missiles removed peacefully. It was preoccupied by priorities at home and in Central America, just as the Soviets were distracted by Poland and Afghanistan.

The U.S. position toward Israel's decision to move forces into Lebanon to expel the PLO and to attempt to install a strong, friendly regime in Beirut remain controversial. The United States advised Israel against such an offensive on several occasions. In May 1982 Israeli Defense Minister Ariel Sharon met with Secretary of State Alexander Haig, and Sharon later claimed that Haig gave some sort of approval for the operation. Sharon had outlined two possible military camapaigns: a limited action in southern Lebanon to repel the PLO, or an advance on Beirut to force a change in the Lebanese political balance. Haig later claimed that he strongly opposed both ideas;[15] Israel should only react proportionately, he said, to a serious provocation.

Schiff and Ya'ari argue that Haig's stance was too mild ever to be taken seriously by the Israeli government. Yet the main evidence cited—Haig's letter of May 25 to the Israeli government—clearly states that he wanted "no ambiguity" as to the need "to impress upon you that absolute restraint is necessary" and that military action might lead to unforeseeable results.[16] Furthermore, in a February 1982 note warning against Israeli action, the Reagan administration argued that Israel's charges of cease-fire violations by the PLO were no justification for a move into Lebanon. Thus, it was already certain that Washington's threshold for a reasonable casus beli was set quite high. Furthermore, the U.S. priority was to ensure successful completion of Israel's withdrawal from the eastern Sinai, as laid down in the Camp David peace accords. One can only suggest that it was Sharon's will to misunderstand—as it was of Badran in 1967—that prevailed.

Once the Israeli army moved into Lebanon, the most striking international factor was Soviet paralysis. There was no apparent political or military coordination between the PLO or Syria and the Soviet Union. Moscow criticized Israel and made vague declarations of support for Syria and the PLO but did nothing on its own.

Again, the superpowers attempted to avoid a direct clash. Brezhnev and Reagan exchanged letters, and Haig commended the Soviets for their behavior, which he termed encouragingly cautious. There was little Moscow could do, even if it wanted to. Soviet options during the invasion were few, even if one could put aside the need for superpower stability. Israel was a significant military power in the region, it had air supremacy, and it was able to destroy even the most advanced Soviet weapons. In addition, Moscow had no secure regional bases from which to dispatch its power.

The Soviets might have sent highly visible aid or even Soviet troops to Syria, but if the other Arab states were not going to rally behind Syria, why should the Soviets take considerable risks to do so? Thus, the Soviets stuck to their anti-U.S. and anti-Israeli propaganda and to denouncing the "feeble and apathetic Arab countries who do not even raise a finger to halt this ugly crime. . . . "[17] Even after warning the United States against sending troops into Lebanon, Moscow backed down when this happened. The Soviets were forced to see two of their main clients defeated, and their most vaunted weapons shown to be useless, although Syria and the PLO still needed Moscow enough to ignore its failure as a patron.

While the U.S. position was stronger, it met with internal conflict and confusion. Publicly, Washington supported U.N. Resolution 508 calling for Israeli withdrawal and a cease-fire. Behind the scenes, however, the handling of the crisis was chaotic. Communication between Haig and National Security Adviser William Clark had broken down. Clark, who lacked experience in international affairs, wanted to support a resolution condemning Israel, failing to understand its implications. Recommendations were sent to Reagan without consultation with Haig, making it impossible to develop a U.S. strategy. In this regard, Haig comments, "In this tragic situation lay the great opportunity to make peace. Syria and the PLO . . . had been defeated. The Syrians and the Soviets were at each other's throats. . . ." Haig wanted to seize the moment to develop a package settlement removing all foreign troops from Lebanon and using the possibility of an "Israeli attack to force the PLO out of Beirut" as a lever to make all sides understand the need for negotiations and the danger of hesitation.[18]

Clark and other high officials either did not understand this strategy or disagreed with it. U.S. policy merely responded to immediate events, while valuable opportunities were lost. In the resulting personal and political friction, Haig was forced to resign in the midst of the crisis. Yet over the longer term the United States again held the diplomatic initiative, eventually producing the Reagan Plan and other efforts. While none of these specific attempts succeeded, due to regional opposition and to the eventually disastrous and tragic dispatch of U.S. marines to Lebanon, the strong U.S. position in the area remained essentially intact.

Conclusions

The history of the outbreak of these three wars shows some common patterns in U.S. and Soviet behavior. Both superpowers acted with relative effectiveness to communicate in the manner necessary to avoid any direct confrontation and to limit any expansion of the wars. Yet the exigencies of supporting their clients also limited superpower cooperation. The United States was able to benefit from the crises far more not only because its most important regional ally, Israel, performed so well militarily but also because it was far better able to take diplomatic advantage of developments. Although to date the United States has not been able to bring about any comprehensive settlement, its holding of assets on both sides of the conflict and its ability to act as mediator remain significant.

The superpower conflict was also secondary in the initiation of these wars, which resulted primarily from regional factors. Mideast clients often exercised disproportionate influence over their patrons because the latter could not afford to lose these assets in the global competition. Yet this counterinfluence can be easily exaggerated. Neither the United States nor the Soviet Union ever acted against their own interests or took significant risks during these crises.

The points outlined at the beginning of this chapter also were borne out. The idea that the Middle East is a playground for a "great game" of projecting superpower influence should be discredited. The region has shown itself to be a "zero-sum game" in which U.S. influence has grown at the expense of Soviet losses and in which almost every country has been forced to tilt toward one superpower or the other. The Soviets have had to scale down their regional ambitions significantly, although times have changed greatly from the period when the Middle East was their only foothold in the Third World. Washington has inherited the difficult task of encouraging regional stability and peacemaking, but given its strategic and economic assets, failure to achieve miraculous results on this front have not led to a concomitant decline in U.S. influence.

Notes

1. Henry Kissinger, "Bureaucracy and Policymaking," in Henry Kissinger and Bernard Brodie, *Bureaucracy, Politics and Strategy*, Security Studies Paper No. 17, Los Angeles, 1968.

2. Daniel Dishon, ed., *Middle East Record 1967* (Jerusalem: 1971), p. 39.

3. Kissinger, "Bureaucracy and Policymaking"

4. Nadav Safran, *From War to War* (New York: 1969), p. 410.

5. Nadav Safran, *Israel the Embattled Ally* (Cambridge, MA: Harvard University Press, 1978), p. 392.

6. Dishon, *Middle East Record 1967*, p. 41.

7. Mohammed Hasanin Heikal, *The Cairo Documents* (London: , 1972), pp. 217–219.

8. Safran, *Embattled Ally*, p. 389.

9. Jon Glassman, *Arms for the Arabs: The Soviet Union & War in the Middle East* (New York: Johns Hopkins, 1976).

10. *Ibid.,* pp. 43–44.

11. Ismail Fahmy, *Negotiations for Peace in the Middle East* (Baltimore: , 1983).

12. Glassman, *Arms for the Arabs,* p. 104.

13. William B. Quandt, *Decade of Decisions: American Policy toward the Arab-Israeli Conflict* (Berkeley, CA: University of California Press, 1977), p. 172.

14. Robert Freedman, "The Soviet Union, Syria, and the Crisis in Lebanon," in David Partington, ed., *The Middle East Annual,* vol. 3 (Boston: 1984), p. 118.

15. Alexander M. Haig, Jr., *Caveat: Realism, Reagan, and Foreign Policy* (New York: Macmillan, 1984).

16. Zeev Schiff and Ehud Ya'ari, *Israel's Lebanon War* (New York: Simon and Schuster, 1984), pp. 63–76.

17. See Robert Freedman, *Middle East Contemporary Survey,* vol. 6 (New York: 1984), pp. 45–47.

18. Haig, *Caveat,* p. 338.

16

Soviet and American Attitudes toward the Arab-Israeli Peace Process

Samuel W. Lewis

Any analysis of Soviet and American approaches toward Arab-Israeli peacemaking must begin by comparing their basic interests and apparent goals. Geography and historical memory play major roles in shaping both.

Soviet interests are grounded in geographic proximity. The Levant region is close enough to Soviet borders to ensure a permanent Soviet sensitivity to Arab-Israeli developments, especially when U.S. involvement produces a threat of strategic encroachment. Soviet interests are far greater in the Northern Tier of Turkey, Iraq, Iran, Afghanistan, Pakistan, and the Persian Gulf region; yet events in Israel, the neighboring Arab confrontation states, and the eastern Mediterranean littoral can pose perceived threats rather analogous to the way in which Central America produces recurrent neuralgia for Washington. Soviet economic interests, even in the Gulf region, are clearly secondary to geostrategic concerns; in the Arab-Israeli arena, they pale to insignificance.

The overriding Soviet interest is to reduce U.S. influence in the eastern Mediterranean region. These are the Soviet goals, pursued tenaciously if often unsuccessfully over the past three decades: preventing the deployment of U.S. military forces and surface-to-surface missiles, constricting U.S. access to airfields and naval facilities, blocking or minimizing cooperative military arrangements between the U.S. and regional military establishments (either Arab or Israeli), hampering the U.S. Sixth Fleet's operational flexibility, and limiting the extent to which Arab-Israeli crises can be exploited by the United States to expand its political influence and military presence. Maximizing Soviet influence, acquiring its own military footholds, and constructing alliances in the region are all corollary strategies to the overarching purpose: to minimize U.S. capabilities for projecting power effectively in a region perceived as dangerously close to the southern Soviet union.

By contrast, fundamental U.S. interests in the region encompass three dissimilar elements: geopolitics, oil, and Israel. Engaged in global competition against a Soviet Union perceived to be intent on expanding its area of political hegemony and expelling American influence from Asia, U.S. strategic planners place high priority on preserving open access to Asian allies and friends through the eastern

Mediterranean and Indian Ocean, on being able to project military force quickly with the cooperation of friendly Arab capitals to protect the weak, oil-rich states of the Persian Gulf against Soviet-supported subversion or proxy attack, and on prolonging internal regime stability in moderate Arab states friendly to the United States. At the same time, however, history, shared democratic traditions and values, religion, and U.S. domestic politics all combine to make permanent security for the state of Israel as absolute a U.S. interest as if Israel were a member of the NATO alliance. For the United States simultaneous pursuit of these oft-conflicting goals becomes extraordinarily difficult in the absence of Arab-Israeli peace.

Alfred Atherton, veteran diplomatic laborer in the vineyard of Middle East peacemaking, summed up the problem well in a recent article in the *Middle East Journal:*

> In the final analysis, there is an underlying asymmetry between American and Soviet interests, objectives, and relationships in the Middle East. American interests will best be served by an end of the Arab-Israeli conflict . . . [as] it creates tension between America's commitment to Israel and its need, for strategic and other reasons, to maintain the best possible relations with key Arab countries or, at a minimum, to prevent their falling under Soviet domination. . . .
>
> The Soviets share . . . an interest in avoiding eruptions of Arab-Israeli hostilities . . . which raise the risk of U.S.-Soviet confrontation. On the other hand, the Soviets have at times gained political advantage from . . . Arab-Israeli tensions. They have never felt the . . . incentive . . . to invest political capital in a peaceful settlement which could eliminate the need for their support among the Arabs.[1]

Thus U.S. policies swing between two poles: certain geostrategic and economic concerns that impel the United States to seek moderate Arab friends and a societal commitment to Israel's security and future. Only Arab-Israeli peace would make it feasible to pursue both goals without recurring confusion and frequent contradiction.

Soviet leaders are, however, also hemmed in by a different ambiguity: on the one hand, a desire to avoid dangerous military explosions that can result in devastating outcomes for their Arab clients, forcing the Soviets to choose between humiliating abstention or an unpredictably dangerous U.S.-Soviet confrontation; on the other hand, a determination to cater sufficiently to Arab priorities so as not to risk losing Soviet footholds in the Arab world, thereby inviting a further expansion of U.S. influence and strategic presence. Soviet behavior, at least since 1967, has reflected this ambivalence.

Contrasting Approaches Toward Peacemaking

The historical record of efforts to bring about a peaceful settlement of the intractable Arab-Israeli conflict already fills acres of library shelves, even though most of the diplomatic archives have yet to be spread before the scholarly community. Description and analysis of the contemporary "peace process" alone encompasses twenty years of intensive if episodic peace initiatives: U.S. shuttle diplomacy, U.N. resolutions and mediators, Arab summit resolutions, U.S.-Soviet collusion, separation of forces agreements, and one Israeli-Egyptian treaty of peace. Among the dozens of books and articles that deal with this recent history, two articles in 1985 by Ambassador Atherton[2] and Professor Robert O. Freedman[3] provide excellent surveys and sound analyses of the approaches followed by the two superpowers in their prolonged diplomatic joust. There is no need to repeat the details here. We should, however, highlight certain aspects of the historical record.

The period of well-nigh continuous negotiations began in the immediate aftermath of the Six Day War in June 1967 and has persisted to this day. Peace prospects often have been dauntingly bleak, but the post-1967 status quo has been too painful for Arab leaders and peoples to digest. Unremitting Arab pressure on Israel to withdraw from the Sinai, the West Bank, East Jerusalem, Gaza, and the Golan, and on the United States to engineer those withdrawals, have been given greater immediacy by recurring warfare, the threat of war, and cross-border terrorism, regularly dramatized in world forums and backed consistently by the Soviet Union. All these have propelled the United States repeatedly back into the Middle Eastern diplomatic fray, albeit often with considerable reluctance, in an effort to try to broker peace or at least to devise some temporary halfway house of partial accommodation. Israel's commitment to withdraw from some occupied territories, grudgingly accepted in United Nations Security Council (UNSC) Resolution 242, was the prelude to the 1969 abortive Rogers Plan, the 1970 cease-fire with Egypt ending the War of Attrition, three separation of forces (partial withdrawal) agreements achieved in 1974 and 1975 following the Yom Kippur War with Egypt and Syria, the Camp David agreement and the Egyptian-Israeli peace treaty, abortive negotiations over autonomy for the West Bank and Gaza, and the stillborn Israeli-Lebanese withdrawal agreement of 1983. This catalogue of failure and success includes only the tip of the diplomatic iceberg of U.S. involvement in attempting since 1967 to broker Arab-Israeli peace.

The U.S. role has frequently become highly uncomfortable. Pressing a friend, whose frustrations and legitimate fears are well understood, to yield strategic territory to seemingly implacable enemies in exchange for intangible promises of acceptance, legitimacy, and peaceful relations is unpleasant business. Yet the United States' conflicting interests in the region have for twenty years left little choice but to persevere.

By contrast, Soviet interests have dictated different tactics, designed to protect or expand Soviet political and military outposts in the Arab World—with major emphasis on Egypt, Syria, Iraq, and the Palestine Liberation Organization (PLO)—while reducing U.S. influence in the region to an irreducible minimum: the unique U.S. bastion in Israel.

The initial Soviet objective following Israel's crushing military defeat of

Egypt, Syria, and Jordan in 1967 was to restore badly tarnished Soviet credibility among its Arab clients, who were bitterly critical of Soviet failure to come to their rescue when the Arab cause turned sour. Rapid military resupply and economic aid were accompanied by an intensive diplomatic campaign to mobilize enough international pressure to force rapid Israeli withdrawal to the pre-1967 armistice lines, as had been achieved after the 1956 Sinai campaign. Only when the Soviets finally understood that, unlike 1956, the United States would this time insist on linking Israeli withdrawal to some formula for a peaceful settlement did they cooperate with the British and the Americans in adopting the compromise embodied in Resolution 242, a text filled with enough "constructive ambiguity" to permit all parties to claim victory. The Soviets, of course, quickly espoused the maximalist Arab interpretation of Resolution 242's key language about withdrawal to reinforce their position with the Arab camp.

Nasser's launching of the War of Attrition in late 1968 did not disturb the Soviets unduly, despite their endorsement of Resolution 242. Renewed but limited hostilities only increased Egyptian military dependence on the Soviet Union and facilitated their acquiring base facilities at Alexandria, Port Said, and an embryo deep-water port at Marsa Matruh. U.S.-Soviet discussions during much of 1969 finally revealed Soviet unwillingness to risk any damage to their position in Egypt by pressing Nasser to accept compromise approaches for carrying out the intent of Resolution 242. When Secretary of State William Rogers finally went public in December 1969 with the U.S. peace proposals, known ever after as the Rogers Plan, immediate rejection by both the Soviet Union and Egypt demonstrated where Soviet priorities lay. One element in Soviet thinking was probably to outbid the United States before the Arab summit meeting then about to be convened. (Incidentally, Soviet tactics spared Israeli-U.S. relations a sharp confrontation, for the Rogers Plan was indignantly rejected by the Israeli cabinet as well.)

By contrast, the Soviets welcomed the Israeli-Egyptian cease-fire of August 7, 1970, which effectively terminated the War of Attrition, despite its having been the product of the so-called "second Rogers initiative" and solely a product of U.S. diplomatic mediation. The explanation seems to be that escalation of the war after Nasser's visit to Moscow in January 1970 had reached a dangerous point. Soviet-supplied SAM-3 missiles, thousands of Soviet military advisors, and Soviet pilots in Egyptian aircraft had helped to blunt the Israeli retaliatory strategy of deep penetration raids. Nonetheless, Egypt's industrial plant had taken harsh blows. The dangers of further escalation were dramatized for Moscow when Israeli pilots downed four Soviet-piloted aircraft on July 30, though no word leaked out publicly at the time. The war had served Soviet interests by binding Egypt's military and leadership closer to the Soviet orbit. Hostilities ceased before they threatened a U.S.-Soviet confrontation. All things considered, a U.S.-sponsored cease-fire must have seemed a good bargain.

The period from 1973 to 1987 provides rich material to illustrate the contrasts in U.S. and Soviet strategies toward peacemaking, but space permits mention of only a few events. Secretary of State Henry Kissinger and Egyptian President Anwar Sadat combined their subtle skills to squeeze the Soviets out of any effective role in the diplomatic process after the 1973 Geneva conference; Kissinger's acrobatic shuttles and Nixon's understanding of how to use the levers of U.S. power to alternatively dangle carrots and sticks before Moscow meshed with Sadat's disillusionment with the Soviets. Moscow's wariness about confronting U.S. power during the 1973 Yom Kippur War again revealed a good deal about Soviet strategic ambivalence toward the Arab-Israeli conflict.

President Jimmy Carter and his secretary of state, Cyrus Vance, reversed course and invited the Soviets back into the Mideast diplomatic game, convinced that, left aside, the Soviets could undermine Carter's ambitious efforts to achieve a comprehensive peace settlement. Not since the abortive Dobrynin-Sisco consultations of 1969 had such energy been invested in reaching an agreed U.S.-Soviet approach to peacemaking. The result, the U.S.-USSR Joint Communique of October 1, 1977, was a disaster for the Soviet Union and an unintended success for the United States. Rather than a superpower-sponsored comprehensive peace conference, at which a bitter U.S.-Israeli confrontation would have been the inevitable outcome,[4] that Joint Communique helped propel Sadat to his historic trip to Jerusalem, a decision which excluded Moscow again from the process and opened the way to Carter's eventual diplomatic triumph at Camp David.

Moscow's response to the Israeli-Egyptian peace treaty was to seek solidarity with Sadat's Arab critics by sniping at its alleged "emptiness" and supporting PLO and Syrian efforts to undermine it, demonstrated most clearly in the Soviet refusal to permit the U.N. Security Council to endorse this first successful peace in the thirty-year history of the Arab-Israeli conflict, much less to deploy a U.N. peacekeeping force in Sinai as desired by both Egypt and Israel to safeguard the treaty. No U.S.-sponsored peace could enjoy a Soviet blessing.

During the first six-and-one-half years of the Reagan administration, mutual ideological hostility prevented any renewal of Carter's effort to achieve a U.S.-Soviet collaborative approach toward the intransigent remaining areas of Arab-Israeli hostility. Moscow's increasing dependence on Syria as its primary ally in the region has effectively subordinated Soviet Middle East policy to Syrian priorities—priorities which do not include reaching a genuine negotiated peace with Israel, at least not in the foreseeable future. Blocking possible U.S. breakthroughs toward an Israeli-Jordanian settlement has been Moscow's major preoccupation; Syrian hostility and PLO machinations have provided effective tools. Israel's ill-conceived Lebanon adventure provided further openings for the Soviets to pursue the creation of a broad Arab alliance against the U.S.-Israeli-Egyptian "peace camp"; yet Moscow's embarrassing lack of military support for Syria and the PLO in the face of Israeli victories limited Soviet ability to enlarge its influence elsewhere in the Arab world. Still, Lebanese President Gemayal's humiliating abrogation of the U.S.-sponsored and brokered Israel-Lebanon Agreement of 1983, under relentless Syrian pressure, added renewed weight to the Soviet insistence that no further steps toward a Middle East settlement can be achieved without the full participation of the Soviet Union and its allies, in particular Syria, and the PLO.

President Reagan announced his own peace initiative on September 1, 1982, aimed at redirecting attention away from the quagmire of Lebanon and back toward a broader peace process grounded in the unfulfilled portion of the Camp David Agreement. The goal was direct negotiations between Israel and Jordan, joined by Egypt, the United States, and non-PLO Palestinian representatives, looking toward an autonomous Palestinian entity in the West Bank and Gaza "linked" in some fashion to Jordan. The timing of Reagan's speech, disastrously inopportune so far as Israel was concerned, was intended to preempt the impending Arab summit meeting at Fez from shutting any doors. While Begin's cabinet angrily rejected Reagan's "Initiative", the Fez summit left it on the diplomatic table together with a new version of an agreed Arab peace proposal, the Fez Plan. Its provisions included the standard Arab demands: total Israeli withdrawal from the West Bank, East Jerusalem, and Gaza, plus calls for an independent, PLO-led state in those areas with Jerusalem as its capital, the dismantling of Jewish settlements in those territories, and "the guarantee of the peace and security of all states in the region,[5] including the Palestinian State by the U.N. Security Council."[6] On September 15, 1982, Soviet Chairman Brezhnev jumped into the competition with a new version of the Soviet Union's earlier peace plan, modifying it to be as similar as possible to the Fez Plan. Brezhnev also repeated the long-standing Soviet call for an international conference on the Middle East to be attended by all interested parties, including the PLO.[7] His purpose was clearly to discourage any Arab temptation to endorse the Reagan Initiative and align the Soviet Union alongside the majority of the Arab states against the U.S. and its Israeli and Egyptian "lackies."

The subsequent period was dominated by prolonged jockeying between King Hussein and Yasser Arafat for dominance in some future joint Jordanian-PLO negotiating team to confront Israel and the United States. Twice they seemed to reach agreement over the future of the occupied territories, in 1983 and again in February 1985; twice Arafat pulled away under pressure from Syria, the Soviet Union, and his more radical PLO colleagues. Meanwhile, the United States worked quietly but intensively, out of the spotlight and whenever possible in labored coordination with Egypt, to encourage King Hussein and Prime Minister Shimon Peres in preparing the ground for the direct negotiations called for in the Reagan Initiative. The Soviet Union worked to thwart U.S.-Israeli-Jordanian efforts, using the PLO and its like-minded ally, Syria, as proxy instruments. Mocow also announced yet another version of its own peace plan on July 29, 1984, this time adding the concept of eventual confederation between Jordan and a Palestinian state to tempt King Hussein. Whenever Hussein and Arafat seemed close to agreement, Soviet attacks on both increased in shrillness; when their negotiations were finally aborted in February 1986, Soviet satisfaction was apparent.

Smugly expressing that reaction was Vladimir Polykov, chief of the Soviet Foreign Ministry's Near East Department:

> We have regarded the Amman Agreement as an unsound step because it does not help the achievement of a just and comprehensive peaceful settlement. The United States has exploited the Amman Agreement to impose the U.S.-Israeli solution on the peoples of the region. The Amman Agreement did not meet with the approval of all the Palestinians. It caused more division and destroyed Palestinian unity. It also aroused fears in many Arab states, many of whom did not support the agreement because it ran contrary to the proposals unanimously approved at the Fez Summit Conference. The events that occurred in the year following the signing of the agreement (February, 1985) show that there were no positive results.[8]

As the tortuous Jordanian-PLO-Israeli-Egyptian-U.S. minuet revolved, King Hussein increasingly stressed to U.S. emissaries his need for an international conference to serve as a diplomatic umbrella for any direct negotiations with Israel. That insistence seemingly reflected two Jordanian convictions: first, that Soviet and Syrian disruptive capabilities were too great to ignore and could be contained only through the conference device; second, that the United States is too closely tied to Israel to merit Jordan's full confidence as a single mediator. A Soviet negotiating team at such a conference could help right the balance. Soviet threats and blandishments have clearly made a major impact in Amman in recent years. Since the Reagan administration has shown little enthusiasm for letting the Soviets back into any substantive role in the Middle East peace process, Jordan's warm espousal of Soviet participation via a conference bodes ill for the changes of launching any direct negotiations at all.

Lessons from History

Looking back over the past two decades, what are some conclusions that one can draw about Soviet and U.S. approaches to the peace process? On the one hand, the Soviet Union has demonstrated an overriding determination to ensure that its role and its interests as a superpower are amply acknowledged in any diplomatic process, and that no Arab-Israeli peace settlement is possible without active Soviet participation. Second, Soviet peace proposals have been calibrated to Arab demands so as to retain for the Soviet Union a favorable position in key Arab capitals. Apparently despairing of driving any wedge into what the Soviets perceive as a firm U.S.-Israeli alliance, the Soviets have utilized their initiatives for tactical purposes to strengthen their influence and undermine that of the United States, not to develop compromise proposals that might possibly lead to a settlement.

Soviet readiness to work constructively with the United States has surfaced but rarely, usually only when the threat of war or military catastrophe for Soviet allies has loomed. Third, when the diplomatic terrain is unpromising, the Soviet Union can readily remain passive about peacemaking. Only the threat that some U.S. initiative might succeed has galvanized a Soviet response.

In the case of the United States, Israel's level of tolerance for risk taking has usually, though not invariably, established the effective boundaries for peace initiatives. Highly sensitized to Israeli resistance to any settlement imposed by outside powers, whether the United States alone or the superpowers acting in tandem, U.S. administrations have, with only two major exceptions, tried to shape their approach to the peace process in ways that would obtain Israeli support or at least acquiescence. (The exceptions were the 1969 Rogers Plan and the 1982 Reagan Initiative, both of which were sharply rejected by Jerusalem and could not therefore produce any concrete results.) This political constraint has produced the phenomenon of successive U.S. mediators, seemingly without number, carrying ideas from Washington around the several capitals of the region, seeking endlessly to prepare the ground for direct Arab-Israeli negotiations. These mediators have been brokering ideas, agendas, and procedures, but with the two exceptions noted avoiding ever putting forward any U.S. peace plan. U.S. diplomats have by now refined to an arcane science the technique of persuading Arab and Israeli leaders to put forward their own proposals, watch them deadlock, then offer American good offices and ideas to keep the process alive. Henry Kissinger and Jimmy Carter both utilized this technique with marked success. But by and large, sturdy conviction, reinforced by public and congressional political realities, has prevented any U.S. president since Dwight Eisenhower from applying any great pressure on Israeli leaders to incorporate U.S. ideas into its policy perimeters. Persuasion, yes; pressure, at least real pressure, no.

Second, acutely conscious of the costs to the United States' regional influence of persistent Arab-Israeli discord, U.S. policymakers cannot leave the diplomatic field for long, no matter how unpromising the prospects for successful diplomacy. The Soviet Union has the luxury of stepping aside from Middle East peacemaking efforts, playing a spoiler's role or dangling before both sides some tantalizing hints of possible constructive collaboration. The United States is condemned to nearly permanent diplomatic engagement to keep a peace process, any peace process, alive. Only when there is at least some appearance of movement can the United States walk the tightrope over its contradictory Arab and Israeli interests.

The Balance Sheet

A number of observers have remarked on the fact that both the United States and the Soviet Union have regarded their contest for influence in the Arab-Israeli part of the Middle East as a zero-sum game.[9] From that perspective, the balance tipped sharply toward Moscow from the mid-1950s until the 1967 war. The late 1960s saw this trend reverse. U.S. diplomacy increasingly set the Middle East agenda. The most important Arab state, Egypt, broke with the Soviet Union, aligned itself with the United States, and made peace with Israel under American auspices; Iraq reestablished diplomatic relations with Washington after years of hostility and effected a more detached view of the Arab-Israeli dispute made necessary in part by its long war with Iran; and several other Arab states maintained or even deepened their relations with Washington, despite frequent predictions that U.S. failure to force Israeli withdrawal from the West Bank and Gaza would turn all the Arab world to bitter anti-American hostility. U.S. military units exercised alongside several friendly Arab forces and in the aftermath of the Lebanon war, Israeli-U.S. strategic cooperation finally has become a reality rather than a slogan, while Israel's forces have acquired unprecedented capabilities to deter or defeat their Arab enemies.

Israel's tragic misadventure in Lebanon and U.S. policy uncertainties there damaged American credibility and prestige enormously. The Iranian Revolution and ouster of all U.S. influence also dealt the United States a staggering blow. There were other mistakes and setbacks. Yet, as Atherton has observed, "It is noteworthy that the Soviets, who have historically sought to exploit regional conflicts and tensions to strengthen their position, have been unable to turn the considerable turmoil in the Middle East over the past several years to their advantage. . . ."[10]

One must ask *why.* Some weight surely must go to the inflexible, unimaginative, reflexive nature of Soviet diplomacy since the early 1970s. Aging Soviet leaders and frequent crises of succession, economic stringencies that have severely constricted Moscow's capacity to emulate Washington's profligate style of resource diplomacy, and ideological confusion—all have made their contribution. The result has been that U.S. diplomacy has had little obstruction from the Soviets in the Arab-Israeli arena for most of the past decade. Its failures could rarely be blamed on the Soviets.

The Gorbachev Era and Its Portents

Typically, analysts of international affairs, especially those within official government institutions, tend to project the future largely as a continuation of the recent past and the present as if the physical law of inertia applied to the behavior of governments. They are sometimes correct; basic national interests and goals change, if at all, very slowly. But with respect to Soviet Middle East policy, inertia could yield to surprising innovation.

Mikhail Gorbachev has already confounded many Soviet watchers with a new style of Soviet diplomacy—more nimble, more attuned to its impact on foreign public opinion, able to shift previous positions with surprising speed, conscious of premiums one gains in multilateral diplomacy by grasping the initiative. Although thus far since assuming power he has displayed this penchant primarily on issues such as arms control negotiations with the United States and Soviet-Chinese relations, it would be unwise to assume that these same characteristics will not soon appear in Soviet policy toward the Arab-Israeli conflict.

For reasons described above, in late 1986 U.S. diplomacy found it increasingly difficult to retain exclusive control of the process. Unlike Sadat, the Arab leader now most central for future peace negotiations, King Hussein, has insisted that the diplomatic arena must be widened to readmit the Soviets. President Reagan has exhibited great wariness about this idea, as has Secretary of State George Schultz. Both learned their lessons well from Nixon and Kissinger. While Soviet policy could suddenly become more daring, U.S. Middle East policy in the final phase of the Reagan presidency seems more likely to stick to well-established patterns. Radical foreign policy initiatives are almost never launched late in any president's term. To the extent Reagan may go against that grain, U.S.-Soviet arms control negotiations provide the more likely arena for U.S. innovation, not the Middle East.

Thus far some small straws have appeared suggesting that Soviet Middle East policy may be in flux, that new initiatives might be impending. Ambiguous overtures to Israel led to an abortive but public meeting between Israeli and Soviet diplomats in Helsinki in August 1986. Then, for the first time in decades, an Israeli prime minister, Shimon Peres, met shortly thereafter with the Soviet foreign minister at U.N. headquarters in New York for what was apparently a lengthy, serious, and amicable discussion. The Soviets have now allowed, or probably even encouraged, their Polish clients to reestablish a diplomatic presence in Tel Aviv. Hungary may follow suit. Even Bulgaria winked toward Jerusalem by inviting Prime Minister Shamir's wife to Sofia on a private visit. A Soviet team of consular experts was scheduled to visit Israel in mid-1987. Tantalizing hints that substantial numbers of Russian Jews may soon be permitted to emigrate have reached Israel through multiple channels. These were merely tentative probes, and nothing substantial may come of them. But the scent of innovation is in the air. What if Gorbachev *were* to decide to launch a major campaign to regain some Soviet influence on Israel?

Soviet-Israeli Relations:—A Blighted Honeymoon

Until the Soviet Union unwisely severed diplomatic relations with Israel in the aftermath of the 1967 war, the Soviet diplomatic mission in Tel Aviv was large, active, and influential. The Soviet Union was early in supporting the establishment of the new Jewish state and was second only to the United States in extending it early recognition in May 1948. Czech arms, undoubtedly smuggled to Palestine with Soviet encouragement, enabled Israel's fledgling, ragtag forces to turn back assaults by the invading Arab armies. Soviet and Russo-Polish political and cultural strains dominated Israel's leadership ranks during the first decades of independence. Marxist ideology strongly infected a substantial slice of the body politic. One of Israel's major political parties in its early years, MAPAM, was stridently pro-Soviet, eventually splitting over that issue. Indeed, a serious concern that, once independent, Israel would swing into the Soviet orbit was one major source of the U.S. Department of State's tenacious opposition to establishment of an independent Jewish state in Palestine.

The Soviet-Israeli honeymoon was brief. By the early 1950s Moscow had evidently concluded that the fishing was better in the Arab pond. David Ben-Gurion's decision to align Israel publicly with the United States and its allies after the outbreak of the Korean War undoubtedly blighted any residual Soviet temptation to regard Israel as a useful pawn. The Czech-Egyptian arms deal of September 1955 marked a watershed; henceforth, Nasser's Egypt would be Moscow's favorite instrument in the Middle East, and the Soviet Union would consistently align its international position with Israel's adversaries.

A great deal of water has now flowed over the dam. Israel is closely allied with and deeply dependent on the United States. For twenty years the Soviet embassy in Tel Aviv has remained shuttered. Soviet spokesmen have led a worldwide crusade against "Zionist-Racism." Soviet-supplied weapons have made first the Egyptian and now the Syrian armies into formidable threats to Israel and the PLO, for a short time, into a conventional army. Those weapons have destroyed many Israeli lives—in 1970, 1973, and 1982–1983. Yet some faint nostalgia lingers, watered by language, culture, and family ties. The large number of Israelis who still speak Russian attests to this continuing tug, even among many Soviet Jews who got out of the Soviet Union only after years of harsh persecution by the KGB.

The Tempting Prospect of Normalization

More telling than nostalgia are other temptations in the thought that Soviet-Israeli relations might again be normalized. The strongest is that a large portion of the vast body of Soviet Jews, vaguely estimated at three million people, might be permitted to emigrate and that a majority would come to Israel to swell the ranks of its Jewish population. Outside the United States, the Soviet Union is the only large reservoir of Jews in the Diaspora, and the only country from which a significant number would be likely to go to Israel if free to do so. During the few years of U.S.-Soviet détente in the second half of the 1970s, hundreds of thousands of Soviet Jews were allowed to leave. The g ates for Soviet Jewry then were tightly shut, and their conditions of life were worsening, until Gorbachev's new policies led to the release from prison of all the well-known Russian Jewish "refusniks" in 1987 and promised some relaxation of pressure on Soviet Jews in general. The temptation to hope for a broader, more dramatic Soviet change of policy will be overwhelming if the new trend continues. Israelis are politically divided on nearly every other issue, but on the need to rescue Soviet Jewry, they are one. That provides the Soviet Union with an ace, if it choses to play it.

Other temptations also are present. Israelis generally admire the United States and like Americans. They are, however, subliminally suspicious of all non-Jews, assume from historical precedent that even their best friends may eventually betray them, and value fiercely their self-reliance and independence. Today's excessive dependence on U.S. aid and goodwill, however cloaked as a strategic alliance, bridles many. Some would prefer to return to the days when both superpowers had ambassadors in Tel Aviv, when the Israeli government had some freedom of diplomatic maneuver by playing one off against the other as other Afro-Asian nations regularly do. Some Likud leaders, such as Prime Minister Shamir, exhibit these tendencies as much or more than those on the Labor side of the aisle. Another consideration is Israel's unceasing search for ways to break down the diplomatic quarantine imposed under Arab pressure by much of the Afro-Asian world and nearly all of Eastern Europe after 1967. Many governments, still hesitating to yield to Israeli blandishments, would feel free to renew diplomatic ties with Israel once the Soviet Union had led the way.

Then there is Syria, today Israel's most implacable Arab enemy, a Soviet client dependent on Soviet weapons and advisors. The Syrians have rebuffed all recent Israeli probes to see whether some explicit or implicit modus vivendi cannot be arranged. U.S. intermediaries have been unsuccessful. Perhaps the Soviets would be better placed to penetrate President Assad's armor.

Consequences of a Soviet-Israeli Rapprochement

Thus, the temptations exist. If Gorbachev chose to exploit them energetically, what would be some of the likely consequences? A decisive Soviet move toward diplomatic normalization, especially if some promised loosening of the bonds on Soviet Jewry were added, would engender turbulence on many fronts.

First, it could disrupt current U.S.-Israeli tactical cooperation in the peace process. The Israeli government's opposition to an international conference and a Soviet role stoutly asserted by Prime Minister Shamir might change, bringing the official Israeli position closer to that of Jordan and Egypt. Foreign Minister Peres and his Labor colleagues in the coalition government have already espoused such a conference, subject to appropriate safeguards for limiting a Soviet role. Reagan would either have to acquiesce grudgingly or risk seeing Gorbachev threaten to take over the role as predominant diplomatic arbiter that Kissinger and Nixon seized in 1973. Indeed, the U.S. has already begun to abandon its opposition to a conference in response to Hussein's and Peres's advocacy.

Second, Soviet relations with its current clients—Syria, Libya, and South

Yemen—could undergo considerable temporary strain. The likely result would be Soviet efforts to reassure and compensate them with more weapons. Other Arab governments would be thrown into some disarray. Those especially close to Washington, such as Egypt, Saudi Arabia, and Jordan, would read the new Soviet move as providing them both the incentive and the freedom to improve their own standing with Moscow, within limits. On the other hand, U.S.-Arab relations might improve. In particular, Syria might well seek a warmer dialogue with Washington to remind Moscow that it too retains some independent diplomatic maneuverability.

Third, the impact on the PLO and conflicted intra-Palestinian politics is unpredictable. Conceivably, the moderate group in Fatah and those PLO leaders who are seemingly tempted toward some form of negotiated settlement could be strengthened at the expense of their harder-line opponents. That could lead to heightened intramural terror among Palestinian factions.

Fourth, possible regional arms limitation agreements might become worth serious exploration. Israeli defense planners are increasingly worried about the heavy economic burden of the regional arms race. Beleaguered U.S. budgeteers, who provide much of the foreign exchange for Israel's defense purchases, would welcome any de-escalation. Shrunken oil revenues give Arab regimes less margin to pay for expensive weapons. Soviet economic woes must make supporting Syria's continuing military buildup increasingly onerous. With Moscow more active across the Arab-Israeli board, some new version of the 1950 Tripartite Declaration Arms Embargo might even become possible, if at the same time the United States and the Soviet Union were making headway in their own bilateral arms control negotiations.

Fifth, prospects for a comprehensive Arab-Israeli peace settlement would not markedly improve. Syrian and Israeli goals would remain too far apart for real compromise. The Jordanian-PLO competition might improve marginally at best. The weight of Likud and its allies in Israel's national camp could well increase as Prime Minister Shamir seized credit for the diplomatic breakthrough with Moscow. That domestic political trend would further weaken the already remote possibility of any Israeli withdrawal from significant portions of the West Bank and Gaza. Egyptian-Israeli relations could become warmer, however, as Israel's diplomatic maneuverability augmented.

Finally, what would happen to the close U.S.-Israel alliance? In all likelihood, not a great deal. Moscow has waited too long to rectify its error in leaving the Israeli field solely to Washington. The cement of diplomatic, military, and economic cooperation has by now set very hard. Israel has become too dependent on its U.S. ally to yield in any fundamental way to Soviet blandishments. Friction could certainly arise, and misunderstandings could be avoided only if Israeli leaders were especially careful to maintain a frank, timely dialogue with Reagan and Shultz. But the U.S.-Israeli partnership can readily adjust to a Gorbachev Middle East initiative, unless idiological warfare in Washington intervenes to put U.S.

diplomacy into a straitjacket. Indeed, a diplomatic thaw between Moscow and Jerusalem might well benefit all the players.

Notes

1. Alfred L. Atherton, Jr., "The Soviet Role in the Middle East: An American View," *Middle East Journal* 39 (Autumn 1985), pp. 708–709.

2. *Ibid.*, pp. 688–715.

3. Robert O. Freedman, "Moscow and a Middle East Peace Settlement," *The Washington Quarterly* 8 (Summer 1985), pp. 143–161.

4. Prime Minister Menachem Begin, then overwhelmingly dominating the Israeli political scene, was fully girded for such a denouement and could have mobilized powerful U.S. political allies against Carter.

5. Moderate Arab interpreters of the Fez Plan assert that this phase embodies an implied form of recognition of the State of Israel. Understandably, Israeli leaders regard it as inadequate for that purpose.

6. Text of the Fez Summit Peace Plan is summarized in *The Middle East Journal* 37 (Winter 1983), p. 71.

7. Freedman, "Moscow and a Middle East Peace Settlement," p. 150.

8. Interview in *Al-Ahali* (Cairo), 16 April 1986, cited in Foreign Broadcast Information Service, *Soviet Union*, 24 April 1986, pp. H9–H11.

9. See, for example, Herbert L. Sawyer, "Moscow's Perception of Recent American Involvement in the Middle East: Implications for Soviet Policy," in Paul Marantz and Blema S. Steinberg, eds., *Superpower Involvement in the Middle East* (Boulder, CO: Westview Press, 1985), pp. 52–53. Also see Freedman, "Moscow and a Middle East Peace Settlement," p. 143.

10. Atherton, "The Soviet Role in the Middle East," p. 706.

17
Soviet and American Attitudes Toward The Iran-Iraq War

Mark A. Heller

A nalysts of the strategic relationship between the United States and the Soviet Union assume that the most likely precipitant of a military confrontation between the superpowers will not be a sudden and premeditated attack of one upon the other, but rather the failure of both to compartmentalize a developing crisis somewhere in the so-called gray areas. The danger of escalatory commitment leading to a direct clash is usually attributed to the endemic instability of domestic and regional political regimes in the Third World, coupled with the competitive alignment of the superpowers on opposite sides of local conflicts.

Because of the heightened superpower tension that has attended a number of Arab-Israeli wars (especially in the termination phase), the Middle East is often cited as the area in which the risk of an escalatory cycle is greatest. In practice, however, the self-evident danger of competitive involvement has led to the evolution of certain informal rules of engagement that tend to reduce the likelihood of a bilateral clash. Foremost of these rules is the tacit recognition that limited, defensive intervention by one superpower to rescue a client in dire straits is a legitimate, nonthreatening action of last resort that should not elicit an interventionary response by the other.

By contrast, the parallel pursuit of seemingly complementary objectives in regional conflicts has been a relatively rare occurrence. Such situations, however, represent a much more dangerous source of superpower confrontation, precisely because experience in managing limited interest symmetries and communicating tolerance thresholds in such instances is lacking. The Iran-Iraq war is the most prominent and pressing case of a regional conflict in which there is some convergence of Soviet and American interests, at least with respect to preferred outcomes.

---

*Portions of this chapter are based on the author's "Sources and Management of the Iran-Iraq War," in Gabriel Ben-Dor and David B. Dewitt, eds., *Conflict Management in the Middle East* (Lexington, MA: Lexington Books, 1987).

Despite the incompatibility of larger, long-term purposes, the common short-term objectives might create the unwarranted illusion that military engagement is tolerable, hence safe, for both. Should the prospect of an undesirable outcome lead one of the superpowers to intervene, its action might easily be interpreted by the other not as a warning against parallel intervention but rather as a signal that such behavior is permissible. In these circumstances the risk of misperception and unintended confrontation would be serious.

It is the possibility of complementary intervention in the Iran-Iraq war that makes the Persian Gulf potentially the most volatile focus of superpower engagement. Although the dangers of direct involvement in the war have thus far been averted, the likelihood of superpower intervention in certain circumstances is far from negligible. And since the consequences of an uncontrolled action-reaction process would be truly catastrophic, bilateral contingency planning for crisis management in the Iran-Iraq arena should be placed near the top of the superpower diplomatic agenda.

Superpower Interests

The littoral states of the Persian Gulf are the focus of long-standing superpower interest and involvement. For the Soviet Union, as for czarist Russia before it, physical proximity virtually dictates intense and sustained interaction, especially with Iran.[1] The latter has frequently been viewed as a source of security threats—because of Iranian irredentism and particularly because of the possible use of Iran by larger powers as an avenue of approach—and therefore also as a logical candidate for inclusion in an expanding Soviet security perimeter.

The area as a whole has also been a major political concern to the Soviets, not only because of the potential opportunities it presents (for the propagation of the Soviet developmental model and the pursuit of influence and presence symbolic of great power status), but also because of the possible challenge of Islam to the validity of the Soviet model in other parts of Asia and Africa and perhaps even in the Muslim-polutation republics of the Soviet Union itself.

Finally, the area has always presented substantial promise as a Soviet trading partner. In the years before the outbreak of the Iran-Iraq war, Soviet political interest in the area was manifested in extremely close relations with Iraq (symbolized by the 1972 Treaty of Friendship and Cooperation). The potential opportunities seemed to multiply in 1979 with the overthrow of the pro-American Shah of Iran and the violent challenges to the pro-American monarchy in Saudi Arabia. The extreme sensitivity to adverse developments along Soviet frontiers was demonstrated in the invasion of Afghanistan at the end of the same year.[2]

American interest in the Gulf region is of more recent origin but of similar intensity. Since World War II, American companies have had a major financial stake in oil in and around the Gulf, and the unimpeded flow of oil from the Gulf has been viewed as a vital national interest. This, by extension, has heightened American concern about the stability, security, and international alignments of the oil-producing states in the area. Moreover, preventing Soviet hegemony in the region has been a constant geopolitical imperative for the United States. Growing challenges to these interests in the late 1970s led the United States to improve its force projection capabilities, to increase its involvement in regional security affairs, and, through the enunciation of the Carter Doctrine in January 1980, to commit itself explicitly to the position that Soviet attempts to gain control of the Gulf would be regarded "as an assault on the vital interests of the United States of America . . . to be repelled by any means necessary, including armed force."[3]

The United States and the Soviet Union tend to measure the success of their policies in the Third World by the extent to which they enhance their political, military, economic, and cultural presence at the expense of the other. This does not imply that their rivalry is a pure zero-sum game, since they do share at least the goal of avoiding a direct superpower clash. Nevertheless, the relationship is predominantly competitive in character. In light of this fact, the attitudes and policies of the superpowers toward the Iran-Iraq war have been surprisingly convergent. The major concern of both is that there be no decisive victory by either belligerent. Both prefer that this be avoided through a political settlement of the war. Failing that, they seek to ensure the maintenance of a balance that will deny either side a war-winning capacity and to minimize the damage of protracted, inconclusive fighting.[4]

Although the Soviet Union is far too strong to be threatened militarily by any local power along its southwestern borders, it has little reason to welcome a decisive victory by either side. A major success by Iraq might lead to the disintegration of central authority in Iran and thus create opportunities for the Soviets to reassert their historical interests in Azerbaijan and perhaps to push south from Afghanistan into Iranian Baluchistan. Soviet attempts to exploit such a situation, however, would have to be tempered by concern about a clash with Pakistan and fear of reactions by U.S. decision makers made more nervous by the impending disintegration of what has always been viewed as an essential buffer against Soviet expansion toward the Indian Ocean. Furthermore, Iraq itself would be unlikely to recall with gratitude the Soviet role in the war or to serve as a vehicle for Soviet influence in the part of the Middle East that it would dominate. In fact, a victorious Iraq would pose a new political and perhaps military challenge to Syria, and this could jeopardize the most important Soviet bastion in the region.

An Iranian victory would be even more dangerous from the Soviet point of view. The Ayatollah Khomeini's venomous anti-Americanism usually overshadows his feelings about the Soviets, but he lumps the Soviet Union together with the satanic Western powers. On one occasion, he even proclaimed, "America is worse than Britain; Britain is worse than America. The Soviet Union is worse than both of them."[5] The triumph of such beliefs is unlikely to advance Soviet interests in the area. On the contrary, the renewed impetus to Islamic revolution given by an Iranian victory would encourage the anti-Soviet resistance in Afghanistan and might further alienate the Muslim population in Soviet Transcaucasia and central Asia. Moreover, the intensified threat to other Arab regimes, including those not currently aligned with the United States, would promote much more intimate security ties with the West and might lead to large-scale U.S. military intervention, which would inevitably be interpreted as a direct threat to Soviet security.

Given the possible consequences of a decisive victory, protracted conflict has represented the lesser of two evils from the Soviet perspective. In fact, there are even some potential benefits to be derived from an ongoing war. Continued fighting maximizes the value of weapons as a lever of influence, and it is precisely as an arms supplier that the Soviets are best able to compete with the West. Soviet oil exports have also generated higher foreign exchange receipts than would have been the case had the war not kept substantial quantities of Iraqi and Iranian oil off the world market. Finally, the Iran-Iraq war has helped to divert Muslim attention from the Soviet war in Afghanistan.

Still, prolonged war in the Gulf implies some weighty costs and risks. First of all, it has confronted the Soviets with difficult choices, since they are eager to cultivate both belligerents. Support for either side, however, threatens to alienate the other, while failure to support either side might drive both to improve relations with China or the West, including the United States. Because of the open split in the Arab world between supporters of Iraq and those of Iran, this Soviet dilemma has to some degree been replicated on a regional scale. The war has been a setback to broader Soviet designs in the Middle East in another sense, as well: It dilutes the preoccupation of some Arab states with the Arab-Israeli conflict and makes it more difficult for the Soviets to use their unqualified support for the Arab side in that conflict as a vehicle to promote their interests in the region as a whole. Moreover, the heightened threat to the other Gulf states posed by a possible spillover of the fighting impels them to maintain more intimate security ties with the United States than would otherwise have been the case, thus facilitating U.S. influence and presence.[6] Given their traditional sensitivity to unstable conditions near their southern borders, this threatens not only a political reverse; it could foreshadow direct U.S. military intervention in the event of severe damage to the regimes of the Gulf states or the oil economy of the area.

These dangers explain why the Soviets have favored a political settlement of the war to its indefinite prolongation, particularly if the Soviet Union itself could play a mediating role and reap some diplomatic benefits. Soviet leaders have therefore endorsed all international appeals for a negotiated settlement, undertaken several mediation efforts of their own, and issued repeated calls to Iran and Iraq to end a war which, they stress, benefits only Israel and the United States.[7]

The primary interest of the United States is accurately reflected in the official position announced at the outbreak of the war and periodically reaffirmed thereafter: support for "the independence and territorial integrity of both Iran and Iraq, as well as that of other states in the region."[8] The United States, of course, is not directly jeopardized by any outcome. There is no conventional military threat from this quarter, except perhaps to U.S. naval and air forces posted to the area. The progressive reduction of oil imports from sources north of the Strait of Hormuz has also rendered the United States itself virtually immune to economic disruption.

The American concept of extended security does, however, require the maintenance of a balance of power in the Gulf. An Iranian defeat might lead to the collapse of central authority in that country and facilitate Soviet penetration; an Iraqi defeat would intensify the fundamentalist threat to other states in the area. In either case, the victor would be able to establish its hegemony at least in the northern Gulf, if not by incorporating the smaller states, then certainly by dictating their foreign and resource policies. This, in turn, would subject the United States' most important global allies in Europe and Japan to serious economic problems. Moreover, a prolonged shutdown of oil exports from the Gulf or the extortion of monopolistic prices by a victorious Iran or Iraq would not leave the United States unaffected, if only because of its obligation to share the burden with its partners in the International Energy Agency.

For the United States, even more than for the Soviet Union, an outright victory by either Iran or Iraq would have no redeeming value. The consequences of an ongoing war, by contrast, have been mixed. In addition to the greater receptivity of the Gulf Cooperation Council (GCC) states to security ties with the United States, some political benefits have accrued as a result of wartime needs of the belligerents themselves. This was particularly true with respect to Iraq, which was forced to abandon its strident anti-U.S. posture and cultivate American goodwill and support. Iraq, initially the major force in the Arab ostracism of Egypt after the Camp David agreement, was also compelled to turn to Egypt for various sorts of assistance, and this facilitated the reengagement of Egypt in mainstream Arab politics, a development that the United States could view only in a positive light. Even Iran, however, has attempted to improve relations with other Western powers (if not with the United States itself) in order to secure the goods, services, and capital that its own economy could not produce.[9]

These gains, however, do not outweigh the permanent risk to the United States that large-scale destruction might spread beyond the immediate war zone to the oil fields, pipelines, terminals, and shipping routes in and around the upper Gulf. In particular, there has been a constant danger that Iran, enraged by Iraqi attacks on Iran's economic infrastructure and convinced that only the support of the Arab Gulf states enabled Iraq to continue fighting, would strike at the economic assets of those states or launch a concentrated campaign of subversion and terrorism against their regimes. If the economic costs or the security threats to those states were to reach truly threatening proportions, the United States might be compelled to intervene. This is an unappealing prospect, not only because of the long-term political repercussions of a direct clash with Iran but also because of the inherent possibility of a superpower confrontation.

Because of the associated perils of a prolonged but unpredictable war, the United States has preferred to see it terminated by political means, even if that means that the regimes in Teheran and Baghdad are not replaced by more savory and responsible alternatives. Like the Soviet Union, the United States has therefore supported U.N. Security Council resolutions calling for a negotiated settlement and the dispatch of a special U.N. representative to the area.

Superpower Policies

Despite their diplomatic efforts (and the even more determined initiatives of other third parties), even the superpowers could not produce negotiations merely by encouragement, for while Iraq soon despaired of its ability to win the war and expressed its willingness to settle for the status quo ante, Iran consistently refused to contemplate an agreement based on the principle of "no victors, no vanquished."

The main obstacle to a negotiated settlement of the war was the millenarian worldview of the Islamic regime in Teheran. However deep-rooted the territorial and geostrategic issues, they were at least sufficiently susceptible to compromise in order to permit a halt to the war, if not to the larger historical conflict. Even the national/racial animosity, exacerbated by the immense casualties and physical destruction of the war itself, could be surmounted. What the Iranian leadership could not concede was reconciliation with the "infidel" Ba'ath rulers in Iraq, whose perfidy was exemplified by, but not confined to, the invasion in 1980. Furthermore, this ideological contradiction was compounded by elements of a personal vendetta. Although Saddam Hussein had unwittingly contributed to the revolutionary process in Iran by responding to the Shah's request and expelling Khomeini from Najaf in November 1978, the Iraqi leader's intentions had hardly been benign, and the Ayatollah was not inclined to forgive simply on the basis of "all's well that ends well." Thus, while Iran did not issue an authoritative statement of its minimal conditions, it consistently rejected every proposal that did not entail at least the removal of Saddam Hussein and the acceptance by Iraq of political terms that implied the elimination of the Ba'ath regime, and neither superpower had the leverage to persuade or induce Iran to change its position.

If persuasion or inducement fail, war termination may conceivably be pursued through coercive means. The Soviet Union and the United States, acting in concert, have always had the capacity to compel Iran to agree to a settlement. This may have been possible through indirect means—that is, the exercise of superpower influence to organize a truly effective economic and military embargo on Iran that would shift the attrition balance decisively in Iraq's favor, although the independent role of China and the limited nature of Soviet or U.S. control elsewhere would have minimized the prospects of success even if the effort had been made. Compelling Iran to agree to a settlement war, however, certainly possible through direct means—that is, military intervention.

Either option would involve risks and costs disproportionate to the objective of war termination. Iraq could not be given the kind of war-winning military capability that might elicit Iranian compromise without jeopardizing the even more important objective of preserving overall equilibrium in the Gulf (and, not incidentally, also precluding the possibility of improved relations with Iran after the end of the war or the demise of Khomeini, or, for the United States, the release of American hostages kidnapped by Lebanese Shiites). In addition, direct military action was too burdened by political, logistical, and operational complications and too fraught with escalatory potential to be considered except in a worst-case contingency: a decisive breakthrough by one side or (at least for the United States) truly unacceptable collateral damage. Given the relatively low-risk, low-cost efforts needed to forestall such contingencies, the superpowers refrained from using their potential capability to impose an end to the fighting and concentrated on the more modest objectives of maintaining a balance between Iran and Iraq and limiting the damage generated by a war their calculus helped prolong.

To avoid the first of these contingencies, the superpowers adapted their policies to the fluctuating fortunes of the war, in the sense of favoring whichever side appeared to be less able to continue in a given set of circumstances. There were, of course, some notable exceptions to this rule, and other considerations also entered into the formulation of policy. In general, however, both the Soviet Union and the United States acted in the manner predicted (or prescribed) by classic balance-of-power theory.

The Soviet Union played an important balancing role throughout the war. Even before the outbreak of fighting, the Soviets, though linked by treaty with Iraq, were working hard to curry favor with the Islamic government in Teheran in order to capitalize on the U.S. "loss" of Iran. The Iranian Communist party (Tudeh) publicly supported Khomeini, and the Soviets, according to some reports, even warned Iran of the impending Iraqi attack in the fall of 1980 and offered to supply weapons and internal security assistance.[10] In the first stage of the war, Soviet behavior objectively helped the side that was militarily weaker. Shipments of major new weapons systems to Iraq were suspended while Soviet allies or proxies (Eastern European countries, North Korea, Libya, and Syria) became the major suppliers of arms and ammunition to Iran. At a GCC foreign ministers meeting in mid-1982, it was claimed that Soviet, East German, and Cuban experts had been present in Iran since the beginning of the year.[11] A Western source later estimated the number of Soviet advisors in Iran at fifteen hundred and reported that they had been shown the sophisticated radar signal processing system in the U.S. F–14 aircraft acquired by the Shah.[12]

The Ayatollah Khomeini's sincere belief in the intrinsic evil of East as well as West, however, meant that substantial Soviet presence or influence in Iran was unattainable, and the main outcome of Soviet policies was the increasing alienation of Iraq. Furthermore, the possibility of an Iranian victory loomed ever larger on the regional horizon. Consequently, the Soviets resumed the sale of major items to Iraq in 1982, thereby enhancing Iraq's ability to persist and contributing to the preservation of the local balance. This pro-Iraqi tilt in Soviet policy continued into the early months of 1984. A Soviet delegation visited Iraq in March and signed a number of economic and technical agreements, including one committing the Soviet Union to constructing a nuclear reactor in Iraq. In April Iraqi Deputy Prime Minister Taha Yasin Ramadan and Foreign Minister Tari Aziz traveled to Moscow and secured major new arms contracts as well as $2 billion in economic credits. These measures undoubtedly helped Iraq sustain its war effort, but they also signaled to Iran that there was a price to be paid for Teheran's strident anti-Soviet propaganda and its support of Afghan resistance forces.

The Iranian reaction was to propose an improvement in Soviet-Iranian relations. This initiative coincided with a change in the overall attrition balance resulting from the increasingly effective Iraqi bombing of Iranian population centers and oil installations. Since that called for some countervailing Soviet action, the Soviet leadership responded positively, and in June 1984 the director general of the Iranian Foreign Ministry was invited to Moscow and discussed the issue of Soviet arms transfers to Iraq with Soviet Foreign Minister Andrei Gromyko. The immediate consequence of this visit was an Iranian-Soviet economic agreement that provided, among other things, for the construction of Soviet power plants in Iran. In April 1985 the Iranian deputy foreign minister traveled to Moscow and secured Soviet agreement to overflight rights for the Iranian national airline.[13] There was no official acknowledgment of direct Soviet arms sales to Iran, but large-scale transfers by North Korea continued—via Soviet airspace and undoubtedly with Soviet approval. In addition, reports surfaced in 1985 suggesting that the Soviets had authorized the sale of surface-to-surface missiles (probably from Libya) in return for access to all Western military technology in the Iranian arsenal.[14] Soviet-Iranian relations continued to improve in 1986. Soviet Deputy Foreign Minister Georgi Kornienko's visit to Teheran in February led to the resumption of direct flights between Teheran and Moscow, the reactivation of the Soviet-Iranian mixed economic commission, and, in August, an agreement to resume the Iranian natural gas exports to the Soviet Union that had been suspended in 1980.[15]

These measures hardly amounted to a second reorientation of Soviet policy on the war, particularly since Soviet aid to Iraq was stepped up in the same period. In fact, they may have been prompted more by the desire to counterbalance Chinese inroads in Iran than by a conscious effort to manage the Iraqi-Iranian balance of forces. Nevertheless, they provided economic reinforcement to Iran at a time when Iraqi actions had inflicted serious hardships. Soviet actions may, therefore, have encouraged Iran to persist in its war, although it is possible that the Soviet intention was to signal Iraq not to place its hopes in an imminent Iranian economic collapse. The latter interpretation is consistent with reports that the Soviets were simultaneously pressing Iraq to show more receptivity to Iranian political demands in order to facilitate a negotiated settlement of the war.[16]

The United States shared the widespread perception of Iraqi military superiority at the beginning of the war and was initially concerned, despite the bitter animosity engendered by the hostage crisis, that Iran might be eliminated as a viable regional actor. At this stage, however, anti-Iranian emotions in the United States made any U.S. support of Iran politically inconceivable. By the time the hostage crisis had been resolved, the immediate threat of an Iranian defeat had passed, and it had become clear that of the two belligerents, Iran was not only more hostile to the United States and more of an obstacle to a political settlement, but it was also more intent on and capable of pursuing a decisive victory. The United States, therefore, geared its policy to preventing such an outcome.

A palpably pro-Iraqi posture was adopted in mid–1982, when the danger of an Iranian victory appeared greatest. In the next two years this tilt resulted in the provision of almost $1 billion in commodity credits to Iraq, a guarantee for 85 percent of the projected cost of an Iraqi pipeline to Aqaba then under consideration, U.S. support of several U.N. Security Council resolutions condemning Iran for attacks on shipping in the Gulf, and, most importantly, pressure on other states to join in the U.S. arms embargo of Iran.[17] Iraq also was removed from the list of countries supporting international terrorism and was therefore no longer subject to the trade restrictions of the Export Administration Act. This enabled it to purchase certain American products, including civilian versions of Bell helicopters.[18] Moreover, there were reports that the United States was supplying Iraq with intelligence information on Iranian army movements.[19] These measures, even the last, contributed less than did Soviet or Arab actions to the neutralization of Iranian advantages, but they provided some material and political-symbolic encouragement to the Iraqi regime.

The Iraqi-U.S. rapprochement was symbolized by the renewal of diplomatic relations, at Iraq's initiative, in November 1984. In a certain sense, this act also represented the limit of the rapprochement. Despite the subsequent authorization of sales of computer technology with possible military applications,[20] the United States was inhibited from becoming an arms supplier to Iraq. This was partly because Iraq no longer urgently needed U.S. weaponry. Indeed, it was Iran that was by then suffering from shortages of military equipment. A porous air defense, in particular, had exposed Iranian cities and economic installations to damaging Iraqi air attacks.

Some U.S. officials were convinced that emerging Iranian vulnerabilities in 1985 and 1986 could facilitate the pursuit of two objectives: first, to secure the release of American hostages held in Lebanon by Shiite fundamentalists subject to Iranian influence; and, second, to lay the groundwork for an eventual improvement in relations with Iran. Iraqi-Iranian enmity would undoubtedly persist whatever the future of the regime in Iran, but the possibility of an Iranian-U.S. reconciliation after Khomeini's death was something that the United States did not wish to foreclose.

Consequently, the Reagan administration surreptitiously sent weaponry and spare parts to Iran, either directly or through Israel. This policy was not adopted to rectify an imbalance in Iraq's favor, but the Iraqi advantage did make it possible for the United States to ship arms to Iran for other reasons without creating an immediate danger of Iranian victory. The aim of compelling Iran to terminate the war was sacrificed for the sake of these other objectives.

The second contingency—avoiding large-scale collateral damage to the oil industry of the Gulf and the security of the Arab Gulf principalities—was of greater urgency to the United States than to the Soviet Union. Although some aspects of horizontal escalation, such as attacks on freighters in the Gulf and Iranian "stop-and-search" interference with neutral shipping, were of concern to both superpowers, the United States, because of the economic and political vulnerability of its local allies to violent instability, was most preoccupied with the general problem of damage limitation.

GCC efforts in the field of defense emphasized the standardization or interoperability of weapons (especially U.S. and French-supplied air defense systems), the distribution of electronic intelligence generated by U.S.-operated AWACS aircraft in Saudi Arabia, and the development of a capacity for operational coordination. These measures undoubtedly contributed to the strengthening of local defense establishments, but they did not enable GCC members to prevent all damage to their economic interests, and they certainly did not create a reliable deterrent against Iranian (or Iraqi) use of force, either during the war or after its termination.

Consequently, the Gulf states also sought, or at least acquiesced in, closer strategic cooperation with the United States. U.S. efforts to acquire a force projection capability in the Gulf area were initially motivated by the overthrow of the Shah and the Soviet invasion of Afghanistan in 1979, but they received an additional stimulus with the outbreak of the Iran-Iraq war and the subsequent threat of its escalation. The overriding convergence of interests and the reality of their own vulnerability obliged the Gulf states to display great receptivity to the U.S. Rapid Deployment Force (later subsumed by Central Command [CENTCOM]) and other manifestations of U.S. power, including the permanent posting of a sizable naval force in the Gulf of Oman.

Only Oman made military facilities available to the United States, although a small naval presence—the five-ship Middle East Force—was maintained in Bahrain; one of the Middle East Force's frigates, the USS *Stark*, was attacked by an Iraqi aircraft in May 1987. In addition, the United States became intimately involved in the Saudi defense program. U.S. personnel operated AWACS aircraft from Saudi bases beginning in September 1980, and they played a crucial role in the Saudi air defense system and were assumed to have participated (via airborne and ground control) in the June 1984 downing of Iranian aircraft. There was also a widespread perception that the overbuilding of the Saudi armed forces, much of it with American equipment, was intended to facilitate the rapid injection of U.S. forces in an emergency.[21]

These damage limitation measures obviously did not produce perfect results; tanker traffic was frequently disrupted, particularly during the spring and summer of 1984. However, the worst of the anticipated dangers—large-scale attacks against major targets on the western side of the Gulf, the overthrow of regimes in the GCC states, and closure of the Strait of Hormuz—did not materialize despite the escalation of the fighting, and there were some grounds for attributing this outcome, at least in part, to the commitment, backed up by the stronger military presence, of the United States.

Conclusions

Despite the generally competitive character of their relationship, the Soviet Union and the United States have at least one shared interest in the Iran-Iraq war: that it not end in the collapse of either belligerent. For a variety of reasons, moreover, both have preferred that this outcome be obviated by a political settlement of the war. Given Iraq's demonstrated inability to compel Iran to stop fighting, however, termination could only have meant persuading the Iranian leadership to moderate its war aims, and the responsiveness of Iranian war policy and war-making capacity to nonmilitary superpower sanctions has been very low, at least until the central personality on one side or both is replaced (and perhaps not even then). This is partly due to Iranian national/religious enthusiasm prolonged after the revolution by Iraq's aggression. Despite occasional indications of popular opposition to the war, including massive public demonstrations in May 1985 following the Iraqi bombing campaign against Teheran, any erosion in this enthusiasm has been insufficient to force the regime to redefine its objectives.

At the same time, third-party pressure on Iran has clearly been neither unremitting in character nor universal in scope. Economic and diplomatic sanctions have been halfhearted, even by the Arab principalities in the Gulf most interested in weakening Iranian resolve to continue the war; Soviet allies have sold to Iran some of what the Soviet Union provided to Iraq; the United States has violated its own embargo in a futile attempt to release a few American hostages; and enough arms have been available on the black market or from various other suppliers to enable Iran to compensate for the refusal of the superpowers to sell it the latest-generation main weapons systems.

The partial and incomplete character of sanctions stemmed from a fairly straightforward calculus: that the consequences of Iran's continuation of the war did not justify the consequences (risks and opportunity costs) to them of the truly severe sanctions that might alter Iranian policy. The same was true, a fortiori, of direct military intervention, since that also involved the risk of a superpower confrontation that might escalate into full-scale war.

In areas outside their recognized spheres of influence, where the possibility of misunderstanding and loss of control is high and domestic or bureaucratic/institutional support for a major commitment cannot be taken for granted, the superpowers have often been inhibited in their use of military force, even when an important interest or asset (such as a friendly regime) was under threat. Nonintervention in the Iran-Iraq war was consistent with this pattern. The prolongation of the war per se did not threaten a vital interest or asset of either superpower, and it would have been astonishing if either had intervened merely in order to stop the fighting.

Perhaps the main reason why the goal of war termination did not lead the superpowers to cross their intervention threshold was, paradoxically, their relative success, together with other third parties, in containing the war. Measures short of direct military involvement could not end the war, but they did help preserve an overall balance that precluded the collapse of either belligerent. In addition, collateral damage remained within tolerable bounds because of the security measures taken by local powers, often in cooperation with the United States.

Nevertheless, the fact that worst-case scenarios have not materialized after seven years of warfare is no guarantee that they never will. An Iraqi defeat may still be triggered by a decisive Iranian breakthrough on the battlefield or by socioeconomic exhaustion and the loss of political authority. If that were to happen, the United States would almost certainly inject military force to deter an Iranian into the Arabian peninsula, and other regional actors might also act to forestall the impending collapse of Iraq. The Soviet Union, inclined for its own reasons to contain Iranian expansion, might well interpret such measures as tacit U.S. acceptance of complementary intervention, perhaps in the form of military pressure on Iran's northern border or hot pursuit of Afghan rebels operating in eastern Iran.

Despite the superficial logic of such an interpretation, however, it is just as likely that the United States, far from condoning Soviet action in the service of a common objective, would feel compelled to "save" Iran in the north even as it deployed military force to restrain it in the south, and while behavior of this sort might seem contradictory, it should be recalled that Great Britain acted with similar inconsistency in 1956: cooperating militarily with Israel against Egypt while remaining committed to help defend Jordan against Israel. It is also conceivable that the imminent disintegration of Iraq would provoke a large-scale Turkish military campaign against the Kurds in northern Iraq and might tempt Ankara to reclaim Mosul province, annexed to Iraq by the British in the 1920s. In that case, the Soviet Union could be expected to respond to appeals for support by any government in Bahgdad, and diversionary Soviet pressure on Turkey's borders or even Soviet-Turkish clashes in northern Iraq could lead to a show of U.S. solidarity with Turkey. In short, the atmosphere surrounding a major Iraqi setback would be rife with confusion and the possibility of misperception, inadvertent escalation, and direct superpower confrontation.

Second, Iraq may accomplish a sustained shutdown of Iran's oil exports, prompting a desperate effort on the part of the latter to close the Strait of Hormuz or convulse the smaller states of the Gulf. Here again, manifestations of U.S. resolve to maintain the flow of oil from the area and to ensure the security of the Gulf principalities could trigger Soviet involvement. Even if this were ostensibly undertaken in support of a common objective—the containment of Iran—rather than to counter U.S. actions, what began as parallel intervention could be quickly transformed into competitive intervention.

Finally, the strains of a prolonged war of attrition, perhaps exacerbated by a succession crisis related to the death or infirmity of Khomeini, may lead to the breakdown of authority in Iran. This could be followed by an armed struggle among different factions for control of the state or the emergence of secessionist movements in various parts of the country. These factions and movements would clearly benefit from foreign assistance, and if one of the superpowers engineered—or even just responded to—a request for such assistance, the other would almost certainly construe this as a challenge requiring a response in kind, thus setting off a process of competitive involvement whose outcome might well be a direct clash.

Whatever the probabilities of such worst-case scenarios, they have to be weighed against potentially catastrophic consequences. For if any of them were to materialize, at least one of the superpowers would act, if not to exploit new opportunities, then certainly to forestall further adverse developments. This would not inevitably lead to parallel intervention by the other. In the case of an Iraqi defeat, for example, the Soviet Union might prefer to let the United States alone bear both the military responsibility for containing Iran and the political ire that this would arouse among Iranians and their ideological acolytes throughout the Middle East.

On balance, however, the importance of the area to the Soviet-U.S. rivalry, coupled with the possible illusion of safety stemming from complementary short-term interests, suggests that intervention in the Iran-Iraq war by one superpower would change the intervention calculus of the other, and it is this prospect, how-ever remote, that obliges the superpowers to focus not only on avoiding worst-case scenarios (which has been done quite successfully) but also on containing a crisis if crisis-avoidance fails. After all, an effort to reach an understanding with the Soviet Union on this problem is at least as urgent as a U.S. overture to Iran ostensibly undertaken for the sake of regional stability.

U.S. administrations have frequently been criticized for ignoring the profes-sional advice of experienced diplomats and other area experts and therefore placing excessive stress on the Soviet role in Middle Eastern problems. This criticism may well be valid insofar as the sources of instability are concerned, as many of the failures in U.S. policy toward Iran must be attributed to the orientation of global-ists in the U.S. national security apparatus. Nevertheless, viewing the implications of regional instability through the prism of superpower relations is fully justified, indeed necessary, because it is only when regional crises are amplified by super-power involvement that they become potential catalysts of global cataclysm. Since complete disengagement is highly unlikely, the most prudent course would appear to be an attempt at prior coordination, including some fairly explicit behavioral guidelines aimed at preventing a critical development in the Iran-Iraq war from becoming an uncontrolled crisis between the superpowers themselves.

Notes

1. For a review of pre-1980 Soviet perceptions and behavior, see Shahram Chubin, *Soviet Policy Towards Iran and the Gulf,* Adelphi Paper No. 157 (London: International Institute for Strategic Studies, 1980).

2. The argument that the invasion was an ill-conceived action of last resort necessitated by the failure to arrest political deterioration by other means is advanced in Mark A. Heller, "The Soviet Invasion of Afghanistan," *The Washington Quarterly* 3 (Summer 1980), pp. 36–59.

3. "State of the Union Address," *Department of State Bulletin* 80 (February 1980), p. B.

4. U.S. Secretary of State Shultz reported that in the course of a meeting with the Soviet foreign minister, "we and Soviet officials agreed that we share a common interest in seeing an end to the Iran-Iraq war." "Shultz Says Soviets Fail to Stem Gulf Arms Flow," *New York Times,* 2 October 1986, p. A–7. For a more detailed treatment, see Mark A. Heller, *The Iran-Iraq War: Implications for Third Parties,* JCSS Paper No. 23 (Tel Aviv and Cambridge: Jaffee Center for Strategic Studies and Harvard Center for International Affairs, 1984), chap. 3.

5. Ruh Allah Khumayni, *Islam and Revolution,* trans. Hamid Algar (Berkeley: Mizan Press, 1981), p. 185.

6. Michael Lenker, "The Effect of the Iran-Iraq War on Soviet Strategy in the Persian Gulf," in Thomas Naff, ed., *Gulf Security and the Iran-Iraq War* (Washington: National Defense University Press, 1985), pp. 85–87.

7. Karen Dawisha, "Moscow and the Gulf War," *The World Today,* January 1981, pp. 11–12.

8. *Department of State Bulletin* 82 (September 1982), p. 59.

9. Heller, *The Iran-Iraq War,* p. 37.

10. Shahram Chubin, "Gains for Soviet Policy in the Middle East," *International Security* 6, (Spring 1982), pp. 140–141.

11. Radio Monte Carlo, cited in Foreign Broadcast Information Service, *Daily Report: Mideast and North Africa* 1, June 1982, p. C2.

12. "New Iraqi Strategy Is Seen in War with Iran," *New York Times,* 31 October 1982.

13. James Chad, "The Deadly Victory," *Far Eastern Economic Review,* 4 July 1985, p. 22.

14. "Soviets Tighten Grip on Iran," *Jane's Defence Weekly,* 23 November 1985, p. 1125.

15. "Iran to Renew Gas Sales to Soviets; Pressure on Iraq Is Seen as Intent," *New York Times,* 26 August 1986.

16. Yediot Aharonot (Tel Aviv), 18 February 1986.

17. U.S. Senate, Committee on Foreign Relations, *War in the Gulf: A Staff Report* (Washington: GPO, 1984), pp. 9–10.

18. Iraq planned to fit these helicopters with Soviet and French armaments. *International Herald Tribune,* 19 July 1983.

19. *Economist Foreign Report,* no. 1925 (26 June 1986), p. 1.

20. Frederick W. Axelgard, "U.S.-Iraq Relations: A Status Report," *American-Arab Affairs,* no. 13 (Summer 1985), p. 9.

21. Harold H. Saunders, "The Iran-Iraq War: Implications for US Policy," in Naff, *Gulf Security and the Iran-Iraq War,* p. 63.

Part VII
The
Global/Regional
Interface

18
Consequences of Superpower Competition in the Middle East for Local Conflicts

Jacob Goldberg

I n discussing the impact of superpower rivalries on local conflicts in the Middle East, one is easily tempted to advance the simple notion that the global confrontation in the Middle East is responsible for the eruption and perpetuation of local and regional conflicts. This one-dimensional approach, however, tends to obfuscate the reality, which is much more complicated than any simple formula may suggest. In fact, the pattern that emerges from a three-decade period of superpower involvement in the Middle East suggests that although superpower competition had aggravating consequences for local conflicts, the latter emerged and evolved primarily as a result of local dynamics inherent in the region itself.

In a way the various manifestations of superpower rivalry in the Middle East may be viewed as variations on a common Cold War theme.[1] From this perspective, the relative marginality of the Middle East to the Cold War becomes conspicuous. Although the region has always been a potential flashpoint, Europe has been and remains the focal point of the global confrontation. The differences between Europe and the Middle East, however, have an obvious bearing on and account for the absence of any pattern of superpower competition in the Middle East, thereby aggravating the consequences for local conflicts.

In Europe the two blocs are arrayed against each other in formal alliances, with the line dividing their spheres of influence officially endorsed. In the Middle East the United States and the Soviet Union, unlike their predecessors—Britain and France—which divided the region between themselves during the better part of the first half of the twentieth century, each competed for influence while refusing to accept or acknowledge the other's claim to a distinct, established sphere of influence. In addition, in terms of regional alliances, the Middle East has undergone numerous configurations of alignments and realignments, preventing—with very few exceptions (such as South Yemen)—any long-term alliance between the superpowers and local client states and thereby making the situation much more fluid, unstable, and susceptible to changes and flare-ups.[2] Finally, the Middle East in the twentieth century is in the midst of a process of transition and change, very much the way Europe in the eighteenth and nineteenth centuries was. This process has resulted in upheavals, turmoil, and inherent instability that affect not only the domestic politics of all the countries but also their foreign policy orientations and shifting alignments with the superpowers.

At stake are the relationships between the superpowers and their local clients, who sometimes are also allies. These relationships present the superpowers with difficult realities, inhibiting or constraining their ability to manipulate conditions in their favor. Both superpowers strive to maintain a delicate balance between their desire to develop a credible military capacity to intervene militarily in the Middle East and a wary recognition that the actual use of force could result in escalation to global confrontation. Accordingly, they put the emphasis on providing military, political, and diplomatic assistance to friendly regimes in the region, hoping to advance their respective interests through the creation of a state of dependence between these regimes and themselves.

Arms supplies, however, inevitably have an impact on conflicts that are rooted in the region itself. How do they affect these local conflicts? The aim of this chapter is not to provide a detailed survey or summary of the impact and influences that the superpower competition has on local and regional conflicts in the Middle East; rather the objective is to provide an overview of the subject in its historical perspective, while providing examples of the influence of the rivalry on regional issues such as the Arab-Israeli conflict, inter-Arab relations, the Iran-Iraq war, and the Lebanese crisis.

Consequences for the Arab-Israeli Conflict

On the whole, it would be accurate to posit that the overwhelming majority of the salient trends and processes in the Arab-Israeli conflict have had their own dynamics. These were inherent in the most fundamental positions and attitudes of the protagonists themselves: Israel and the Arab participants in the conflict. At the same time, however, it must be emphasized that superpower competition in the Middle East affected—in various forms, periods, and directions and in varying degrees—the evolution of the Arab-Israeli conflict and had a profound impact on its perpetuation and, conversely, the chances for its resolution. Methodologically, generally one can safely classify superpower rivalries as contributing factors to the Arab-Israeli conflict, whose basic causes and features are rooted in local and regional dynamics pertaining to three major fields: Arab attitudes toward Israel, political and national priorities within the Arab confrontation states, and the state of inter-Arab relations.

Basically, the Arab-Israeli conflict was utilized by the superpowers to strengthen each one's position at the expense of the other. Thus, in the late 1940s the Soviet Union used the conflict as a means of reducing and eliminating British influence in the Middle East by supporting Israel against the Arabs.[3] Conversely, since the mid-1950s the Soviets have supported the Arab states against Israel as a means of eroding the U.S. position in the Arab world and of promoting their own stature. The United States has sought the opposite goal: the consolidation of its position in the Middle East at the expense of the Soviets by playing the role of sole arbitrator and mediator who enjoys the confidence of both sides. Being locked in what both superpowers perceive to be a zero-sum game, their competition has influenced the temperature of the Arab-Israeli conflict, prevented wars from being conclusive (thereby prolonging the conflict), and had considerable unsettling consequences throughout the past three decades. Indeed, it has accounted for the conflict remaining high on the international agenda and in part for its perpetuation and intensity. This was especially conspicuous between 1967 and 1970, when the superpowers transformed the Arab-Israeli dispute from a troublesome regional conflict into one with global, and dangerous, implications.

Numerous instances exemplify how, on the one hand, superpower competition inflamed the conflict at various stages but, on the other, did not constitute the cause of its most salient developments. In 1955, the Soviet Union, through the Czech-Egyptian arms deal, penetrated the Arab world and polarized Arab-Western relations. It also ignited the Egyptian-Israeli rivalry by enhancing Israeli anxieties concerning President Nasser's offensive designs. It was finally Israel's perception of Nasser's strategy that led it to launch the 1956 war, but the massive Soviet-orchestrated arms deliveries to Egypt certainly played the role of a catalyst that reinforced the Israeli interpretation of Nasser's intentions.[4] Likewise, in 1967 the eruption of the Six Day War had much to do with long-term processes emanating from local factors: the rise to power of the Ba'ath regime—and particularly its radical wing—in Syria; the exacerbation of the Egyptian-Syrian rivalry; and the emergence of the al-Fatah Palestinian movement, its alliance with Syria, and the beginning of its armed operations against Israel. Soviet warnings and threats about Israeli military concentrations along the Syrian border in May 1967 also were one of the major events that led to the swift escalation toward war in early June.[5]

The post-1967 period can be characterized by the same features. While President Nasser conceived and launched the War of Attrition in March 1969, it was the Soviet decision in early 1970 to commit pilots and missile crews to the air defense of Egypt that marked the most severe juncture in the war. Soviet involvement triggered the first and only direct combat between Israeli and Soviet military personnel, ending in the loss of Soviet jets and pilots. Moscow's intervention not only aggravated the situation militarily, but it also signified for Nasser the complete political support of the Soviets, something that enabled him to be more adamant in his demands and terms for the termination of hostilities, thereby further prolonging and exacerbating the War of Attrition.[6]

There were only two periods in which relations between the superpowers had an opposite, relaxing effect on the Arab-Israeli conflict, but both cases reflected superpower cooperation and not competition. The most conspicuous period was, of course, 1971–1973—"détente" in terms of East-West relations, "no war, no peace" in the context of the Arab-Israeli dispute. The relaxation, however, was not in the conflict per se but in its most violent manifestation—war. But even as such, the tranquility was rooted in local, not global, considerations: the death of Nasser, the time Anwar Sadat needed to consolidate power, and the lack of offensive weapons deemed by Sadat as indispensable for launching a major war against Israel.[7]

The same paradigm repeated itself in the first 10 months of 1977, when President Jimmy Carter's idea of a "comprehensive settlement" envisaged the inclusion of the Soviet Union in the peace process. Although cooperation between the two superpowers helped create an atmosphere conducive for negotiations, the general relaxation of the conflict in 1977 emanated from changes in the strategies and positions of the two central Arab confrontation states, Egypt and Syria, and of Israel.[8] The common denominator in these two periods, 1971–1973 and 1977, is that both were marked not by superpower competition but rather by détente and attempted cooperation. Thus, these two exceptional cases would tend to reinforce the general rule that superpower rivalries and competition had clearly aggravating consequences for the Arab-Israeli conflict.

Other exacerbating consequences were caused by massive Soviet arms supplies to Arab confrontation states. Such supplies provided these states with a military option and made war possible in 1967, 1969–1970, and 1973. The availability of increasing quantities of highly sophisticated weaponry to certain Arab states stiffened their opposition to compromise settlements. Furthermore, the Soviet willingness to replenish Arab losses in battle had political effects; it eased the pressure on more radical Arabs to consider negotiations as a possible way out of the impasse with Israel. The massive Soviet resupply of Syria in the aftermath of the 1982 war in Lebanon is a case in point. It considerably hardened the Syrian position in subsequent negotiations and caused the Syrian leadership to contemplate initiating war even without other regional allies. Indeed, much of the Syrian goal of achieving strategic parity with Israel is predicted on the expectation, if not the assumption, that given its huge investments in Syria, the Soviet Union would have to stand firmly behind Damascus.[9] U.S. arms supplies to Israel usually had the opposite effect. They demonstrated Israel's complete dependence on the United States for its security and thus made the Israeli leadership more amenable to U.S. efforts to bring about Israeli concessions. The U.S. airlift during the 1973 war is a case in point.[10]

Another perspective that illuminates the impact of superpower competition on the Arab-Israeli conflict is revealed by the examination of the superpowers' attitudes toward a possible settlement. The Soviet Union has traditionally benefited from the continued existence of a controllable and manageable Arab-Israeli conflict simmering on a low flame. Conversely, the United States perceived its interests to be better served by the relaxation and, ideally, the termination of the conflict. In addition, the Soviets have a political interest in not being excluded from the politics of the Arab-Israeli conflict because their ability to play a major role is symbolic of their superpower status and their claim to parity with the United States. Moreover, such exclusion would automatically create a Pax Americana and by definition erode, if not eliminate, Soviet influence in the region. Thus, the Soviets have a vested interest in frustrating a settlement, let alone one based on U.S. terms.

Nevertheless, there is another side of the coin, as the Soviet interest in sustaining Arab-Israeli hostility is balanced by Moscow's desire to minimize risks of a global confrontation in the region. The Soviets have considerable experience concerning the difficulties of controlling the dynamics of the conflict and of the possibility that events beyond their control may force them into assuming risks they wish to avoid. A settlement of the Arab-Israeli conflict could respond to such concerns. Yet the Soviets are unwilling to accept a settlement that would undermine their presence while enhancing the influence of the United States. If a settlement were orchestrated and guaranteed by both superpowers, however, it could institutionalize and legitimize the Soviet role in regional politics and satisfy their desire for equal status with the United States. Is this, however, a probable scenario and a feasible contingency?[11]

Such assymetry between the superpowers has another angle as well. The Geneva conference, which was convened briefly in late December 1973 under the auspices of both superpowers and thus involved not only the United States but also the Soviet Union, did not lead to successful Arab-Israeli negotiations but quickly became a debating forum that went nowhere. Likewise, the 10-month efforts of the Carter administration in 1977, culminating in the joint Soviet-American communiqué, collapsed even before its Geneva conference got off the ground. Conversely, the U.S.-sponsored interim agreements between Israel and Egypt and between Israel and Syria, as well as the Camp David Egyptian-Israeli peace process, were crowned with success.

The ambiguities of the superpowers' attitudes toward a settlement are best reflected in the fact that their competition would seem to have led to opposite consequences. In 1974–1976 the United States sought to take advantage of the 1973 war to buttress its position and launched a major thrust aimed at supplanting the Soviets. This step-by-step approach, which culminated in three successful interim agreements between Israel, Egypt, and Syria, completely excluded the Soviets from the process. True, the United States did not impose these agreements on the local powers, and the process resulted from the local powers' perception of their own interests, which converged in utilizing the United States as a sole mediator. But it was remarkable that under certain circumstances superpower competition and one power's desire to exclude the other could pave the way for a settlement, albeit limited.

The years 1978–1981 witnessed the repetition of the same phenomenon, this time resulting not merely in an interim agreement but in a full-fledged peace treaty between Israel and the most important Arab state, Egypt. Once again, the basic initiative, considerations, and dynamics were all rooted in Egyptian and Israeli preferences. Still, for reasons pertaining to superpower competition in the Middle East and in a deliberate attempt to exclude the Soviets from the process, the United States played a central and crucial role in the conclusion of the first peace treaty between Israel and an Arab country. The paradox is even more highlighted when this success is contrasted with the failure of the strategy of the same administration in the 10 months preceding Sadat's visit to Jerusalem. A joint Soviet-American approach led nowhere; a process dominated by the United States and based on the exclusion of Moscow resulted in success.

Despite the successes noted above, superpower competition also has aborted U.S. efforts to reach a settlement. The Reagan Plan of September 1982 was predicated on a Jordanian-Palestinian mechanism that deprived the Soviet Union and its client (Syria) of any role in the process.[12] One of the main reasons for the plan's failure to get off the ground was, and still is, major Soviet efforts to torpedo it. The avenues and means of pressure that Moscow has utilized to obtain this goal have varied, including a massive rearmament of Syria in order to enhance its stature as a Middle Eastern power capable of exercising leverage on Jordan and the Palestine Liberation Organization (PLO); heavy pressure on Yasser Arafat, dissuading him and "his" PLO from joining Jordan and the U.S.-sponsored process; and pressure on Jordan not to embrace the Reagan Plan without Syria.

What can account for U.S. success in 1974–1976 and 1978–1979 and for its failure since 1982? Do the results emanate from the superpower rivalry? Or are they due to the fact that Soviet pressure and efforts after 1982 were more effective than those exercised in the 1970s? A close examination reveals that the differences are not rooted in the global competition but rather in local considerations. The United States succeeded in consummating the Egyptian-Israeli peace process because the two local interlocutors had a vested interest in the accords and because Egypt was strong enough to withstand Arab pressure and condemnation. The Reagan Plan, in contradistinction, did not muster the necessary local support—not because of Soviet pressure but because of the Syrian factor. The Soviets managed to exercise influence in this respect only because they had a local client who wished to frustrate the plan to advance its own interests and had the necessary power to do so because of its leverage on Jordan and the PLO. Without Syria, Moscow's ability to thwart the plan would have been very limited.

In sum, it would be fair to conclude that even though the basic determinants of any settlement pertain primarily to policies of the local protagonists, the very involvement of the superpowers makes the arrival at an accommodation all the more complicated. This is even more conspicuous when the superpowers are involved in their own competition because it broadens the circle of the Arab-Israeli conflict and adds a number of dimensions that also must be addressed in the context of a settlement.

This brings us to the third and final aspect of the problem. Despite the general observation made earlier, one can think of four cases in which the policies of the superpowers influenced basic and central junctures in the Arab-Israeli conflict and had a profound impact on its evolution.

First, Soviet support for the establishment of Israel, both in 1948 and during the preceding years, was crucial. Indeed, were it not for the votes of the Soviet Union and its Eastern European satellites in November, 1947, the U.N. General Assembly would not have mustered the required two-thirds majority to approve Israeli nationhood. Second, it was the basic shift in the U.S. position in the aftermath of the 1967 war that frustrated the Soviet desire to repeat the 1956 scenario. Unlike then, when both superpowers forced Israel to withdraw from the whole of the Sinai in the context of some vague verbal assurances, in 1967 the United States basically accepted Israel's position that any withdrawal from occupied Arab territories must come only in the framework of a peace settlement, and that in the absence of Arab willingness to negotiate a settlement, Israel could actually continue to hold on to the occupied territories. It was this U.S. position that largely accounted for the completely different evolution of the conflict in the post-1967 period compared to the post-1956 one. Third, firm U.S. support of Israel over the years was probably one of the salient factors in the growing recognition in Egypt that Israel was not to be destroyed militarily and that there was no escape from a settlement. Fourth, the Arab-Israeli conflict would probably have existed and persisted even without the superpower competition, but the fact that the conflict produced six major wars in the course of 34 years also must be attributed to the superpowers: without their massive arms supplies, there could hardly have been such large-scale wars.

Consequences for Inter-Arab Relations

The inability and unwillingness of the superpowers to divide the Arab world among themselves, and their recurrent attempts to undermine each other's footholds there, have significantly contributed to the escalation of conflict in inter-Arab relations. Conceptually speaking, the postwar penetration of the Middle East by the United States and the Soviet Union influenced and, in turn, was affected by inter-Arab relations much more than the Arab-Israeli conflict.

In the context of Western strategy, the first major move in the region was the attempt in 1954–1955 to create a pro-Western Baghdad Pact, which would serve as an adjunct to the Northern Tier and the Central Treaty Organization (CENTO). This strategy was predicated on the perception that the "expansionist Soviet Union" had to be contained by a network of pro-Western alliances, and the Middle East was just one link, albeit crucial, in this policy. In addition, turning Baghdad into a pivotal Middle East asset for the West coincided with the Iraqi leadership's own aspirations to play a central role in Arab politics.

From the Soviet perspective, the Western strategy was viewed as an aggressive one aimed at encircling the Soviet Union and threatening the Soviet regime and the security of the country. Soviet desires to abort it converged with Nasser's determination to destroy the Baghdad Pact because it symbolized Iraq's challenge to his aspirations to become the Arab world's indisputable leader. This convergence of Soviet and Egyptian interests created the background for the 1955 Czech-Egyptian arms deal. Nasser figured that he stood a good chance of confronting Western-supported Iraq only if he could create a strong counterweight in the form of Soviet penetration into the Middle East, which would prove his ability to withstand Western designs and make Egypt the hub of the new Arab world. From the Soviet standpoint, the goal was to undermine Western positions in the Middle East, establish a Soviet presence in the region, and strengthen the anti-Western components of Arab nationalism. When the Soviet strategy, implemented by its Middle East surrogate, Nasser, seemed to have made some considerable inroads throughout the region, the United States responded in the form of the Eisenhower Doctrine, offering U.S. support for any country ready to resist the encroachment of Soviet communism. Thus, all the characteristics of the global Cold War were transplanted into the Middle East equation.[13]

In the context of inter-Arab relations, what followed was one of the stormiest and most bellicose periods, characterized by an increasing polarization that led to turmoil and upheavals in most Arab countries. This Arab cold war was, of course, anchored in its own local and regional dynamics; the Iraqi-Egyptian rivalry was bound to erupt even without the superpowers' manipulation of local conflicts. In a way, it was the continuation of the two-decade-old Hashemite-Egyptian competition for hegemony over the Middle East, intensified and aggravated by the rise of a radical regime in Egypt. At stake were nothing less than the fundamental issues of Arab unity, leadership of the Arab world, global orientation, and, last but not least, a personality clash between the conservative Nuri Sa'id and the radical Nasser. The superpower competition exacerbated the inter-Arab rivalry by instilling it with a whole new dimension: an attempt to turn Iraq into a major Arab center, which was rooted in Western designs against the Soviet Union, aggravating inter-Arab rivalries and accelerating the polarization of the Arab world along East-West lines. It strengthened the Nasserist front and placed it in a position superior to that of the weakened pro-Western camp, which could easily be depicted as a collaborator with Western imperialism. Finally, it enhanced the process of the radicalization of the inter-Arab system and helped institutionalize the Arab cold war. Malcolm Kerr had, most probably, two foci of cold wars in mind when titling his book *The Arab Cold War* and starting the narrative in 1955.[14]

Thus, the pattern that emerges out of this crucial year is one in which global and local factors played the role of both causes and effects. The West's recruitment of Baghdad—due to global considerations—positioned Iraq against Egypt; but Nasser's resolve to challenge and supersede Iraq—a local inter-Arab factor—prompted him to bring the Soviets into the Middle East. Without Nasser's perception of Moscow's role in his strategy, the Soviets would not have been able to appear on the Middle Eastern scene in 1955.

The picture was more consistent in the 1960s, when the inter-Arab system was characterized by a bipolar Arab world divided into conservative (or reactionary) regimes supported by the United States and radical (or progressive) states with close ties to the Soviet Union. The major processes—the war in Yemen, the Saudi-Egyptian struggle, and the rise of the Ba'ath party in Syria and Iraq—clearly emanated from regional developments, and the superpowers mainly wished to manipulate them in their favor. The same relationship repeated itself in the multipolar post-1973 Arab world. The Egyptian shift to the U.S. camp, Syrian-Egyptian friction, the eruption of the Lebanese crisis, Sadat's peace initiative, and the Iran-Iraq war all were anchored in regional factors, the superpowers were presented with faits accomplis that they could accelerate, intensify, or slow but not control or direct.

Consequences for the Iran-Iraq War

The Iran-Iraq war is one of the very few cases of local and regional conflicts that was hardly affected by the superpower competition in the Middle East. This is all the more remarkable in view of two factors: the longevity of the war (now in its seventh year), which should have provided the superpowers with ample time and abundant opportunities to affect its course, and the strategic importance of the Persian Gulf and its proximity to Soviet boundaries. Against this background, one would have expected both superpowers to attempt to manipulate the war in their favor; instead, the attitudes have been characterized by extreme caution and a reluctance to intervene, sometimes presenting a picture of virtual passivity.

The Soviet Union has not sought to intervene or escalate the war, if only because it wishes to maintain good relations with both the protagonists. Indeed, one of the characteristic features of Soviet behavior has been the attempt to walk a tightrope between a "natural" sympathy toward the Ba'ath regime in Baghdad and the desire not to alienate the leadership in Teheran. In addition, Moscow was apprehensive that, if either side faced defeat, it might turn to the West for help. Finally, the Soviets were worried that their involvement might trigger the intervention of the U.S. Rapid Deployment Force.

The United States, for its part, wishes to avoid any entanglement that might place Washington clearly in one of the two camps. This passivity can be adhered to so long as there are no signs that either side is about to win the war, precisely because the administration wishes to see neither belligerent emerge as the predominant power in the Persian Gulf. For Washington, the war represents a choice between two evils—Arab radicalism emanating from Baghdad and Islamic fundamentalism emanating from Teheran an antipathy fueled by the hostage crisis. Two contingencies might force a U.S. response: if the war were to spill over into Saudi Arabia and the small Persian Gulf states, or if freedom of navigation through the Strait of Hormuz were threatened. Indeed, when there were initial signs that these contingencies were crystallizing in the spring of 1954 during the "tanker war," Washington demonstrated its willingness to intervene, something that forced Iran to back off. Thus, with the exception of some periodic tilts toward Iraq—caused both by fear of Iraqi defeat and by attempts to exploit Baghdad's weakness to draw it closer to the pro-Western Arab camp—the United States has maintained a policy of nonintervention in the war.[15]

What has reinforced this situation is the fact that the superpowers lack leverage over the basic policies of both Iran and Iraq. Neither the United States nor the Soviet Union can, even if they so wished, bring an end to the war; they are incapable of persuading Iran to revise its terms for a cease-fire and are unable to force Saddam Hussein to step down. However, even their ability to influence the course of the war, let alone its outcome, is extremely limited. One may conceivably argue that by their very decision *not* to intervene, the superpowers have influenced the evolution of the war, but then one has to bear in mind that even if they wished to intervene, the superpowers could hardly affect the war's basic trends and consequences for lack of influence over the two belligerents. Thus, the combination of objective realities (lack of leverage) and subjective factors (reluctance to intervene) has created a unique situation whereby the superpower competition has hardly affected this major Middle Eastern conflict. The dynamics of the war remain distinctly local and regional.

Consequences for the Crisis in Lebanon

The Lebanese crisis, as it has evolved over the past 11 years, consists of two dimensions. On the local level, there have been consistent demands by Muslim groups to do away with the power-sharing formula agreed upon in 1943 and replace it with a new power structure that would reflect changing demographic realities, something the major Christian groups have vehemently opposed. On the regional level, Syrian, PLO, and Israeli intervention and embroilment in Lebanese politics—each trying to exploit the internal conflict to advance its own interests—have created a secondary circle that has further exacerbated the civil war. The 18-month-long U.S. involvement in Lebanon (1982–1984) added a third, global circle to the Lebanese equation, aggravating not only the internal struggle but also the regional confrontation.[16]

Initially, the Reagan administration was tempted to intervene in Lebanon, hoping that the Israeli operation would make it possible to expel Syria, a Soviet client, and install a pro-Western regime. The signing of the Israeli-Lebanese agreement in May 1983 was to symbolize and institutionalize this achievement. After this involvement gradually turned from an asset to a liability, however, the administration began to justify the U.S. presence in Lebanon in terms of a zero-sum game—that is, "cutting and running" would signify a major Soviet gain. Shortly thereafter, President Reagan expressed the explanation in appropriate strategic vocabulary: "The US has vital interests in Lebanon, which is key to the region's stability. If Lebanon ends up under the tyranny of hostile forces, not only will our strategic position in the eastern Mediterranean be threatened, but also the stability of the entire Middle East, including the vast resources of the Arabian Peninsula."[17]

The Soviet Union responded by resupplying Syria with massive quantities of armaments. This emboldened President Assad and enabled him to deepen his intervention in Lebanon and stand up to the U.S. challenge. In the context of the Lebanese crisis, the U.S. presence and cooperation with the Maronites further intensified sectarian conflict and strife. U.S. bombardment of Shiite and Druze strongholds deepened their alienation from the Christians and made reconciliation even more elusive.

Conclusions

The most instructive way to summarize the impact of superpower competition on local conflicts in the Middle East is by examining three core issues: the *degree* of the impact, its *nature and consequences,* and its *centrality or marginality* relative to the other components of local conflicts.

The degree of superpower influence on local Middle East rivalries varies from one conflict to another. In some cases, such as the Arab-Israeli dispute, the competition of the superpowers has had a broad impact. This could be a function of the importance of the issues or the arena to the superpowers' interests; the predisposition of local parties to bring about superpower intervention; or the fact that the conflicts are by definition susceptible to superpower involvement. In other cases, such as the Iran-Iraq war, superpower competition has had a very limited effect on the various aspects of the war. As noted above, it resulted from both an absence of leverage and an unwillingness to get embroiled.

On the whole, however, superpower involvement in an influence on local conflicts is inherently limited by two sets of reasons. Objectively, there is a profound, deep-seated reluctance in Middle Eastern countries to let the superpowers enjoy too large a degree of influence. This is particularly true for the United States, given the vestiges of Western presence in the area in this century, but it also applies to the Soviet Union because of Middle East fear of both Soviet communism and expansionism. Hence, there is a strong desire to stay free of any foreign control or influence. Subjectively, despite their desire to manipulate local conflicts in their favor, the superpowers are cautious lest their involvement draw them into confrontations beyond their control. Thus, for all their support of Syria, the Soviets have shown no enthusiasm for being dragged into Assad's regional conflicts.

Nevertheless, despite the incentive of their shared interest in avoiding the risks of confrontation, the superpowers' latitude to act on it is very limited. On many occasions their intervention has taken into consideration several factors and envisaged certain goals, but in reality the consequences of their actions did not coincide with the expectations. Thus, there unqualified support of a local power could prompt the client to take actions that might set off an unintended general war, embroiling the superpowers in a confrontation they wish to avoid. The Soviet role in the events of May 1967, which led to the Six Day War, is a case in point.

As far as the consequences of the competition are concerned, the record shows that the attempts by each superpower to strengthen its position in the Middle East while weakening the influence of the other has injected a major destabilizing element into the web of local and regional conflicts. The unsettling consequences of superpower competition have been made worse by the absence of any agreement between them concerning the division of the region into mutually recognized spheres of influence, thereby creating gray areas in which the holder of influence is undefined. Thus, their competition has generally had the effect of inflaming local conflicts and polarizing crisis situations, making the resolution of disputes all the more difficult.

Finally, is the superpower rivalry central or marginal in the making and evolution of local conflicts? With a few exceptions, local disputes tend to emerge, evolve, and perpetuate as a result of factors indigenous to the region itself. Superpower rivalry, then, serves as a catalyst, adding a contributing element to the equation. The superpowers can exercise a restraining or inflammatory influence on their local allies, but they cannot force them into war, nor can they prevent them from going to war. Furthermore, one can make a good case by arguing that rather than looking at the impact of superpower competition on local disputes, one should concentrate on the reverse relationship. The almost-confrontation of the United States and the Soviet Union at the end of the 1973 war—a war conceived and carried out through a local initiative—is one such example. One could speculate that the same paradigm might evolve in the future should one of the following scenarios materialize: the disintegration of the Iranian regime, a complete Iranian victory over Iraq, or an Iranian offensive against the small Gulf states and/or Saudi Arabia. All represent contingencies whereby local disputes might prompt the intervention of one or both superpowers, creating the danger of a global confrontation. Superpower competition and local disputes in the Middle East are, thus, mutually infectious.

Notes

1. J.C. Hurewitz, "Super Power Rivalry and the Arab-Israeli Dispute: Involvement or Commitment?," in M. Confino and S. Shamir, eds., *The USSR and the Middle East* (Jerusalem: Israel University Press, 1973), pp. 155–160.

2. Sanford Lakoff, "Power and Limit: US Strategic Doctrine in the Middle East," in Aurel Braun, ed., *The Superpower Conflict in the Middle East* (Boulder, CO: Westview Press, 1986).

3. Ya'acov Ro'i, "Soviet-Israeli Relations, 1947–1954", in M. Confino and S. Shamir, eds., *The USSR and the Middle East*, pp. 126–132.

4. See Nadav Safran, *From War to War* (New York: Pegasus, 1969), pp. 49–53.

5. Bernard Reich, *Quest for Peace: United States-Israel Relations and the Arab-Israeli Conflict* (New Brunswick, NJ: Transaction Books, 1977), pp. 41–47.

6. For details on the Soviet role, see Yaacov Bar-Siman-Tov, *The Israeli-Egyptian War of Attrition, 1969-1970* (New York: Columbia University Press, 1980), pp. 145–174.

7. See Reich, *Quest for Peace*, pp. 186–207.

8. William Quandt, *A Decade of Decisions* (Berkeley, CA: University of California Press, 1977), pp. 281–286.

9. See Irit Abramski-Bligh, "Soviet-Syrian Relations, 1982–1984," *The Jerusalem Quarterly*, 37, (1986), pp. 40–56.

10. See Reich, *Quest for Peace*, pp. 241–244.

11. For a discussion of this question, see S.N. MacFarlane, "The Arab-Israeli Conflict in Soviet Strategy," *Middle East Focus*, September, 1985, pp. 9–12; and A. Ben-Zvi, "The Prospects of a Superpower Condominium in the Middle East: A Critical Analysis," *Middle East Focus*, November 1985, pp. 16–17.

12. Robert Neumann, "Finally—A US Middle East Policy," *The Washington Quarterly 6*, Spring 1983, pp. 199–208.

13. See Uri Ra'anan, *The USSR Arms the Third World* (Boston: MIT Press, 1969).

14. Malcolm Kerr, *The Arab Cold War* (London: Oxford University Press, 1971).

15. Ali R. Rustum, "Holier Than Thou: The Iran-Iraq War," *Middle East Review 17*, Fall 1984, pp. 50–57.

16. Itamar Rabinovich, *The War for Lebanon, 1970-1985* (Ithaca, NY: Cornell University Press, 1985), pp. 183–186.

17. "Vital Interests of U.S. at Stake," *Washington Post*, 25 October 1983.

19
Mutual Encroachment: The United States and the Soviet Union in Syria and Jordan

Itamar Rabinovich
Asher Susser

The classic pattern of superpower rivalry in the Middle East and its ramifications for the local actors was established in the 1950s. As happened in other parts of the postcolonial Third World, the decline of Western power and the appearance of the Soviet competitor provided Middle East states with hitherto unfamiliar room for maneuver. It was Gamal Abdel Nasser of Egypt who, more than any other Arab leader, exploited the new opportunities in the mid- to late 1950s. Nasser's international policies, however, were not the product of pure political calculation. Revolutionary Arab nationalism, which he developed and symbolized, had built into it a powerful anti-Western bias, which at most times overshadowed the movement's shying away from Marxism.

The actual competition between the two superpowers in the Arab world passed through three main phases. First, in the mid- and late 1950s the Soviet Union, following the West's failure to build a regional defense organization, succeeded in establishing its influence in Egypt and Syria. The Western powers retained their influence in the conservative Arab states, such as Iraq (before 1958), Jordan, and Saudi Arabia. The anti-Western, nonaligned ideology of the Soviet Union's new Arab friends was matched by the rigid anti-Soviet, anti-Marxist, pro-Western positions of the conservative Arab regimes.

Second, whatever fluidity there was in this array of forces disappeared in the early and mid-1960s. Egypt lost its ability to maneuver between the superpowers and became a Soviet client. A clear symmetry emerged between a group of radical, pro-Soviet Arab regimes on the one hand and a group of conservative, pro-Western regimes on the other. Although an abortive effort was made to establish an Egyptian-American dialogue, and although Jordan agreed in 1963 to establish diplomatic relations with the Soviet Union, on the whole the demarcation between the two groupings remained stable.

Third, the events of 1967 were the single most important catalyst for change in this state of affairs, which surfaced in full force by 1972. They underlined the Soviet role as the Arabs' unambiguous supporter against Israel and as the primary supplier of weapon's systems to the main confrontation states. The Soviet Union proved incapable, however, of retrieving the Arab territories lost in 1967. Furthermore, some 15 years after establishing its influence in the region, the Soviet Union had lost its advantage of being a fresh, noncolonial power and was now seen as just another great power with certain colonial trappings. At the same time, the ideology of revolutionary Arab nationalism suffered a historic defeat, while the prestige and standing of the conservative Arab regimes was considerably reinforced. These developments, coupled with U.S. willingness, in principle, to act as a broker in Arab-Israeli settlements, introduced a major change in the pattern described above.

This change was demonstrated by Egypt's reorientation from 1972 to 1974. Although the seeds of change were already evident during Nasser's last years, Anwar Sadat effected the change gradually. For example, even though he expelled the Soviet advisors in July 1972, Egypt continued to receive sophisticated Soviet weaponry (some of which had been denied it earlier), and during the October war Sadat was supported by the Soviet Union as if he remained a prime client. Only in 1974 was his partnership with the United States fully developed, and his relations with the Soviet Union began to deteriorate.

It is against this background that the next phase of the Soviet-American competition for influence in the Arab world should be seen. As part of this competition, the two superpowers have sought to take advantage of the new fluidity to expand their influence at each other's expense. With certain obvious differences, Syria has been the object of U.S. efforts, while the Soviet Union has focused on Jordan. Given the principal concerns of these two Arab states, the Arab-Israeli settlement process and the issue of arms supply have been the two main channels of competition.

A New U.S.-Syrian Relationship

For some 15 years, from the formation of the United Arab Republic (UAR) in February 1958 to the aftermath of the October war in 1973, a significant U.S.-Syrian relationship did not exist. Relations were mostly hostile and briefly (September 1961 to March 1963) indifferent and awkward. Syria was not a target of U.S. policy nor did it fit into any larger U.S. scheme for the region on those rare occasions when such schemes were formulated. Syria severed diplomatic relations with the United States after the Six Day War, and the two countries did not even have the benefit of interest sections as channels of communication.

This state of affairs changed radically in December 1973, primarily as a result of the October war and other related developments, which gave rise to an Arab-Israeli settlement process and inaugurated a new phase of U.S. policy toward the Middle East. This policy was defined not only by Washington's determination (and ability) to orchestrate the Arab-Israeli settlement process but also by the need to address the new realities in the region (particularly the need to bring an end to the oil embargo) and to manage superpower competition with the Soviet Union within the larger framework of détente.

These various considerations required the development of a new relationship with Syria. Syria was an important Arab state capable of influencing the trend of Arab politics and the collective policy of the Arab states. As Egypt's wartime ally, it possessed, in the war's immediate aftermath, an actual veto power over Egypt's ability to participate in the settlement process. Although Sadat was clearly anxious to proceed with the settlement process, it was politically impossible for him to negotiate with Israel and regain Egyptian territory while Syria was boycotting the process and criticizing his conduct. Likewise, conservative Arab states, willing to end the oil embargo, found this difficult to accomplish in light of Syrian and other radical Arab opposition.[1] Therefore, it was deemed necessary to bring Syria into the settlement process.

In any event the task proved to be easier than expected. Syrian President Hafiz al-Assad was anxious to join the process. He had led his country into war on the assumption that he could recapture most of the Golan Heights within 48 hours and that a cease-fire could and would be imposed by the Soviet Union in the U.N. Security Council before Israel would have time to regroup. This was a gross miscalculation. He did take much of the Golan Heights, but Sadat did not want an immediate cease-fire, and the Soviets preferred Egypt's interests over those of Syria. After Israel did regroup and a cease-fire finally was imposed (again with Soviet-Egyptian cooperation and without consultation with Syria), the Israeli Defense Face (IDF) had actually captured new Syrian territory beyond the 1967 cease-fire lines. Syria had paid dearly in human lives and a devastated infrastructure, only to end up with a new loss, and it did not take long for Assad to understand that the only way for him to regain lost territory and obtain achievements comparable (though not equal) to those of Egypt was to join the U.S.-sponsored peace process.[2]

This conclusion was reinforced by larger considerations. Since coming to power in November 1970, Assad had run his own particular foreign policy. He did not contemplate a volte-face similar to that of Sadat, but he did want to diversify Syrian foreign policy and at least open a dialogue with the United States. This trend was accentuated by the October war. It was obvious that the United States and the conservative Arab oil-producing states were going to play a much more prominent role in the region, and Syria's policies would have to adapt to that new reality. Nor was Assad beholden to the Soviets for what he regarded as shabby treatment during the war.[3] Consequently, he was willing to deal with the United

States, to normalize and improve Syrian-U.S. relations, and even to collude and cooperate with Henry Kissinger in limiting the Soviet Union's role in the settlement process to a bare ritualistic minimum.[4]

All this was accomplished between December 1973 and June 1974, culminating in President Nixon's visit to Damascus. The U.S.-Syrian rapprochement was expedited by the personal bond that developed between Kissinger and Assad and by Kissinger's high regard to Assad's leadership and pragmatism. While the secretary of state was constrained by broader considerations of the U.S.-Soviet relationship, his memoirs are quite explicit with regard to his hopes for luring Syria away from the Soviet orbit. Having said to Assad on November 15, 1973, that "you can talk to the Soviets, we don't want to influence Syrian-Soviet reations," Kissinger hastened to add, "This was less than the full truth, of course; it was not a statement of reality. We wanted to influence Soviet-Syrian relations. We preferred them to be less close than they were. But Assad would loosen his ties with the Soviets for his reasons, not ours, and we could affect Syrian-Soviet relations best by giving Damascus a stake in closer relations with the United States."[5]

The realism of this passage was fully borne out by the actual course of events. It would have been easy to be swayed by some of the unusual aspects of the new U.S.-Syrian relationship as it evolved during the first half of 1974. The sight of Soviet Foreign Minister Gromyko humiliated by Assad and his foreign minister, Abd al-Halim Khaddam, in order to accommodate his U.S. counterpart could have given rise to unfounded American expectations for a reorientation in Syrian foreign policy. This was not a serious possibility, however. For one thing, however pragmatic Assad may have been, he was still the head of a Ba'athist regime and could not diverge too radically from the policies for which his party stood. There was also a limit to U.S. support. It could not replace the Soviet Union as chief arms supplier and external supporter. U.S. relations with the Soviet Union, Israel, Egypt, and the conservative Arab states imposed significant restraints on the development of its relationship with Syria. Finally, even the one fruitful area of U.S.-Syrian cooperation—the settlement process with Israel—had to be abandoned. In the summer of 1974, and even more clearly in 1975, it became clear that the pattern of the immediate postwar period could not be repeated and that a second round of an Egyptian-Israeli agreement legitimized by a parallel Syrian-Israeli agreement was not feasible. Kissinger opted for a separate Egyptian-Israeli agreement. The minor Israeli concessions he could propose to Assad as compensation[6] were not acceptable to the Syrians. When the interim agreement on the Sinai was signed on September 1, 1975, the Syrians launched a political offensive not only against that agreement but also against the notion that the United States could conduct a successful regional policy unacceptable to Syria.

These events clearly marked the end of this formative phase of the new U.S.-Syrian relationship. So far the intimacy of that period has not been recaptured and, as will be shown, has often been replaced by acute enmity. Its legacy has, however, survived. U.S. leaders and diplomats have continued, as a rule, to have high esteem for Assad and his leadership. Even during periods of intense rivalry and hostility, many of them continued to believe that Syria was not a Soviet satellite and that, at some point, U.S.-Syrian cooperation could be revived. Elias Sarkis, the Lebanese president from 1976 to 1982, referred to this state of mind as a "true riddle." "The relations between the United States and Syria confuse me," he complained. "Syria is acting as if it had a real conflict with the United States and the Americans behave as if they had common interests with Syria."[7]

Phases of U.S.-Syrian Relations

In the decade following the summer of 1975, the U.S.-Syrian relationship passed through four main phases.

The Balance of Kissinger's Period

Sharp disagreement over the Interim Agreement and Syrian efforts to obstruct this U.S. venture did not prevent a quest for further U.S.-Syrian dialogue. In the fall of 1975 Washington cooperated with a Syrian initiative to have the Palestine Liberation Organization (PLO) invited to a U.N. Security Council discussion of the Palestinian issue. The quid for this quo was Syrian willingness to extend the mandate of the U.N. force on the Golan Heights by another six months.

This and other aspects of the Arab-Israeli conflict were, however, soon overshadowed by the evolution of the Lebanese crisis and particularly by Syrian actions during that crisis. Syria intervened directly in the crisis, shifted its policy from support of the revisionist coalition to virtual support of the status quo, and did all that in close coordination with the United States. There was a dual U.S. dimension to Syrian policy in Lebanon. In the first place, Syria's intervention in Lebanon was motivated, among other things, by a desire to demonstrate to Washington that it had become the effective regional power, at least in its part of the Arab world. Second, there was the obvious need to secure U.S. agreement to the Syrian's military intervention and to obtain U.S. aid in obtaining Israeli acquiescence to this act. This was accomplished in the winter of 1976, resulting in what came to be known as the Red Line Agreement.[8]

The turn in Syrian policy toward Lebanon and Assad's determination and ability to proceed in the face of open Soviet disapproval strained Soviet-Syrian relations during the summer of 1976. Once again, as in 1973–1974, Assad's willingness to engage in a fairly intimate coordination of policies with Washington and to antagonize his Soviet patrons in the process could have created false expectations of a possible Syrian reorientation. Once again, however, this was a tactical move dictated by expediency, and it was not in all likelihood a genuine realignment. By 1977, in fact, Syrian-Soviet relations had been restored to their earlier state. At the same time, the episode had some lasting effects. It reinforced the feeling in Washington that Assad's pragmatism and authority meant that sometime in the future a more significant rapprochement could be successfully attempted.

The Carter Administration and Syria

An entirely new phase in U.S.-Syrian relations began with the Carter administration and its formulation of a new Middle Eastern policy. The Carter administration decided to seek a comprehensive settlement of the Arab-Israeli conflict (including the Palestinian question), giving this high priority on its foreign policy agenda. This meant, among other things, that a U.S.-Syrian dialogue had to be established, as Syria was an important Arab state with a good deal of regional influence. Its endorsement and participation were deemed essential for the implementation of administration policy.

Early efforts to win Syrian support revealed a number of difficulties. Assad had his own ideas as to a prospective settlement, asserted his claim as the defender of the Palestinian cause, and was ever suspicious of Egypt's interest and Washington's acquiescence in a separate Egyptian-Israeli deal.

President Carter tried to overcome these difficulties through a direct personal meeting with Assad. It was one of a series of meetings with all the pertinent heads of government, but unlike the others, Assad refused to come to Washington, and Carter met him on neutral ground, in Geneva, on May 9, 1977. Assad also stood his ground vis-à-vis the Soviets. He would not come to Moscow before his meeting with Carter, so as not to be forced into a coordination of positions. He went to Moscow after his meeting with Carter, presumably to render his own version of the meeting. This was typical of the way in which Assad sought to maneuver between the superpowers. He has rarely been as successful.

Several American participants have provided interesting accounts of this meeting, and although they diverge on several important points, a number of common themes emerge. Carter was impressed by Assad and quite taken with him, and a good personal rapport was established. For his part, Assad was insistent on matters he regarded as essential, but he also displayed his pragmatism.[9] Carter emerged from the meeting quite hopeful, but he discovered during the next few weeks that Assad was the single most important obstacle to the implementation. Carter's memoirs are quite explicit on this point:

> I found him to be very constructive in his attitude and somewhat flexible in dealing with some of the more crucial items involving peace, the Palestinians, the refugee problem and borders. He said that a year or two ago it would have been suicidal in his country to talk about peace with the Israelis, but they have come a long way and were willing to cooperate. . . . This was the man who would soon sabotage the Geneva peace talks by refusing to attend under any reasonable circumstances and who would, still later, do everything possible to prevent the Camp David accords from being fulfilled.[10]

One must assume that Assad's version of this meeting and the misunderstanding it bred was quite different from Carter's. We also know of another encounter between President Carter and the Syrian foreign minister, from which the two emerged with very different impressions and interpretations.[11] In any event, Syrian suspicions of U.S. policy and its actual consequences persisted, and Syria clearly obstructed that policy. Nor did the U.S. effort to deal with Syria through its Soviet patron prove to be very successful. This marked a significant shift from earlier efforts to deal directly with Syria, but this approach also was to no avail.[12] In the fall of 1977, the Carter administration was patently cross with Assad and subsequently willing to proceed with the Camp David accords despite Syria's exclusion. This did not develop, however, into an overall hostility. The Carter administration continued to support Syria's role in Lebanon, was not particularly moved by the signing in October 1980 of a formal Soviet-Syrian treaty, and, with more pressing issues on its Middle Eastern agenda, did not pay further particular attention to Syria.

Alexander Haig and Syria

The transition from the Carter to the Reagan administration signified, among other things, a change of attitude toward Syria. The new administration and its first secretary of state tended to view the Middle East through a geopolitical or East-West lens, which placed Syria in the rubric of Soviet proxies. Its role in Lebanon was now perceived and presented as negative, and Secretary Haig in his public speeches clearly stated that a solution to the Lebanese crisis would have to include a Syrian withdrawal.[13] Haig's greater Middle Eastern policy was based on the concept of strategic consensus, within which the divergent concerns of Israel and Washington's Arab friends would be reconciled. Syria had no place within this scheme, and Damascus was not included in Haig's first tour of the region in the spring of 1981.

Syria was later seen by the Reagan administration primarily in the context of the looming war in Lebanon. By the end of 1981 and certainly by the winter of 1982, the United States knew that the Israeli prime minister had decided on a large-scale operation in Lebanon. Washington was opposed to that operation and until May 1982 expressed that opposition to its Israeli interlocutors in very clear terms. In May 1982, however, the United States changed its position. The degree of that change is still a matter of controversy,[14] but as Haig himself points out in his memoirs, a proportionate Israeli response to a major provocation had become acceptable. Haig must have reached the conclusion that Israel was bound to act and that in this case the United States might as well take advantage of this and seek to implement its own ideas of settlements in both Lebanon and the Arab-Israeli conflict. The possibility of an Israeli-Syrian clash had to be taken into account and with it Soviet sensitivity to any threat to the safety of its principal client. A clash limited to Lebanon, however, must have seemed manageable.

The actual course of events proved to be more complex. The Israeli operation was extensive and much less successful and decisive than expected. Haig's position in the Reagan administration was eroded, and he was finally forced to resign against the background of the Lebanese war.

Haig argued that despite everything, he had twice been very close to arranging a solution to the Lebanese crisis, which included a Syrian (as well as an Israeli and a Palestinian) withdrawal, and that the incompetence of his bureaucratic rivals had obstructed it.[15] It is idle to speculate on the impact such an agreement could have had on U.S.-Syrian relations, although it is important to note the Kissingerian influence on Haig's thinking. A defeated Syria, depending on the United States to protect it from a victorious Israel, should have been far more cooperative, but as is well known, events developed in a quite different direction.

The Reagan Administration and Syria, 1982-1984

Soon after George Shultz succeeded Haig, he engineered two efforts to implement U.S. plans in the region that simultaneously affected and excluded Syria. Damascus defeated both.

On September 1, 1982, the administration released the Reagan Plan, which sought to take advantage of recent events in order to promote a U.S. solution to the Palestinian problem through Jordanian participation. This failed due to a number of reasons, not the least of which was Syrian opposition, as it thought it was equally important to demonstrate that any effort to solve the Palestinian problem without Syrian endorsement and participation was bound to fail. Its influence on the PLO in the aftermath of the Lebanese war enabled Syria to exert effective pressure and to contribute in April 1983 to the collapse of the first Jordanian dialogue with the PLO.

It was still more important for Syria to obstruct U.S. policy in Lebanon. Both U.S. efforts to prop the administration of Amin Jumayyil and the U.S. Israeli-Lebanese agreement of May 17, 1983, which was signed under U.S. auspices, were anathema to Assad, and by the winter of 1984 he had succeeded in obstructing both. Assad operated mostly by proxy, but he failed to avoid a direct clash with the United States. American aircraft and artillery were used against Syrian forces, but this too was to no avail.

The episode left a mixed legacy. Some U.S. officials emerged with hostile sentiments toward Assad and Syria. Others were impressed by Assad's effectiveness and have since argued that the lesson to be learned is that Syria cannot be ignored.

Since 1984 there have been few opportunities to address or ignore Syria in the context of regional initiatives. Partly as a consequence of its failures during 1982–1984, the Reagan administration has been reluctant to sponsor new regional initiatives, and the only such initiative it has supported—to bring about Israeli-Jordanian-Palestinian negotiations—never gathered sufficient momentum to become the object of serious Syrian opposition. In the absence of new U.S. initiatives, Syria's claim to indispensability has not been tested, while Syria's relative decline in regional standing during this same period may even have undermined this claim.

A muted U.S.-Syrian dialogue of sorts has continued, based on a fairly limited bilateral relationship. Through this the United States was also able to exert some moderating influence over the Syrian-Israeli rivalry in Lebanon, while concern for terrorism came to play an unusually prominent role in U.S.-Syrian relations. This new form of dialogue was predicated on Syria's hegemonial role in Lebanon and on Lebanon's centrality to this issue. As a rule Assad's regime has skillfully straddled the line, supporting some Palestinian and Shiite organizations while opposing or maintaining a measure of influence over others. Therefore, Syria played a helpful role during the hijacking of a TWA airliner in June 1985, although it could not obtain release of all the hostages without Iranian help.

Credit for such helpfulness must go to a diluted version of earlier policies that depended on the Assad regime's ability to influence and harness radical Middle Eastern elements, including its own. That policy, however, soon ran its course and began to backfire by the spring of 1986, eventually leading Britain to sever diplomatic relations with Syria and causing the United States and the EEC to impose sanctions. The manner in which the United States imposed sanctions on Syria was characteristic of Washington's ambivalence. The statement published by the White House on November 14, 1986, contained a specific warning, explaining that the measures being taken "are intended to convince the Syrian government that state support of terrorism will not be tolerated by the civilized world. We will continue to monitor the situation and take additional steps as necessary." The same statement ended with a revealing sentence, however: "Syria can play an important role in a key region of the world but it cannot expect to be accepted as a responsible power or to be treated as one as long as it continues to use terrorism as an instrument of its foreign policy." This was the other side of the aforementioned threat: that should Syria change its ways, a U.S.-Syrian dialogue that would recognize and perhaps even enhance Syria's regional role could be renewed.

The Soviet Union and Jordan

The role that Jordan has played in the superpower competition in the Middle East in recent years can be fully understood only against the background of the Jordanians' own perception of their position in the region and the policy requirements that stem from this perception. Perceiving themselves to be "living in the eye of an ever-blowing storm,"[16] the Jordanians are clearly concerned as to the potentially negative political and economic impact of various interrelated sources of regional tensions and instability, including the Arab-Israeli conflict, the Iran-Iraq war, the rise of Muslim fundamentalism, the subversive capacity of Syria and the Palestinians, and possible superpower confrontation deriving from their strategic interests in the Arab-Israeli conflict and the Gulf.

Jordanian fears of radicals and potential sources of radicalism, of whatever nature, are not new and have always governed Jordan's policies in the Arab arena as well as its great power orientation. This is equally true of Jordan's attitudes toward Nasserism, Ba'athism, communism, and Khomeiniism. What did change significantly after 1967 were the modes of combat against these radical or potentially destabilizing influences, which developed as a corollary of the transformation of inter-Arab and great power relationships.

The Arab world in the post-1967 era is very different from the one that existed in the heyday of Nasserism. Simultaneously, great power relations emerged from the Cold War period as the new, however tenuous, détente evolved during the 1970s. In the dichotomized Arab world of the 1950s and 1960s—clearly divided between the so-called progressive or revolutionary Arab regimes (aligned with the Soviet Union) and the pro-Western conservative regimes—Jordan was unequivocally entrenched in the conservative camp, locked in an uncomfortable and almost incessant confrontation with its pro-Soviet Arab adversaries, who actively sought the overthrow of the monarchy. Under those circumstances Jordan's alliance with the West was vital for the kingdom's survival as an independent state. King Hussein, therefore, was eager to join the anti-Soviet and anti-Nasserite Baghdad Pact in late 1955 and drew back only in the face of ferocious domestic opposition fanned by Egypt. In early 1957 Hussein welcomed the Eisenhower Doctrine, and shortly thereafter he dismissed the oppositionary Nabulsi cabinet, which he accused of planning to open the country to communist infiltration, an accusation based in part on Nabulsi's intention to establish diplomatic ties with the Soviet Union.[17] In those days it was only natural for the stalwarts of the Hashemite regime to express their genuine fear of "communist imperialism"[18] and to align themselves wholeheartedly with the Western powers.

Thus, when U.S. troops landed in Lebanon in 1958 at the time of the Lebanese civil war and shortly after the overthrow of the Hashemite regime in Iraq, Hussein welcomed the presence of British troops in Amman for a few months as a gesture of Western resolve to protect Jordan. The brief respite in the Arab cold war,[19] when Nasser instituted Arab summitry in 1964, soon gave way to a return to the old pattern of a clear distinction between the revolutionaries and the reactionaries that persisted until the outbreak of the Six Day War in 1967.

The Six Day War was a crucial watershed in inter-Arab relations that shattered accepted "truths" of Nasserite policies. Arab salvation was clearly not in the hands of the Soviet Union, Soviet weaponry, or Arab socialism. The conservative camp's arguments against the pseudo-Marxist "imported ideologies" now seemed to carry much more weight. The decline of Nasser's charismatic appeal and his death in 1970 left the Arab world leaderless and disoriented. The previously dichotomized Arab world now became increasingly diffuse and amorphous as inter-Arab relations entered a new phase of fluidity and rapidly alternating ad hoc alliances in which the old progressive and reactionary terminology became irrelevant. The erstwhile mortal enemies, Nasser and Hussein, were now close allies. After having fought and lost together, both were equally interested in cooperating to regain the territories Israel had occupied in 1967, while both facilitated access to each other's respective superpower patron. Although Jordan was still wary of Soviet influence in the Middle East, the Soviet Union no longer fulfilled its former role of patron of a clearly defined group of Arab states bent on the Hashemite regime's demise.

As the Soviet Union sought increasing involvement in the Middle East peace process following the passage of Resolution 242 by the U.N. Security Council and the four-power and two-power talks on the Middle East in the late 1960s, a mutual Soviet-Jordanian interest in improved relations began to evolve, and gained momentum after the October war. The Soviets appeared to have concluded by this time that their previous policy of keeping the Arab-Israeli conflict on a low flame as a convenient means of penetration into the Middle East, based on arms sales to the Arab states, was ineffective. They lacked the necessary control or influence over the Arabs to prevent the outbreak of war, and these wars, particularly the October war, brought the very real danger of a Soviet-U.S. confrontation, threatening Soviet achievements in the Middle East. A settlement of the conflict to which the Soviets could be a party, for which the Soviet Union would be a guarantor or a coguarantor, might promise greater stability in the long run for the Soviet presence in the Middle East.[20]

In the aftermath of the October war, however, Kissinger elbowed the Soviets out of the Middle East peace process in the disengagement agreements achieved between Israel, Egypt, and Syria. The Egyptians and even the Syrians could not but conclude that the road to the retrieval of territory went through Washington. The Soviets, having suffered a deterioration of their position, were particularly keen to secure their own participation in the peace process by demanding that subsequent talks be conducted in the Geneva conference framework.[21]

Paradoxically, it was Jordan, the long-standing regional ally of the United States, that was most disappointed by U.S. policy. The Jordanians were left out of the disengagement agreements and gained nothing from Soviet exclusion from the peace process. Furthermore, Jordan felt humiliated when it was forced to accept significant operational restrictions on the Hawk air defense system it had procured from the United States shortly after the October war. At the instigation of Israel and its U.S. supporters, the Jordanians had to agree to the installation of an immobile system, which, in their view, did not satisfy their needs. The Jordanians now began to see Soviet involvement in the peace process as particularly conducive to their own national interests: as a balance to what they regarded as a strong U.S. bias toward Israel.

Jordan's attitude toward Soviet involvement was also a function of Hussein's Arab policy. The Arab arena after 1967 was more congenial for Jordan. Jordan's legitimacy had been enhanced by its participation in the Six Day War, and even though this legitimacy suffered a serious setback during the Black September episode of 1970, the leaderless and amorphous Arab world gave Jordan greater room for maneuver. Hussein was no longer forced into persistent confrontation with an often well-orchestrated camp of adversaries, and his self-confidence consequently increased. This was reinforced further by the fact that Hussein had matured from the "Boy King" of the 1950s into a respected senior statesman who had survived in power for longer than the most vociferous of his former detractors in the Arab world. Jordan could not, however, change the simple reality that it was a relatively weak state, and Hussein could not defy Arab opinion as easily as could Egypt, the most powerful Arab state. He has, therefore, followed an extremely cautious policy, trying to forge an Arab consensus on controversial issues related to Arab-Israeli conflict.

The era of Arab confrontation in the 1950s and 1960s was a harrowing experience for the Jordanians, one they do not wish to undergo again. The fact that Jordan has a massive, potentially volatile Palestinian population and very powerful, potentially hostile neighbors such as Syria and Iraq makes it particularly vulnerable to subversion or even outright military attack. Even though Jordan's room for maneuver has increased, it is still very limited by Hussein's desire to avoid actions that could lead to the formation of a new hostile anti-Jordanian Arab coalition.

It is, therefore, imperative in the Jordanian view to conduct a policy of accommodation and conciliation with the other major Arab parties in the conflict—Syria and the PLO—and to enjoy the support of at least one of them in any future negotiating process. Neither the Syrians nor the PLO would subscribe to a Pax Americana, and for both Soviet involvement is almost an article of faith. Jordan does not wish to antagonize either local Soviet ally or the Soviet Union itself by denying the Soviets their role. In particular, Hussein loathes the notion of facing a Soviet-supported confrontation with Syria—unless the United States could "deliver Israel" by compelling it to return to the 1967 boundaries. Only such a Pax Americana would be a reasonable counterweight to the damage Jordan would probably suffer in the Arab arena, since this type of settlement is not in the offing, the Jordanians will not accept a settlement without the Soviet Union.

The Jordanians do want a settlement, however, and the sooner the better. Their fear of Israel has grown considerably since the Likud came to power in 1977. Whether justifiably or not, they genuinely believe that those Israeli political forces who assert that "Jordan is Palestine" would take any opportunity to step up Jewish settlements on the West Bank and to induce the Palestinian population to emigrate to Jordan as a prelude to or consequence of annexation. This kind of "demographic aggression,"[22] as they call it, is a nightmare for the Jordanians, who fear that it would have a disastrous, destabilizing effect on the kingdom, and Israeli withdrawal from the West Bank has thus become an urgent imperative. Furthermore, the Jordanians fear that lack of a settlement will only feed the forces of militant Palestinian or Muslim radicalism and eventually lead to war, endangering the very existence of the regime on the East Bank.

This genuine desire for a settlement, coupled with the view that the Soviet Union should be involved in such a process, has made Jordan particularly suscepti- ble to Soviet encroachment, influence, and pressure. Moreover, Jordan's inability to obtain from the United States a sophisticated air defense system led to its first arms deal with the Soviet Union. This deal, concluded in 1981, was for twenty batteries of sixteen SA-8 low-level missiles, together with radar-guided guns. Another Jordanian-Soviet arms deal may be in the offing following the Jordanians' failure in 1985 to purchase advanced fighter aircraft and antiaircraft missiles from the United States.

Such purchases, if made in the 1950s or 1960s, would have been interpreted as an admission of weakness by Jordan, which would have been seen to be bowing to pressure from the "revolutionary" states to realign itself with the Soviets. By the 1980s, however, the purchases carried no such meaning, and indeed they have not signified any change in Jordan's fundamentally pro-Western orientation. The Jordanians were quick to explain after their first arms deal with the Soviets that they would have preferred a deal with the United States, and Hussein made it quite clear that the weapons would be manned by Jordanians, without the need for any "sizeable . . . presence" of Soviet advisors. Israeli sources did report the arrival of several dozen Soviet experts in Jordan in connection with the missile deal, but Jordan's commander in chief, Lieutenant-General Zayd Bin Shakir, noted that Jordan hired the foreign experts for no longer than six months.[23] Al- though the deal did not signify a major change in Jordan's superpower orientation or afford a Soviet presence in the country, this new dependency relationship, how- ever limited, left the Jordanians with even less reason to antagonize the Soviet Union.

Considering Israeli and U.S. positions toward the PLO, Jordan's massive Pal- estinian population, and its long border with the West Bank and Israel, Jordan is the linchpin of any compromise over the Palestinian problem. Therefore, since the mid-1970s the Soviets have consistently made Jordan a focus of their attention, driving home the message that Soviet participation in this process was necessary. Although the Jordanians have generally been receptive, there have been some fleet- ing exceptions.

To the Jordanians the question of Soviet participation in the peace process is one of tactics and not as it is for Syria and the PLO, one of principle. Thus, in the aftermath of the Sadat initiative, they did not join the Syrian-led and Soviet- supported anti-Egyptian Steadfastness Front, instead waiting to see whether the United States and Egypt could produce a formula for Israeli withdrawal from the West Bank. When this did not materialize, however, it was the Jordanians who took the lead in promoting an alternative to the Camp David process based on returning the peace process to either the U.N. Security Council or an international conference in which the United States, the Soviet Union, and representatives of the European Community would take part.

The Lebanese war of 1982 offered Jordan a historic opportunity to take advantage of the PLO's political plight. Hussein made an unscheduled and unofficial visit to the Soviet Union at the end of June 1982 in what was described by the Jordanians as an exchange of views aimed at "reinvigorating efforts for the achievement of comprehensive peace."[24] It appears, however, that this move was only an attempt to reassure the Soviet Union at a time when Jordan's real objective was to prod the United States to come forth with a new Middle East peace initiative. In early 1982, as the Israeli withdrawal from the Sinai approached its final implementation, the Jordanians began urging the United States to make new proposals. The Reagan Plan, announced in September 1982, bore a strong imprint of Jordanian influence and corresponded to a large extent with Jordanian aspirations. It was not at all surprising, therefore, that the Jordanians welcomed the Reagan initiative as "the most courageous stand taken by an American Administration ever since 1956."[25] Now, for the first time since the October war, the Jordanians were seriously considering a settlement under U.S. auspices, explicitly stating that an international conference with the participation of both superpowers was not a realistic alternative. While the Soviet Union's local clients, the PLO and Syria, were still reeling from the blows they had received from Israel, Hussein was now prepared to argue that the U.S. initiative, although ambiguous on certain points, was indeed the best avenue by which to pursue peace under the existing circumstances.[26]

The Soviet Union responded firmly to derail this initiative. When Hussein visited Moscow in December 1982 at the head of a seven-man committee formed by the Arab League at the Fez summit in September, he was warned by Soviet Union leader Yuri Andropov that the Soviet Union would oppose the Reagan Plan with all its resources. If Hussein chose to participate in the U.S. initiative, the full weight of responsibility would be on Hussein's shoulders, and according to Andropov, they were "not broad enough to bear it." At the end of March 1983, on the eve of Yasser Arafat's visit to Amman that was to decide the fate of his negotiations with Hussein on cooperating with the Reagan Plan, Oleg Grenevsky, the head of the Soviet Foreign Ministry's Near East Department, arrived in Jordan for talks with the king, intending to dissuade him from joining the U.S.-backed peace process.[27] Soviet pressure also was brought to bear on Arafat not to cooperate with Hussein and not to "fall into the trap set by the Reagan plan."[28] Furthermore, while the Soviets do not control Syrian foreign policy, Soviet and Syrian interests in regards to the Reagan Plan tended to converge. Damascus, either in league with the Soviets or on their own accord, also pressured Arafat and warned the Jordanians that it would use force to prevent a "second Sadat" from emerging on its border. The Jordanians did, in fact, believe that if the Syrians felt that Hussein and Arafat were developing a realistic initiative, Jordan could expect Syrian-inspired subversion or even a direct military threat.[29] Afterward, Hussein complained that Soviet opposition to the Reagan Plan had been one of the main reasons for the failure of his talks with Arafat. The Soviet Union, he maintained, had constantly worked against the plan through its Syrian surrogates.[30]

Soviet obstructionism was one of the main reasons, but not the most important one, that the talks had failed. Instead, Hussein's major complaints were levelled against the United States. Jordanian hopes that the Reagan administration would impose its plan on Israel were soon dashed. After his talks with Arafat in April 1983 broke down, Hussein was particularly severe in his condemnation of U.S. policy in the Middle East. The United States, he argued, had become a "direct ally of one of the parties" and had thus "chosen to disqualify itself" as the sole force in the area that could help the parties move toward a joint and durable peace. The United States, according to Hussein, was "not free to move except within the limits of what AIPAC [the American-Israel Political Action Committee] the Zionists and the State of Israel determine for it."[31] Renewed disappointment with the United States and first hand experience with Soviet obstructionism put an end to Jordan's brief deviation from the Geneva-type formula, and it was no coincidence that the article in which Crown Prince Hasan referred to Jordan being in the "eye of an ever-blowing storm" was titled "Return to Geneva," a process to which the Jordanians are probably more committed now than ever before.

The international conference the Jordanians now have in mind is one that would include all five permanent members of the U.N. Security Council. The Jordanians attach great importance to the European role, which they feel would be necessary to balance the U.S.-Israeli and Soviet-Syrian alliances.[32] The Hussein-Arafat agreement of February 1985 made specific reference to an international conference of this nature as the principal forum for negotiations. Although this agreement was directed primarily at the United States in order to obtain U.S. recognition of the PLO as a prerequisite to progress in the peace process, it was equally intended to bring about a change in the U.S. and Israeli positions on the question of Soviet participation. All the same, the Soviet Union made no secret of its disapproval of the accord, suspecting that Jordan and the PLO were on the verge of being drawn into some form of Pax Americana. The Soviets even refused to meet with a joint Jordanian-PLO delegation that was to explain the accord to them. Soviet coolness, again backed up by Syrian hostility and by pressure on Arafat from within the PLO, served to keep the Jordanians up to the mark and prevent them from bowing to U.S. pressure to enter direct negotiations with Israel.

The accommodating mode and mood of Jordanian policy-making in the post-1967 era, in regard to as many Arab states as possible and, consequently, to both superpowers, has exposed Jordan to Soviet encroachment, influence, and obstructionism in regard to the peace process. Jordan's fear of reaping a whirlwind by antagonizing the Soviet Union and its local allies also has instilled a greater sense of caution in Jordanian policy in regard to other regional issues pertaining to the superpowers. If in the 1950s the Jordanians were keen to join an anti-Soviet regional defense pact and even welcomed the Eisenhower Doctrine, in the 1980s they are not prepared to do anything of the kind. Although they were obviously disturbed by the menacing Middle Eastern posture of the Soviet Union after the invasion of Afghanistan, they were obviously disturbed by the menacing Middle

Eastern posture of the Soviet Union after the invasion of Afghanistan, they were quick to reject the notion that the Arabs should now seek U.S. protection or that Jordan should supply the United States with facilities for military staging areas in the region. Hussein explained that he would "not like to see" either U.S. or Soviet bases in the area,[33] which could turn the Middle East into a theater for superpower confrontation and "proxy conflict," in which the Arabs would end up as "pawns in a bigger game."[34]

Jordanian anxieties were compounded by the evidence of superpower polarization on their own borders—Syria bound to the Soviet Union by a Treaty of Friendship and Israel with its on-again off-again strategic alliance with the United States.[35] The Jordanians were not prepared to accept the U.S. contention that the major threat to the area came from the Soviet Union and argued that the Arab-Israeli conflict and Israel's policies were far more immediate threats to regional security. These threats, they contended, could be best addressed not by confronting the Soviet Union but by accommodating its own desire for participation in a regional settlement. As for Gulf security, the Jordanians dismissed the idea of a U.S. Rapid Deployment Force (RDF) and called upon the superpowers to declare the Gulf to be a neutral zone defended by the local powers without external interference.[36] This policy of accommodation, while not inviting the Soviets in, did at least serve the Soviet interests by keeping the United States out.

The Jordanians did, however, share U.S. interest in preserving the stability of the Gulf states, and they were prepared to serve as a strategic hinterland for the Gulf, if not as a staging area for U.S. forces. During 1983 there were reports of a Jordanian RDF being established with U.S. assistance that included the use of U.S. Air Force transports to airlift the Jordanian force to crisis areas. The Jordanians denied that such a force being formed, as it gave the impression that it would operate on behalf of the United States. They did, however, admit that they would be willing to give aid to any Arab state that requested it and that in order to be able to do so, modern equipment and transport facilities were being sought from the United States. They emphasized, however, that any support would be "not on behalf of any in this world" but in regard to its own national interests.[37] Probably in deference to Jordanian sensitivities, the project became known as Joint Logistic Planning between Jordan and the United States. In July 1985 Jordan's armed forces conducted air defense and field training exercises, backed by U.S. aircraft and nine hundred U.S. military personnel. According to a U.S. embassy spokesman in Amman, the United States was providing "expertise, assistance, and guidance," plus some equipment, including F-16 jet fighters, support aircraft, and AWACS radar planes.[38] U.S. publicity given to the joint exercises was minimal, while the Jordanian media, made no mention of the U.S. role.[39] At the same time, a Jordanian official let it be known that Jordanian-Soviet relations were steadily improving.[40] It was quite clear that the Jordanians had no intention of giving the impression of forming an anti-Soviet alliance with the United States, and it would indeed seem that the maneuvers were related primarily to Jordan's apprehensions in regard to Iran and Gulf stability rather than to the Soviet Union.

Jordan's policy of accommodation toward the Soviet Union and its regional allies has indeed made Jordan more susceptible to Soviet encroachment and influence. It would be wrong to conclude, however, that Jordan has developed a policy of neutrality between the superpowers. The Jordanian policy of accommodation is a direct result of its deeply felt suspicion and distrust of the Soviet Union and its local protégés, and Amman realizes that, when the chips are down, it can really rely only on the United States for support and protection. After all, local Soviet allies, such as Syria and the PLO, are potentially the most dangerous threats to Jordan's future stability. Indeed, when tensions mounted on the Syrian-Jordanian frontier in late 1980, Jordanian leaders expressed concern that the Syrian military buildup may have been motivated by a new Soviet drive for regional influence at a time when Soviet involvement was growing in Iran, South Yemen, the Horn of Africa, and Libya. Although relations with the Carter administration were particularly strained at this time (because of Camp David), it was to the United States that Jordan turned for support. The State Department responded by issuing a statement to the effect that Jordan was a friend whose security was important to the United States, and Washington also agreed to speed up delivery of already purchased spare parts and ammunition. Jordan could hardly have expected a similar response from the Soviet Union in a situation of this kind.

Jordanian policy toward the Soviet Union can thus be described as one of calculated accommodation in clear preference to confrontation. In sum, however, this is only a tactical change in the mode of contending with the Soviet Union and its local allies and not a shift in superpower orientation.

Notes

1. See Henry Kissinger, *Years of Upheaval* (London: Weidenfeld and Nicolson, 1982), pp. 760–761 and *passim.*

2. See I. Rabinovich, "The Impact of the October War on Syria's Position and Policy in the Conflict with Israel," in A. Cohen and E. Karmon, eds., *In the Shadow of the October War* (Haifi, Israel: University of Haifa, 1974), pp. 211–222 (Hebrew).

3. G. Golan and I. Rabinovich, "The Soviet Union and Syria: The Limits of Cooperation," in Y. Ro'i, ed. *The Limits of Power* (London: London, Crom Helm, 1979), pp. 213–231.

4. Kissinger, *Years of Upheaval*, pp. 782, 944–945 and *passim.*

5. *Ibid.*, p. 782.

6. Assad himself referred to these proposals and his rejection of them in the revealing speech he delivered on July 20, 1976. The text is reproduced in the appendix to I. Rabinovich, *The War for Lebanon 1970–1985*, rev. ed. (Ithaca, NY: Cornell University Press, 1985).

318 • *The Global/Regional Interface*

7. Quoted in Karim Pakradouni, *La Paix Manques* (Beirut: Al-Sharq Lil Mainshuvat, 1984), p. 144.

8. See Rabinovich, *The War for Lebanon,* p. 106.

9. See Jimmy Carter, *Keeping Faith* (Toronto: Bantam Books, 1982), p. 286; Cyrus Vance, *Hard Choices* (New York: Simon and Schuster, 1983), p. 176; Zbigniew Brzezinski, *Power and Principle* (London: Weidenfeld and Nicolson, 1985), pp. 94–95; and William B. Quandt, *Camp David* (Washington, DC: Brooklyn Institute, 1985), pp. 56–58.

10. Carter, *Keeping Faith,* p. 286.

11. See Quandt, *Camp David,* pp. 56–58, 116–117, for the Carter-Khaddam misunderstanding.

12. This approach is reflected most clearly in Brzezinski, *Power and Principle,* see particularly p. 106. The joint U.S.-Soviet communiqué of October 1, 1977, was in part inspired by the hope that Syria might be induced to join the envisaged process.

13. See Alexander Haig, *Caveat* (New York: Macmillan, 1984), pp. 171, 317–321.

14. *Cf.* Rabinovich, *The War for Lebanon,* p. 126.

15. Haig, *Caveat,* p. 321.

16. Crown Prince Hasan, "Return to Geneva," *Foreign Policy* 57 (Winter 1984–1985), p. 8.

17. This was not the sole reason for the dismissal of the cabinet but one of the indications that the king's authority was being rapidly eroded. See Uriel Dann, "Regime and Opposition in Jordan Since 1949," in M. Milson, ed., *Society and Political Structure in the Arab World* (New York: Humanities Press, 1973), pp. 164–165.

18. A. Susser, *Between Jordan and Palestine: A Political Biography of Wasfi al-Tall* (Tel Aviv: HaKibbutz Hameuhad Publishing House, 1983), p. 29 (Hebrew).

19. The term coined by Malcolm Kerr in his widely known book *The Arab Cold War: Gamal Abd al-Nasir and His Rivals, 1958-1970* (New York: Oxford University Press, 1971).

20. Galia Golan, "The Soviet Union and the Arab-Israel Conflict," *The Jerusalem Quarterly* 1 (Fall 1976), p. 15.

21. *Ibid.,* p. 16.

22. Crown Prince Hasan in interview to *Le Figaro,* 22 May 1984.

23. A. Susser, "Jordan," in C. Legum, H. Shaked, and D. Dishon, eds., *Middle East Contemporary Survey (MECS)* N.Y. and London: Holmes and Meier Publishers Inc., vol. 6 (1981–82), p. 693.

24. *Ibid.,* p. 694.

25. *Ibid.,* p. 683.

26. A. Susser, "Jordan," *MECS,* vol. 7 (1982–1983), p. 632.

27. *Ibid.,* p. 648.

28. A. Susser, *The PLO After Lebanon* (Tel Aviv: HaKibbutz Hameuhad Publishing House, 1985), pp. 75–76 (Hebrew).

29. A. Susser, "Jordan," *MECS,* vol. 7, pp. 643–644.

30. *Ibid.,* p. 648.

31. Hussein in interviews to *Al-Hawadith,* 6 January 1984; *New York Times,* 14 March 1984.

32. Hussein to *Le Figaro,* 22 May 1984; and on Jordan TV, 17 June 1984, cited in Foreign Broadcast Information Service (FBIS), 18 June 1984.

33. A. Susser, "Jordan," *MECS*, vol. 4 (1979–1980), p. 585.

34. A. Susser, "Jordan," *MECS*, vol. 5 (1980–1981), p. 653.

35. A. Susser, "Jordan," *MECS*, vol. 7 (1982–1983), p. 632.

36. A. Susser, "Jordan," *MECS*, vol. 5 (1980–1981), pp. 652–654.

37. Jordan TV, 28 January 1984, cited in FBIS, 30 January 1984.

38. "Jordan, with Help from U.S., Is Holding Military Exercises," *New York Times*, 2 July 1985.

39. Radio Amman, 9 July 1985, cited in BBC Summary of World Broadcasts, 12 July 1985.

40. *Al-Talia al-Arabiyya*, 1 July 1985.

20

The Lebanon War and the Soviet-American Competition: Scope and Limits of Superpower Influence

Bruce W. Jentleson

Compared to past wars in the Middle East, the 1982 Israeli invasion of Lebanon had much less of an escalatory effect on relations between the United States and the Soviet Union. Diplomatic demarches were exchanged between Washington and Moscow, and the hot line even was used. There was nothing, however, like the threats of military intervention during the 1956 Suez crisis and the 1967 war, let alone the ominous escalation of the 1973 war.

Yet while they avoided escalation, the superpowers were hardly disinterested observers to the events in Lebanon. Both perceived important interests as being at stake, and both sought to exert their influence through varying strategies in order to defend and advance their interests.

What were these strategies? Did they achieve their objectives? Why or why not? What are the lessons of Lebanon for the ongoing superpower competition for influence in the Middle East? This chapter will focus on these questions.

Superpower Strategies and the Lebanon War

It is very difficult to place precise dates on the Lebanon war. Itamar Rabinovich traces its origins back to 1970, and even then notes that its roots run much deeper.[1] For present purposes, this chapter will concentrate on the three stages most directly related to the superpowers' roles in and responses to the crisis set off by the Israeli invasion:

1. The prelude, from the beginning of the Reagan administration to the Israeli invasion (June 6, 1982).

I would like to acknowledge the research assistance of Charles Dannehl and Alfonso Lara.

2. The war, from the Israeli invasion through the Sabra and Shatila massacres (September 18, 1982), including the first Multinational Force (MNF) and the enunciation of the Reagan Plan.

3. The "peace," corresponding to the period of the second MNF (September 20, 1982 to February 7, 1984), including the bombing of the U.S. Marine barracks.

Prelude: January 20, 1981 to June 6, 1982

Despite the historic accomplishments of the Camp David accords, the Reagan administration was determined to replace the priority given by its predecessor to the regionalist strategy of brokering peace with the more globalist strategy of strategic consensus. Basically, the logic of strategic consensus, was that the enemy of my enemy, if not my friend, at least no longer will be my enemy. Arab states such as Egypt, Saudi Arabia, Jordan, Oman, and Morocco were to be made to realize that, whatever their conflicts with Israel, they all shared an overriding threat from the common enemy of the Soviet Union. Recent Soviet military involvement in Angola and Ethiopia and their outright invasion of Afghanistan had demonstrated both their will and their capacity to project their conventional military power far beyond the traditional theater of the Eurasian heartland. These actions could only portend what Secretary of State Alexander Haig, the principal architect of the strategic consensus strategy, called "a basic and ominous objective: to strike at countries on or near the vital resource lines of the Western world."[2]

Implicit in all this was the additional assumption that at the same time that it deterred the Soviet threat, strategic consensus would also accomplish what neither Kissinger's shuttle diplomacy nor Carter's personal diplomacy could—regional peace. For a number of reasons, however, this proved not to be the case. One was that it misdiagnosed Soviet strategy. Rather than being poised for an imminent thrust into the Middle East, Soviet foreign policy had entered a period of consolidation.[3] It was not that the Soviets had necessarily abandoned their hegemonic aspirations, but to a certain extent their recent geostrategic gains made their military posture less reliant on their position in the Middle East than in the past.[4] Moreover, the Soviets now found themselves operating under a number of constraints. They were bogged down in Afghanistan, preoccupied by Solidarity in Poland, and burdened with sick and aging leaders. In addition, amidst the rise of Islamic fundamentalism and having been discredited by their own invasion of Muslim Afghanistan, they had lost at least some of the ideological advantage they had traditionally enjoyed as a function of anti-Western Arab nationalism.

Soviet motivations for disrupting the U.S.-led regional peace process, however, were stronger than ever. Soviet propaganda stressed the Palestinians' rights to self-determination, but basic Soviet calculations held that any peace agreement for which the United States would get credit, irrespective of its details, was inimical to their interests. Consequently, they tightened their political bonds with Syria through a Treaty of Friendship and Cooperation (in October 1980) and with the Palestine Liberation Organization (PLO) by upgrading its office in Moscow to full diplomatic status (in October 1981). They also increased economic aid, arms shipments, and tacit as well as direct support of terrorism. Increasingly, they strove to make not just Israel but the United States itself the target—in effect, to foster the logic among Arab radicals that the "friend of my enemy is my enemy."

Thus, during this period Soviet strategy was more political than military. They played the role of spoiler, more intent on blocking U.S. influence than adding new satellites or surrogates. While this was no less of a challenge to U.S. interests, it was very different from the one on which the strategic consensus strategy was premised.

A second problem with this new U.S. strategy was its designated Middle Eastern allies. While many moderate Arab governments shared U.S. concerns about the Soviet threat and were willing to strengthen their bilateral military ties to the United States, only Egypt was willing to go even part of the way toward sublimating its conflict with Israel.[5] The assassination of Anwar Sadat by Islamic fundamentalists in October 1981 left other Arab leaders who might have been inclined to agree analytically with the U.S. strategy fearful of the domestic consequences. As to the Israelis, while they particularly appreciated the new American resolve to take a hard line toward Syria and Libya, they found other aspects of the policy, such as the AWACS sale to Saudi Arabia, quite disturbing. Nor were they prepared to give up their independence of action against their Arab adversaries, as they demonstrated in June 1981 by bombing the Iraqi nuclear reactor and in December 1981 by extending Israeli law to cover the Golan Heights (a de facto annexation).

Lebanon itself proved to be the third and ultimately most serious problem. For strategic consensus to be viable, Lebanon had to be confined, in William Quandt's terms, to a "mere sideshow."[6] Toward this purpose, during 1981 Ambassador Philip Habib was dispatched through four rounds of shuttle diplomacy in an effort to negotiate settlement of the Syrian-Israeli missile crisis and the intensified PLO-Israeli border skirmishes. Yet Lebanon would not remain a sideshow, and when it moved to center stage, it was regional dynamics and not the Soviet Union that brought it there. The Soviets, while not particularly disposed to cooperating with the Reagan administration, in actuality had not been all that averse to keeping the lid on Lebanon. They continued to supply arms to the PLO in southern Lebanon and provided Syria with the SAM missiles it moved into the Bekaa Valley in April 1981. The basic thrust of their policy, however, was to restrain Syria from provocations that ran a high risk of escalation to war with Israel.[7] Even after the Israeli annexation of the Golan Heights, a Syrian military delegation left Moscow with less than it requested.[8]

Whether or not the United States gave Israel the green light to invade Lebanon, it at least seems fair to say that there was no red light.[9] But the most interesting part of this argument is less who said what to whom than the traceable connections between the essential logic of the strategic consensus strategy and the realpolitik benefits the United States could anticipate from the Israeli invasion, at least in its "Operation Peace for Galilee" version. For Israel to defeat the PLO and to intimidate the Syrians would not only alleviate an immediate threat to Israeli security, but it was also seen as sending a global signal of power and resolve that by association stood to enhance the credibility of U.S. power.

For Ariel Sharon, however, the East-West strategic consensus was more cover than context. What the United States ended up with, particularly in the eyes of the moderate Arab states with which it had been trying to build this heralded consensus, was at best guilt by association and at worst charges of collusion and deception.

War: June 6 to September 18, 1982

The Israeli invasion of Lebanon shocked the Reagan administration into dealing much more directly with the immediate problems at hand. Ambassador Habib was again dispatched to mediate, humanitarian assistance was extended to victims of the war, and rather substantial pressure was placed on Israel, including a suspension of sales of cluster bombs and such unusually candid criticism as the "sternly worded statement" issued by President Reagan calling on Prime Minister Begin to observe the truce in Beirut.[10]

By late August U.S. diplomacy had brokered an agreement for the PLO's withdrawal from Beirut. The United States was to join with France and Italy in providing troops for an MNF that would enforce the safe passage guarantees given to the PLO. While only eight hundred marines were involved, and while their mission was quite explicitly defined as noncombatant, this first such deployment of U.S. troops since the Vietnam War was felt to have important symbolic value. More importantly, the MNF proved quite successful in accomplishing its immediate mission. The PLO evacuation from Beirut took place without incident and on schedule, neither of which could be considered a foregone conclusion. The cease-fire held, thus averting the fearsome prospect of war between Israel and Syria. In addition, to a greater extent than in almost a decade, there appeared to be genuine hope within Lebanon that all foreign occupying forces would be removed and that internal reconciliation might be possible.

While these were limited and (as soon became all too apparent) temporary successes, they took on added importance relative to the setbacks incurred by the Soviet Union. The stinging defeats suffered by their PLO and Syrian surrogates did obvious damage to the Soviet position. The greatest damage, however, came from the way the Soviets responded—or more to the point, failed to respond—to the crises faced by their allies. While the PLO was "in its moment of greatest need," the Soviets had done nothing.[11] With respect to Syria, the Kremlin stuck to its strict constructionist interpretation of the limits of its commitments under their 1980 treaty.

It is true that, historically, Soviet behavior during Middle East wars has tended to be fairly cautious and particularly circumspect about the risks of escalation. In the past Soviet threats, as Francis Fukuyama observes, "were always made relatively late in the crisis when it was clear that they would not have to be carried out."[12] This time, however, they did not even offer their allies a belated threat to intervene on their behalf. According to Karen Dawisha, the most severe threat Brezhnev managed to make during the actual crisis period was to warn that if U.S. troops were sent in, the Soviet Union would "build its policy with due consideration of this fact."[13]

The reasons for Soviet reticence during the Israeli invasion are not totally clear. Lebanon itself had never been a critical part of either Soviet global or regional strategy. Now they also could (and did) point to the disunity with which the Arab world itself responded to the Israeli invasion. In addition, while they might glorify the PLO in their propaganda, the Soviets still could conveniently draw the distinction between it and a nation-state ally. Nevertheless, it would be mistaking rationalizations for rational strategy to attribute to the Kremlin in any sort of pragmatic wisdom. The fact of the matter was that their passivity cost them a great deal of prestige, especially in the Arab world.[14]

Nor could there be any denying what the military scorecard showed. In the first week of the invasion, the Israeli Air Force shot down seventy-nine Syrian MiGs and destroyed nineteen SAMs while losing one plane.[15] The Kremlin tried to blame this on the human factor (the Syrian pilots and SAM crews), while the Syrians derogated the quality of Soviet-made equipment.[16] The question of blame obviously could not be resolved, but the public flack only made the consequences worse for both the Soviets and the Syrians.

Given this correlation of forces (a favorite Soviet term in the 1970s, now seemingly tilting against them), the Reagan administration concluded that this was a propitious time to, as the president put it, "seize the moment."[17] On September 1 President Reagan proposed in a speech a comprehensive new initiative for Arab-Israeli peace talks. While the specific terms differed somewhat from the Camp David accords, the Reagan Plan marked a return to a regionalist peace-brokering strategy.[18] It ran head-on into two problems, however. One, which also had stalled the Camp David process, was Israeli and Arab opposition. Prime Minister Begin wasted no time in denouncing the Reagan Plan and in pushing through the Knesset funds for new West Bank settlements (precisely what the Reagan Plan had called upon him not to do). The Arab League was no more receptive, proposing instead its own plan calling for an independent Palestinian state. Jordan's favorable reaction kept the Reagan Plan alive, but just barely.

The other problem, and again the most serious, was Lebanon. The whole idea of seizing the moment was based on the Lebanon war being on its way to resolution. As an expression of his faith in this, President Reagan had announced in this speech that U.S. marines would be withdrawn ahead of schedule. Instead of a Lebanese settlement laying the foundation for regional peace, however, their opposition to the Reagan Plan only gave Syria, the PLO, and Israel additional reason for perpetuating their conflict in Lebanon. Within days of the MNF's departure, Israel, citing renewed PLO attacks from Syrian-held territory, bombarded Syrian and PLO positions in central and eastern Lebanon. The next day, the newly chosen president of Lebanon, the pro-Israeli Phalange leader Bashir Gemayel, was assassinated. Then followed the massacres at the Sabra and Shatila refugee camps, in the wake of which there could be little doubt that the Lebanese conflict remained unresolved.

The Peace That Never Was: September 20, 1982 to February 7, 1984

Responding to the urgent plea of the new Lebanese president, Amin Gemayel, the Reagan administration sent U.S. marines back to Beirut as part of a second MNF. In the crisis atmosphere following Sabra and Shatila, there seemed to be no other choice than to reinject international authority into an increasingly volatile situation. Beyond that, however, the precise mission of the second MNF was unclear. The formal statement issued by the Joint Chiefs of Staff was no more specific than "to establish an environment which will permit the Lebanese Armed Forces to carry out their responsibilities in the Beirut area."[19] Moreover, this time no promises were made that the marines would be home within 30 days.

It soon became evident that "establishing an environment" translated into two principal objectives. First, all foreign forces were to be withdrawn from Lebanon. This included, according to Secretary of State George Shultz, "foreign armies" (Syria and Israel), "foreign paramilitary forces" (the PLO), and "foreign terrorist groups" (Syria and Iran). The withdrawal of these forces was an obviously important objective in its own right. It also was deemed a necessary precondition for the second objective of internal reconciliation. "Whatever the indigenous barriers to national reconciliation," Shultz argued, "that process can never really get under way so long as Lebanon remains occupied."[20]

The MNF was to be the principal instrument for achieving both these objectives, but it was to do so more through political than military means. The very presence of the MNF, and particularly of the contingent of U.S. marines, was expected both to reinforce diplomatic efforts to negotiate the withdrawal of all foreign forces and to buy time for the Gemayel government to establish its internal authority. The MNF was not to attempt to defeat any of the foreign forces or the Lebanese militias; rather, the Lebanese Army was to be trained and equipped so that it would be better able to do so. Beyond that, the only specific military task given to the marines was to keep Beirut International Airport open. Even this was to be done within the peacetime rules of engagement.[21]

The Reagan administration thus claimed that the U.S. presence was not as an interventionary or expeditionary force but rather in the service of politically neutral objectives. The United States was in Lebanon only to uphold the sanctity of the nation's internationally recognized borders against foreign encroachments and to allow its duly elected government to exercise its constitutional authority within those borders against domestic factions who raised up arms against it. Moreover, when the second MNF arrived, it received (by most accounts) a generally positive and hopeful reception from the Muslim as well as Christian communities.[22]

In the view from the Kremlin, however, the U.S. strategy was anything but neutral peacekeeping and disinterested brokering. It was an effort to create another U.S. client state in the Middle East. Moreover, the Soviets were bent on recouping the losses they had already suffered. Thus, shortly after the second MNF had been deployed, the Soviets sent SAM-5 batteries to Syria.[23] The SAM-5s were one of the first installments on what amounted to an estimated $2.5 billion in arms transfers over the next 18 months. Even more significant than the total dollar figure was the fact that this was the first time Soviet SAM-5s had ever been deployed outside the Warsaw Pact. Soon thereafter, and again for the first time outside the Warsaw Pact, the Soviets armed the Syrians with SS-21 missiles.

The Soviets were active on the diplomatic front as well. They countered the Reagan Plan with their own purported peace plan. In addition, as Itamar Rabinovich and Asher Susser point out, they pressured Jordan's King Hussein not to join the Reagan Plan. With regard specifically to Lebanon, they rebuffed a request by Secretary of State Shultz for assistance in gaining Syrian assent to the May 1983 withdrawal agreement between Israel and Lebanon. The new Soviet leadership under Yuri Andropov instead was quite outspoken in its denunciation of the agreement.[24] The Soviets feared that if Lebanon joined Egypt in the U.S. camp, as it appeared to be doing, the Reagan Plan might lead other Arab states to follow. Moreover, an Israeli-Lebanese alliance could threaten Syrian security at a time when, as one Soviet official put it, Syria was "the fundamental link in the present situation in opposing U.S.-Israeli plans."[25]

It also should be noted, however, that while the Soviets were once again playing the role of spoiler of U.S.-led peace efforts, they did not throw caution totally to the wind. During the May 1983 crisis over the Israeli-Lebanese agreement, the Soviet ambassador to Lebanon rejected the Syrian foreign minister's request for a pledge of support if war broke out as a purely "hypothetical question."[26] In September 1983, when Syria tangled directly with U.S. military forces, the Soviets denounced the United States but also urged restraint on the part of Syria. As to the arms flow, while varying interpretations are possible, it is important to note that in manning the SAM-5s with their own crews, the Soviets retained control over their use. In the same vein, the SS-21 missiles were shipped to Syria only after the cease-fire with the United States was in place and reportedly with the stipulation that they be used only in self-defense.[27]

For its part, Syria was not at all ambivalent. Lebanon remained integral to

Assad's irredentist-imperial vision of a "Greater Syria," with its ambition for both dominance within the Arab world and the capability (finally) to defeat Israel.[28] Lebanon, thus, was not to be allowed even to resume its traditional quasineutrality, let alone make peace and tacitly ally with Israel. In addition, at a somewhat more mundane but hardly insignificant level, Syria also had an interest in protecting an estimated $1 billion drug trade in the Bekaa Valley.[29]

A third foreign force that had to be reckoned with was Iran. While no official Iranian armies were in Lebanon, the government of the Ayatollah Khomeini provided the inspiration and the material for a number of terrorist acts, including the October 23, 1983, bombing of the U.S. Marine barracks.

In the wake of the 241 lives lost as a result of this bombing, the Reagan administration sought to deflect the ensuing domestic political pressure by shifting attention away from the issue of what was (or, more to the point, was not) being achieved in Lebanon to the damage that a forced withdrawal would do to U.S. credibility on a global scale. The immediate consequence, Secretary of Defense Caspar Weinberger predicted, would be a "completely Soviet-dominated enclave right in Lebanon."[30] To this President Reagan added that "not only will our strategic position in the eastern Mediterranean the threatened but also the stability of the entire Middle East, including the vast resource areas of the Arabian Peninsula."[31] Even more than the geostrategic specifics, however, it was U.S. resolve that was being tested. If the United States failed that test, "if we are driven out of Lebanon," warned Secretary of State Shultz, "our role in the world is that much weakened everywhere. . . . The message will be sent that relying on the Soviet Union pays off and that relying on the United States is a fatal mistake."[32]

Nevertheless, by early February the Reagan administration found itself with no other choice but to withdraw the marines. Not only was pressure building in Congress, but political advisors within the administration were becoming increasingly conscious of the election now less than a year away. Even more to the point was the virtual collapse of the Lebanese Army, amidst mass defections of Druze and Shiite troops and officers. The Lebanese Army now controlled little more than the grounds of the presidential palace at Baabda, and as a French magazine characterized his lot, Amin Gemayel had become "le President otage."[33] President Reagan tried to save face by terming the withdrawal a "redeployment," but there could be little denying the fact that the United States was in retreat. This was clear from what was said, as Egyptian President Hosni Mubarak and Jordan's King Hussein, were quite outspoken in their criticisms of the dependability of the United States' word and the reliability of its power. It also was clear from what was not said. At a Republican luncheon in mid-February, President Reagan "was interrupted nine time by applause in his comments on the economy and other subjects, but his discussion of foreign policy was met with silence, including his claim that 'there's a new sense of purpose and direction to American foreign policy.'"[34]

The Lebanon War and Superpower Influence

As so often has been the case in Lebanon, the losers were easier to identify than the winners. The United States clearly had lost. Its efforts to forge a regional anti-Soviet alliance and to rebuild Lebanon into an ally had both failed, while its attempt to broker a regional peace remained barely alive. On balance, the United States had lost prestige, influence, and credibility.

Relative to this, the Soviet Union could be considered to have "won." In ways and for reasons that will be discussed below, however, the Soviet victory was, at best, a qualified one.

Why the United States Lost in Lebanon

The Structure of the Conflict. The first point to be made concerns the disadvantages that the structure of the conflict imposed on U.S. policy. The United States was attempting nothing less than (1) to deter the Soviet Union, (2) to compel Syria to withdraw its forces from where they had been for almost a decade, and (3) to induce the Arabs and the Israelis to make peace. However, as the general international relations literature shows, each of these objectives was inherently more difficult to accomplish than it was to block.

1. One of the central conclusions reached by Alexander George and Richard Smoke based on their study of eleven cases of nonnuclear deterrence is that the "initiator" has an inherent advantage over the "defender."[35] The defender (the role the United States was playing in Lebanon) has the initial problem of making its commitment to carry out its threat credible. Moreover, even if a commitment is perceived as credible, George and Smoke argue that "it is not a sufficient condition for deterrence success." The structure of the situation still leaves the initiator with "multiple options," from which it can choose those for which the balance between risks and benefits is the most favorable.[36]

2. A second general axiom, developed in particular in the works of Thomas Schelling, is that compelling a country to change its existing behavior is even more difficult than detering it from taking some future proscribed action. "The threat that compels rather than deters," Schelling writes, "often requires that the punishment be administered *until* the other acts, rather than *if* he acts."[37] To do so, however, increases the risks of escalation to the compeller no less than to the compellee, especially given factors faced by both sides (again, irrespective of their national or political system identities), such as bureaucratic inertia, potential challenges at home from disaffected rivals, and the basic psychological disposition against losing face. In Lebanon the compellence objective was further complicated by the peacetime rules of engagement under which the United States was operating—against an adversary who had no inhibitions about resorting to terrorism, including suicide bombings.

3. As to inducement, suffice it to say that international relations scholarship still treats cooperation as a special case that needs to be explained.[38] This is true even among countries whose basic relationship is a nonconflictual one, let alone those whose conflict stirs the passions and has done so for centuries.

Internal Sources of Conflict. Even the sum of these structural disadvantages, however, cannot by themselves fully explain the U.S. defeat in Lebanon. A second set of factors concerns the internal sources of the Lebanese conflict. As noted earlier, the Reagan administration kept looking outward for sources of conflict: to the Soviet Union, to Syria, and to Iran. In its retrospective analyses, its failure was attributed principally to opposition from these three sources. The foreign forces were not forced out, so there could no internal reconciliation. The problem with this analysis is that it ignores the extent to which the most fundamental sources of the Lebanese conflict stemmed from the internal fissures of Lebanese society.[39] This, after all, was the country about which almost 20 years earlier Edward Shils had written:

> Lebanon is not a civil society. . . . The politically relevant members of Lebanese society are not inclined to allow the obligations which arise from their membership in the society to supervene when they feel that interests which they regard as vital are threatened. These interests are the integrity of their communities of belief and primordial attachments—of kinship and loyalty—and the opportunities and possessions of the constituent groups or individual members of these communities. . . . The consequences of these actions for the Lebanese society as a whole are too frequently regarded as being of secondary significance.[40]

It was in this respect that the National Salvation Front (NSF), formed with the Syrians by Druze, Shiite, and even disaffected Christian leaders, can be seen to have been motivated by much more than just shared opposition to the agreement with Israel signed by President Amin Gemayel. The NSF is more accurately the product of the interactive relationship—an all too potent synergy—between the internal and external dimensions of the Lebanese conflict. While Amin Gemayel initially had been viewed with at least a degree of openness by other confessional groups, once in power he too ruled more like the leader of a faction than the leader of the nation.[41] He spurned early overtures for discussions toward a new national pact from Shiite Amal leader Nabih Berri and Druze leader Walid Jumblaat, and instead sought to use the Lebanese Army to impose "reconciliation." He sent the army into West Beirut to disarm the Muslim militias, a move that could hardly be considered an evenhanded effort to reestablish central authority when no comparable confiscatory raids were conducted in Christian East Beirut. Moreover, in both its command structure and its missions, the Lebanese Army became more closely linked to the Phalange.

Yet right up to the bitter end the Reagan administration kept insisting that "we support no faction or religious community, but we are not neutral in our support of the legitimate government of Lebanon."[42] Such a position may have had legalistic validity, but it was too formalistic to fit the Lebanese reality. This was especially true with regard to the idea that a program of professional training would be sufficient to depoliticize the Lebanese Army. As Ze'ev Schiff writes:

> The Lebanese Army can play a part in consolidating the power of the government only if a *prior* political agreement can be reached between the central government and at least one of the major confessional groups, in addition to the Christians. History shows that without that agreement the army crumbles when asked to fight either Shiites or Druze.[43]

Nevertheless, U.S. Defense Department officials contended that "dealing with Lebanese factional politics was not their job; they were simply to train the Lebanese to be good soldiers." State Department officials also begged off, claiming "they felt unqualified to do more than urge the Lebanese in a general sense to reconcile their factional politics."[44]

At minimum, then, as Daniel Pipes argued in early 1983, "any U.S. policy designed to deal with the Lebanese crisis must address the country's domestic situation, particularly the deep antipathies that exist among the country's religious communities."[45] It may even have been that the Reagan policy had things backwards—that, as William Quandt asserted, "political reconciliation is more important as an immediate objective than the withdrawal of all foreign forces and is probably a condition for subsequent achievement of that more ambitious goal."[46] What was clear was that instead of internal reconciliation being able to wait until the external forces had been removed, the exacerbation of the internal conflict caused by the policies of the Gemayel government was making resolution of the external problem all the more difficult. This in turn intensified the internal conflict, and the vicious cycle that is Lebanon was joined once again.

Policy Instruments. The third factor contributing to the U.S. defeat was the ineffectiveness of the policy instruments through which U.S. objectives were to be achieved. As already noted, the principal instrument, the second MNF, was intended as a political use of military force. As such, its mission was more of the "signalling, bargaining, negotiating character" that Alexander George calls "coercive diplomacy" than of the more traditional "quick, decisive military strategy" of defeating an adversary.[47] For such an instrumentality to be effective, however, the adversary also has to be more interested in sending signals than in wreaking havoc. As stated more generally by Robert Osgood, both sides have to be willing to confine the conflict "within the boundaries of contrived mutual restraints."[48]

This was presumed to be, but most definitely was not, the case in Lebanon. According to the Long Commission, the deployment of the second MNF had proceeded from the assumption that it would be operating in a "relatively benign environment." Yet long before the October 23 bombing of the marine barracks, there were signs that "the environment could no longer be characterized as peaceful." The terrorism to which the marines were being subjected was "tantamount to an act of war," yet the battalion never was "trained, organized, staffed or supported to deal effectively with the terrorist threat in Lebanon."[49] It continued to be seen as a political and not a military instrument. As a result, when the terrorist truck bomber attacked in the middle of the night, he encountered sentries who, in accordance with the peacetime rules of engagement under which they were still operating, were carrying unloaded weapons.

The other problem in terms of policy instruments, although less one of misuse than lack of use, was the limited leverage the Reagan administration exercised over the Gemayel government. To be sure, maintaining leverage over another government, even that of a small ally, is not an easy task. As the numerous disputes with Israel demonstrated, the ally will often go its own way despite protests, pressures, and even sanctions. As Fouad Ajami rightly points out, however, the unconditionality of U.S. support made it possible for the Gemayel government to try to substitute "the support of a foreign power. . . . for a social contract at home."[50] In this respect, the unwillingness of the Reagan administration to bring its leverage to bear ended up being counterproductive to its own interests and objectives. Defense Secretary Weinberger might continue to claim, as he did on the eve of the marines' withdrawal, that the U.S. role had been little more than that of "a stabilizing interposition force."[51] Far more accurate and insightful, though, was the conclusion of the Long Commission that as a result of U.S. policy, "the image of the USMNF, in the eyes of the factional militias, had become pro-Israel, pro-Phalange and anti-Muslim."[52]

Domestic Constraints. Finally, there were the domestic constraints on U.S. policy. The explicit limitations on both MNFs to noncombatant roles reflected the Reagan administration's concern for congressional and public misgivings about becoming too deeply involved in Lebanon. In this respect, domestic constraints had always had an effect on policy, although not until after the marine barracks bombing did domestic pressure really mount. Prior to that, even though some American lives had been lost, Congress (with House Speaker Thomas P. "Tip" O'Neill working with the administration) had authorized the marine deployment for an additional 18 months. While the president was able to draw on his "great communicator" skills to stir a rally around the flag, however, the rally did not last very long.[53]

Too much emphasis should not be put on the domestic constraints. Even an extraordinarily well-executed policy would have encountered difficulties because the structure of the conflict made the objectives that the United States sought to achieve inherently problematic. On top of that, by paying too little attention to the internal sources of the Lebanese conflict and by essentially choosing the wrong policy instruments, the Reagan administration contributed rather substantially to its own failure. The constraints that Congress did impose cannot be dismissed as reflexive isolationism or pure partisan politics. In fact, the Reagan policy left plenty of room for reasonable people to disagree.

Explaining the Limits of the Soviet Victory

For the Soviet Union, as Harold Sawyer has commented, the forced withdrawal of the U.S. Marines from Lebanon represented "a substantial and multi-faceted loss for the United States."[54] The United States did not get its client state; instead, with the marines gone, Syria moved into the vacuum left by their departure. Only a few weeks after the U.S. withdrawal, President Gemayel abrogated his treaty with Israel, and soon thereafter, after traveling to Damascus to consult with Assad, he appointed the avowedly pro-Syrian Rashid Karami as his prime minister. In addition, Israel did not attain another separate peace; in fact, with Syria now armed with more sophisticated weaponry and with the Shiites of southern Lebanon increasingly radicalized (and the PLO reinfiltrating Lebanon), Israel's northern border still was not secure. "Most important of all," as Sawyer emphasized, *"the chances for a peace settlement on American terms have been weakened."*[55]

As significant as these gains were, however, they also have had their limitations. The "completely Soviet-dominated enclave" predicted by Secretary Weinberger has yet to appear. Moreover, Lebanon has once again proven itself resistant to becoming anyone's client, even Syria's. Additionally, while Syria was militarily stronger than ever before, a powerful Syria is a double-edged sword for the Soviet Union. Clearly, having Syria act as "another Cuba" serves Soviet purposes not only in the Middle East but also, given Syria's central role in international terrorism, globally.[56] In other respects, however, Soviet and Syrian objectives are not nearly so complementary. Under Assad Syria, as noted earlier, has aspired to regional hegemony. The Soviet Union has sought to temper Assad's hegemonic aspirations on a number of occasions and at times has opposed them outright. Galia Golan notes that when Syria invaded Lebanon in 1975–1976, "the Soviets very directly demonstrated their disapproval," both through verbal condemnations and a suspension of arms shipments.[57] In addition, while the Israeli invasion of Lebanon revealed the hypocrisy of Soviet comradeliness toward the PLO, when Syria then sought to extend its dominance over the PLO, the Soviets suddenly rediscovered their commitment to Yasser Arafat. A balance of power needed to be preserved within the Soviet sphere of client states for fear that too much power in the hands of any single state would increase its independence of Moscow.

Syrian strength also has once again raised the spectre of war with Israel. Here, too, the pattern of the past has been one of a considerable degree of Syrian-Soviet tension. Syria has gone to war with Israel more than any other Arab state. It remains committed, perhaps even more so now than in the past, to the destruction of Israel. Therefore, another war, especially one in which for the first time Israel may not have the margin of military superiority needed to compensate for its other strategic vulnerabilities, has the potential to serve Syrian objectives quite well. The Soviets, however, while far from being a promoter of peace, have consistently tended to be much less sanguine about the prospects of war.[58] This undoubtedly is partly due to the fact that, given the historical record, the Soviets have little reason to be particularly confident that the Arabs would win. Moreover, there is the concern that any Arab-Israeli war inherently carries with it the potential for drawing in the superpowers and escalating to nuclear war. Even short of such eventualities, a war at the present would likely undermine further developments toward a new détente with the United States, which seems to be a high priority for the Gorbachev regime.

That the Soviets helped create the current unstable situation by providing Syria with SAM-5s and SS-21s points out the contradictions in their position and underlines the dilemma they face. These weapons were intended to strengthen Syria so as to reinforce and perpetuate the state of "nonpeace" that the Soviets traditionally have seen as serving their interests. Perhaps they believed that by attaching the precautionary conditions of their own crews manning the SAM-5s and the self-defense stipulation for use of the SS-21s they could threaten Israel while still controlling the risks of war. If so, they clearly miscalculated. According to most reports, the Soviet crews are gone, but the SAM-5s and SS-21s are still there. Moreover, from the Israeli perspective (as Hirsh Goodman makes quite clear), the strategic realities are such that security planning has to be based on the military capabilities in the possession of its adversaries.[59] Thus, with Syria possessing and Israel facing missiles with the extreme accuracy and long range of the SS-21s, the incentives for either side to launch a preemptive strike are now greater than before.

A final point concerns the limited ability of the Soviet Union to capitalize diplomatically on the discrediting of the United States by its Lebanon intervention. They did manage to take some advantage of the openings this created. In April 1984 diplomatic ties were restored with Egypt after a three-year lapse, and in 1985, relations were established for the first time with Oman and the United Arab Emirates. There also have been reports of unofficial contacts and improved relations with Saudi Arabia. While these initiatives are quite important and could become even more important in the future, thus far the Soviets have been hindered by the burdens of their own reputation from achieving major diplomatic breakthroughs. They still face a combination of fear and contempt for their invasion of Muslim Afghanistan. They also carry their own historical legacy of being implicated by Qaddafi's aggression against other Arab states, in the coups in South Yemen, and in at least some of the Arab-against-Arab terrorism. Finally, as far as Islamic fundamentalists are concerned, atheistic communism is second only to the United States as a great Satan.

In addition, the Soviets face very pragmatic doubts as to their value as an ally. They have had a difficult time recouping the credibility they lost during the Israeli invasion as a dependable protector during crises. Moreover, there are now grave doubts about their economic value as an ongoing ally. Whereas 30 years ago the combination of their economic and technical assistance and the attractiveness of their economic model helped them gain entree into the Middle East, now their own severe economic problems have left them with much less to offer in terms of aid, trade, investment, and technology, or even as a model.

Perhaps the most revealing expression of the limits on Soviet gains in the aftermath of the Lebanon war has been its recent diplomatic overture to Israel. While substantive progress has been slow, the very occurrence of a meeting between Israeli Prime Minister Shimon Peres and Soviet Foreign Minister Eduard Shevardnadze in September 1986 had tremendous symbolic significance. As Ambassador Samuel Lewis observes in chapter 16, this may only be a "tentative probe," but "the scent of innovation is in the air." Serious discussions of Soviet participation in a multilateral peace conference have been renewed for the first time in almost a decade. From one respective this represents a gain for the Soviet Union. However, given the vituperativeness of Soviet rhetoric, as well as the hostility of their policies toward Israel over the past two decades, this nevertheless amounts to a significant shift in Soviet strategy. What it points to is that despite the damage done by the Lebanon war, the U.S. and Israeli positions still set the basic terms for Middle East politics. Despite everything, the U.S.-led peace process remains the principal alternative to another war. The Soviet Union may now recognize its need to participate.

Final Observations

If there is a single central lesson from the Lebanon war for the superpower competition in the Middle East, it is in accentuating the limits of superpower influence. These limits are in part inherent in the structure and nature of the Middle East conflict, which has historically made it difficult for any great power at any time to work its will in the region. As the Lebanon war attested, however, these limits also have been in part self-inflicted. The policies of both the United States and the Soviet Union were plagued by mistakes, tensions, and contradictions before, during, and after the Israeli invasion of Lebanon.

Thus, the beginning of a more realistic policy (defined as one that stands a greater chance of achieving its intended objectives while also minimizing the risks of escalation to nuclear war) lies in an objective assessment of the limits of influence. The implication here, however, is not in the direction of noninvolvement, for while acknowledging the limits, the scope of superpower influence in the Middle East remains significant. Moreover, continued involvement in the politics of the Middle East is an inescapable reality for both superpowers. It would be inimical to their overall global positions not to be involved. Even more than that, the Middle East has its own way of making sure it is not ignored.

The critical question, therefore, is not *whether* to be involved but how best to achieve the objectives for which one is involved. Lebanon showed that neither superpower has yet found the answer to this question.

Notes

1. Itamar Rabinovich, *The War for Lebanon, 1970–1983* (Ithaca: Cornell University Press, 1984), p. 9.

2. Statement to the U.S. Congress, House of Representatives, Committee on Foreign Relations, *Foreign Assistance Authorization for Fiscal Year 1982*, Hearings, 97th Congress, 1st session, 1981, p. 7.

3. On the general shift in Soviet foreign policy toward Third World regional conflicts in the early 1980s, see Francis Fukuyama, *Moscow's Post-Brezhnev Reassessment of the Third World* (Santa Monica, CA: RAND Corporation, 1986); Jerry Hough, *The Struggle for the Third World* (Washington, DC: Brookings Institution, 1986); Carol R. Saivetz and Sylvia Woodby, *Soviet-Third World Relations* (Boulder, CO: Westview Press, 1985); and Elizabeth Kridl Valkenier, *The Soviet Union and the Third World: An Economic Bind* (New York: Praeger, 1983).

4. The Soviet Air Force and Navy now had access to facilities in Ethiopia, South Yemen, Mozambique, and Angola. Moreover, as Marxist-Leninist regimes, these governments also were deemed more reliable allies than "bourgeois nationalists" such as Gamal Abdel Nasser and Anwar Sadat in Egypt or more independent military dictators such as Saddam Hussein in Iraq and Hafiz Assad in Syria (Louis J. Andolino and Louis R. Eltscher, "Soviet Naval, Military and Air Power: Projecting Influence in the Third World," in Robert W. Clawson, ed., *East-West Rivalry in the Third World* [Wilmington, DE: Scholarly Resources, 1986], pp. 55–76). In his chapter in this book Francis Fukuyama also makes the point that Soviet technological advances made forward basing less critical ("Soviet Military Power in the Middle East; or, Whatever Became of Power Projection?" (chap. 10).

5. Nimrod Novik, *Encounter with Reality: Reagan and the Middle East* (Boulder, CO: Westview Press, 1985), pp. 41–47; Herbert L. Sawyer, "Moscow's Perceptions of Recent American Involvement in the Middle East: Implications for Soviet Policy," in Paul Marantz and Blema S. Steinberg, eds., *Superpower Involvement in the Middle East; Dynamics of Foreign Policy* (Boulder, CO: Westview Press, 1985), p. 60.

6. William B. Quandt, "Reagan's Lebanon Policy: Trial and Error," *The Middle East Journal* 38 (Spring 1984), p. 238.

7. One such effort was the Soviet insistence during the 1981 missile crisis that their treaty commitment applied only to Syria proper and not to Syrian troops in Lebanon. Moreover, unlike the treaties of friendship and cooperation with countries such as India and Vietnam, in which the mutual security guarantee became operative immediately and automatically upon "an attack or threat of attack," the treaty with Syria promised only contact and coordination (Stephen T. Hosmer and Thomas W. Wolfe, *Soviet Policy and*

Practice Toward Third World Countries (Lexington, MA: Lexington Books, 1983), p. 216 n. 47, pp. 249–250 n. 21).

8. Robert O. Freedman, "Moscow, Damascus and the Lebanese Crisis of 1982–1984," in Marantz and Steinberg, *Superpower Involvement in the Middle East,* p. 94.

9. The strongest statement of this argument is Ze'ev Schiff, "The Green Light," *Foreign Policy* 50 (Spring 1983), pp. 73–85. See also Schiff and Ehud Ya'ari, *Israel's Lebanon War* (New York: Simon and Schuster, 1984), pp. 62–77; Amos Perlmutter, "The Middle East: A Turning Point?," *Foreign Affairs* 61 (Fall 1982), p. 74; Quandt, "Reagan's Lebanon Policy," p. 239; and Alexander M. Haig, Jr., *Caveat: Realism, Reagan and Foreign Policy* (New York: Macmillan, 1984), pp. 317–352.

10. This characterization is used in the chronology published in the *America and the World 1982* edition of *Foreign Affairs* 61(3), p. 729.

11. *Strategic Survey, 1982–83* (London: International Institute for Strategic Studies, 1983), p. 2.

12. Fukuyama, *Moscow's Post-Brezhnev Reassessment,* p. 65; see also *Strategic Survey 1982–83,* p. 66.

13. Karen Dawisha, "The U.S.S.R. in the Middle East: Superpower in Eclipse?," *Foreign Affairs* 61 (Winter 1982–1983): 440–441.

14. One illustrative incident was the reprimand delivered to the Soviet ambassador by Muammar Qaddafi as reported on Tripoli Radio (*Ibid.,* pp. 439–440). Of course, Qaddafi's sagelike advice was for the PLO leaders to commit suicide so as to help their cause with their own martyrdom.

15. *Strategic Survey 1982–83,* p. 72.

16. Dawisha, "The U.S.S.R. in the Middle East," pp. 439–440, cites an October 1982 interview granted Western journalists by the Syrian minister of information in which he complained that Soviet weaponry was inferior to U.S. technology.

17. There were additional reasons other than just its defeat by Israel for the perception that Syria was at the moment quite weak. There had been a great deal of domestic unrest, including an attempted coup in January 1982 and the revolt of the Muslim Brotherhood, leading to the massacres in the city of Hama in February 1982. Mounting tensions with Iraq had forced the closing of the borders in April 1982. Its support of Iran had caused Kuwait to try to reduce the Syrians' funding from the Gulf states. And there had been friction with Saudi Arabia over both the Iran-Iraq war and Syria's rejection of the Fahd Plan (*Strategic Survey 1982–83,* p. 64).

18. Beyond the specific details, the most significant change was that the United States now was not just mediating and facilitating but putting on the table its own detailed set of proposals. "The United States thus far has sought to play the role of mediator," President Reagan stated. "But it has become evident to me that some clear sense of America's position on the key issues is necessary to encourage wide support for the peace process" (*Department of State Bulletin,* September 1982, pp. 23–25).

19. *Report of the DOD Commission on Beirut International Airport Terrorist Act, October 23, 1983,* 20 December 1983 (hereafter cited as *Long Commission Report*), p. 35.

20. Statement before the House Foreign Affairs Committee, September 21, 1983, reprinted in *Department of State Bulletin,* November 1983, p. 24.

21. *Long Commission Report,* p. 36.

22. Daniel Pipes, "Lebanon: The Real Problem," *Foreign Policy* 51 (Summer 1983), pp. 157–158; Thomas Friedman, "Ceders of Lebanon" (review of Rabinovich, *War for*

Lebanon), The New Republic, 14 October 1985, p. 35; Helena Cobban, "Lebanon's Chinese Puzzle," *Foreign Policy* 53 (Winter 1983–1984), p. 40; Quandt, "Reagan's Lebanon Policy," p. 241; Augustus Richard Norton, "Shi'ism and Social Protest in Lebanon," in Juan R. I. Cole and Nikki R. Keddie, eds., *Shi'ism and Social Protest* (New Haven: Yale University Press, 1986), p. 171.

23. The SAM-5s did not arrive until January 1983, but the decision to deploy them probably was made in September or October 1982. See Francis Fukuyama's "Soviet Military Power," chap. 10 in this book.

24. Freedman, "Moscow, Damascus and the Lebanese Crisis," pp. 102–103.

25. Karen Brutents, deputy head of the International Department of the Central Committee, cited in Sawyer, "Moscow's Perceptions," p. 70.

26. Freedman, "Moscow, Damascus and the Lebanese Crisis," p. 103.

27. *Ibid.,* pp. 98, 108, 129 n. 85.

28. See Assad's speech of July 20, 1976, reprinted as an appendix in Rabinovich, *The War for Lebanon, 1970–1983,* pp. 183–218.

29. Pipes, "Lebanon: The Real Problem," p. 139.

30. Statement on Meet the Press, 12 February 1984, reprinted in *Department of State Bulletin,* April 1984, p. 60.

31. Remarks and Question-and-Answer Session, 24 October 1983, reprinted on *Department of State Bulletin,* December 1983, p. 41.

32. Statement before the Senate Foreign Relations Committee and the House Foreign Affairs Committee, 24 October 1983, reprinted in *Department of State Bulletin,* December 1983, p. 44.

33. "Liban: le Président Otage," *Le Point,* 23 September 1985, p. 24.

34. "Reagan Denies U.S. Failed in Lebanon," *Washington Post* 18 February 1984, p. 1.

35. Alexander L. George and Richard Smoke, *Deterrence in American Foreign Policy: Theory and Practice* (New York: Columbia University Press, 1974), pp. 519–533 and *passim.*

36. *Ibid.,* pp. 526, 532.

37. Thomas Schelling, *Arms and Influence* (New Haven: Yale University Press), p. 70 (emphasis in original) and *passim.*

38. George and Smoke, *Deterrence in American Foreign Policy,* pp. 588–613; Robert Jervis, "Cooperation under the Security Dilemma," *World Politics* 30 (January 1978), pp. 167–214; Robert O. Keohane, *After Hegemony: Cooperation and Discord in the World Political Economy* (Princeton, NJ: Princeton University Press, 1984); Kenneth A. Oye, ed., *Cooperation under Anarchy* (Princeton, NJ: Princeton University Press, 1986).

39. Rabinovich, *The War for Lebanon, 1970–1983, passim;* Pipes, "Lebanon: The Real Problem," pp. 139–159; Friedman, "Ceders of Lebanon," pp. 34–36; Cobban, "Lebanon's Chinese Puzzle," pp. 34–48; Norton, "Shi'ism and Social Protest in Lebanon," pp. 156–178; David Ignatius, "How to Rebuild Lebanon," *Foreign Affairs* 61 (Summer 1983), pp. 1140–1156; Adam Zagorin, "A House Divided," *Foreign Policy* 48 (Fall 1982), pp. 111–121; Fouad Ajami, "Lebanon and Its Inheritors," *Foreign Affairs* 63 (Spring 1985), pp. 778–799.

40. Edward Shils, "The Prospect for Lebanese Civility," in Leonard Binder, ed., *Politics in Lebanon* (New York: John Wiley, 1966), p. 2.

41. Thomas Friedman, who won a Pulitzer Prize for his reporting from the Middle East, takes a particularly scathing view of Gemayel. In his review of the Rabinovich book, he characterizes the Lebanese president as "a man of boundless mediocrity. . . . Petty, vain, mean-spirited, totally lacking in vision, Amin turned out to be the wrong man at the right time" ("Ceders of Lebanon," p. 35).

42. Statement by Under Secretary of State Kenneth Dam in U.S. Congress, Senate Foreign Relations Committee, *Policy Options in Lebanon*, Hearings, 98th Congress, 2d session, 1984, p. 26.

43. Ze'ev Schiff, "Dealing with Syria," *Foreign Policy* 55 (Summer 1984), pp. 109–110 (emphasis added).

44. "The Collapse of Lebanon's Army: U.S. said to Ignore Factionalism," *New York Times*, 11 March 1984, pp. 1, 6.

45. Pipes, "Lebanon: The Real Problem," p. 141.

46. Quandt, "Reagan's Lebanon Policy," p. 254.

47. Alexander L. George, "The Development of Doctrine and Strategy," in A. L. George, David K. Hall, and William E. Simons, *The Limits of Coercive Diplomacy* (Boston: Little, Brown, 1971), pp. 16–19.

48. Robert E. Osgood, *Limited War Revisited* (Boulder, CO: Westview Press, 1979), p. 11.

49. *Long Commission Report*, pp. 39–40, 4, 133.

50. Ajami, "Lebanon and Its Inheritors," p. 790.

51. Statement on Meet the Press, reprinted in *Department of State Bulletin*, April 1984, p. 60.

52. *Long Commission Report*, p. 41.

53. For example, an ABC News/*Washington Post* public opinion poll showed an increase in those calling for withdrawal of the marines from 40 percent (September 26, 1983) to 45 percent three days after the barracks bombing. The day after the president's speech, this figure dropped to 37 percent. But by mid-December it had surged back up to 48 percent. "Marines in Beirut," *National Journal*. 3 December 1983, p. 2548; and "Marines in Lebanon," *National Journal*, 21 January 1984, p. 136.

54. Sawyer, "Moscow's Perceptions," p. 56.

55. *Ibid.* (emphasis in original).

56. Daniel Pipes, "Syria: The Cuba of the Middle East?," *Commentary* 82 (July 1986), pp. 15–22.

57. Galia Golan, "The Soviet Union and the Israeli Action in Lebanon," *International Affairs* 59 (Winter 1982–1983), p. 9.

58. William B. Quandt, *Decade of Decisions: American Policy Toward the Arab-Israeli Conflict, 1967-1976* (Berkeley, CA: University of California Press, 1977), pp. 37–71; George W. Breslauer, "Soviet Policy in the Middle East, 1967–1972: Unalterable Antagonism or Collaborative Competition?," and Alexander L. George, "The Arab-Israeli War of October 1973: Origins and Impact," both in A. L. George, *Managing U.S.-Soviet Rivalry: Problems of Crisis Prevention* (Boulder, CO: Westview Press, 1983), pp. 65–106, 139–154, respectively.

59. Hirsh Goodman, *Israel's Strategic Reality: The Impact of the Arms Race* (Washington, DC: Washington Institute for Near East Policy, 1986).

Part VIII
Dealing
with the
Consequences

21

The Management of Superpower Conflict in the Middle East

Abraham Ben-Zvi

Though need to regulate and manage the web of superpower relations in the Middle East is the direct outcome of the big powers' inability to overcome at least some of their long-standing regional conflicts of interest. Against the background of continued competition and the failure to terminate local disputes or to reach agreement to avoid unilateral action, to limit conventional arms transfers to the area or to carefully and explicitly delineate and define interests and areas of involvement, the question arises as to the informal procedures and ways by which the big powers attempted in practice to regulate and moderate their rivalry in the region. Although these behavioral ways can be elucidated by the analysis of certain noncrisis events and episodes, it is the unique characteristics and dimensions of regional wars and acute crises that provide, as we shall soon witness, the most appropriate setting for clearly identifying the dynamics by which both Washington and Moscow continuously sought to reconcile continued support for their regional allies with the types of restraint needed to avoid being drawn into dangerous confrontations and military clashes.[1]

The issue of conflict management in the Middle East during acute regional crises can be thought of as both an extension and an exception to the overall patterns of superpower relations in the area. In the first place, it is an extension and an intensification of a basic dilemma that haunts both the United States and the Soviet Union in their pursuit of certain incompatible policy objectives. This dilemma can be formulated as the desire to compete successfully and consolidate new bases of influence in an area defined by Alexander George as one of "disputed high-interest symmetry"[2] without, however, crossing the threshold from coercion to actual violence.[3] In this respect, conflict management in the Middle East approximates the model of coercive bargaining, which is intended primarily to gain or retain for each side the whole, or at least the essence, of whatever is in dispute, while at the same time avoiding the excessive risk of a direct confrontation.[4]

Unlike the situation in areas of high-interest symmetry, such as Europe, where an elaborate system of confidence-building measures helps stabilize and regulate Soviet-American rivalry, no such formal arrangements, procedures, or demarcation lines exist in the Middle East to reduce the risks of dangerous confrontations and military clashes. (The superpower discussions on the Middle East held in Vienna in February 1985, in Geneva in November 1985, and in Stockholm in June 1986 fell considerably short of any systematic effort to define the rules of the superpower game in the region, amounting merely to an exchange of views.[5])

Indeed, in the context of the acute and protracted Arab-Israeli dispute, the United States and the Soviet Union have been unable in the course of the past two decades to cooperate effectively to prevent the outbreak of two major regional conflagrations (as well as several local wars) that threatened to drag them into war with each other. Incapable of either jointly formulating certain explicit norms of behavior that would effectively "circumscribe the means by which they might advance their unilateral interests," or of defining and delineating their interests and areas of involvement, the two powers limited their conflict-management activity to a considerably less comprehensive and ambitious endeavor. This endeavor was designed to identify and maintain certain tacit "tolerance thresholds," the crossing of which could result in an uncontrolled escalation.[6] This informal, highly fragile structure of thresholds or demarcation lines has comprised norms and understandings such as the mutual recognition that both superpowers are entitled to advance their own regional interests in a variety of political, economic, and military ways, as long as their actions do not threaten a brutal and rapid change in the region's overall balance of power.[7]

Although the emerging system of mutual expectations and thresholds has established several behavioral norms and patterns of legitimate conduct, the fact that it is largely a tacit and implicit cluster of norms, surrounded by misunderstanding, controversy, and intense rivalry, explains why these patterns of restraint could not provide the panacea for lasting regional stability. The fact that in the Middle East, unlike the situation in Europe, "there is no clear geographical line dividing East and West that separates each side's area of predominant interests," further complicates the efforts to define and delimit the superpowers' interests.[8]

For all its centrality and prominence, the intensely conflictual facet of superpower crisis behavior constitutes but one element, fully integrated into a wider, multidimensional behavioral complex. Paradoxically, the core of this highly differentiated cluster is characterized by a remarkable degree of symmetry, parallelism, and even occasional collaboration and partnership between the superpowers rather than by unwavering animosity and tension. This parallel crisis behavior is inherent in the mutual desire to control the risks of escalation and thus to help defuse an acutely menacing regional situation. When this desire to avoid disaster takes precedence over the concurrent desire to support regional clients and proxies (and to maximize pressures on the other superpower or its allies), the overall structure of the bargaining process becomes essentially accommodative rather than coercive.[9]

To paraphrase George, when the tension between the requirements for prudent crisis management and for effective coercive diplomacy is resolved by giving priority to the requirements of crisis management, a "window of opportunity" is opened toward terminating the crisis. Indeed, with the collaborative aspects of the bargaining process becoming increasingly central and dominant, the stage is set for a compromise settlement, which may require at least one of the parties to settle for less than its maximum objectives.[10]

Against the backdrop of this basic duality, of this continued shift in emphasis and dominance between the desire of the superpowers to cooperate in order to effectively restrain the combatants, and their concurrent wish to unilaterally "defect" by aiding their respective clients, it is clear why this aspect of superpower behavior deserves a separate analytical treatment. Whereas in several noncrisis or precrisis forms of superpower regional activity, the competitive dimension in general overshadows and dwarfs collaborative elements and facets, conflict management situations defy any such clear-cut categorization. Indeed, the sphere of conflict management is the sphere of the apparent contradictory, with the global parties constantly fluctuating and shifting between conflicting proclivities, preferences, and constraints.

In a variety of noncrisis situations, the superpowers continuously tended, in the course of the past two decades, to operate primarily—though within limits—as the patrons of their regional clients in pursuit of certain unilateral advantages. In a number of acute conflict-management situations, however, they repeatedly combined the role of the partisan patron with the less parochial and considerably wider perspective of the superpower, whose uppermost concern remained to avoid a dangerous disruption of the overall stability of the global international system.[11] In other words, in numerous noncrisis or even precrisis situations of controlled superpower competition, alliance politics calculations repeatedly emerged as the dominant factor dictating partisan behavioral patterns (in areas such as military assistance). During regional conflicts, however, considerations related to patron-client relations, or to intra-alliance politics, comprised but one element within a considerably more complex and multifaceted decision-making process and were on occasion modified by wider, systemic priorities.

The purpose of the following analysis is to elucidate more systematically the recurrent superpower patterns of interaction on the eve of and in the course of severe regional conflicts in the Middle East. Two major conflict episodes will be juxtaposed: the Six Day War of June 1967 and the Yom Kippur War of October 1973. By virtue of their magnitude and ramifications, along with the intensive superpower conflict-management activity they precipitated, these events, although by no means identical, are depicted as the lens through which an entire complex of superpower rules of engagement and norms of behavior can be illuminated and explained.

The Structure of Precrisis and Crisis Superpower Diplomacy

A juxtaposition of the plethora of noncrisis and even precrisis messages and signals that the superpowers exchanged, or sought to exchange, within the confines of the Arab-Israeli predicament, with those conveyed in the course of the 1967 and 1973 wars, highlights and underscores the unique nature and particular characteristics of superpower bargaining as it developed during the period immediately following the outbreak of hostilities in the Arab-Israeli sphere.

On the eve of the 1967 war, notwithstanding President Lyndon Johnson's request that Moscow caution and restrain its Egyptian ally, the Soviet prewar posture—at least during the early phase of the crisis—remained on the whole partisan and provocative, as Moscow passed on to Egypt misleading information concerning Israel's plan for a large-scale attack on Syria. By transferring to Egypt what may have been merely an Israeli contingency plan (and thus by encouraging President Nasser to take threatening measures against Israel), the Soviet leadership presumably sought to demonstrate its loyalty to the Syrians, and thus assigned priority, at least at the outset of the crisis, to patron-client considerations over the complex of factors and concerns related to global, systemic stability.[12]

Six years later, notwithstanding the emerging climate of détente and the conclusion, in May 1972, of the Basic Principles Agreement between the superpowers, the actual dynamics of superpower relations in the Middle East were determined—during the period preceding the outbreak of the Yom Kippur War of October 1973—by the fact that both sides continuously had in this locale very strong, if not vital, interests, on the relative balance of which they were unable to agree.[13] Thus, although both parties signed a set of general working principles for an overall Middle East settlement (in addition to the Basic Principles Agreement) at the May 1972 Moscow summit, this ambiguous document quickly proved to be merely a facade under the cover of which both superpowers have consistently sought unilateral regional advantages.[14]

Against this background of incompatible regional objectives and policies, it is clear why the superpowers, on the eve of war, failed to carry out any form of a collaborative crisis avoidance design, instead confining their precrisis activity, particularly in 1973, to the dissemination of highly ambiguous and ambivalent warning signals. Indeed, during the period preceding the 1967 and 1973 wars, this basic ambiguity prevented those warning signals that were transmitted from leading to an open and explicit superpower dialogue. Surrounded by and embedded in a welter of distracting noise of irrelevance (and, in 1967, of deception), these messages could not penetrate the perceptual barriers and screens of preconceptions, expectations, and established beliefs of the other side.[15]

Contrary to this vision of a dyad permeated with confusion, misunderstanding, and ambiguity during noncrisis and precrisis periods, the picture that emerges once an acutely menacing crisis is perceived by both parties is one of relative symmetry and parallelism, which on occasion precipitates limited superpower collaboration. Therefore, a juxtaposition of the predominant precrisis or noncrisis superpower behavioral patterns in the area, with those evident in the course of acutely threatening regional crises and wars, suggests a clear dichotomy in terms of both the structure and content of the strategies and tactics pursued.

Whereas, during the precrisis stage, considerations related to the superpowers' relations with their allies were in general dominant, such considerations were at least partially subordinated to considerations related to global and regional stability, which determined much of the superpowers' behavior during periods of severe regional crisis and war. Specifically, as soon as Washington and Moscow recognized that the ongoing regional conflagration could well be coupled and elevated to the global level, they proceeded rapidly to improve and upgrade their bilateral communication system in the hope of injecting an element of clarity, certainty, and explicitness into a highly complex, emotion-laden regional situation. Indeed, once they perceived the dangers of escalation and the costs of a direct superpower clash—which were inherent in an unabated regional war to which they were inextricably linked as patrons of the protagonists—they took immediate steps to minimize the prospects of misperception and miscalculation.[16]

Thus, in sharp contrast to some of the tentative, unclear, and occasionally obscure messages that the superpowers exchanged before a highly menacing perception of war permeated their respective cognitive maps, superpower crisis signaling was characterized in both episodes by an abiding desire to increase both the salience and credibility of the messages exchanged. For this purpose, special methods and channels of communication were used. Direct communication links between the national leaders of both powers, such as the hot line, continuously augmented and accompanied the more traditional methods of bilateral communication, thus signaling that a dire emergency had arisen.

During the Six Day War, the superpowers resorted to the hot line as a special communication channel as early as June 5 and through it reached a quick understanding on the need to avoid direct involvement and to work jointly for an early cease-fire. On the following day they again resorted to the hot line as the most appropriate means of clarifying intentions and minimizing the shared risks of escalation or misunderstanding. This occurred when Soviet Premier Alexei Kosygin called for an immediate cease-fire and for a U.S. action to halt Israel's advance in the Sinai Peninsula. President Johnson responded quickly on the hot line and recommended that the U.N. Security Council be used as the appropriate mechanism for terminating hostilities (as was subsequently done).[17]

This superpower sensitivity to the dangers of misperception, communication gaps, and bureaucratic procrastination (which are inherent in an exclusive reliance on standard and routine channels and methods of communication during nonroutine periods of acute regional crises) remained unabated throughout the war, with both Washington and Moscow relying on the hot line as an extraordinary, most trusted communication device. (A particularly illuminating illustration of the use of the hot line as an uncertainty-reducing mechanism is provided by the *Liberty* incident of June 8.[18])

In addition to transmitting information and conveying reassurances, superpower communication in June 1967 (both verbal and nonverbal) was designed to deliver warnings. Seeking to clarify and reinforce several tacit rules of superpower regional conduct by explicitly defining its threshold tolerance and limits beyond which it would have to resort to military action in support of a regional ally, the Soviet Union, confronted on June 10 by what was perceived in Moscow as the imminent collapse of its Syrian client, threatened to take "the necessary actions, including military" unless Israel unconditionally halted all operations on the Golan front. Kosygin's warning, which amounted to a signal to Washington of an irrevocable commitment to the Damascus regime, stated further that a "very crucial moment" had arrived and that a "grave catastrophe" lay ahead unless the preservation of the Syrian regime was guaranteed.[19]

Believing that the Kremlin would not acquiesce in the face of the impending destruction of a major local ally, the Johnson administration was quick to adopt a coercive posture toward Israel, designed to compel the government to agree to an immediate cease-fire with Syria. The pressure proved effective, and shortly thereafter, on June 11, the President informed Kosygin of Israel's decision to stop its military advance.

A similar picture of the superpowers' determination to eliminate the screen of distracting and misleading background noise by engaging in an uninterrupted and intensive dialogue at the highest level emerges from an analysis of the Yom Kippur War of October 1973. Seeking to upgrade and improve their communication system, they resorted to the hot line as well as to summit diplomacy as their major communication mechanism. For example, in view of Egypt's rapidly deteriorating military situation, on October 19, Soviet leader Leonid Brezhnev sent an urgent message over the hot line to President Richard Nixon in which he called for immediate negotiations on procedures to end the fighting. The subsequent dispatch of Secretary of State Henry Kissinger to Moscow enabled the parties to engage in direct and uninterrupted bargaining, and thus provided the impetus for a rapid understanding on the parameters of a cease-fire formula.

Furthermore, as has already been shown in the context of the Six Day War, superpower communication during the confrontational phase of the crisis was intended to reinforce a major norm of conduct, namely, the recognized right of a superpower to intervene in a regional war in order to save its local ally from defeat. When the regional ally of a superpower is faced with imminent defeat, "the balance of interests clearly shifts in favour of the superpower backing the regional actor that is in serious difficulty, making it both 'legitimate' and credible that the superpower would intervene, if necessary [on its behalf]."[20] Indeed, for all its menacing nature, the fact that the Soviet threat to intervene in the 1967 war was directly communicated to the United States at all, and that it was not carried out automatically as soon as a profound and acute threat to basic Soviet values and strategic objectives was diagnosed, indicates that the Soviets were anxious to avoid any unilateral, irrevocable military commitment or move, which would have precipitated a deepening superpower retaliation.

In the context of the 1973 war, a similar illustration of this Soviet propensity to manipulate the risk of escalation in situations where a regional ally is on the verge of a complete military collapse is provided by Brezhnev's October 24 message to Nixon. As was the case with Kosygin's dispatch of June 10, 1967, Brezhnev's note was quite explicit in threatening to intervene unilaterally in order to impose a cease-fire and thus prevent the destruction of the encircled Egyptian Third Army unless the United States agreed to the dispatch to Egypt of "Soviet and American military contingents to ensure the implementation of the Security Council cease-fire resolutions." Brezhnev's threat precipitated an equally explicit message from Nixon, in which a unilateral superpower military action was categorically and unequivocally rejected (concurrent with this response, a worldwide military alert was declared by the United States).[21]

Notwithstanding these highly threatening and conflictual interactions, it is clear that the Soviet warning (which was augmented by a variety of communication moves) was essentially a deterrent move, calculated to achieve "maximum impact on Israeli decisions to cease hostilities." As such, it appears as "a classic instance of the demonstrative manipulation of military force for political ends."[22] Indeed, seeking to define the boundaries or thresholds of its tolerance, Moscow still avoided any irreversible military move in the face of highly adverse regional circumstances, and thus resorted to a belligerent, combative language as a substitute for the actual use of force.

Viewed from this perspective, the welter of communication moves that supplemented Moscow's harsh rhetoric (which included the alert of the airborne troups command, the preparation of aircraft for the transport of Soviet troops, and the strengthening of the Soviet naval force in the Mediterranean) amounted to additional warning signals, intended to lend both salience and credibility to Brezhnev's October 24 verbal message. Hoping that these demonstrative, highly visible actions would prompt Washington to intensify the pressure on Israel to agree to an immediate cease-fire without destroying the encircled Egyptian Third Army, Moscow's preparatory actions thus formed "a signal of intent" without commiting the Soviets to any final irrevocable commitment.[23]

Against this background it is clear that behind the facade of saber rattling and the plethora of coercive and deterring threats by the superpowers (and in particular by the Soviet Union), both consistently attempted in 1967 and 1973 to preserve for themselves a margin of maneuverability so as to maximize the chances of avoiding disaster. In other words, the coercive threats and warnings (both verbal and non-verbal) were always moderated by the parties' overriding desire to avoid any irreversible committal moves that were bound to trigger highly dangerous counter-commitments.

The Content of Precrisis and Crisis Superpower Diplomacy

The central finding that emerges from the foregoing structural analysis of the recurrent predominant communication patterns in both episodes is that the cluster of considerations derived from the goal of minimizing the risks of direct confrontation overshadowed the complex of factors related to the objective of securing victory for regional allies. A similar picture of the superpowers' determination to scrupulously refrain from crossing the threshold between coercion and violence appears when the overall content of the messages exchanged is examined.

A comparative analysis of the cases of 1967 and 1973 indicates that in both, each superpower was confronted with essentially the same policy dilemma: how far to go in assisting its local ally without risking a dangerous confrontation.[24] In this context, considerations related to alliance politics and to the desire of both global powers to project an image of resolve by honoring either formal or implicit commitments to their regional clients occasionally contradicted considerations pertaining to the stability of both the global international system and the Middle East subsystem.

In seeking to reconcile this recurrent contradiction between their roles as patrons and superpowers, the two parties were in general predisposed to assign priority to the cluster of global-systemic considerations over those related to alliance politics.[25] It was only during the climatic confrontational phases of each crisis, however, that one of them—the United States—was induced to curb its ally for the sake of reducing the risk of global instability.[26]

Indications of parallel superpower crisis behavior (which on occasion has led to collaborative action) in the context of the two cases under review abound. During the Six Day War, for example, both parties expressed an intention to work for a cease-fire as early as June 5. Notwithstanding this mutual wish to see the war terminated as soon as possible, the Soviets (who feared not only a possible escalation but a military debacle for their regional clients unless it was brought to a rapid conclusion) were unable to persuade Egypt to stop the fighting. It was only in the course of the following day, in view of Egypt's rapidly deteriorating military situation, that Moscow opted to translate its initial understanding with Washington into a concrete U.N. Security Council resolution, which called for a cease-fire in place. On June 8, facing a desperate military situation, Egypt finally yielded to continued Soviet pressure and accepted an unconditional cease-fire.[27]

Concurrent with this search for an early cease-fire, the superpowers reached an understanding that they would refrain from intervening militarily in the conflict. Since neither the United States nor the Soviet Union considered the interests involved worth a world war, their supreme concern at this stage of the crisis was to avoid a direct confrontation. Thus, each managed, through formal and informal contacts, to communicate to the other that it did not intend to intervene directly provided the other side followed a similar course. This relationship of mutual restraint was established as soon as the war started. It was bolstered, not undermined, by various declarations of support of the clients, as well as by warnings issued by each the superpower to the other side and nonverbal gestures such as naval movements. The distinction between coercive tactics and violent actions was thus scrupulously maintained.[28]

While anxious to avoid a major war, the Soviet Union also was motivated in its persistent support of an early cease-fire by a growing fear that an overwhelming defeat of its Egyptian ally might adversely affect its prestige and reputation as a patron. In this respect, and in the context of Soviet-Egyptian and Soviet-Syrian relations, considerations pertaining to patron-client relations further reinforced and merged with a cluster of global concerns and priorities.

Turning to the U.S.-Israeli dyad, it is clear that as the war progressed, increasing signs of friction and disunity clouded the scene. Ultimately, in view of the rapid Israeli advances in the Golan Heights area and the subsequent Soviet warning that it would intervene unilaterally unless Israel unconditionally halted all operations, the Johnson administration, on June 10, 1967, resorted to coercive tactics vis-à-vis its Israeli ally. Convinced that the Kremlin would not acquiesce in the face of the complete military defeat of yet another of its regional clients and anxious to defuse a highly dangerous situation, Washington's high-policy elite moved apace to press Israel to stop its military campaign without delay.

Thus, the complex of considerations that were inextricably linked to the U.S.-Israeli dyad was subordinated to those pertaining to U.S.-Soviet relations. Concern for global and regional stability clearly took precedence over the requirements and needs of the U.S.-Israeli informal alliance. In other words, in view of the apparent incompatibility between its role as superpower and that of patron, the Johnson administration ultimately opted to sacrifice alliance politics calculations for the sake of averting a direct superpower confrontation.[29]

As soon as Kosygin's warning on June 10 reached Washington, both the White House and the State Department launched an intensive effort "to convince Israel to work out an effective cease-fire with Syria."[30] As the president concedes in his memoirs, "every diplomatic resource" was used by the administration to ensure "that the Israelis would implement the ceasefire resolution."[31] The pressure proved effective, and all fighting on the Syrian front came to a halt on June 11.

A similar picture of concerted as well as uncoordinated parallel superpower crisis behavior emerges from an analysis of the 1973 war. Overall, not only did the superpowers share the objective of preventing the war from engulfing them directly, but they were anxious not to let the conflagration severely damage the fragile détente structure. Thus, as early as October 7, Nixon and Brezhnev exchanged messages in which they called for mutual restraint. On numerous occasions thereafter, the two superpowers directly or implicitly reiterated their desire to contain the crisis and avoid escalation. The only deviation from this pattern was the sharp confrontation of October 24–25, which was precipitated by Brezhnev's threats to intervene unilaterally (which, in turn, led to the U.S. worldwide alert). As was the case in the 1967 war, only when the Soviet leadership was faced with the prospects of a humiliating defeat of a regional client did it deliberately and self-consciously manipulate the risk of superpower confrontation through its threats of military intervention.[32]

During earlier phases of the war, however, both Washington and Moscow operated cautiously and, while resupplying their local allies, attempted to terminate the fighting (albeit in ways that were capable with their clients' interests and objectives). Seeking to avoid the destabilizing effects and ramifications of a prolonged war, while at the same time anxious to consolidate Egypt's initial gains in the war by securing an early cease-fire before the pendulum could swing in Israel's favor, Soviet Ambassador to Egypt Vinogradov urged President Sadat to agree to a cease-fire in place as early as the evening of October 6. Confronted with an Egyptian refusal, the Soviets nonetheless resumed their efforts the following evening. Maintaining that the war had already succeeded in changing the balance of political and military power in the region, Vinogradov strongly recommended that Egypt agree to terminate the fighting, but again to no avail.[33]

Not until October 16, in the wake of the failure of Egypt's October 14 offensive toward the Mitla and Gidi passes (at the cost to Egypt of more than two hundred tanks),[34] did the Soviets decide to intensify the pressure for a rapid cease-fire. On the following day, in view of an urgent Soviet appeal, Secretary of State Kissinger proceeded to Moscow in order to coordinate efforts for terminating the war. On October 22 Kissinger and Brezhnev agreed to a simple cease-fire-in-place, coupled with a call for the implementation of U.N. Security Council Resolution 242 and, at U.S. insistence, to negotiations between the parties under appropriate auspices.[35] All regional protagonists agreed to this formula, although Israel, which needed additional time to complete its offensive on the southern front, did so most reluctantly.[36]

Finally, as was the case in 1967, the administration exerted considerable pressure on Israel, demanding that it refrain from any additional violations of the cease-fire agreement and immediately halt all fighting in the wake of Brezhnev's threat of October 24 to intervene unilaterally in the war. The U.S. deterring reaction to this threat (the worldwide alert) was thus coupled with a coercive posture toward Israel designed to compel it to stop its advance and to permit the resupply of the encircled Third Army. On October 26 Kissinger warned Israeli Ambassador Dinitz that "there was a limit beyond which we could not be pushed" by Israel, maintaining further that the United States would not permit the destruction of the Third Army.[37]

Although alliance politics considerations were once again subordinated in this confrontational phase of the crisis to the overriding U.S. concern for global stability, this incompatibility between the roles of superpower and patron is valid only within the framework of U.S.-Israeli relations. In this context an element of strain was indeed injected into an essentially consensual dyad, with Israel reacting with frustration and disenchantment in the face of an intensive, highly coercive U.S. effort to deny it a decisive victory.

Viewed from a different perspective, however, Kissinger's diplomatic drive of late October to ensure that the war was not terminated in an asymmetrical fashion (as was the case in 1967) was fully compatible with his ambitious design to bring about a reversal of regional alliances by demonstrating to President Sadat the advantages inherent in a realignment with the United States.[38] In this respect, while the alliance with Israel was clearly compromised, it was subordinated both to the compelling globel need to minimize the risks of superpower confrontation and to the desire to impress upon Egypt the fact that the United States was the only power possessing adequate diplomatic leverage vis-à-vis Israel.

Alliance calculations and considerations, albeit of a more subtle nature, thus merged with and further reinforced the cluster of considerations pertaining to the overall stability of the global international system.

Crisis Management and Conflict Resolution

It is precisely in this area of alliance politics that the distinction between conflict management activity and conflict resolution behavior is most significant. For if one is to proceed beyond the constrained, delimited parameters of superpower crisis collaboration (which is intended to defuse acutely threatening regional conflagrations) and tackle head-on the deep-rooted origins of regional turbulence and cleavage, the recurrent superpower propensity during a crisis to ultimately subordinate support for regional allies to the need to preserve global stability must be extended and applied as a prerequisite to the area of crisis prevention and, even more importantly, to the sphere of conflict resolution. In other words, for any superpower peacemaking drive to have any prospect of success, it is essential that both Washington and Moscow be prepared (and capable) to exert upon their respective allies and clients pressures of the same magnitude and order as were exercised during the confrontational phase of the 1967 and 1973 wars.

However, in view of the historical record and the structural systemic realities (which are conducive to the establishment and maintenance of "influence parity" relationships between the superpowers and their regional allies),[39] the prospects of any spillover from the realm of conflict management to the wider area of conflict resolution are fraught with uncertainty and doubt. Indeed, a review of some of the noncrisis superpower peacemaking moves and initiatives on the Arab-Israeli front clearly demonstrates that on those rare occasions (such as in the case of the joint U.S.-Soviet communique of October 1, 1977) when the two global sides managed to set aside their differences and jointly define the parameters of a Middle East settlement, they were unable to control their allies' behavior completely or to press efforts to impose a settlement. Confronted with a recalcitrant, defiant regional environment (as well as with a hostile domestic environment, in the case of the United States), whose major actors remained adamantly and irrevocably opposed to the superpowers' designs, they were forced to reconsider their priorities and ultimately abandon their collaborative plans.

In view of the superpowers' inability in a variety of noncrisis situations to impose their will on their regional clients, it is clear why the issue of conflict or crisis management in the Middle East can be thought of as an isolated and deviant facet of superpower relations. To rephrase the opening proposition, it can therefore be argued that situations of conflict management, and in particular their most confrontational phase, constitute an exception more than an extension of the recurrent prevalent noncrisis superpower behavioral patterns.

By virtue of their magnitude and potentially destabilizing systemic ramifications, such acutely threatening episodes comprise the compelling incentive for superpower action, which is incompatible with certain alliance commitments and partisan goals. Thus it is only against the backdrop of a highly threatening regional conflict that a departure from certain established patron-client modes of behavior is likely to occur. In the absence of this unique setting, and as long as the overall structure of the international system remains essentially bipolar, it is safe to expect that the United States and the Soviet Union will find the task of jointly establishing an explicit, formal, and comprehensive regional system of crisis avoidance and conflict resolution a difficult, if not an insurmountable, one.

Thus, at least in the foreseeable future, the superpowers will continue to rely largely on certain partial, tacit understandings and informal patterns of restraint in approaching the Arab-Israeli predicament.[40] The fact that such norms are invariably precarious, unstable, and uncertain in anything but the short run guarantees that the Middle East will continue to be permeated with tension and fraught with misunderstanding and animosity.

Notes

1. Alexander L. George, "Crisis Prevention Reexamined," in Alexander L. George, ed., *Managing U.S.-Soviet Rivalry: Problems of Crisis Prevention* (Boulder, CO: Westview Press, 1983), p. 377.

2. *Ibid.*, pp. 381–382.

3. Phil Williams, *Crisis Management: Confrontation and Diplomacy in the Nuclear Age* (London: Martin Robertson, 1976), pp. 102, 147, 195.

4. Glenn H. Snyder and Paul Diesing, *Conflict Among Nations: Bargaining, Decision Making and System Structure in International Crisis* (Princeton, NJ: Princeton University Press, 1977), pp. 209–243.

5. President Reagan's News Conference of February 21, 1985. For the full text of the President's words see: "President's News Conference or Foreign and Domestic Issues," *The New York Times*, 22 February 1985, p. A14. It is interesting to note that on February 15, 1985 (on the eve of the Vienna metting), State Department spokesman Bernard Kalb refused even to label the talks as negotiations. Kalb added, "These talks are not the precursor of any agreements, nor are they going to seek any agreements in Vienna." The statement is quoted in Bernard Gwertzman, "U.S. Tells Syria of Appreciation in Hostage Case," *The New York Times*, 16 February 1985, pp. A1–A2.

6. Alexander L. George, "Political Crises," in Joseph S. Nye, Jr., ed., *The Making of America's Soviet Policy* (New Haven, CT: Yale University Press, 1984), p. 150. See also Yair Evron, "Great Powers' Military Intervention in the Middle East," in Milton Leitenberg and Gabriel Sheffer, eds., *Great Power Intervention in the Middle East* (New York: Pergamon Press, 1979), pp. 22–23; Raymond Cohen, *International Politics: The Rules of the Game* (London: Longman, 1981), p. 57.

7. Evron, "Great Powers' Military Intervention," p. 23.

8. Alexander L. George, "Mechanisms for Moderating Superpower Competition," *AEI Foreign Policy and Defense Review* 6 (no. 1, 1986), p. 7.

9. The terminology in this section is based on Snyder and Diesing, *Conflict Among Nations*, pp. 208, 446–450.

10. Alexander L. George, "Crisis Management: The Interaction of Political and Military Considerations," *Survival* 26 (September/October 1984), pp. 231–233.

11. Snyder and Diesing, *Conflict Among Nations*, p. 447. See also Janice Gross Stein, "Proxy Wars—How Superpowers End Them: The Diplomacy of War Termination in the Middle East," *International Journal* 35 (Summer 1980), pp. 488–489.

12. Carsten Hollbraad, *The Superpowers and International Conflict* (New York: St. Martin's Press, 1979), pp. 79–84.

13. George, "Crisis Prevention Reexamined," pp. 381–382.

14. Alexander L. George, "Détente: The Search for a 'Constructive' Relationship," in George, *Managing U.S.-Soviet Rivalry*, p. 24.

15. Major illustrations of this communication failure are provided by Brezhnev's unsuccesful attempt of May 1973 to warn Nixon about the imminent danger of war in the Middle East and Gromyko's similarly ambiguous warning of September 25, 1973.

16. Alan Dowty, *Middle East Crisis: U.S. Decision Making in 1956, 1970, and 1973* (Berkeley, CA: University of California Press), p. 307.

17. Hollbraad, *The Superpowers and International Conflict*, pp. 88–89.

18. Lyndon Baines Johnson, *The Vantage Point: Perspectives of the Presidency, 1963–1969* (New York: Holt, Rinehart and Winston, 1971), pp. 300–301; Steven L. Spiegel, *The Other Arab-Israeli Conflict: Making America's Middle East Policy, From Truman to Reagan* (Chicago: The University of Chicago Press, 1985), p. 151.

19. Johnson, *Vantage Point*, pp. 301–302.

20. George, "Mechanisms for Moderating Superpower Competition," p. 9.

21. Henry Kissinger, *Years of Upheaval* (Boston: Little, Brown, 1982), pp. 583–584, 591.

22. Cohen, *The Rules of the Game*, p. 59.

23. Williams, *Crisis Management,* p. 142.

24. George, "Crisis Prevention Reexamined," p. 377.

25. Stein, "Proxy Wars," pp. 479, 489, 494–495.

26. George, "Political Crises," p. 135.

27. Johnson, *Vantage Point,* p. 297; Stein, "Proxy Wars," p. 389.

28. Hollbraad, *The Superpowers and International Conflict,* pp. 84, 88; William B. Quandt, *Decade of Decisions: American Policy Toward the Arab-Israel Conflict, 1967–1976* (Berkeley, CA: University of California Press, 1977), pp. 60–61.

29. Stein, "Proxy Wars," pp. 494–495.

30. Johnson, *Vantage Point,* p. 301.

31. *Ibid.*

32. Stein, "Proxy Wars," pp. 494–495.

33. *Ibid.,* pp. 500–501.

34. Quandt, *Decade of Decisions,* p. 186; Spiegel, *The Other Arab-Israeli Conflict,* p. 250.

35. Quandt, *Decade of Decisions,* p. 192.

36. Spiegel, *The Other Arab-Israeli Conflict,* p. 261.

37. Kissinger, *Years of Upheaval,* pp. 602–609.

38. Alexander L. George, "The Arab-Israeli War of October 1973: Origins and Impact," in his *Managing U.S.-Soviet Rivalry,* pp. 147, 149.

39. Christopher C. Shoemaker and John Spanier, *Patron-Client State Relationships: Multilateral Crises in the Nuclear Age* (New York: Praeger, 1984), pp. 33–34.

40. Cohen, *The Rules of the Game,* p. 52; Joanne Gowa and Nils H. Wessell, *Ground Rules: Soviet and American Involvement in Regional Conflicts* (Philadelphia: Foreign Policy Research Institute, 1982), p. 3.

Part IX
Conclusion

22
Soviet-American Competition in the Middle East

Aharon Yariv

Soviet-American competition in the Middle East dates back to the mid-1950s, although the United States displayed a keen interest in Saudi oil much earlier. Russia also had an imperial interest in the area, which predates the United States by far, but the Soviet Union entered the competition directly and openly only in 1955, with the so-called Czech-Egyptian arms deal. Since its beginning, Soviet-American competition in the Middle East has been part and parcel of their global struggle, in which coexistence is accepted while a zero-sum game is played by both sides.

The superpowers' strong interest in the area is due to the region's location, its resources and their salience in the global struggle, and the absence of clearly defined spheres of influence. The significant factors include, first and foremost, oil and then the area's position as the nexus of global communications, its proximity to the Soviet Union's southern borders and NATO's southern flank, its function as a bridge to Africa, its market potential, and last but not least, the role of Middle Eastern states in the Third World.

The Soviet Union possesses the advantage of proximity, but that does not necessarily translate into directly concrete gains, as is clearly shown by the Soviets' spotty record in the Middle East over the past three decades. Heavyhandedness has not been unique to the Soviets, although it has been much more pronounced on their side than on the side of the Americans.

The Soviet military presence in the area is significant, comprising naval forces, bases, facilities, advisors, and experts. But the United States also maintains a relatively strong military capability in the Middle East. The establishment of Central Command, with its Rapid Deployment Force, as well as the various bases at U.S. disposal in the Middle East and the fact that these are all backed by the overall U.S. strategic deterrent, compensate for the great distance of the United States from the area. Considering the changes taking place in the Soviet Union with regard to power projection and the role of the navy—both of which are increasingly limited—the U.S. military posture should more than balance the Soviets'.

For obvious reasons, the Soviet Union appeals more to radical regimes and elements such as Syria, Libya, South Yemen, and the Palestine Liberation Organization (PLO), whereas the United States appeals mainly to more moderate and conservative regimes such as Saudi Arabia, Jordan, and Egypt. Both superpowers have experienced serious ups and downs in their patron-client relationships with the states in the area; Egypt is a glaring example for both superpowers. In this respect, the United States enjoys a certain advantage over the Soviets due to Israel's inevitable and proven reliability. From the superpowers' point of view, their influence over their respective clients is limited by the fact that these clients tend to follow their national priorities and interests over those of their respective patrons. Syria's heavy involvement in Lebanon in 1976 against the wishes of the Soviets is a case in point, as is the extension of Israeli law over the Golan Heights in 1981 vis-à-vis the United States. Still other instances abound, and this often goes even farther, such as when a superpower feels constrained to support the actions of a client, at least up to a certain point.

Thus, war between superpower clients can be and has been initiated without the prior consent, although generally not without the prior knowledge, of the relevant patron, who probably also endowed his client with the military capability to start such a war. A patron may feel constrained from stopping his client early on, and this can increase the risk of escalation and confrontation. So far, when this risk has become perceived and palpable, the two superpowers have succeeded, with different degrees of difficulty, in managing the crisis and finding a common formula for its resolution. In working out this formula, each superpower naturally acts according to its own interests, taking into account the interests of its client that are consonant with the current military situation. This happened in 1956, 1967, the 1969–1970 War of Attrition, the brief 1970 Syrian-Jordanian conflict, the 1973 Yom Kippur War, and the 1982 Lebanon war—an impressive record of successful superpower crisis management and resolution and confrontation avoidance. Unfortunately, this record has not been matched by an ability to prevent most conflicts. Prior concerted superpower efforts necessary for crisis prevention in many cases surpassed the parameters determined by the combined national interests of patron and client. In those cases where these parameters can coincide, such as in Syrian-Israeli relations, superpower cooperation for crisis prevention can succeed, and such joint efforts can be mutual (such as a U.S.-Soviet effort) or of a superpower–"other client" nature (such as U.S.-Syrian or U.S.-Israeli). In this context of crisis management, the United States has been playing the leading role.

Clearly, both superpowers have a strong interest in crisis management, since their main (but not sole) motive is to avoid escalation and confrontation. This is not the case as far as conflict resolution is concerned, and the differing and conflicting interests of both patrons and clients render the issue much more complex. The Arab-Israeli conflict clearly attests to this. The Iran-Iraq conflict, although of a different nature, provides further evidence of superpower superiority in crisis management over conflict resolution.

As for the Arab-Israeli conflict, the United States has a definite advantage over the Soviet Union because it is able to deal with both parties. Therefore, it has been playing a leading role in everything concerning the peace process. One cannot deny the Soviets' spoiler role, however, mainly because of the Soviets' influence over the PLO and Syria, and one can assume that they did play a part in the failure of the 1982 Reagan plan. Once also can assume that in the future the Soviets will do their best to prevent the resolution of the Arab-Israeli conflict by a Pax Americana.

Another aspect of the Arab-Israeli conflict concerns direct superpower military involvement. Soviet military involvement in Egypt in 1970 and that of the United States in Lebanon in 1982–83 clearly point to the risk entailed when the application of limited force is counterproductive and yet the use of sufficient force can lead to confrontation. Both superpowers' patron-client relationships in the area are based on political, strategic, military, and economic support. As mentioned before, the nature of the client's political regime to a large degree determines its choice of patron. This already endows the United States with a certain advantage in the area. As to the strategic element, both superpowers have to contend with the prevalent memories of colonial times, reflected in a sensitivity to direct superpower presence in the region and a high-profile patron military presence. As a result, no lasting regional strategic structure has been established thus far. In the area of economic and technological (nonmilitary) aid, the United States again has a clear advantage. The Soviets have performed poorly, thus helping to bring about (together with political, strategic, and military support) the present overall U.S. superiority in the competition.

As far as military support—mainly arms transfers—is concerned, there are no constraints except financial ones on the client's side, while there are a number on the patron's side, including political (especially for the United States) and financial contraints and the need to maintain a certain balance among the various recipients. Unfortunately (although inevitably), arms transfers are the main instrument of superpower policy in the Middle East, and both superpowers employ this instrument on a massive scale. Between 1974 and 1983, military assistance deliveries to the Middle East, including Iran, totaled about $180 billion in 1985 dollars (about $70 billion from 1974 to 1978 and $110 billion from 1979 to 1983). The lion's share was obtained from the superpowers (about 77 percent in the period 1974–1978 and about 50 percent in the period 1979–1983). The rest was acquired from Western Europe (France, the United Kingdom, West Germany and Italy)—15 percent in 1974–1978 and approximately 27 percent in 1979–1983—and from the People's Republic of China and the Soviet bloc countries (Czechoslovakia, Rumania, and Poland)—more than 1.2 percent in 1974–1978 and 6 percent in 1979–1983. The growing share of other powers in arms transfers is due to increased availability as well as to the Arab diversification of their armament sources. All this does not decrease the importance of arms transfers as an instrument in the superpower competition, but it does increase the room for maneuvering by clients in regards to their particular patron and can thereby limit the latter's influence.

Besides the question of quantitative escalation (which was even steeper in 1984–1986), the qualitative, high-technology factor also plays an important role, escalating the per unit cost, with important implications for client and patron. To a large degree, the quantitative and qualitative escalation since 1974 has been fueled by petrodollars and the need to recycle them. The recent drop in oil prices has already started to bring about a certain slowdown, although not a radical change. In view of Soviet economic difficulties, the United States enjoys an advantage in this sphere as well, but it has to contend with the impact of high-technology arms transfers on the local balance of power, especially concerning the Arab-Israeli balance. The Soviet need for hard currency will not permit it to cut arms transfers severely in the foreseeable future. The benefits that accrue to both superpowers from testing their weapons systems on the Middle Eastern battlefield is counterbalanced by the increased potential for instability that these weapons can bring to the area and by the competition between the military and civilian sectors for restricted technological resources. The latter presents a problem to both patrons' clients, except perhaps Israel.

Considering the inherent instability of the region and the active and latent conflicts, the huge amounts of sophisticated weapons present a serious danger to regional and international security. This danger is even more difficult to overcome due to the large number of suppliers. It could, perhaps, be successfully confronted by patient efforts, based on a prior in principle agreement between the United States and the Soviet Union, to be followed by other suppliers. Unfortunately, arms transfers constitute an important source of hard currency, which might make the Soviet Union, as well as other suppliers, reluctant to go along with these restrictions, especially if the Iran-Iraq war drags on, with its attendant threats to neighboring states and a consequent increasing interest in arms acquisitions.

Connected with arms transfers is the danger linked to the massive arms transfers, both quantitatively and qualitatively, from the Soviet Union to Syria. These serve Assad's highly touted doctrine of strategic parity, as it permits a strong increase in the Syrian armed forces' order of battle and their being equipped with sophisticated weapons systems. Thus, the threat of a Syrian-Israeli war is increased and, with it, the risk of a superpower confrontation.

Another important aspect of the superpower competition is terrorism. This, of course, is an international problem. Nevertheless, the Middle East as a region and Middle Eastern terrorist organizations (mainly Palestinian and Shiite ones) play a major role. The growing ferocity of terrorist incidents, in particular international ones, and the relatively new phenomenon of state-supported terrorism, where once again the central actors are from the Middle East (Syria, Iran, and Libya), have emphasized the dangerous importance of the issue. In these cases, however, there is no symmetry between the superpowers. True, for both countries it is a question of *how*, but for the United States, a target of terrorism, it is "how to defend and how to prevent," while for the Soviets it is "how to support and gain or maintain clients." The Soviets do not have any direct control over the terrorist organizations they support and are generally not involved in any terrorist operations. This support extends mainly to politics, training, and arms, and except for two incidents in Lebanon, no Soviet targets have been attacked—a fact that speaks for itself.

Under the guidance of President Reagan and Secretary of State Shultz, the present U.S. administration has taken a strong stand on terrorism, which, among other things, led to the air attack on Libya in 1986. It seems that the U.S. stand, its activity, and the physcial blow delivered to Libya also served as a background to Britain's sharp action against Syria in the wake of the Hindawi trial. This trial, as well as that of his brother in West Germany, in which the latter was accused of intending to blow up an El-Al plane, highlighted Syria's role in terrorism, as a clear connection between Syrian intelligence and the accused was revealed. Hindawi was sentenced to 45 years in prison, and Britain severed its diplomatic relationship with Syria. Assad's Syria is the Soviet Union's most important client in the region. Should Syria persist in its role as an actor in international terrorism, including acts against U.S. targets, this could lead to a U.S. military reaction. As Soviet and U.S. interests regarding terrorism generally—and in the case of Syria in particular—are diametrically opposed, this could lead to a dangerous confrontation. Such a possibility might seriously influence U.S. deliberations and restrain its actions. On the other hand, Syria might reduce its role in terrorism and might be "encouraged" by the Soviets to do so.

Another potential peril lies in the Iran-Iraq war. As an Iraqi victory seems to be out of the question, the superpower interests are more or less identical, up to a point: to prevent an Iraq collapse as well as an Iranian victory. Iraq is a Soviet client, but in view of Iran's present stance and in view of the dangers Iraq and the Gulf states supporting it are facing, the United States has adopted a tilt towards it. At the same time each superpower wants to prevent a post-Khomeini Iran from becoming the other's client, and while it is possible that such a regime will continue Iran's present neutralist stance, it is not impossible that a situation will arise in which Iran will be up for grabs. No doubt the competition for such a prize may be hot, leading to a confrontation.

Recent revelations and events have shown the continued U.S. and Soviet interest in the other's involvement in the Gulf war. The Soviets continue to supply massive amounts of arms to the Iraqis and have recently signed a trade agreement with Iran. The United States has undertaken a number of arms deals, which were destined, according to the President, to serve long-range strategic interests. At the same time, the United States supplied Iraq with intelligence useful in its air attacks on Iran to avoid an Iraqi defeat. Evidently, therefore, there are common interests between the two superpowers—that there be neither an Iranian nor an Iraqi victory and that each superpower preserves its chances for a future patron-client relationship.

These thorny issues (arms transfers, Syria, terrorism, the Iran-Iraq war) emphasize the importance and the urgency of promoting the Arab-Israeli peace process and of the U.S. role. The U.S. advantage in this context has already been mentioned. Its relations with Israel are closer than ever, especially due to the U.S.-Israeli strategic understanding. Yet the United States also has the tools to deter Arab aggression and can, if needed, take advantage of Israel's heavy dependence on it. Both these factors can be conducive to the promotion of the peace process, although they require that the leaderships of both patron and client be finely attuned to one another.

Real progress in the peace process depends to a large degree on the possibility of solving the Palestinian problem, which must involve the PLO and Syria—a feat that perhaps cannot be accomplished without the participation of the Soviet Union.

Here we come to the Soviet disadvantage of one-sidedness—that is, the problem of talking only to the Arab side. With Israeli readiness to consider international accompaniment to peace talks, and with various signs pointing to the possibility of the Soviets being prepared to start rebuilding relations with Israel, overcoming that disadvantage may be feasible. Nevertheless, Soviet participation in the peace process—that is, at an international conference—is not dependent on Israeli consent alone but is linked to Israeli, Soviet, and U.S. attitudes. Progress in the area of U.S.-Soviet strategic relations is the *conditio sine qua non* for serious progress in the peace process.

If an overall U.S.-Soviet agreement on the strategic issues is reached, then it might lead to success in the peace process and eventually open the way to an agreement on arms transfers. Such achievements might moderate the struggle between the superpowers in the region, even though it will not eliminate it—if for no other reason than that local conflicts will continue to persist and upheavals will continue to occur. Oil, with all its associated problems, could again become a critical issue in the 1990s. Nevertheless, taking all pertinent factors into account, the United States should be able to maintain its present advantage in the competition.

At present, after the Reykjavik summit meeting in November 1986, U.S.-Soviet relations are not exactly at their best, and we do not yet know whether there will be another summit meeting and what will happen there. The importance of such a meeting in November 1987 and its consequences need not be stressed. If successful, it also will influence superpower competition in the Middle East and help propel the peace process on its course. Failure will seriously slow down any efforts to advance the process and will increase the danger of war. Even were a summit to occur and be crowned with success, however, it would not necessarily bring about an abrupt and all-encompassing change in superpower competition in the Middle East. In that case, one should expect emerging nuances, gradual changes, and a slowly improving climate, and under these circumstances, a nimble adaptation of policy and its mutual coordination will be of great importance.

For the foreseeable future, Soviet-American competition in the Middle East will continue. The United States should be able to maintain its present advantage even in light of the spirited activity by the Gorbachev regime in developing the area, with the caveat, so characteristic of the region, of some unforeseen and far-reaching local change.

Index

About the Contributors

Abraham S. Becker, staff member of The RAND Corporation in Santa Monica, California, since 1957, is now Senior Economist and Associate Director of the National Security Strategies Program. He has also served as visiting professor of economics at UCLA in 1985 and 1987 (also 1963, 1967, 1968, 1970). He has also been a consultant to the CIA and the ACDA, and a U.S. member of the United Nations Expert Group on Reduction of Military Budgets, in 1974 and 1986. His publications include *Economic Relations with the USSR: Issues for the Western Alliance* editor and contributor, (Lexington Books, 1983) "Sitting on Bayonets: The Slowdown of Soviet Defense Spending," in R. Kolkowicz and E. Mickiewicz, eds., *The Soviet Calculus of Nuclear War,* (Lexington Books, 1986); "U.S.– Soviet Trade and East-West Trade Policy," in A. L. Horelick, ed., *U.S.-Soviet Relations: The Next Phase,* (Cornell University Press, 1986); and "The Soviet Union and the Third World: The Economic Dimension" *Soviet Economy* 2:3 (July-September 1986).

Abraham Ben-Zvi is an associate professor in the Department of Political Science and a senior researcher at the Jaffee Center of Strategic Studies, Tel Aviv University. Professor Ben-Zvi received his Ph.D. from the University of Chicago in 1973 and has published extensively on issues related to surprise attack, threat, perception, and U.S. foreign policy. His most recent book is *The American Approach to Superpower Cooperation 1973-1986* (Westview Press, 1986).

Shai Feldman is a senior research associate at Tel Aviv University's Jaffee Center for Strategic Studies (JCSS). He is a graduate of the Hebrew University of Jerusalem and received his Ph.D. from the University of California, Berkeley. Among Dr. Feldman's publications are *Israeli Nuclear Deterrence: A Strategy for the 1980s* (Columbia University Press, 1983) and *Consensus, Deception, and War: Israel in Lebanon* (JCSS, 1984).

Francis Fukuyama is a member of the Political Science Department at The RAND Corporation in Santa Monica, California. He also served on the Policy Planning Staff at the U.S. Department of State in 1981–1982.

Dore Gold is a senior research associate at the Jaffee Center for Strategic Studies at Tel Aviv University, where he specializes in U.S. strategic interaction with the Middle East. He is the author of numerous studies on U.S. national security policy, including the Strategic Defense Initiative (SDI), rapid deployment problems in the Middle East, and terrorism. He is a regular contributor to the Moshe Dayan Center's *Middle East Contemporary Survey*, writing on regional and international developments in the Persian Gulf states.

Robert E. Harkavy is a professor of political science at The Pennsylvania State University. He has served on the Atomic Energy Commission and the Arms Control and Disarmament Agency and was recently a visiting research professor at the U.S. Army War College. He is currently a consultant to the Office of the Secretary of Defense.

Brian M. Jenkins, head of The RAND Corporations's Political Science Department, is one of the world's leading authorities on international terrorism. He has served as a consultant to a number of U.S. government agencies and major corporations and is the author or coauthor of more than a hundred RAND research reports and papers on various aspects of terrorism. He also is the author of *International Terrorism: A New Mode of Conflict* (Crescent Publications, 1975) and the editor and coauthor of *Terrorism and Personal Protection* (Butterworth Publishers, 1985).

Bruce W. Jentleson is an assistant professor of political science at the University of California, Davis. He is the author of *Pipeline Politics: The Complex Political Economy of East-West Energy Trade* (Cornell University Press, 1986) and is currently writing another book, tentatively titled *Entangled Alliances: The United States in Third World Revolutions and Regional Conflicts.* In 1987–1988 he will be an International Affairs Fellow of the Council on Foreign Relations.

Eliyahu Kanovsky is a professor of economics at Bar-Ilan University, Israel, and visiting Ludwig Jesselson Professor of Economics at Yeshiva University, New York. His recent publications include "Another Oil Shock in the 1990s? A Dissenting View" (Washington Institute for Near East Policy, 1987); "Saudi Arabia's Dismal Economic Future" (Moshe Dayan Center for Middle Eastern Studies, Tel Aviv University, 1987); "What's Behind Syria's Current Economic Problems?" (*Middle East Contemporary Survey*, 1986); and "Jordan's Decade of Prosperity: Will it Persist?" (*Middle East Contemporary Survey, 1986*).

Efraim Karsh is a lecturer in the Department of Political Science and a senior research associate at the Jaffee Center for Strategic Studies, Tel Aviv University. In 1985–1986 he was a research associate at the International Institute for Strategic Studies in London.

Sanford Lakoff is a professor of political science at the University of California, San Diego, and a member of the steering committee of the Institute on Global

Conflict and Cooperation (IGCC). He has written extensively on the history of political thought and on issues of science and public policy. Most recently, he has coedited *Strategic Defense and the Western Alliance* (Lexington Books, 1987).

Samuel W. Lewis was a career Foreign Service officer for thirty-one years until his retirement in 1985, serving in a number of foreign and domestic posts. From 1977 to 1985 he was the U.S. ambassador to Israel under Presidents Carter and Reagan. Since his retirement, Ambassador Lewis has been Diplomat-in-Residence at the Johns Hopkins Foreign Policy Institute in Washington, D.C., Senior International Fellow at the Moshe Dayan Center for Middle Eastern and African Studies, Tel Aviv University, and Guest Scholar at the Brookings Institution, Washington, D.C.

Ariel Merari is the head of the Project on Terrorism at Tel Aviv University's Jaffee Center for Strategic Studies and a former chairman of that university's Psychology Department. He is the editor of the Jaffee Center's yearly review of international terrorism, *Inter,* as well as of *On Terrorism and Combating Terrorism* (University Publications of America, 1985).

Stephanie G. Neuman is a senior research scholar at Columbia University's Research Institute on International Change and the director of the Comparative Defense Studies Program. She is also a consultant to the U.S. Department of State. Dr. Neuman has coedited and contributed to volumes 1 and 2 of *Lessons of Recent Wars* (Lexington Books, 1985 and 1987) and has contributed many chapters for collections on national security. Her articles have appeared in a number of academic and popular journals and newspapers.

Gur Ofer is a professor in the Department of Economics and the Department of Russian Studies at the Hebrew University of Jerusalem. He is also a consultant to The RAND Corporation and has written several pieces, including the book *The Service Sector in Soviet Economic Growth* (Harvard University Press, 1973).

Joseph Pelzman is a professor of economics at the George Washington University. He spent the academic year 1984–1985 doing research on Soviet military and economic assistance to the Middle East at Hebrew University, Jerusalem, where he was a Lady Davis Fellow. His publications and current research are focused on Soviet–Eastern European trade, Soviet military and economic assistance to the Middle East, and U.S. commercial policy.

Alan Platt has served as a senior staff member of The RAND Corporation, and is now a consultant based in Washington, D.C. During 1978–1980, Dr. Platt was chief of the Arms Transfer Division at the U.S. Arms Control and Disarmament

Agency. He also has served as chief foreign policy aide to former U.S. Senator Edmund Muskie and as a lecturer at Stanford University, UCLA, and Georgetown University.

Itamar Rabinovich is the Incumbent of the Ettinger Chair in Contemporary Middle Eastern History at Tel Aviv University and head of that university's Moshe Dayan Center for Middle Eastern Studies. He is the author of *Syria under the Ba'th 1963–1966* (Transaction Books, 1972) and *The War for Lebanon, 1970–1985* (Cornell University Press, 1984), among other works.

Barry Rubin is a fellow at the Foreign Policy Institute of Johns Hopkins University. His books include *Modern Dictators: Third World Strongmen* (McGraw Hill, 1987), *Secrets of State: The State Department and the Struggle Over U.S. Foreign Policy* (Oxford University Press, 1985), *Paved with Good Intentions: The American Experience and Iran* (Penguin, 1981), and *The Arab States and the Palestine Conflict* (Syracuse University Press, 1981). He is also coeditor of *The Arab-Israeli Reader.*

Gerald M. Steinberg teaches political science and public policy at Hebrew University and at Bar-Ilan University. He specializes on the links between science, technology, and politics and his articles have appeared in *Comparative Politics, Policy Sciences,* and other publications. He is the author of *Satellite Reconnaisance: The Role of Informal Bargaining* (Praeger, 1983) and is currently editing *The Domestic Politics of SDI* (Lexington Books, 1987) in conjunction with the Institute on Global Conflict and Cooperation at the University of California.

Asher Susser is a research associate at the Moshe Dayan Center for Middle Eastern and African Affairs and a lecturer in the Department of Middle East History at Tel Aviv University. He is the author of *Between Jordan and Palestine: A Political Biography of Wasfi Al-Tall* and *The PLO After the War in Lebanon* (both in Hebrew).

Aharon Yariv is head of the Jaffee Center for Strategic Studies at Tel Aviv University. Having served in the Israeli Defense Forces for twenty-five years, he rose to the rank of Major General, and his last position was director of Military Intelligence. He was also minister of transportation, and minister of information, as well as a member of the Israeli parliament. He is the author of numerous works on Israel's security, the military balance in the Middle East, and intelligence issues.

About the Editors

Steven L. Spiegel is a professor of political science at UCLA. His latest book, *The Other Arab-Israeli Conflict: Making America's Middle East Policy, from Truman to Reagan* (University of Chicago Press, 1985), received a National Jewish Book Award for 1986. He has published widely on American policy in the Middle East in leading journals and periodicals, including *Commentary, Orbis, Journal of International Affairs,* and *Middle East Review,* and has written and edited several books on international relations.

Mark A. Heller is a senior research associate at the Jaffee Center for Strategic Studies (JCSS), Tel-Aviv University. From 1984 to 1986, he was deputy director of the JCSS, and in 1986–1987 he was Visiting Associate Professor of Government and a research fellow in the Peace Studies Program at Cornell University. Dr. Heller is editor and coauthor of *The Middle East Military Balance* (Tel Aviv University, 1984). His other recent publications include *A Palestinian State: The Implications for Israel* (Harvard University Press, 1985), *The Iran-Iraq War* (Jaffee Center for Strategic Studies, 1984) and, with Nadav Safran, *The New Middle East Class and Regime Stability in Saudi Arabia* (Harvard University Press, 1985).

Jacob Goldberg teaches Middle East history at Tel Aviv University and is senior research fellow at the university's Moshe Dayan Center for Middle Eastern and African Studies. He is the author of *The Foreign Policy of Saudi Arabia: The Formative Years, 1902–1918* Harvard University Press, 1986) and has been a visiting professor at Cornell University, George Washington Unviersity, and the University of California, San Diego.

Publications of Contributing Institutes

Institute on Global Conflict and Cooperation
University of California

Sanford Lakoff and Randy Willoughby, *Strategic Defense and the Western Alliance* (Lexington Books, 1987).

Jaffee Center for Strategic Studies
Tel Aviv University

Mark A. Heller, ed., *The Middle East Military Balance* (*The Jerusalem Post* and Westview Press, 1984 and 1985).

Joseph Alpher, ed., *War by Choice* (HaKibbutz HaMeuchad, 1985) (Hebrew).

Zvi Lanir, ed., *Israeli Security and Economics in the 1980s* (Ministry of Defense Publishers, 1985) (Hebrew).

Ariel Merari, ed., *On Terrorism and Counter-Terrorism* (University Publishers of America, 1985).

Ariel Merari, Tamar Prat, Sophia Kotzer, Anat Kurz, and Yoram Schweitzer, *In Ter 85 A Review of International Terrorism* (*The Jerusalem Post* and Westview Press).

Aryeh Shalev, *The West Bank: Line of Defense* (Praeger, 1985).

Ariel Merari and Shlomi Elad, *The International Dimension of Palestinian Terrorism* (HaKibbutz HaMeuchad, 1986) (Hebrew).

Moshe Dayan Center for Middle Eastern
& African Studies
Tel Aviv University

Michael G. Fry and Itamar Rabinovich, *Despatches from Damascus: Gilbert MacKereth and British Policy in the Levant 1933–1939* (Moshe Dayan Center, 1986).

Israel Gershoni and James Jankowski, *Egypt, Islam and the Arabs: The Search for Egyptian Nationhood, 1900–1930* (Oxford University Press, 1986).

Jacob Goldberg, *The Foreign Policy of Saudi-Arabia: The Formulative Years 1902–1918* (Harvard University Press, 1986).

Joel L. Kraemer, *Philosophy in the Renaissance of Islam: Abu Sulayman al-Sijistani and His Circle* (E.J. Brill, 1986).

Joel L. Kraemer, *Humanism in the Renaissance of Islam: The Cultural Revival during the Buyid Age* (E.J. Brill, 1986).

Martin Kramer, *Islam Assembled: The Advent of the Muslim Congresses* (Columbia University Press, 1986).

Haim Shaked and Daniel Dishon, eds., *Middle East Contemporary Survey, Volume 8, 1983–1984* (Westview Press, 1986).

Ami Ayalon, *Language and Change in the Arab Middle East* (Oxford University Press, 1987).

Martin Kramer, ed., *Shi'ism, Resistance and Revolution* (Westview Press, 1987).

Uriel Dann, ed., *The Great Powers in the Middle East Between 1919–1939* (Holmes and Meier, forthcoming).

Milton J. Esman and Itamar Rabinovich, eds., *Ethnicity, Pluralism and the State in the Middle East* (Cornell University Press, forthcoming).

Itamar Rabinovich and Haim Shaked, eds., *Middle East Contemporary Survey, Volume 9, 1984–1985* (Westview Press, forthcoming).

Center for International and Strategic Affairs
University of California, Los Angeles

William C. Potter, ed., *Verification and SALT* (Westview Press, 1980).

Bennett Ramberg, *Destruction of Nuclear Energy Facilities in War: The Problem and Implications* (Lexington Books, 1980); revised and reissued as *Nuclear Power*

Plants as Weapons for the Enemy: An Unrecognized Military Peril (University of California Press, 1984).

Paul Jabber, *Not by War Alone: Security and Arms Control in the Middle East* (University of California Press, 1981).

Roman Kolkowicz and Andrzej Korbonski, eds., *Soldiers, Peasants, and Bureaucrats* (Allen & Unwin, 1982).

William C. Potter, *Nuclear Power and Nonproliferation: An Interdisciplinary Perspective* (Oelgeschlager, Gunn, and Hain, 1982).

Steven L. Spiegel, ed., *The Middle East and the Western Alliance* (Allen & Unwin, 1982).

Dagobert L. Brito, Michael D. Intriligator, and Adele E. Wick, eds., *Strategies for Managing Nuclear Proliferation—Economic and Political Issues* (Lexington Books, 1983).

Bernard Brodie, Michael D. Intriligator, and Roman Kolkowicz, eds., *National Security and International Stability* (Oelgeschlager, Gunn, and Hain, 1983).

Raju G.C. Thomas, ed., *The Great Power Triangle and Asian Security* (Lexington Books, 1983).

R.D. Tschirgi, *The Politics of Indecision: Origins and Implications of American Involvement with the Palestine Problem* (Praeger, 1983).

Giacomo Luciani, ed., *The Mediterranean Region: Economic Interdependence and the Future of Society* (Croom Helm, St. Martin's Press, 1984).

Roman Kolkowicz and Neil Joeck, eds., *Arms Control and International Security* (Westview Press, 1984).

Jiri Valenta and William C. Potter, eds., *Soviet Decisionmaking for National Security* (Allen & Unwin, 1984).

Rodney W. Jones, Cesare Merlini, Joseph F. Pilat, and William C. Potter, eds., *The Nuclear Suppliers and Nonproliferation: International Policy Choices* (Lexington Books, 1985).

Gerald Bender, James Coleman, Richard Sklar, eds., *African Crisis Areas and U.S. Foreign Policy* (University of California Press, 1985).

Rodney Jones, Joseph Pilat, Cesare Merlini, William C. Potter, eds., *The Nuclear Suppliers and Nonproliferation: Dilemmas and Policy Choices* (Lexington Books, 1985).

William C. Potter, ed., *Verification and Arms Control* (Lexington Books, 1985).

Neil Joeck, ed., *Strategic Consequences of Nuclear Proliferation in South Asia* (Frank Cass, 1986).

Bennett Ramberg, *Global Nuclear Energy Risks: The Search for Preventative Medicine* (Westview Press, 1986).

Ragu G.C. Thomas, *Indian Security Policy* (Princeton University Press, 1986).

——, *Dilemmas of Nuclear Deterrence* (Frank Cass, 1987).

Roman Kolkowicz, ed., *The Logic of Nuclear Terror* (Allen & Unwin, 1987).

Michael D. Intriligator and Hans-Adolf Jacobsen, eds., *East-West Conflict: Elite Perceptions and Policy Options* (Westview Press, forthcoming).

DATE DUE